Math Principles for Food Service Occupations

FOURTH EDITION

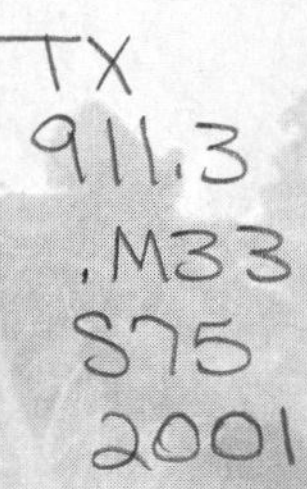

Math Principles for Food Service Occupations

FOURTH EDITION

Anthony J. Strianese and Pamela P. Strianese

Delmar
Thomson Learning™

Africa • Australia • Canada • Denmark • Japan • Mexico • New Zealand • Philippines
Puerto Rico • Singapore • Spain • United Kingdom • United States

NOTICE TO THE READER

Publisher does not warrant or guarantee any of the products described herein or perform any independent analysis in connection with any of the product information contained herein. Publisher does not assume, and expressly disclaims, any obligation to obtain and include information other than that provided to it by the manufacturer.
The reader is expressly warned to consider and adopt all safety precautions that might be indicated by the activities described herein and to avoid all potential hazards. By following the instructions contained herein, the reader willingly assumes all risks in connection with such instructions.
The publisher makes no representations or warranties of any kind, including but not limited to, the warranties of fitness for particular purpose or merchantability, nor are any such representations implied with respect to the material set forth herein, and the publisher takes no responsibility with respect to such material. The publisher shall not be liable for any special, consequential, or exemplary damages resulting, in whole or part, from the readers' use of, or reliance upon, this material.

Delmar Staff:
Business Unit Director: Susan L. Simpfenderfer
Executive Editor: Marlene McHugh Pratt
Acquisitions Editor: Erin O'Connor Traylor
Developmental Editor: Melissa Riveglia
Editorial Assistant: Alexis Ferraro
Executive Marketing Manager: Donna Lewis
Channel Managers: Nigar Hale, Eleanor J. Murray
Executive Production Manager: Wendy A. Troeger
Production Editor: Elaine Scull
Cover Design: Joseph Villanova
Cover Images: Digital Imagery® Photo Disc, Inc., Thomas Stock, Stock Studios Photography

Printed in the United States of America
1 2 3 4 5 6 7 8 9 10 XXX 05 04 03 02 01 00

For more information, contact Delmar, 3 Columbia Circle, PO Box 15015, Albany, New York 12212-5015; or find us on the World Wide Web at http://www.delmar.com or **http://www.Hospitality-Tourism.delmar.com**

Library of Congress Cataloging-in-Publication Data
Strianese, Anthony J.
Math principles for food service occupations / Anthony J. Strianese and Pamela P. Strianese.—4th ed.
p. cm.
Rev. ed. of: Math principles for food service occupations / Anthony J. Strianese. 3rd ed. ©1996.
Includes index.
ISBN 0-7668-1317-7
1. Food service—Mathematics. I. Strianese, Pamela P. II. Haines, Robert G. Math principles for food service occupations III. Title.
TX911.3.M33 S75 2000
647.95'01'513—dc21 00-030682

Contents

Foreword

Math plays a major role in the daily life of a hotelier. Too often it seems to be taken for granted. I started my career in the field of accounting. Today, I am directly involved in hotel operations. I am so fortunate to have had exposure to accounting because that experience helps me to better understand the financial results of our operation and enables me to evaluate our cost controls and make adjustments as needed.

The SHERRY-NETHERLAND is on the corner of 59th Street and Fifth Avenue in New York City. We have more than 400 rooms, of which 150 are individually decorated and furnished, including one- and two-bedroom suites, and are available for transient hotel occupancy. The Louis Sherry Room is used for meetings, luncheons, and cocktail parties. Our full-service restaurant also provides full room service for our guests. The building is a landmarked neo-Romanesque hotel built in 1927 by ice cream magnate Louis Sherry and Lucius Boomer, the founder of Cornell University's School of Hotel Management and former president of the Waldorf-Astoria. A three-year, $18 million renovation has just been completed, which restored our historic architectural treasures. The hotel has been a favorite New York residence of many Hollywood legends including Jack Warner, Danny Kaye, George Burns, Dean Martin, Sammy Davis Jr., and Jim Henson. The SHERRY-NETHERLAND is surrounded by galleries and museums, the city's most exclusive shopping (Tiffany's, Bergdorf Goodman), and the world's best in entertainment, including Broadway, Carnegie Hall, and Lincoln Center. Our hotel offers our guests a haven that combines European elegance and service with 21st century amenities.

Since 1995, The SHERRY-NETHERLAND has earned the **Sine Qua Non Award** from the *GOLDBOOK,* a prestigious international travel and life-style publication. It is one of only six U.S. hotels, and the only hotel in New York City, to earn this honor. The award, translated from Latin, means, "without which there is no other." As Patricia Slesinger, the publisher of the *GOLDBOOK* writes "certainly without them there would be no standard by which to measure the best at all. This 5-STAR rating is earned by those who approach perfection with creativity and consistency. It is about the best."

I hope you who are reading this book will come to appreciate the role math plays in determining the cost of a meal or the required rate to be charged for a hotel room. Customer service is obviously of great importance in the hospitality industry. However, without understanding the numbers, one could find themselves in serious financial difficulty. Imagine, for example, selling a steak dinner for $20.00 when the cost of the food and labor to produce and deliver that meal exceeds $20.00. Or, renting a hotel room for $100.00 when the cost of maintaining the room, selling it, providing amenities etc. exceeds $100.00.

Math plays an integral part in all of our lives. It is a valuable tool. Even the simplest business transactions affect the financial condition of a business. Knowing the place of business in our society and knowing how to manage wisely our own personal business affairs is of considerable importance. The study of math contributes to everyone's general education and prepares people for employment in business.

Louis N. Ventresca
Executive Vice President & Chief Operating Officer
The SHERRY-NETHERLAND
781 Fifth Avenue
New York, New York

Preface

Many students, when told they are required to take a math course, react with fear due to the poor math experiences they have had in the past. Once students realize how important and relevant math is in the food service, they become motivated to learn, understand, and use math correctly to accomplish their goals of becoming a chef, baker, manager, or any of the many occupations in the Food Service Industry. The authors of this fourth edition have had great success in teaching their students math skills and applications.

In researching this book, we have received interesting and passionate responses about the role that math plays in food service careers from chefs and managers throughout the United States and Canada. In conversations with these individuals, one fact became clearer and clearer: the more successful an individual was in his or her career, the more passionate he or she was in wanting to get the message to students about the importance of learning and using math to become a success in business. One common theme was articulated repeatedly by chefs and managers interviewed by the authors: with a knowledge and the proper usage of math, a business will succeed and the individual will succeed. Like cooking or baking, math is a sequential process. They pointed out that an individual must first master the basic skills before he or she can create a gourmet meal or spectacular dessert.

The fourth edition has been completely revised by the new authors of the book. We have read and reread the third edition and have calculated every example and problem in the book. All examples have been checked for accuracy. New problems have been added to challenge the students. Step-by-step instructions for problems and concepts have been included. Throughout the book, the authors have added a series of TIPS (To Insure Perfect Solutions) to assist the student in solving problems and understanding concepts of math. Each chapter has a Chef Sez feature, which is a quote from a manager or chef about the importance of math in their own particular operation. The chapter on computers (Chapter 12) has been completely revised and updated to reflect the math skills a student must possess to use a spreadsheet software program. New areas and explanations have been added concerning costing out a menu and food cost procedures. We have added behavioral objectives for the skills and strategies that are covered in each chapter. Throughout the book, the summary reviews have been developed to provide a written assessment for student mastery of the objectives. Of special interest and importance to the instructors who are using this new edition, the Instructor's Manual has been revised and all answers have been checked and double-checked for accuracy. Finally, this book is a "keeper." We have added an appendix with all formulas used in the book. This will be a valuable reference tool as you climb the career ladder.

As in the third edition, *Math Principles for Food Service Occupations* opens with a **Pretest** and concludes with a **Posttest** for the purpose of evaluating the student's math skills prior to, and upon completion of, the course. The Pretest and Posttest consist of 40 different math skills that are associated with a food service career.

The content of the text has been divided into five coordinated parts to demonstrate subject association and simplify learning.

Part I, **The Calculator,** is placed at the beginning of the book. The authors believe that the calculator is an essential tool for math computation, just as a knife is a tool for the culinary professional. Since calculator skills and the use of calculators are being taught in elementary education, this chapter is placed in the front of the book. If the instructor does not feel that the chapter on calculators should be introduced until after the fundamentals are mastered, he or she can insert it into the class where appropriate.

Part II, **Review of Basic Math Fundamentals,** consists of three chapters intended to refresh and sharpen the student's math skills. The emphasis is placed on methods used to solve mathematical problems related to food service situations. This information should be thoroughly reviewed, with exercise problems worked and referred back to whenever necessary. The authors know that learning math is a sequential process. The student must have mastered the fundamentals and have an understanding of basic math concepts and computational skills before moving into more complicated problem solving.

Part III, **Math Essentials in Food Preparation,** consists of five chapters which focus on the math necessary to function as part of the preparation crew. This part includes weights and measures, portion control, converting and yielding recipes, and production and baking formulas. An expanded Chapter 9 (Using the Metric System of Measure) explains why the baker's balance scale is important to the individual considering baking as a career.

Part IV, **Math Essentials in Food Service Recordkeeping,** consists of four chapters concentrating on the math necessary for keeping important records accurate and current. This part includes sections on daily production reports, purchasing and receiving, waiting tables, guest checks and tipping, and a revised chapter on computer applications used in a food service operation.

Part V, **Essentials of Managerial Math,** includes the types of math procedures that are typically the responsibility of management. It consists of seven chapters intended to assist in managerial decision making. The information on calculating food cost has been revised and expanded. A new technique, The Chef's Magic Circle, will assist the students in remembering formulas. New methods of pricing the menu by using the multiplier method have made this section more detailed than in the third edition. Also included are chapters on daily cash receipts and bank deposits, exploring recipe and food costing, pricing the menu, inventory procedures, financial statements, personal tax and payroll, and simple and compound interest.

The material contained in this text will provide the student with sufficient math knowledge to demonstrate confidence and utilize skills that will lead to rapid job advancement in his or her career. Math, along with culinary skills and proper friendly service, is an essential part of the equation that makes a food service operation a success. Many talented chefs have succeeded in business, while others have failed. The authors want to emphasize that there is more to operating a successful food service operation than putting quality food before the guest.

Acknowledgments

When we were contacted to undertake the task of writing the fourth edition of *Math Principles for Food Service Occupations,* we knew that we would need help acquiring examples, information, and illustrations. We were fortunate that our travels have taken us to many locations where we could interview chefs and managers. Because of our many interests and participation at conventions and conferences, we have made important and meaningful contacts with influential leaders in the American Culinary Federation, New York State Hospitality and Tourism Association, New York State Restaurant Association, the Albany County Convention and Visitors Bureau, and graduates of the Hotel, Culinary Arts and Tourism program at Schenectady County Community College. Our experience in writing the two editions of *Dining Room and Banquet Management* and *The Food Service Industry Video Series,* as well as numerous articles for local business publications has allowed us many research opportunities. Both of us have Masters' degrees: Pam in Education and Toby in Educational Psychology. Toby has also been certified by the American Culinary Federation as a Certified Culinary Educator.

When undertaking this fourth edition we asked ourselves what would make this book stand out from other math books in our field. We knew we could bring a positive perspective about math to the student because of our combined 44 years of teaching experience at the elementary and college level. Also, we knew that we could call upon our hospitality experience throughout our various careers as cook, chef, bookkeeper, waitperson, food and beverage manager, butler, bartender, and banquet manager to reflect the importance of math in the food service industry to the student. But we wanted something more—we wanted to make the math meaningful. So in each chapter we added a section called Chef Sez in which the leaders in this industry explain to the reader why math is important. In alphabetical order we list the following contributors and their titles:

Greg Benamati, 50's Prime Time Restaurant, M.G.M. Studios at Walt Disney World, Lake Buena Vista, Florida;

James V. Bigley, President, Quality Food Management, Inc., Latham, New York;

Jill K. Bosich, American Culinary Federation Culinary Team 2000, Chef-Instructor, Orange Coast College, Costa Mesa, California;

Bert P. Cutino, Certified Executive Chef, American Academy of Chefs, Co-Founder and Chef, Sardine Factory Restaurant, Monterey, California;

Robert S. Faller, Director of Sales and Marketing, The Otesaga Resort Hotel, Cooperstown, New York;

Kevin Gee, Certified Executive Chef, Corporate Executive Chef, Organic Foods Inc., Little Rock, Arkansas;

Charlie Gipe, Executive Chef and Pippins Manager, Hersheypark, Hershey, Pennsylvania;

George R. Goldoff, Director of Food and Beverage, Bellagio Hotel and Resort, Las Vegas, Nevada;

John Harasty, Executive Chef, ARAMARK Corporation, Churchill Downs, Louisville, Kentucky;

Charles E. Henning, Managing Director, Sonoma Mission Inn & Spa, Sonoma, California;

Peter Huebner, President and Owner of Canada Cutlery Inc., Scarborough, Ontario, Canada;

Matthew J. Kaperka, Division Manager, Concessions, Sports & Entertainment, ARAMARK Corporation, Flushing Meadows, New York;

William Leaver, Supervisor, Correctional Food Procurement & Distribution, State of New York, Department of Nutritional Services, Albany, New York;

Noble Masi, Certified Master Baker, Senior Chef Instructor, The Culinary Institute of America, Hyde Park, New York;

Harold Qualters, General Manager, Troy Pub & Brewery, Troy, New York;

Milford Prewitt, National Reports Editor, *NATION'S RESTAURANT NEWS,* New York City, New York;

Rodney Renshaw, Executive Chef, The Savoy, Washington, DC;

Thomas Rosenberger, Certified Executive Chef, Director, Food and Beverage Management Programs, Department of Resorts and Gaming, Community College of Southern Nevada, North Las Vegas, Nevada;

Rick Schofield, Manager, Beverage Operations, The Culinary Institute of America, Hyde Park, New York;

Andre Soltner, Founder and former owner of Lutece, Master Chef, Senior Lecturer, The French Culinary Institute, New York City, New York;

Fritz Sonnenschmidt, Certified Master Chef, Chairman of the American Academy of Chefs, Culinary Dean, Culinary Institute of America, Hyde Park, New York;

Michael Thompson, Professional Culinary Recruiter, Walt Disney World, Disney Worldwide Services, Lake Buena Vista, Florida;

Louis N. Ventresca, Executive Vice President & Chief Operating Officer, The Sherry-Netherland, New York, New York.

We were fortunate to have several editors at Delmar who assisted us with this project. Jeff Burnham and Judy Roberts, who recruited us to write the book; our current Acquisitions Editor, Erin O'Connor Traylor, who ALWAYS returns phone calls from wherever she is in the United States; Melissa Riveglia, our Developmental Editor; and Alexis Ferraro, Editorial Assistant. We thank the previous author of the first three editions, Robert G. Haines, for all of his prior research and writing. The authors also wish to thank the reviewers of this book: Doug Armstrong, BS, Chef, Instructor, New Hampshire Community Technical College, Laconia, New Hampshire; Joseph Crompton, CCC, CCE, Chef, Instructor, Heyward Career and Technology Center, Culinary Arts Department, Columbia, South Carolina; William Gibson, BS, Instructor, Kauai Community College, Culinary Arts, Lihue, Hawaii; Linda Jaster, BS, Instructor, Dietitian, Texas State Technical College, Food Service/Culinary Arts, Waco, Texas; Ron Jones, BS, CCE, Chair of Hospitality Studies, McIntosh College, Culinary Arts, Dover, New Hampshire; Mary Petersen, MS, Executive Director, Foodservice Educators Network International, Annapolis, Maryland; and Barbara Van Fossen, MS, Associate Professor, Jefferson Community College, Food Service Management Program, Steubenville, Ohio.

Special thanks must be given to two individuals who provided us with gracious hospitality in their hotels, which allowed our thoughts to flow freely. Paul Puzzanghero, the General Manager of the Boston Marriott Newton in Newton, Massachusetts, and Cristina Lussi, the Director of Sales and the staff at the Lake Placid Resort Hotel and Golf Club in Lake Placid, New York. We were able to write, edit, and finish the drafts of this edition in the picture-perfect area of Lake Placid with the warm hospitality of the Lake Placid Resort Hotel and Golf Club.

We would like to thank these individuals from Schenectady County Community College in the Department of Hotel, Culinary Arts, and Tourism. Susan Hatalsky, Assistant Professor Certified Executive Chef (C.E.C.)/Certified Culinary Educator (C.C.E.) who assisted us with new and updated information on production and baking formulas; Associate Professor Gary Brenenstuhl and Senior Technical Assistant Ann Parks who gave us ideas and suggestions for changes; Carol L. Chiarella, CPA, Professor and Chairperson of the Business and Law Department who answered our questions concerning taxes and accounting and made valuable suggestions for the text; and Terry Treis, the duplicating machine operator who assisted and advised us with the duplication process of our copies.

The authors are indebted to the following people who planned and participated with our photography: Melissa Riveglia, our Developmental Editor (A REAL PRO) who guided us through the photo shoot and our final edits; Elaine Scull, the art director; and Tom Stock the photographer from Stock Studios. There are not enough kind words to express our gratitude for the superb dedication and work that our food stylist, Teri Scholtz, and her employer Price Chopper Advertising provided for this project.

From the Department of Hotel, Culinary Arts and Tourism at Schenectady County Community College we thank our models, students Elsa Suarez, and Benjamin Blandon, and C.E.C./C.C.E. Susan Hatalsky. Students Nicole Gaudin, Nicole Pesta and Shawn McDowell kept us fed with their culinary creations during our photo shoot. Finally to Professor Paul Krebs C.C.E. and Technical Specialist Paul Hiatt C.C.E. for their insight, experience, ideas and suggestions for the photo shoot.

Finally, we would like to thank our employers for the support and encouragement they have given us to undertake this project: The North Colonie Central School District in Loudonville, New York, and Schenectady County Community College in Schenectady, New York. A special thanks goes to our sons, Mike and Larry, and to our family.

If you would like to contact us with questions, comments, or suggestions or any other pertinent information, you may contact either Delmar Thomson Learning or us directly by e-mail at strianaj@gw.sunysccc.edu.

Pamela P. Strianese Anthony (Toby) J. Strianese

Pretest: Math Skills

The pretest evaluates a student's math skills before the student begins the food service math course. This pretest helps both the student and the instructor to focus on the areas of greatest concern.

To earn a competency in each of the 40 math exercises presented, a student must work three of the four problems of each type presented correctly. If this is achieved, the student will earn a + (plus) for that particular exercise. If this goal is not achieved, a – (minus) will be recorded. A profile sheet on both the pretest and posttests are kept on file by the instructor for reference by either the student or instructor. The pluses are recorded in either blue or black ink on the profile sheet under the proper exercise. The minuses are recorded in red ink.

1. Add the following numbers.

$$\begin{array}{r} 27 \\ +49 \\ \hline \end{array} \qquad \begin{array}{r} 17 \\ 46 \\ +13 \\ \hline \end{array} \qquad \begin{array}{r} 6555 \\ 2265 \\ +8085 \\ \hline \end{array}$$

38 + 127 + 5678 + 42975 = ______________

2. Subtract the following numbers.

$$\begin{array}{r} 48 \\ -\ 26 \\ \hline \end{array} \qquad \begin{array}{r} 658 \\ -\ 96 \\ \hline \end{array} \qquad \begin{array}{r} 82723 \\ -\ 3430 \\ \hline \end{array}$$

34228 − 16767 = ______________

3. Change the mill to the nearest cent.

$0.034 ______________ $6.857 ______________

$0.126 ______________ $725.683 ______________

4. Multiply the following numbers.

$$\begin{array}{r} 54 \\ \times\ 9 \\ \hline \end{array} \qquad \begin{array}{r} 68 \\ \times\ 45 \\ \hline \end{array} \qquad \begin{array}{r} 981 \\ \times\ 127 \\ \hline \end{array}$$

2520 × 36 = ______________

5. Divide the following numbers.

$12\overline{)192}$ $18\overline{)1350}$

$122\overline{)76860}$ $2125\overline{)518750}$

6. Reduce the fractions to the lowest terms.

$\frac{4}{12}$ ______ $\frac{16}{96}$ ______ $\frac{56}{64}$ ______ $\frac{60}{108}$ ______

7. Convert each mixed number to an improper fraction.

$6\frac{1}{8}$ ______ $16\frac{3}{7}$ ______ $7\frac{3}{8}$ ______ $41\frac{5}{8}$ ______

8. Convert each improper fraction to a whole number or a mixed number.

$\frac{41}{9}$ ______ $\frac{192}{64}$ ______ $\frac{27}{6}$ ______ $\frac{270}{24}$ ______

9. Find the equivalent fractions.

$\frac{5}{6} = \frac{}{30}$ $\frac{6}{15} = \frac{}{60}$

$\frac{5}{9} = \frac{}{36}$ $\frac{2}{3} = \frac{}{21}$

10. Add the following fractions and reduce each answer to its lowest terms.

$\frac{3}{7} + \frac{2}{7}$ $3\frac{7}{8} + 1\frac{1}{4}$ $1\frac{3}{16} + 4\frac{3}{4}$ $2\frac{1}{2} + 4\frac{3}{4} + 8\frac{1}{12}$

11. Subtract the following fractions and reduce each answer to its lowest terms.

$\frac{9}{12} - \frac{5}{12}$ $8 - 3\frac{5}{8}$ $12\frac{1}{4} - 6\frac{5}{16}$ $42\frac{23}{32} - 26\frac{15}{16}$

12. Multiply the following fractions and reduce each answer to its lowest terms.

$\frac{3}{5} \times \frac{5}{6} =$ ________________ $1\frac{3}{4} \times 2\frac{3}{8} =$ ________________

$8 \times \frac{4}{9} =$ ________________ $8\frac{2}{3} \times 2\frac{1}{4} =$ ________________

13. Divide the following fractions and reduce each answer to its lowest terms.

$\frac{2}{9} \div \frac{1}{3} =$ ________________ $1\frac{3}{4} \div \frac{2}{3} =$ ________________

$1\frac{1}{4} \div \frac{3}{8} =$ ________________ $12\frac{3}{4} \div \frac{1}{3} =$ ________________

14. Convert each decimal to a fraction.

0.7 __________ 0.009 __________ 4.15 __________ 0.89 __________

15. Convert each fraction to a decimal.

$\frac{3}{10}$ __________ $5\frac{1}{6}$ __________ $\frac{3}{8}$ __________ $14\frac{5}{8}$ __________

16. Convert each fraction to a percent.

$\frac{3}{5}$ __________ $\frac{7}{8}$ __________ $1\frac{2}{5}$ __________ $\frac{3}{10}$ __________

17. Convert each decimal to a percent.

23.4 __________ 0.67 __________ 0.0065 __________ 49.3 __________

18. Convert each percent to a decimal.

8.5% __________ 12.6% __________ 228% __________ 25% __________

19. Add the decimals.

$$\begin{array}{r} 9.6 \\ 4.6 \\ +\ 0.8 \\ \hline \end{array} \qquad \begin{array}{r} 8.085 \\ +\ 12 \\ \hline \end{array}$$

0.6 + 8.4 + 10 = ________________

0.9946 + 0.023 + 0.0425 = ________________

20. Subtract the decimals.

$$\begin{array}{r} 9.08 \\ -\ 3.57 \\ \hline \end{array} \qquad \begin{array}{r} 221.06 \\ -\ 9.2 \\ \hline \end{array}$$

42.3 − 10.63 = ________________

8 − 0.04 = ________________

21. Multiply the decimals.

$$\begin{array}{r} .275 \\ \times\ 15 \\ \hline \end{array} \qquad \begin{array}{r} 7.38 \\ \times\ 2.9 \\ \hline \end{array}$$

$6.5 \times .043 =$ ______________

$10.85 \times .034 =$ ______________

22. Divide the decimals.

$0.06\overline{)0.855}$ $9.5\overline{)0.4832}$

$0.44\overline{)5853}$ $18\overline{)9.683}$

23. Use percents to find the total number.

20% of what number is 10? ______________

18% of what number is 36? ______________

60% of what number is 45? ______________

40% of what number is 20? ______________

24. Find the following numbers.

36% of 8 = ______________

6.8% of 36 = ______________

112% of 200 = ______________

14.5% of 85 = ______________

25. Find the following percentages.

What percent of 40 is 20? ______________

What percent of 200 is 88? ______________

What percent of 150 is 90? ______________

What percent of 360 is 126? ______________

26. Find the measurement equivalents—ounces.

32 ounces = How many quarts? ______________

128 ounces = How many gallons? ______________

16 ounces = How many pints? ______________

8 ounces = How many cups? ______________

27. Find the measurement equivalents—cups.

2 cups = How many pints? __________

4 cups = How many quarts? __________

6 cups = How many quarts? __________

16 cups = How many gallons? __________

28. Find the measurement equivalents—spoons.

3 teaspoons = How many tablespoons? __________

48 teaspoons = How many cups? __________

8 tablespoons = How many cups? __________

16 tablespoons = How many cups? __________

29. Find the measurement equivalents—pounds.

1 pound = How many pints? __________

2 pounds = How many quarts? __________

4 pounds = How many gallons? __________

8 pounds = How many gallons? __________

30. Using a comma, separate the following numbers into periods.

2 4 5 8 3 2 4 2 5

5 2 4 6 1 3 6 4 7 5

4 6 2 2 8 9 7 4 5 2 3 6 0 7

6 9 0 0 0 0 0 0 0 0 0

31. Find the cost per serving.

A 5-pound box of frozen peas costs $2.90. How much does a 3-ounce serving cost?

____

A $2\frac{1}{2}$-pound box of frozen corn costs $2.10. How much does a $3\frac{1}{2}$-ounce serving cost?

____

A $2\frac{1}{2}$-pound box of frozen carrots costs $0.55 per pound. How much does a 3-ounce serving cost?

____

If frozen asparagus spears cost $10.90 for a 5-pound box, how much does a 3-ounce serving cost?

____

32. Use a calculator for these four basic functions.

$48 + 54 + 97 =$ ______________

$48922.56 - 31825.67 =$ ______________

$1628 \times 52 =$ ______________

$7135 \div 145 =$ ______________

33. Determine the total cost of each meal.

A tip of $2.00 was 15% of the cost of the meal. ______________

A tip of $8.00 was 20% of the cost of the meal. ______________

A tip of $5.00 was 20% of the cost of the meal. ______________

A tip of $12.00 was 15% of the cost of the meal. ______________

34. Using ratios, find how much water is required in each of the following.

How much water is required to cook $1\frac{1}{4}$ quarts of barley using a ratio of 4 to 1?

____

How much water is required to bake $\frac{3}{4}$ quart of rice using a ratio of 2 to 1?

____

How much water is required to soak $\frac{3}{4}$ gallon navy beans using a ratio of 3 to 1?

____

How much water is required to convert $1\frac{3}{4}$ quarts of orange concentrate to orange juice using a ratio of 3 to 1?

____

35. What are the customary measures?

1 gram = ______________ ounces

1 kilogram = ______________ pounds

28 grams = ______________ ounce or ounces

1 liter = ______________ quart or quarts

36. How much interest is paid?

Find the simple interest on $425.00 at 6 percent interest for 1 year.

____

Find the simple interest on $980.00 at $5\frac{1}{2}$ percent interest for 1 year.

____

Find the amount of compound interest at the end of 2 years on a principal of $3000.00 compounded annually at 3 percent interest.

____

Find the amount of compound interest at the end of 3 years on a principal of $2500.00 compounded annually at 3.5 percent interest.

____

37. Use a calculator for these chain calculations.

$69 + 225 - 68 \div 2 =$ _______________

$1250 - 685 + 245 \div 2 \times 4 =$ _______________

$265 \times 21 - 180 + 442 =$ _______________

$\$32584.50 - 21522.25 \times 0.05 =$ _______________

38. Determine the following serving portions.

How many 5-ounce Swiss steaks can be cut from a beef round weighing 48 pounds (A.P.) if 6 pounds 5 ounces are lost in boning and trimming?

____

A 13-pound (E.P.) pork loin is roasted, 1 pound 6 ounces are lost through shrinkage. How many 3-ounce servings can be obtained from the cooked loin?

____

A 1-pound (A.P.) beef tenderloin is trimmed, 8 ounces are lost. How many 6-ounce filet mignons can be cut from the tenderloin?

____

A 6-pound (E.P.) beef tenderloin is roasted, 14 ounces are lost through shrinkage. How many $2\frac{1}{2}$-ounce servings can be obtained from the roasted loin?

____

39. Using 1 cup of gelatin powder for each quart of liquid, determine the amount needed when preparing the following amounts:

    2 gallons flavored gelatin: __________

    $2\frac{1}{2}$ quarts flavored gelatin: __________

    3 pints flavored gelatin: __________

    3 quarts flavored gelatin: __________

40. Determine each menu price:

    Raw food cost is $1.85 and mark-up rate is $\frac{3}{4}$.

    ____

    Raw food cost is $2.25 and mark-up rate is 35 percent.

    ____

    Raw food cost is $2.58 and mark-up rate is $\frac{2}{3}$.

    ____

    Raw food cost is $2.95 and mark-up rate is 45 percent.

    ____

Math Skills—Profile Sheet

The following should be listed on the profile sheet:

1. Addition
2. Subtraction
3. Mills
4. Multiplication
5. Division
6. Reducing fractions
7. Converting to improper fractions
8. Improper fractions to mixed numbers
9. Finding equivalent fractions
10. Addition of fractions
11. Subtraction of fractions
12. Multiplication of fractions
13. Division of fractions
14. Converting decimals to fractions
15. Converting fractions to decimals
16. Converting fractions to percent
17. Converting decimals to percent
18. Converting percent to decimals
19. Addition of decimals
20. Subtraction of decimals
21. Multiplication of decimals
22. Division of decimals
23. Percents to find number
24. Finding percent of a number
25. Finding percent of two given numbers
26. Measurement equivalents—ounces
27. Measurement equivalents—cups
28. Measurement equivalents—spoons
29. Measurement equivalents—pounds
30. Separating periods
31. Cost per serving
32. Basic functions—calculator
33. Cost of meal
34. Ratio
35. Metric conversion
36. Interest, simple/compound

37. Chain calculations—calculator
38. Serving portions
39. Using a formula
40. Menu price

PART I

THE CALCULATOR

CHAPTER 1
Using the Calculator

Chapter one introduces the calculator as an important tool in food service occupations. This chaper will provide instruction on the use of the calculator utilizing the operations of addition, subtraction, multiplication and division. Problem solving will be illustrated by using chain calculations, the constant function, the percent key, the memory function and the plus/minus key to convert a positive number to a negative number and vice versa.

Using the Calculator

OBJECTIVES

At the completion of this chapter, the student should be able to:

1. Find sums, differences, products, and quotients.
2. Solve problems by using chain calculations.
3. Multiply or divide repeatedly using the constant function.
4. Find sums and differences by using a percent.
5. Find products and quotients by using a percent.
6. Solve problems using the memory function.
7. Use the plus/minus key to convert a positive number to a negative number and vice versa.

The calculator is the single most important tool used in food service occupations. It is portable, which means that an employee/owner can use it on the loading dock to check invoices, as well as in the kitchen to convert recipes. Calculators are easy to use and accurate. There are so many different types of calculators on the market today that it becomes a major decision when a purchase must be made. To help reach a decision, it is best to read literature on the various kinds before finalizing your choice. In this age of electronics, there are many choices: solar-powered calculators, scientific calculators, full-featured solar-powered scientific calculators, solar mini-desktop calculators and inexpensive hand-held calculators, just to name a few.

PURCHASING A CALCULATOR

If the calculator you use is for normal functions, it would be an advantage to purchase a solar calculator with fair-sized solar panels that can be used in just about any light. The solar calculator is recommended by the authors in order to obtain the most accurate answers. A good-sized keyboard is another plus as it is easier to calculate using the finger rather than the end of a pencil, which must be used on very small keyboards. The features required for most food service math functions can be found in most of the inexpensive hand-held calculators. This is the kind of calculator used in this chapter to explain the necessary functions employed most often in the food service industry. Our intent is to help the student become more familiar with the main calculator functions and more comfortable using them. Every calculator does not have the same features, and even the keyboards vary from one model to the other. For this reason, you should always read and study your calculator instruction booklet.

Figure 1-1 Hand calculator

T I P S . . . ***To Insure Perfect Solutions***

Calculators work differently. Read *all* directions that come with your calculator.

USING A CALCULATOR

The face of the small hand-held calculator usually contains the keys listed in Figure 1-2. However, the operation key may have a different placement, depending on the calculator. Also listed are the functions these keys perform.

The instructions provided in this chapter will apply to most calculators. However, remember that some differences will exist between models. The following calculator functions are those that you will use during your food service career. The functions that would be of little use, such as the square root key, will not be discussed. The student should calculate all examples presented to acquire practice and a complete understanding of the functions explained.

The first step in the use of any calculator is to make sure it is cleared and ready to receive calculations. This is done by depressing the **ON** key, meaning the power is "on" and the calculator is "clear." At this point, it is also wise to do a few simple problems to make sure the batteries and

ON/OFF	Press to activate the power and turn the calculator on or disconnect power by turning it off. The off key usually clears the calculator including the memory register. Not all solar calculators have an on/off switch.
C	When the power is on, this key is pressed to clear the calculator of all functions except the memory function.
CE	Press to clear an incorrect keyboard entry that has not been entered into the function. It does not clear the memory function.
CA or AC	If it is included on the keyboard, this key clears the calculator of all functions including the memory function.
0–9	Numeral entry keys.
.	Decimal point key. Used to enter a decimal point into a number.
=	Equal or result key.
+	Plus or addition key.
−	Minus or subtraction key.
×	Times or multiplication key.
÷	Division key.
%	Percentage key — moves the decimal point two places to the left in the result.
√	Computes the square root of the number in the display. Not used in food service calculations. Used in scientific calculations.
+/−	Change sign key. Does not appear on all calculators. Used to convert a positive number to a negative number and vice versa.
M+	Memory plus key. Adds display number to the memory.
M−	Memory minus key. Subtracts a number from the memory.
RM MR	Recall Memory or Memory Recall Key Displays content in memory. Does not clear memory.
CM MC	Clear Memory or Memory Clear Key Displays memory figures and clears the memory.
MRC	Memory Recall and Clear Key. Recalls the memory and also clears the memory. When key is depressed once, memory is recalled. Depressed twice memory is cleared.

Figure 1-2 *Calculator keys*

the calculator are functioning properly. The simple test problems may be addition and percent. For example:

Enter 7 + 5 = 12 (Addition test)
Enter 600 + 30% = 780 (Percent test)

Think of this as 30% (600) + 600 = 780.

(600) 30% + 600 = 780

Note: On some calculators you may use this equation: 600 + 30% = 780.

The Four Basic Methods of Operation

The four basic methods of operation—addition, subtraction, multiplication, and division—are carried out on the calculator in the order that you would do the problem manually, or say the problem verbally. For example, to add 8 and 6, you would enter 8 + 6 =. The answer, 14, would then appear in the display window. To subtract 6 from 14, you would enter 14 − 6 =. The answer, 8, would again appear in the display window.

Try the following practice exercises to see if you have mastered how to use a calculator for the four basic operations. Correct answers are given.

Addition practice exercises

a. 37 + 46 + 54 = (*Answer:* 137)

b. 48 + 52 + 78 = (*Answer:* 178)

c. 3463 + 225 + 2218 + 4560 = (*Answer:* 10466)

d. 32.5 + 519.43 + 2226.06 + 18.03 = (*Answer:* 2796.02)

e. 26423 + 22.08 + 2946 + 3220 + 445.046 = (*Answer:* 33056.126)

Subtraction practice exercises

a. 33682 − 18620 = (*Answer:* 15062)

b. 3895.28 − 1620.29 = (*Answer:* 2274.99)

c. 48920.56 − 32826.69 = (*Answer:* 16093.87)

d. $8668.78 − $4878.28 = (*Answer:* $3790.50)

e. 956 − 482.739 = (*Answer:* 473.261)

Multiplication practice exercises

a. 86 × 256 = (*Answer:* 22016)

b. 1620 × 62 × 18 = (*Answer:* 1807920)

c. 4482 × 22 × 6.8 = (*Answer:* 670507.2)

d. 46.5 × 7 × 12.2 × 18.4 = (*Answer:* 73068.24)

e. $438.75 × 34.5 = (*Answer:* $15136.875)

Division practice exercises

a. 2175 ÷ 15 = (*Answer:* 145)

b. 7137 ÷ 156 = (*Answer:* 45.75)

c. 6256.25 ÷ 175 = (*Answer:* 35.75)

d. 82.9 ÷ 4.5 = (*Answer:* 18.422)

e. 6.5 ÷ .25 = (*Answer:* 26)

SUMMARY REVIEW

Addition

1. 48 + 59 + 212 = ____________
2. 78 + 135 + 389 = ____________
3. 269 + 458 + 678 = ____________
4. 3263 + 298 + 2229 + 4680 = ____________
5. 35.6 + 626.42 + 2430.07 + 15.03 = ____________

Subtraction

6. 23583 − 16420 = ____________
7. 4596.26 − 2725.23 = ____________
8. 56750.35 − 31998.67 = ____________
9. $7567.75 − $5428.46 = ____________
10. 987 − 462.634 = ____________

Multiplication

11. 89 × 368 = ____________
12. 1586 × 82 × 15 = ____________
13. 4556 × 23 × 7.6 = ____________
14. 46.8 × 8 × 13.3 × 16.4 = ____________
15. $656.76 × 32.5 = ____________

Division

16. 1675 ÷ 18 = ____________
17. 6280 ÷ 166 = ____________
18. 8245.25 ÷ 186 = ____________
19. 92.7 ÷ .52 = ____________
20. 7.5 ÷ 23 = ____________

Chain Calculations

Chain calculations involve a series of numbers and a variety of math procedures. Many chain calculations involve all four basic operations. Chain calculations are carried out on the calculator in the same order you would say the problem verbally. For example:

$$29 + 120 - 38 \times 3 \div 3 =$$

The answer 111 appears in the display window.

Chain calculation practice exercises

a. 97 + 120 − 38 × 5 ÷ 4 = (*Answer:* 223.75)

b. 1440 − 1200 + 45 ÷ 2 × 2 = (*Answer:* 285)

c. 395 × 42 − 225 + 448 = (*Answer:* 16813)

d. $53785.25 − $32726.85 × .05 = (*Answer:* $1052.92)

e. 596 × 58 − 24568 + 1420.6 = (*Answer:* 11420.6)

SUMMARY REVIEW

1. 67 + 230 − 89 × 6 ÷ 2 = ____________
2. 1260 − 1051 + 290 ÷ 2 × 3 = ____________
3. 365 × 52 − 290 + 545 = ____________
4. $42685.50 − 31628.75 × .05 = ____________
5. 592 × 65 − 28562 + 1325.8 = ____________

Constant Function

The **constant function** may be used to multiply or divide repeatedly by the same number. *The constant is entered first when multiplying and becomes the multiplier.* The multiplier remains in the calculator as a new multiplicand is entered. The = key is depressed to get the result. For example, find the product for each of the following:

What is the amount of sales tax on the following purchases if the 6.5 percent sales tax rate is used as the constant?

a. $ 252.00

b. $ 79.00

c. $2456.92

Remember that 6.5 percent must be changed to the decimal 0.065 (the decimal moves two places to the left when the % sign is removed) and entered first, followed by the × sign and then the multiplicand. Pressing the = key will give each product. The constant and × sign are entered only once. Now try these three calculations. Answers are rounded to the nearest cent.

a. 0.065 × $252.00 = $16.38

b. $79.00 = $5.14

c. $2456.92 = $159.70

As you can see, the constant and × sign are entered only one time. New multiplicands are entered without reentering the constant or sign.

Summary Review

What is the amount of sales tax on the following amounts, if the 6.5 percent sales tax rate is used as the constant? Round answers to the nearest cent.

1. $286.00 ______________
2. $79.50 ______________
3. $2460.95 ______________
4. $5235.45 ______________
5. $8164.34 ______________

In division, the constant is entered after the first dividend is entered. It becomes the divisor and remains in the calculator as each new dividend is entered. For example, find the quotient in the following:

Using 82 percent as the percent of cost, find the selling price based on the wholesale price of each of these:

a. $692.25

b. $46.93

c. $2253.86

Remember that 82 percent must first be changed to the decimal 0.82 (the decimal moves two places to the left when the % sign is removed) and entered after the first dividend. The procedure for entering would be the dividend followed by the ÷ sign, which is entered only once, as is the constant which is entered last. Pressing the = key will give each quotient. Now try these calculations. Answers are rounded to the nearest cent.

a. $692.25 ÷ .82 = $844.21

b. $46.93 = $57.23

c. $2253.86 = $2748.61

Summary Review

Using 65 percent as the percent of cost, find the selling price based on the wholesale price of each of the following items. Round answers to the nearest cent.

1. $695.25 ______________
2. $58.65 ______________
3. $2255.75 ______________
4. $3140.35 ______________
5. $4480.65 ______________

◆ *Chef Sez . . .*

"The use of calculators in food service is just as important to the success of an operation as the quality of its food. Without calculators or more important, the proper use of them, no establishment will be successful."

William Leaver
Supervisor, Correctional Food Procurement & Distribution
State of New York
Department of Nutritional Services

The Office of Nutritional Services establishes all menus, portion sizes, equipment requirements, and purchases of all food items for the 70 correctional facilities (with a population of over 70,000) in New York State. This amounts to almost 40 million dollars a year. Mr. Leaver supervises the par stocks and all purchasing for the correctional facilities. He is a member of the executive team at a cook-chill plant that produces 130,000 portions of food per day. They currently ship their products to 41 correctional facilities and the Training Academy.

Adding and Subtracting by a Percent

It is necessary to understand the steps taken when adding or subtracting a number or amount by a percent to find a given number. Remember that percentage is the language used quite often in the food service industry to convey the importance of a certain figure. The more practice you acquire dealing with percent the greater your advantage.

Adding a Percent

Problem: The Showboat Restaurant purchased $593.51 worth of kitchen equipment. The sales tax was 5.5 percent. What was the total cost of the equipment?

1. Enter $593.51 × .055 = $32.64
2. $593.51 + 32.64 =
3. $626.15 appears in the display window. This is the total cost.

$626.15 + 5.5% = $626.15

Subtracting a Percent

Kelly Hart purchased a new slicing machine for $2,560. She was given a 15 percent discount. What was the total cost?

1. Enter $2560.00 × .15 = $384.00
2. $2560 − 384.00 =
3. $2176.00 appears in the display window. This is the total cost.

$2560 − 15% = $2176.00

Summary Review

1. $284.62 + 6.5% = ____________
2. $4892.15 + 15.8% = ____________
3. $636.22 − 5.5% = ____________
4. $4192.14 − 10.6% = ____________
5. $982.40 − 6.5% = ____________

Multiplication and Division by a Percent

Multiplication and division by a percent are functions that are performed similarly to the four basic operations in that they are performed just as you would express the problem orally. For example, you would say $580 times 5.5 percent, so on the calculator you would enter 580 × 5.5%, and the correct answer appears in the display window as 31.9 (this is 31.90). Or you can change 5.5 percent to the decimal 0.055 and proceed to find the solution by entering 580 × 0.55 = 31.90. The calculator will automatically place the decimal point, but the dollar sign must be added.

Exercises:

Try the following practice exercises to see if you have mastered this function. Answers are rounded to the nearest cent.

a. $896.25 × 7.5% or 0.075 = (*Answer:* $67.22)

b. $652.40 × 6.7% or 0.067 = (*Answer:* $43.71)

c. $2900 × 35% or 0.35 = (*Answer:* $1015.00)

d. $7200.00 × 15.6% or 0.156 = (*Answer:* $1123.20)

e. 958.20 × 7.9% or 0.079 = (*Answer:* 75.70)

When dividing by a percent, as stated before, the problem is entered just as you would express it orally. For example, you would say $580 divided by 5.5%, and the correct answer appears in the display window as 10545.454, or you can change the 5.5 percent to the decimal 0.055 and proceed to find the solution by first entering 580 ÷ 0.055 =. Again, the calculator will automatically place the decimal point, but the dollar sign must be added.

Exercises:

Try the following practice exercises to see if you have mastered this function. Answers are rounded to the nearest cent.

a. $896.25 ÷ 75% or 0.75 = (*Answer:* $1195.00)

b. $652.40 ÷ 6.7% or 0.067 = (*Answer:* $9737.31)

c. $2900.00 ÷ 35% or 0.35 = (*Answer:* $8285.71)

d. $7200.00 ÷ 15.6% or 0.156 = (*Answer:* $46153.85)

e. $958.20 ÷ 7.9% or 0.079 = (*Answer:* $12129.11)

Summary Review

1. \$996.30 × 7.5% = ________
2. \$565.45 × 6.5% = ________
3. \$2800.00 × 15.4% = ________
4. \$7452.85 × 5.8% = ________
5. \$788.99 × 6.75% = ________
6. \$425.60 ÷ 75% = ________
7. \$352.75 ÷ 6.4% = ________
8. \$2890.00 ÷ 14.2% = ________
9. \$7252.80 ÷ 5.4% = ________
10. \$956.26 ÷ 7.9% = ________

The Memory Function

The **memory function** is used to retain figures in the calculator. Even when the power is turned off, some calculators will retain figures. This function makes totalling an invoice or figuring other totals simpler when multiplying by a percent. Since the keys of some calculators may vary slightly, it is wise to check a calculator's instruction booklet before using its memory function. For example:

Before starting, press the C and CM keys to clear the calculator and its memory. The following is a step by step outline of how to use the memory function to complete an invoice. (See Figure 1-3.) Each step corresponds to a line of the invoice as shown in Figure 1-4.

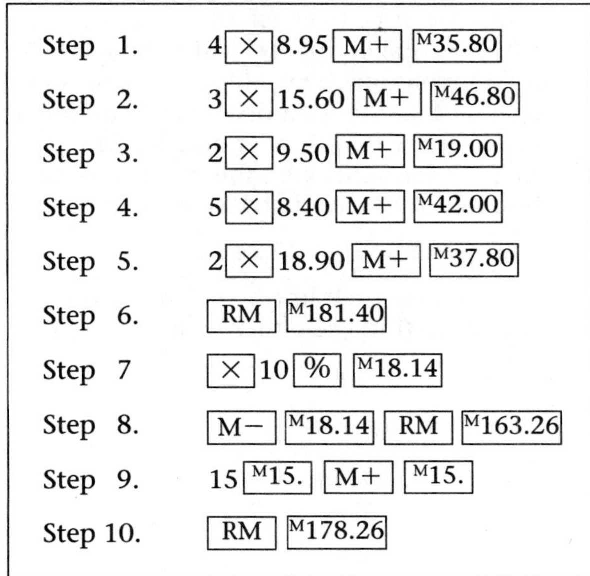

Figure 1-3 *Step-by-step outline for use of the memory function*

Distributor:	Haines Foods, Inc.			Phone: 771-8800 Date: April 20, 20___	
Address:	70 Greenbrier Avenue Ft. Mitchell, KY 41017				
	Distributors of Fine Food Products — Wholesale Only				
No. of Pieces 5	Salesperson Joe Jones			Order No. 2860	Invoice # J 2479
Packed by: R.H.	Sold To: Mr. John Doe Street: 120 Elm Avenue City: Covington, KY				

Case	Pack	Size	Canned Foods	Price	Amount
4	6	#10 can	Sliced Apples	8.95	35.80
3	6	#10 can	Pitted Cherries	15.60	46.80
2	12	#5 can	Apple Juice	9.50	19.00
5	24	1 lb.	Cornstarch	8.40	42.00
2	24	#2$\frac{1}{2}$ can	Asparagus	18.90	37.80
			Total Amount		181.40
			Less: Special Discount 10%		18.14
			Total Net Price		163.26
			Plus: Delivery Charge		15.00
			Total Invoice Price		178.26

Figure 1-4 *Invoice form*

Using the calculator, check the accuracy of the completed invoice of M&D Foods Company, Inc. (Figure 1-5). Multiply the number of cases times the price to check the accuracy of the amount given on each line. When mistakes appear, make the necessary corrections. Also check the total invoice price by adding all figures in the amount column. You may do this exercise with or without the memory function. However, using the memory function for practice will increase your confidence in the future. To start checking the invoice using the memory function, the first line would be calculated as follows:

6 × 20.87 M + 125.22 M   Display Window

Complete each line by following the procedure given in the above example. To find the total invoice price, press the RM key (recall memory).

DISTRIBUTORS OF

Mrs. Kay's

finest foods

Professionally Prefered Food Products

M & D

FOODS COMPANY, INC.

Manufacturers and Distributors of Quality Food Specialties

9888 N 600 East
Wilkinson, IN 46186

Invoice № 13503

OFFICE
Wilkinson . . . . (317) 326-3115

NAME			SHIP TO Houston Park Nursing Home	
STREET & NO.			STREET & NO. 254 Houston Road	
CITY	STATE	ZIP	CITY Florence	STATE KY ZIP 41042

ORDER NO.	DEPT.	BUYER	SALESMAN	WHEN SHIP	TERMS	HOW SHIP	DATE
2863		RG	CK		charge	UPS	11/12/01

CASE	SIZE		UNIT	PRICE	AMOUNT	
6	#10	sliced apples	case	20.87	125	22
4	#10	sliced pineapple	case	17.27	69	08
8	#10	tomato puree	case	13.85	110	80
7	#10	green beans, cut	case	11.58	81	06
3	#10	tomatoes, whole peeled	case	16.98	50	94
2	10 lbs	fettuccine, long	lbs	6.56	13	12
4	10 lbs	vermicelli, cut	lbs	5.20	20	80
2	13 oz	pickling spices	oz	4.18	8	36
3	6 oz	rubbed sage	oz	5.42	16	26
2	11 oz	thyme, ground	oz	5.89	11	78
5	46 oz	cranberry juice cocktail	case	22.66	113	30
3	50 lbs	granulated sugar	bag	16.70	50	10
		Total invoice price			$670	82

Figure 1-5 *Completed invoice form (Courtesy of M & D Foods Company, Inc.)*

SUMMARY REVIEW

1. Complete the following invoice, using your calculator and its memory function.

Distributor:	Miller Foods, Inc.			Phone: 772-9654 Date: April 22, 2000	
Address:	2033 Elm Avenue Norwood, Ohio 45212				
	Distributors of Fine Food Products — Wholesale Only				
No. of Pieces 4	Salesperson James Jones			Order No. 2861	Invoice # J 2480
Packed by: R.H.	Sold To: Street: City:	Mr. Tim O'Connell 916 Montague Street Cincinnati, Ohio 45202			

Case	Pack	Size	Canned Foods	Price	Amount
5	6	#10 can	Sliced Pears	$10.95	______
3	6	#10 can	Sliced Peaches	12.85	______
6	12	#5 can	Tomato Juice	9.50	______
4	24	1 lb.	Cornstarch	8.40	______
3	24	#2$\frac{1}{2}$ can	Asparagus	18.90	______
			Total Amount		______
			Less: Special Discount 12%		______
			Total Net Price		______
			Plus: Delivery Charge		$12.00
			Total Invoice Price		______

Multiplying by a Percent Using the Memory Function

Remember that percentage is a key function when developing a food service career. It is, as previously stated, the language of the food service industry. When discussing labor costs, food costs, etc., the figures are given by percent. With this in mind, you can see the importance of understanding and developing confidence in using this function and dealing with percent. For example:

Mr. O'Toole purchased five food items at $18.50 each and three food items at $12.60 each. If the sales tax on the total purchase was 6.5 percent, what was the total cost?

Step 1: 5 × 18.50 M+ = 92.5 M	display window
Step 2: 3 × 12.60 M+ = 37.8 M	display window
Step 3: RM 130.30 M	display window
Step 4: × 6.5% = 8.4695 M	display window
Step 5: M + RM = 138.77 M	display window

Summary Review

1. Chenusa Jones purchased 12 items at $12.60 each. Sales tax was 5.5 percent. What was the total cost?

   ____

2. Bob Shirley purchased 8 items at $6.25 each, and 6 items at $8.95 each. If the sales tax on the total purchase was 6.5 percent, what was the total cost?

   ____

3. Bill Thompson made purchases costing $10.40, $54.80, $7.35, $8.98, and $0.56. If the sales tax was 6.75 percent of the total amount, what was the total cost?

   ____

4. Hillary Meyers purchased 15 items at $16.20 each and 4 items at $20.50 each. If the sales tax on the total purchase was 4.25 percent, what was the total cost?

   ____

5. Sheryar Khan purchased items costing $89.95, $16.75, and $9.25. If the sales tax was 5.75 percent of the total amount, what was the total cost?

   ____

Using the Plus/Minus Key

This change sign key is used to convert a positive number to a negative number and vice versa. The key is only used on certain occasions and would not be considered a popular key like the 3 or 1 key. For example:

The Blue Bird Restaurant purchased some used equipment for $2,800. It was given a special discount of 8 percent plus a sales tax of 6.5 percent. What was the total cost?

Enter 2800.00 × 8% 224 – 2800 = 2576– ±2576 + 6.5 %
2743.44 appears in the display window. This is the total cost.

In the above calculation, the 2576 appears with a minus sign, which is a negative number. To add the 6.5 percent sales tax, that negative sign must be converted to a positive sign so the sales tax amount can be added to the cost. This is accomplished by pressing the plus/minus key after the amount 2576– appears in the display window.

SUMMARY REVIEW

1. The Chateau Restaurant purchased a dessert cart for $1,680. Because the cart was slightly damaged, they were given a 7.5 percent discount. A sales tax of 5.5 percent was added to the purchase price. What was the total cost?

   ____

2. The Sky Lark Restaurant purchased new china for $4,868.54. Because they chose a discontinued pattern, they were given an 8 percent discount. A sales tax of 6.5 percent was added to the purchase price. What was the total cost?

   ____

3. A party was catered for 60 people. The bill came to $480. A senior citizen discount of 4.5 percent was given. A sales tax of 6 percent was added to the bill. What was the total bill?

   ____

4. A party for 90 people was served. The bill was $810. A discount of 3.5 percent was given because it was a school group. A sales tax of 6.5 percent was added to the bill. What was the total bill?

   ____

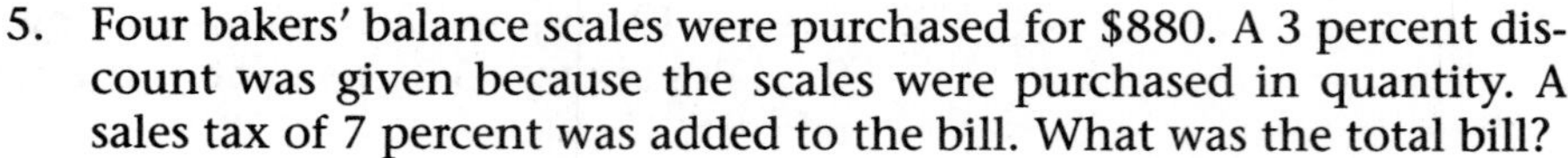

5. Four bakers' balance scales were purchased for $880. A 3 percent discount was given because the scales were purchased in quantity. A sales tax of 7 percent was added to the bill. What was the total bill?

   ____

PART II

REVIEW OF BASIC MATH FUNDAMENTALS

Part II contains a review of the basic math fundamentals used in most food service operations. Whole numbers, fractions, decimals, and percents are among the topics covered. Competency in each area of this review section is essential for ensuring accuracy in working the math exercises presented in this work text and for accurate recordkeeping when performing math functions in the food service industry.

Numbers, Symbols of Operations, and the Mill

OBJECTIVES

At the completion of this chapter, the student should be able to:

1. Read and write numbers.
2. Identify the symbols for the four basic operations of addition, subtraction, multiplication, and division.
3. Identify the mill and use it in solving problems.

The information presented in this chapter is intended to refresh your knowledge of basic mathematical terms and principles that you have learned in your early school years, but may not have put into practice often enough to retain. These terms and principles are important to all math functions. They will be used throughout the book. If they are not fully understood, it will be impossible for you to increase your math skills, and without math skills it is difficult to function effectively in the workplace.

The food service industry, in the 21st century, will continue to require employees to possess math skills. The industry is extremely competitive, and controlling cost (e.g., food, beverage, labor, etc.) is vital to the survival of any business venture.

Math skills start with the understanding of terms such as *whole numbers, units, numerals,* and *digits.*

You may feel you fully understand all these terms, but it is still important that you study this chapter, if only to adjust your attitude to a more enthusiastic approach toward refreshing your math skills.

Chef Sez . . .

"What is your labor cost, your food cost, your beverage cost, your increase in covers over last month, your variable expenses, your overhead, your break-even, your cost of capital, your revenue per square foot, your inventory turnover or your profitability? All of these are questions, which you will need to know to operate an effective and profitable business. All of these questions can be answered by having the ability to understand and analyze numbers through mathematics. But many food service operators have difficulty interpreting these relationships; thus they are only able to make decisions based on limited knowledge of the situation. A food service manager does not need to be an accountant to operate a profitable enterprise, but a food service manager does need to have a working knowledge of basic mathematics to make daily decisions on the health of their business."

George R. Goldoff
Director of Food and Beverage
Bellagio
Las Vegas, Nevada

Mr. Goldoff oversees the success of the 21 restaurants and outlets that serve food, along with the four bars and nine service bars at this prestigious hotel, resort, and gaming complex. Revenue from food and beverage sales is $175,000,000 (yes, that's right 175 million dollars). Bellagio employs 750 cooks and 2,700 food and beverage employees.

NUMBERS

Whole numbers are numbers such as 0, 1, 2, 3, 4, 5, 6, 7, 8, and 9, that are used to represent whole units rather than fractional units. A **unit** is a standard quantity or amount. Units, of course, are not limited to manufactured products. A unit may be a single quantity of like products such as a case of apple juice. Units are often established by producers or manufacturers. The unit they establish is usually a quantity that is convenient for both the consumer and producer. Some convenient and sensible units for individuals could include a quart or gallon of milk, a pound of butter, a pint or quart of strawberries, or a dozen oranges. In the food service industry, convenient and sensible units might include a #10 can of fruit or vegetables, a 100-pound bag of flour, or a 5-pound box of bacon. Convenient and sensible units also help a manufacturer or business keep track of inventories.

Numerals are used to represent or express numbers. For example, 8, 21, 450, II, and X are numerals because they express numbers. The individual numbers on a clock are numerals as well.

Digits are any of the numerals that combine to form numbers.

There are 10 digits, as shown in Figure 2-1, with the names that you should be quite familiar with.

0	1	2	3	4	5	6	7	8	9
zero	one	two	three	four	five	six	seven	eight	nine

Figure 2-1 *Digits*

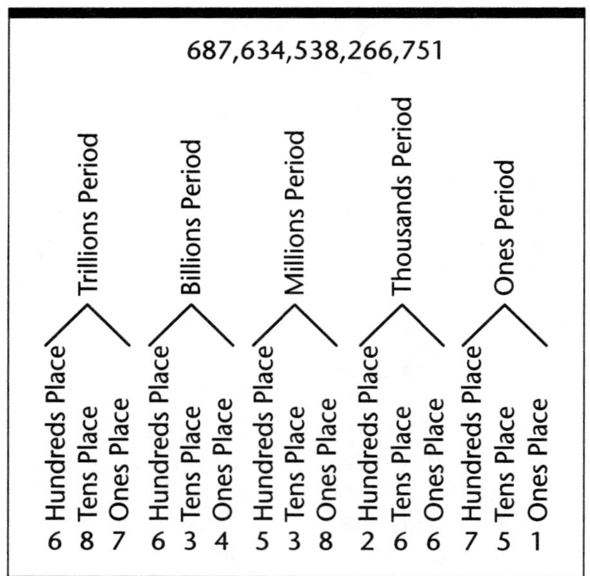

Figure 2-2 *Place value columns within each period*

Digits can be combined in various ways to produce different numbers. For example, 457 and 745 are both combinations of the digits 7, 5, and 4. The value of each digit depends on where it is placed in the combination of numbers. Each place has a different name and therefore a different value, as shown in Figure 2-2.

In large groups of numbers made up of four or more digits, the digits are placed into groups of three. Each of these groups is called a **period,** as shown in Figure 2-2. Periods are separated with commas. (In the metric system, to be discussed later in this text, periods are separated by space rather than commas.) The value of each digit is determined by its position in the place value columns. In Figure 2-2, the digit 5 is used twice. When it appears in the tens place of the ones period, the 5 represents 50. When it is used in the hundreds place of the millions period, it represents 500 million. As you can see, *place* is very important when numbers are grouped.

In the food service industry, the billions and trillions periods are very seldom or ever required. These periods are used by big business and our government when discussing budgets and the national debt. Major restaurant chains and some popular restaurant establishments will present and use figures in the millions place, but that is usually the extent of profit or loss figures.

Commas are used to separate periods. They are used for financial records such as profit and loss statements and balance sheets. Commas are also used when writing checks, both professionally and personally.

T I P S . . . ***To Insure Perfect Solutions***

When placing commas, start at the right then count three places and insert a comma.

SUMMARY REVIEW

Separate the following numbers into periods. Then show how the number should be written. Example: 539,256,750. Five hundred thirty nine million two hundred fifty six thousand seven hundred fifty.

1. 4956 ____________________
2. 10495 ____________________
3. 245620425 ____________________
4. 26495 ____________________
5. 218873296 ____________________
6. 48973 ____________________
7. 210000000 ____________________
8. 41213728 ____________________
9. 97822732642 ____________________
10. 8725351280 ____________________

Large numbers are also expressed with the names shown in Figure 2-3. The digit 0 in the ones column is needed to hold a place and to give the other digits their proper value. The digit 6 in the tens place would be 6, not 60, without the zero. The complete number shown in Figure 2-3 is read "eight billion nine hundred twenty five million four hundred fifty one thousand two hundred sixty." Zeroes are not read. The number 149,000,000 is read "one hundred forty nine million." The word "and" is not used in reading whole numbers.

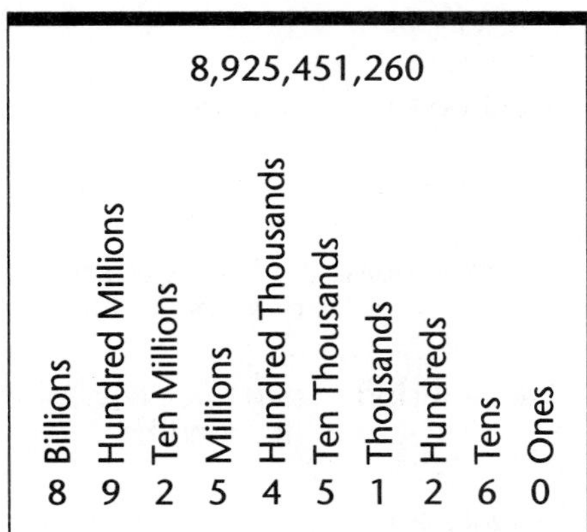

Figure 2-3 *Place values*

Symbols of Operations

There are four basic arithmetic operations: addition, subtraction, multiplication, and division. Math symbols are used to indicate which of these four operations is required in any given transaction or arithmetic problem. The importance of math symbols can be demonstrated by selecting two numerals and setting up problems using each of the four basic math symbols. The problems appear to be similar until the symbol is added.

(a) $\begin{array}{r} 10 \\ +\,2 \\ \hline 12 \end{array}$ (b) $\begin{array}{r} 10 \\ -\,2 \\ \hline 8 \end{array}$ (c) $\begin{array}{r} 10 \\ \times\,2 \\ \hline 20 \end{array}$ (d) $10 \div 2 = 5$ or $\frac{10}{2} = 5$

As you can see, the math symbol used will yield different results and dictates the direction the problem will take.

Example (a), of course, is addition, (b) is subtraction, (c) is multiplication, and (d) is division. Figure 2-4 provides the names, meaning, and some examples of the symbols commonly used in the food service industry.

Symbol	Name	Meaning	Examples
+	plus sign	add to, or increase by	8 + 99 = 107 2 + 19 = 21 361 + 12 = 373
–	minus sign	subtract from, take away from, decrease by, or less	17 – 9 = 8 23 – 5 = 18 49 – 9 = 40
×	multiplication or times sign	multiply by, or the product of	2 × 12 = 24 9 × 3 = 27 5 × 25 = 125
÷	division sign	divided by	4 ÷ 2 = 2 27 ÷ 9 = 3 100 ÷ 20 = 5
___	fraction bar	separates numerator and denominator	$\frac{6}{3} = 2$ $\frac{10}{5} = 2$ $\frac{20}{5} = 4$
.	decimal point	indicates the beginning of a decimal fraction	0.321 1.877 117.65
%	percent sign	parts per 100, by the hundredths	15% 12% 6%
=	equal sign	the same value as, or is equal to	1 = 1
$	dollar sign	the symbol placed before a number to indicate that it stands for dollars	$12.00
@	at or per	used to indicate price or weight of each unit when there is a quantity of a unit	5 doz. doughnuts @ $1.15/doz. 25 bags of potatoes @ 10 lb./bag 100 ice cream cones @ $0.25 per cone

Figure 2-4 *Mathematical symbols*

SUMMARY REVIEW

In the problems or statements following, the symbol of operation has been omitted. In each instance, determine the symbol that should be placed in the blank.

1. Meaning by the hundredths. ________________
2. Used to indicate price of each unit. ________________
3. Used to separate the numerator from the denominator when dealing with fractions. ________________
4. Indicates the beginning of a decimal fraction. ________________
5. A symbol placed before a monetary figure. ________________
6. 24 ____ 15 = 360
7. 284 ____ 4 = 71
8. He purchased a dozen ____ $1.99 per dozen.
9. 28 × 2 ____ 56
10. A waitress is usually tipped 15 ____ of the total bill.
11. 1540 ____ 5 = 308
12. 1850 ____ 360 = 1490
13. 2075 ____ 190 = 2265
14. The food cost for the month was 38 ____.
15. The restaurant purchased six cases of sliced apples ____ $12.50 per case.

THE MILL

When dealing with monetary numbers, **cent** is used to represent the value of one hundredth part of a dollar. The third place to the right of the decimal is called a **mill** and represents the thousandth part of a dollar, or one tenth of one cent.

When the final result of a monetary number includes a mill, it is usually rounded to a whole number of cents. To round a number to the nearest cent, the third digit (the mill) is dropped if it is less than 5. If that digit is **5 or more,** another cent is added to the digit before it. For example:

> $4.626 rounded to the nearest cent is $4.63 because 6 mills are more than 5.
>
> $4.623 rounded to the nearest cent is $4.62 because 3 mills are less than 5.

The mill is an important figure in the food service industry because the production cost of an item and the cost of menu food items are figured to the mill to obtain the exact cost of the item. The exact cost is very important when figuring a menu or selling price. For example, when producing rolls, it is necessary to know that each roll may cost $0.043 to produce, making the cost of one dozen rolls $0.516 or $0.52. In the case of a menu item the manager must determine the cost of a serving before he or she can determine a selling or menu price.

T I P S . . . *To Insure Perfect Solutions*

Find the answer to the problem. The *LAST* step is rounding to the mill.

Summary Review

Answer the following questions about the mill.

1. How many mills are contained in one cent? ______________
2. How many mills are contained in 10 cents? ______________
3. How many mills are contained in $1.00? ______________
4. What is the rule to follow if the mill is 4 or less? ______________. Five or more? ______________

Change the following amounts to the nearest cent.

5. $0.045 ______________
6. $0.57 ______________
7. $0.058 ______________
8. $0.042 ______________
9. $0.073 ______________
10. $0.064 ______________
11. $0.012 ______________
12. $0.124 ______________
13. $638.514 ______________
14. $8,425.783 ______________
15. $542.237 ______________

Addition, Subtraction, Multiplication, and Division

OBJECTIVES

At the completion of this chapter, the student should be able to:

1. Find sums.
2. Find differences.
3. Check subtraction by adding.
4. Find products using the multiplication table.
5. Use a step-by-step procedure to find products.
6. Check the accuracy of the multiplication product.
7. Find quotients.
8. Find the remainder.
9. Check the accuracy of the division quotient.

In this chapter, the four most basic, and essential, math functions—addition, subtraction, multiplication, and division—will be covered. In these pages you will not only revisit the foundation of all computation, but you will also see how these computations are integral to food service operations.

TIPS . . . ***To Insure Perfect Solutions***

We read words from left to right. We solve math problems working from right to left.

Chef Sez . . .

"As professionals in the culinary profession one must possess, in addition to the necessary culinary skills, the knowledge and expertise of the "numbers." This means that when calculating costs and percentages of departments, it is important that those figures are precise in order to achieve financial success. Therefore, it is important to have education, specifically math, for it is an attribute for achievements in anyone's career."

Bert P. Cutino, Certified Executive Chef,
American Academy of Chefs,
Co-Founder and Chef
SARDINE FACTORY RESTAURANT
Monterey, California

Chef Bert Cutino, along with Ted Balestreri, started the SARDINE FACTORY RESTAURANT on October 2, 1968 with 72 seats in a nearly abandoned area known as Cannery Row. The restaurant was located in a building that once fed sardine workers. The restaurant has expanded to include five different dining rooms that seat 250, and it has sales of 4 million dollars a year. It is one of the most successful, widely recognized, and highest grossing dining establishments in the United States. The SARDINE FACTORY has been the recipient of virtually every major restaurant and wine award in the industry, including the prestigious DiRoNA Award since 1993. With its inventory of 30,000 wine bottles and 1,375 labels, the restaurant has earned the Wine Spectator's Grand Award since 1982; the Nation's Restaurant News Hall of Fame Award (1981); Restaurant and Institutions Ivy Award (1980); and the list continues.

Mr. Cutino attributes his success through the years to his unwavering commitment to quality. He feels that each person on staff, from waitpersons to kitchen staff, must be able to present himself or herself as a professional and strive for excellence.

ADDITION

Addition can be considered one of the most popular math functions because it means an increase is taking place. In any business venture it is the desire of the operator that the increase shows up in the form of a nice profit.

Addition is the act of putting things together, or combining things or units that are alike, to obtain a total quantity. This total quantity is called the **sum.** If you have \$6.00 and are given \$10.00, you have a total of \$16.00. This simple addition problem can be written two different ways. For example:

$$\$6.00 + \$10.00 = \$16.00$$

Written with the numbers placed in a row or line, it is called the *horizontal position.* The horizontal position is seldom used in a problem involving large numbers because the way the numbers are positioned makes it difficult to calculate the answer.

This same problem can also be written in what is called the *vertical* or *column position.*

$$\begin{array}{r} \$\ 6.00 \\ +\ 10.00 \\ \hline \$16.00 \end{array}$$

In both instances the plus sign, a symbol of operation, is used to indicate that the numbers are to be added. Figure 3-1 shows an example of how addition is used in food service.

Figure 3-1 *How many servings of Zabaglione? This is an example of the use of addition (2 + 3 = 5) in food service.*

T I P S . . . ***To Insure Perfect Solutions***

Addend plus Addend equals Sum

or

$$\begin{array}{r} \text{Addend} \\ +\ \underline{\text{Addend}} \\ \text{Sum} \end{array}$$

As another example, when serving a sirloin steak dinner, if there are 25 steaks ready to be served, 18 on the broiler cooking, and 125 stored in the refrigerator, the food service establishment has a total of 168 steaks on hand. Since all of the units to be added are alike, it is unnecessary to write out what the units are. Therefore, the addition can be written in either of the following ways:

$$25 + 18 + 125 = 168 \quad \text{(or)} \quad \begin{array}{r} 25 \\ 18 \\ \underline{+125} \\ 168 \end{array}$$

It is not necessary to use the plus sign when three or more numbers are added together in the vertical position because it cannot be confused with any other arithmetic operation. Remember that each digit must be placed in the correct column to give it the proper value.

Computing addition problems manually may be considered a task of the past because everyone uses calculators today. Nevertheless, it is still wise to understand the rules and proper steps for solving addition problems this way because situations may arise when a calculator is unavailable or, worse yet, the battery may go dead while you are performing an important calculation. It is never wise to depend entirely on calculators or adding machines. Absorb the information and examples presented in this chapter so that you can add rapidly and accurately should automation ever fail you.

Guidelines

There are several basic guidelines that can be followed in arithmetic problems to save time and to improve accuracy.

Be Neat. If you are interested in a food service career, neatness is essential in both your physical appearance and personal hygiene. Neatness is also important in math. It does not require additional time to write neatly and carefully, placing each number in the proper column directly under the number above it, as shown below.

$$\begin{array}{r} 2\,1\,5\,8 \\ 3\,6 \\ 5\,2\,6 \\ 2\,0\,9 \\ 8\,5 \\ +\ 1\,9\,2\,2 \\ \hline 4\,9\,3\,6 \end{array}$$

T I P S . . . ***To Insure Perfect Solutions***

Always write down trades (carryovers).

Neatness is also important when trading (carrying) numbers over from one column to the next. The sum of the ones column in the preceding problem is 36 and not 6. The 3 (actually 30) is traded (carried over) to the tens column. When the trade (carryover) 3 is written, it is placed neatly at the top of the tens column so that it is not overlooked when counting that column. The sum of the tens column is 23 (actually 230). The 2 is traded (carried over) to the hundreds column. Again, place the 2 neatly over the top of the hundreds column. Follow this procedure for each column in the problem as shown below:

$$\begin{array}{r} ①\ ②\ ③\ \ \\ 2\,1\,5\,8 \\ 3\,6 \\ 5\,2\,6 \\ 2\,0\,9 \\ 8\,5 \\ +\ 1\,9\,2\,2 \\ \hline 4\,9\,3\,6 \end{array}$$

Check Your Work. All work must be checked, even when using a calculator, to be sure your addition is correct. Mistakes can be made even when calculating automatically. Even if you find, through checking, that your work is always correct, the practice should still be continued. The penalty for mathematical errors in the classroom is only a lower grade; the penalty for errors in a food service operation can result in a monetary loss for both you and your employer.

The common method of checking addition is to add the individual columns in reverse order. For example, if you originally added the columns from top to bottom, which is the usual practice, you can check your work by adding a second time, from bottom to top. Just reverse your procedure.

Increase Your Accuracy and Speed. Addition is often simplified if numbers are combined and then added. For example, in the problem 7 + 3 +

8 + 2 + 5 + 3 = 28, the addition is greatly simplified by combining 7 and 3 into 10, and 8 and 2 into 10, which adds up to twenty. Adding the remaining numbers (5 and 3) gives 8, which makes a total of 28.

Eliminate unnecessary steps when adding. One method of increasing your speed and accuracy is that instead of thinking seven plus three equals ten, automatically see the seven and three combination as ten. When adding the problem in the previous paragraph, do not think that ten plus ten equals twenty, plus five equals twenty-five, plus three equals twenty-eight. Think, ten, twenty, twenty-eight.

If these guidelines are followed, it will help you to ensure the accuracy and speed required for any type of addition problem, especially those related to food service. Some of these guidelines, such as neatness and checking your work, apply to all arithmetic operations.

SUMMARY REVIEW

Find the sum of each of the following addition problems. Use the methods and guidelines suggested in this chapter. To improve your math skills, calculate these problems manually and then check your work.

1.
```
  6
+ 9
---
```

2.
```
  4
  7
  6
+ 3
---
```

3. 3 + 5 + 8 + 11 = ____

4. 24 + 19 + 12 + 28 = ____

5.
```
  259
+ 147
-----
```

6.
```
  338
  225
+ 648
-----
```

7.
```
 $56.17
  49.54
  26.38
+ 18.52
-------
```

8.
```
  312
  422
  345
  239
+ 751
-----
```

9.
```
 $366.26
  441.31
  374.43
  223.23
+152.43
-------
```

10.
```
     8
    28
   335
  2765
   222
   589
    17
   259
+  126
------
```

11.
```
 $ 43.16
   42.19
   41.20
   38.72
   31.42
   29.73
   25.42
   27.63
   18.64
+  16.25
--------
```

12.
```
 $555.25
  216.11
  140.18
  310.20
  713.14
  726.12
  289.82
  326.22
  129.10
+ 222.12
--------
```

13. If a person's guest check includes an omelette @ $2.80, French toast @ $2.75, and coffee @ $0.55, how much is the total check?

____

14. When preparing a fruit salad bowl the following items were used: oranges $1.98, apples $0.79, grapes $0.92, bananas $1.69, strawberries $2.68, peaches $1.47, and pineapple $0.98. What was the total cost of the fruit salad bowl?

____

15. The restaurant had 203 orders of chicken in the freezer—126 in the walk-in refrigerator and 59 in the reach-in refrigerator. How many orders of chicken did they have on hand?

____

SUBTRACTION

Subtraction means to take away. It is the removal of one number of things from another number of things. (See Figure 3-2.) The word "subtract" is very seldom used except in its mathematical sense. The popular word used in the business world is "deduct," which also means to take away. For

Figure 3-2 *Subtraction is taking place when a serving portion is removed from others (8 − 1 = 7).*

example, instead of saying "he *subtracted* a discount of $2.00 from my bill," the statement would be, "he *deducted* a discount of $2.00 from my bill."

If you have $12.00 and spend $8.25, the subtraction problem is written as follows:

$12.00
− 8.25
$ 3.75

The minus sign (−) must always be used so that the problem is not confused with another mathematical operation.

Each of the factors in subtraction has a name. The original number before subtraction, or before anything is removed, is called the **minuend.** In the example above, the minuend is $12.00. The number removed from the minuend is called the **subtrahend.** Finally, the amount left over or remaining after the problem is completed is called the **difference.**

1585	Minuend
− 742	Subtrahend
843	Difference

Trading (Borrowing)

Subtraction frequently requires **trading (borrowing).** When trading add ten to the ones column of the minuend, at the same time diminish the number in the tens column by one. Although the minuend is usually a larger number than the subtrahend, a particular digit in the minuend may be less than the digit beneath it in the subtrahend, so trading (borrowing) is required. Example: 1,723 − 688 = 1,038. When this problem is set up in the vertical position, it looks like this:

	thousands	hundreds	tens	ones	
	1	7	2	3	Minuend
−		6	8	8	Subtrahend
	1	0	3	5	Difference

T I P S . . . ***To Insure Perfect Solutions***

Minuend minus Subtrahend equals Difference

or

Minuend
− Subtrahend
Difference

T I P S . . . ***To Insure Perfect Solutions***

Always write down trades (carryovers).

The minuend (1,723) is clearly a larger number than the subtrahend (688). However, the digit 8 in the ones column of the subtrahend is larger than the digit 3 in the ones column of the minuend. Since 8 cannot be subtracted from 3, it becomes necessary to trade (borrow) from the tens column.

To indicate that a ten has been traded (borrowed), cross out the 2 in the tens column and write 1 above it. If this step is neglected, you may sometimes forget that you traded (borrowed).

$$\begin{array}{rrrrr} & & & 1 & 13 \\ & 1 & \cancel{7} & \cancel{2} & \cancel{3} \\ - & & 6 & 8 & 8 \\ \hline \end{array}$$

Add the traded (borrowed) ten to the 3 in the ones column, which increases the 3 to 13. Then subtract $13 - 8 = 5$. The five is written beneath the bar in the ones column.

$$\begin{array}{rrrrr} & & & 1 & 13 \\ & 1 & \cancel{7} & \cancel{2} & \cancel{3} \\ - & & 6 & 8 & 8 \\ \hline & & & & 5 \end{array}$$

In the tens column, 8 cannot be subtracted from 1 (actually 80 from 10), so it is necessary to trade (borrow) a hundred from the hundreds column. This is done by crossing out the numeral 7 in the hundreds column and writing 6 above it.

$$\begin{array}{rrrrr} & & 6 & 11 & 13 \\ & 1 & \cancel{7} & \cancel{2} & \cancel{3} \\ - & & 6 & 8 & 8 \\ \hline & & & & 5 \end{array}$$

Return to the tens column, subtract 8 from 11 (actually 80 from 110) to get 3 (actually 30). Write the 3 in the tens column beneath the bar.

$$\begin{array}{rrrrr} & & 6 & 11 & 13 \\ & 1 & \cancel{7} & \cancel{2} & \cancel{3} \\ - & & 6 & 8 & 8 \\ \hline & & & 3 & 5 \end{array}$$

Moving to the hundreds column, 6 can be subtracted from 6 (which is actually 600 from 600). Even though nothing will remain, a zero is used to hold a place. Trading (borrowing), therefore, is unnecessary in this column.

$$\begin{array}{rrrrr} & & 6 & 11 & 13 \\ & 1 & \cancel{7} & \cancel{2} & \cancel{3} \\ - & & 6 & 8 & 8 \\ \hline & & 0 & 3 & 5 \end{array}$$

The problem is completed by bringing down the 1 that remains in the thousands column. The completed problem appears below:

$$\begin{array}{rrrrr} & & 6 & 11 & 13 \\ & 1 & \cancel{7} & \cancel{2} & \cancel{3} \\ - & & 6 & 8 & 8 \\ \hline & 1 & 0 & 3 & 5 \end{array}$$

Checking Subtraction

Checking any math problem is always a wise step to take even when using a calculator because errors are so easily made. The common way of checking a subtraction answer is to add together the subtrahend and the difference. The sum of these two numbers should equal the minuend.

Subtraction:		Check:	
3 6 4 2	Minuend	2 1 3 2	Subtrahend
− 2 1 3 2	Subtrahend	+ 1 5 1 0	Difference
1 5 1 0	Difference	3 6 4 2	Minuend

SUMMARY REVIEW

Find the difference in the following subtraction problems. Calculate these problems manually and then check your work.

1. 955 − 214 = ________ 2. 688 − 520 = ________

3. 4925 − 1647 = ________

4. 743 − 526 5. 828 − 612 6. 5197 − 2058

7. \$24.43 − 15.20 8. \$76.32 − 56.54 9. \$132.77 − 57.99

10. \$7,333.64 − 6,132.45 11. \$221,004.03 − 74,623.07

12. The bill for the wedding party came to \$1,585.21. They were given a discount of \$121.00 because the guaranteed number of people attended. What was the total bill?

____

13. The restaurant thought they had 76 live lobsters on hand. Taking a quick inventory, it was discovered that 18 were dead. How many live lobsters did the restaurant have left?

____

14. A restaurant had 240 chickens in the freezer. They used 31 for a special party. How many did they have left?

____

15. A restaurant purchased 268 pounds of sirloin. Thirty-six pounds were lost in boning and trimming. How many pounds were left?

____

MULTIPLICATION

Multiplication is another math operation where an increase takes place. Methods that bring forth an increase such as addition seem to be most popular especially if the increase is spelled "profit" or carries a dollar sign. Multiplication can be thought of as a shortcut for a certain type of addition problem. In **multiplication,** a whole number is added to itself a specified amount of times. For example, $4 \times 2 = 8$ is another way of expressing $4 + 4 = 8$. The number 4 is added to itself two times.

Since a relationship exists between addition and multiplication, it does not matter which operation is used in simple problems such as the one above. However, when the problem consists of problems involving large numbers (such as $4531 \times 6580 = ?$), addition is an impractical way of solving the problem. This is when multiplication becomes useful as a shortcut for addition. Working out the preceding problem is quite lengthy using multiplication, as shown in the following example. Now just imagine what would be involved if done by addition:

$$
\begin{array}{r}
6580 \\
\times \quad 4531 \\
\hline
6580 \\
19740 \\
32900 \\
26320 \\
\hline
29813980
\end{array}
$$

TIPS . . . ***To Insure Perfect Solutions***

Multiplier times Multiplicand equals Product

or

$$
\begin{array}{r}
\text{Multiplier} \\
- \ \text{Multiplicand} \\
\hline
\text{Product}
\end{array}
$$

Each number involved in the multiplication process has a name. The number which is added to itself (4 in the example, $4 \times 2 = 8$) is called the **multiplicand** (which means "going to be multiplied"). The number representing the amount of times the multiplicand is to be added to itself is called the **multiplier** (number 2 in the example). The result of multiplying the multiplicand by the multiplier is called the **product.** The product in our example is 8.

The following example gives the names and functions of the various numbers involved in the multiplication operation.

362	Multiplicand
× 32	Multiplier
724	Subproduct
10860	Subproduct
11584	Product

Function	**Name**
Number to be added to itself	Multiplicand
Number of times to be added to itself	Multiplier
Product of the ones column	Subproduct
Product of the tens column	Subproduct
Final result (answer)	Product

In this example, subproducts are shown. **Subproducts** (sub meaning under, below, or before; product being the result of multiplying) occur whenever the multiplier consists of two or more digits. In this case, the multiplier is 32. The first subproduct is the result of the product 362 × 2 = 724. The second subproduct (10,860) is the result of multiplying 362 × 30. The zero at the end of this subproduct is not necessary because 4 + 0 = 4. It does not affect the outcome of the problem, and is only shown here to illustrate that the product of multiplying 362 × 30 is 10,860 and not 1,086. It also helps keep all of the digits in their proper columns (ones in the ones column, tens in the tens column, and so forth), as mentioned earlier in relation to subtraction.

Once all of the subproducts are determined, they are added together to obtain the final total or product (in this example, 11,584). The multiplication sign (also called the times sign) is always used in a multiplication problem to distinguish it from any other type of arithmetic operation.

The Multiplication Table

It has now been demonstrated to you through examples that multiplication is a shortcut for certain types of addition problems. A shortcut method is only valuable if it can be used efficiently and accurately. The key to using multiplication efficiently is the multiplication table. (See Figure 3-3, giving products up to 12 × 12). Accuracy depends on your efforts and how well you have developed your multiplication skills.

Practice the multiplication table until it is memorized. To test how well you have memorized this table, write each problem on one side of an index card and the product on the other side. You should be able to look at a problem and know its answer within five seconds without looking at the other side.

T I P S . . . ***To Insure Perfect Solutions***

Remember the old saying, practice makes perfect.

1 × 1 = 1	5 × 1 = 5	9 × 1 = 9
1 × 2 = 2	5 × 2 = 10	9 × 2 = 18
1 × 3 = 3	5 × 3 = 15	9 × 3 = 27
1 × 4 = 4	5 × 4 = 20	9 × 4 = 36
1 × 5 = 5	5 × 5 = 25	9 × 5 = 45
1 × 6 = 6	5 × 6 = 30	9 × 6 = 54
1 × 7 = 7	5 × 7 = 35	9 × 7 = 63
1 × 8 = 8	5 × 8 = 40	9 × 8 = 72
1 × 9 = 9	5 × 9 = 45	9 × 9 = 81
1 × 10 = 10	5 × 10 = 50	9 × 10 = 90
1 × 11 = 11	5 × 11 = 55	9 × 11 = 99
1 × 12 = 12	5 × 12 = 60	9 × 12 = 108
2 × 1 = 2	6 × 1 = 6	10 × 1 = 10
2 × 2 = 4	6 × 2 = 12	10 × 2 = 20
2 × 3 = 6	6 × 3 = 18	10 × 3 = 30
2 × 4 = 8	6 × 4 = 24	10 × 4 = 40
2 × 5 = 10	6 × 5 = 30	10 × 5 = 50
2 × 6 = 12	6 × 6 = 36	10 × 6 = 60
2 × 7 = 14	6 × 7 = 42	10 × 7 = 70
2 × 8 = 16	6 × 8 = 48	10 × 8 = 80
2 × 9 = 18	6 × 9 = 54	10 × 9 = 90
2 × 10 = 20	6 × 10 = 60	10 × 10 = 100
2 × 11 = 22	6 × 11 = 66	10 × 11 = 110
2 × 12 = 24	6 × 12 = 72	10 × 12 = 120
3 × 1 = 3	7 × 1 = 7	11 × 1 = 11
3 × 2 = 6	7 × 2 = 14	11 × 2 = 22
3 × 3 = 9	7 × 3 = 21	11 × 3 = 33
3 × 4 = 12	7 × 4 = 28	11 × 4 = 44
3 × 5 = 15	7 × 5 = 35	11 × 5 = 55
3 × 6 = 18	7 × 6 = 42	11 × 6 = 66
3 × 7 = 21	7 × 7 = 49	11 × 7 = 77
3 × 8 = 24	7 × 8 = 56	11 × 8 = 88
3 × 9 = 27	7 × 9 = 63	11 × 9 = 99
3 × 10 = 30	7 × 10 = 70	11 × 10 = 110
3 × 11 = 33	7 × 11 = 77	11 × 11 = 121
3 × 12 = 36	7 × 12 = 84	11 × 12 = 132
4 × 1 = 4	8 × 1 = 8	12 × 1 = 12
4 × 2 = 8	8 × 2 = 16	12 × 2 = 24
4 × 3 = 12	8 × 3 = 24	12 × 3 = 36
4 × 4 = 16	8 × 4 = 32	12 × 4 = 48
4 × 5 = 20	8 × 5 = 40	12 × 5 = 60
4 × 6 = 24	8 × 6 = 48	12 × 6 = 72
4 × 7 = 28	8 × 7 = 56	12 × 7 = 84
4 × 8 = 32	8 × 8 = 64	12 × 8 = 96
4 × 9 = 36	8 × 9 = 72	12 × 9 = 108
4 × 10 = 40	8 × 10 = 80	12 × 10 = 120
4 × 11 = 44	8 × 11 = 88	12 × 11 = 132
4 × 12 = 48	8 × 12 = 96	12 × 12 = 144

Figure 3-3 *Multiplication Table of Numbers from 1 through 12.*

1	2	3	4	5	6	7	8	9	10	11	12	13	14	15	16	17	18	19	20	21	22	23	24	25
2	4	6	8	10	12	14	16	18	20	22	24	26	28	30	32	34	36	38	40	42	44	46	48	50
3	6	9	12	15	18	21	24	27	30	33	36	39	42	45	48	51	54	57	60	63	66	69	72	75
4	8	12	16	20	24	28	32	36	40	44	48	52	56	60	64	68	72	76	80	84	88	92	96	100
5	10	15	20	25	30	35	40	45	50	55	60	65	70	75	80	85	90	95	100	105	110	115	120	125
6	12	18	24	30	36	42	48	54	60	66	72	78	84	90	96	102	108	114	120	126	132	138	144	150
7	14	21	28	35	42	49	56	63	70	77	84	91	98	105	112	119	126	133	140	147	154	161	168	175
8	16	24	32	40	48	56	64	72	80	88	96	104	112	120	128	136	144	152	160	168	176	184	192	200
9	18	27	36	45	54	63	72	81	90	99	108	117	126	135	144	153	162	171	180	189	198	207	216	225
10	20	30	40	50	60	70	80	90	100	110	120	130	140	150	160	170	180	190	200	210	220	230	240	250
11	22	33	44	55	66	77	88	99	110	121	132	143	154	165	176	187	198	209	220	231	242	253	264	275
12	24	36	48	60	72	84	96	108	120	132	144	156	168	180	192	204	216	228	240	252	264	276	288	300
13	26	39	52	65	78	91	104	117	130	143	156	169	182	195	208	221	234	247	260	273	286	299	312	325
14	28	42	56	70	84	98	112	126	140	154	168	182	196	210	224	238	252	266	280	294	308	322	336	350
15	30	45	60	75	90	105	120	135	150	165	180	195	210	225	240	255	270	285	300	315	330	345	360	375
16	32	48	64	80	96	112	128	144	160	176	192	208	224	240	256	272	288	304	320	336	352	368	384	400
17	34	51	68	85	102	119	136	153	170	187	204	221	238	255	272	289	306	323	340	357	374	391	408	425
18	36	54	72	90	108	126	144	162	180	198	216	234	252	270	288	306	324	342	360	378	396	414	432	450
19	38	57	76	95	114	133	152	171	190	209	228	247	266	285	304	323	342	361	380	399	418	437	456	475
20	40	60	80	100	120	140	160	180	200	220	240	260	280	300	320	340	360	380	400	420	440	460	480	500
21	42	63	84	105	126	147	168	189	210	231	252	273	294	315	336	357	378	399	420	441	462	483	504	525
22	44	66	88	110	132	154	176	198	220	242	264	286	308	330	352	374	396	418	440	462	484	506	528	550
23	46	69	92	115	138	161	184	207	230	253	276	299	322	345	368	391	414	437	460	483	506	529	552	575
24	48	72	96	120	144	168	192	216	240	264	288	312	336	360	384	408	432	456	480	504	528	552	576	600
25	50	75	100	125	150	175	200	225	250	275	300	325	350	375	400	425	450	475	500	525	550	575	600	625
1	2	3	4	5	6	7	8	9	10	11	12	13	14	15	16	17	18	19	20	21	22	23	24	25

Figure 3-4 *Multiplication Table of Numbers from 1 through 25.*

Another method of presenting the multiplication table is shown in Figure 3-4. This unique table gives the products of numbers up to 25 × 25 = 625. It is relatively simple to use. For example, to find the product of 8 × 9, locate the number 8 in the vertical (up and down) column to the far left. Then move your finger to the right until the nine is located in the horizontal (left to right) column at the top of the table. The number 72 is in the place where the 8 column and the 9 column intersect. Therefore, 72 is the product of 8 × 9. Look one place below the 72 and find the number 81. This is the product of 9 × 9. Drop down another place to find that 10 × 9 = 90.

T I P S . . . ***To Insure Perfect Solutions***

Using a card or sheet of paper across the table horizontally is helpful in locating the products of the various numbers.

Simplifying Multiplication by a Step-By-Step Procedure. This multiplication example is intended to illustrate the step-by-step procedures involved in finding the product. As mentioned earlier, multiplication is a variation of, and has a very close association with, addition. In this example, it will be shown that the product of the problem is the result of adding together the subproduct of each step of the problem.

Example:	924
	× 65
Ones column:	
Step 1. 5 × 4 =	20
Step 2. 5 × 20 =	100
Step 3. 5 × 900 =	4,500
Subproduct of ones column	4,620
Tens column:	
Step 4. 60 × 4 =	240
Step 5. 60 × 20 =	1,200
Step 6. 60 × 900 =	54,000
Subproduct of tens column	55,440
Add subproducts:	
Step 7. 4,620 + 55,440 =	60,060 (Product)

This example shows the steps in finding the product of 924 × 65. Generally when the problem is worked, the unneeded zeros are eliminated, but carryover numbers are used, as shown in the following example:

9 2 4	Multiplicand
× 6 5	Multiplier
4 6 2 0	Subproduct of ones column
5 5 4 4	Subproduct of tens column
6 0 0 6 0	Product

2 is the carryover number for the ones column.
1 is the carryover number for the tens column.

Notice that the subproduct of the ones column in both methods of working the problem is 4,620. The same is true for the subproduct of the tens column, 55,440. The zero is left off the subproduct in the second method because its only purpose is to hold a place. As long as the other figures are in their proper places, the zero is unnecessary.

Checking the Product

The accepted and common method of checking the accuracy of a multiplication product is to invert, or turn over, the multiplicand with the multiplier and work the problem from a reverse position.

Original Multiplication

3 4 8	Multiplicand
× 5 4	Multiplier
1 3 9 2	Subproduct
1 7 4 0	Subproduct
1 8 7 9 2	Product

Problem Checked

5 4	Multiplier
× 3 4 8	Multiplicand
4 3 2	Subproduct
2 1 6	Subproduct
1 6 2	Subproduct
1 8 7 9 2	Product

If the problem is worked accurately in both instances, the products will be the same. If two different products are obtained, invert the problem back to its original form and try again with a little better effort. Today checking can be done on a calculator. However, it is a good practice to work problems through manually and then double check the work on a calculator. Remember that doing problems manually sharpens your math skills, and that times will arise when you must function without automation.

Guidelines

A few guidelines are offered here to help provide speed and accuracy to multiplication work.

Be Neat. Neatness is very important, as pointed out earlier in this Chapter. The customary method of multiplying eliminates end zeros (zeros that appear at the end of a number), and therefore you must be very careful in writing each number in its proper place.

Be Careful with Carryover Numbers. Remember that carryover numbers are added to the product of the two numbers being multiplied. The carryover numbers are not multiplied, as pointed out in the following example. (Note: It is unnecessary to write the carryover numbers as shown in the following example.)

```
  ④ ⑤
  7 5 8
×     7
-------
5 3 0 6
```

The first numbers to multiply are 7 × 8 = 56. Write the 6 in the ones column beneath the bar and carry the 5 over to the tens column. Next, 7 × 5 = 35. To this we add the carryover number 5. So 35 + 5 = 40. Write the zero in the tens column beneath the bar and carry the 4 to the hundreds column. Next step in proper order is 7 × 7 = 49. To this add the carryover number 4. This becomes 49 + 4 = 53. Write the 3 in the hundreds column beneath the bar and the 5 in the thousands column beneath the bar. 7 × 758 = 5,306.

T I P S . . . ***To Insure Perfect Solutions***

When the multiplier consists of two or more numerals, be careful to note the carryover numbers.

To Quickly Determine the Product When Multiplying by 10, 100, 1000, etc., Add the Correct Number of Zeros to the Multiplicand. For example: 10 × 222 = 2,220. Since there is one zero in 10, add one zero to 222 to obtain the product. When multiplying by 100, two zeros would be added. 100 × 222 = 22,200. When multiplying by 1000, three zeros are added.

Use Units in the Product When They Are Used in the Multiplicand. A unit was explained in a previous lesson as a single quantity of like things. Most multiplication problems in the world of work involve some sort of designated units. If a chicken processing plant has 45 chickens in 15 separated pens, how many chickens does it have on hand? (45 × 15 = 675.) The product is not simply 675, but 675 chickens. This type of unit does not have to be written next to the multiplicand when working the problem, but remember what type of units are being multiplied so the result will be a certain number of those designated units.

SUMMARY REVIEW

Find the answer to the following multiplication problems. If units are indicated, write the unit in the answer. Do these problems manually and then check your work. Round to the nearest cent.

1. 156 × 4

2. 5682 × 76

3. 3562 × 27

4. 372 × 121

5. 9763 × 1845

6. $355.46 × 32

7. $5,351.44 × 48

8. $8,421.55 × 1.69

9. A side of beef weighs 323 pounds and costs $1.83 per pound. How much does the side cost?

    ____

10. If a foresaddle of veal weighs 46 pounds and costs $7.60 per pound, what is the total cost?

    ____

11. Jim's catering truck gets 13 miles to every gallon of gas. How many miles can it travel on 78 gallons of gas?

    ____

12. When preparing meat loaf, it is required that 4 pounds of ground beef goes into each loaf. How many pounds of ground beef must be ordered when preparing 65 loaves?

    ____

13. Ribs of beef weigh 24 pounds and cost $2.24 per pound. What is the total cost of the ribs?

____

14. A wedding reception is catered for 575 people. The caterer charges $8.50 per person. What is the total bill?

____

15. A cook earns $65.00 a day. How much is earned in a year if the cook works 328 days?

____

DIVISION

Division is the act of separating a whole quantity into parts. It is a sharing of that whole part, a process of dividing one number by another. It is basically the method of finding out how many times one number is contained in another number. It is, in a sense, a reverse of multiplication, as shown below:

Multiplication	$5 \times 8 = 40$
Division	$40 \div 8 = 5$
	$40 \div 5 = 8$

Look at division from another viewpoint. Assume that your employer promises to pay you $8.00 per hour. After putting in 8 difficult hours, you receive a check for only $56.00, before deductions of course. Just looking at the total you know something is wrong. A simple division problem will show you that $56 ÷ 8 = $7. You were only being paid $7.00 an hour, or you were paid only for 7 hours. Using division can thus help you find out that a mistake was made.

Division is frequently used in the food service business because foods are constantly being divided. A strip sirloin is divided into steaks, vegetables into portions, cakes into servings, etc. (See Figure 3-5, which shows another example.) An example illustrating the division of food can be seen by observing how a solution is found to the following problem:

A No. 10 can of applesauce contains about 105 ounces. How many guests can be served if each guest receives a 3-ounce portion?

$$105 \div 3 = 35$$

Thirty-five guests can be served from the 105-ounce can of applesauce. Using division has helped the cook to know how many cans must be opened when serving a certain number of people.

Figure 3-5 *Division is the method of operation used when dividing roll dough into units.*

In division, the number to be divided is called the **dividend.** In the problem 80 ÷ 4 = 20, the number 80 is the dividend. The name for the number by which the dividend is divided (number 4 in this example) is the **divisor.** The result of dividing the dividend by the divisor is called the **quotient.** The quotient in this example is the number 20.

TIPS . . . *To Insure Perfect Solutions*

Dividend divided by Divisor equals Quotient

$$\text{Divisor}\overline{)\text{Dividend}}^{\text{Quotient}}$$

TIPS . . . *To Insure Perfect Solutions*

When dividing using the calculator, enter the dividend *first*.

In situations where the divisor is not contained in the dividend an equal or exact number of times, the figure left over or remaining is called the **remainder.** For example: 83 ÷ 4 = 20 with 3 left over because 4 is too large to be contained in 3. In this problem, 3 is the remainder.

There are several division signs that can be used when working division problems. Usually the sign selected depends on how long or difficult the problem may be. Up to this point in our examples of the division operation, division has been indicated by a bar with a dot above and below (÷). This symbol is mainly used when the problem is simple or when first stating a division problem that is to be solved. Simple problems are also written using the fraction bar. For example, 84 ÷ 7 = 12 can also be written $\frac{84}{7} = 12$.

For what is known as a long division problem, the accepted sign to use has the appearance of a closed parenthesis sign with a straight line coming out of the top:

$$\overline{)\quad\quad}$$

Step-By-Step Division

When reviewing basic mathematical operations, division is usually discussed last because it involves both multiplication and subtraction in its operation (including carryover numbers and trading). For example: 8,295 ÷ 15 = ?

Since this problem would be considered a lengthy one, the long division form is used.

		thousands	hundreds	tens	ones	
						Quotient goes here
Divisor	15)	8	2	9	5	Dividend

A long division problem is started from the left, rather than from the right, as in addition, subtraction, and multiplication. The first step is to estimate how many times 15 is contained in 82 (actually 8200). It is known that 5 × 15 = 75, so your first estimate would be 5. The 5 is written above the division bar in the hundreds place.

	thousands	hundreds	tens	ones	
		5			Start of quotient
15)	8	2	9	5	Dividend

To make sure that 5 is the correct figure, it is multiplied by 15. The product is 75. The 7 is written in the thousands column, under the 8, and the 5 in the hundreds column, under the 2. Then 75 is subtracted from 82. If the difference is less than 15, the estimate of 5 in the hundreds place of the quotient is correct. 82 − 75 = 7. Since 7 is less than 15, the estimate is correct.

	thousands	hundreds	tens	ones	
		5			
15)	8	2	9	5	Dividend
	7	5			Product of 5 × 15
		7			(82 − 75 = 7)

The next step is to bring the 9 in the tens place of the dividend down to the right of the 7, giving 79. We estimate that 79 contains 15 only 5 times. 79 − 75 = 4, which is smaller than 15. (Note that sometimes the estimate is too low or too high. When this happens, the estimate must be increased or decreased accordingly.)

So far our problem has advanced to this point:

```
     5 5
15)8 2 9 5        Dividend
   7 5
     7 9
     7 5          Product of 5 × 15
       4          (79 − 75 = 4)
```

The next step is to bring down the remaining figure 5 from the ones column and place it to the right of the 4 (left over from subtracting 75 from 79). Again estimate how many times 45 contains 15. It is easy to see that 3 should be the estimated figure, making the problem come out even. The completed problem is shown as follows:

```
     5 5 3        Quotient
15)8 2 9 5        Dividend
   7 5
     7 9
     7 5
       4 5
       4 5        Product of 3 × 15
```

The Remainder

As explained earlier, the figure in a division problem that may be left over when the dividend does not contain the divisor exactly is called the remainder. For example:

```
                  6 5      Quotient
Divisor   33)2 1 6 3       Dividend
             1 9 8         Product of 6 × 33 = 198
               1 8 3
               1 6 5       Product of 5 × 33 = 165
                 1 8       Remainder
```

At this point, there are no more numerals to bring down from the dividend. There are no 33s contained in the number 18. Therefore, the leftover 18 is called the remainder. The remainder can also be written in fractional or decimal form, as shown below:

$$2{,}163 \div 33 = 65\tfrac{18}{33} \text{ (a fraction) or } 65.545 \text{ (a decimal).}$$

Checking Division

The common method of checking division is to multiply the quotient by the divisor. The product of multiplying the divisor and quotient together should be the same as the dividend.

Division:

```
                 1 3 2      Quotient
Divisor   22)2 9 0 4      Dividend
             2 2
               7 0
               6 6
                 4 4
                 4 4
                   0      Remainder
```

To check the division:

```
   1 3 2      Quotient
 ×   2 2      Divisor
   2 6 4
 2 6 4
 2 9 0 4      Dividend
```

When the quotient includes a remainder, multiply the quotient by the divisor as shown in the previous example, then add the remainder to the product.

```
                2 7 5      Quotient
Divisor 31   )8 5 4 4      Dividend
              6 2
              2 3 4
              2 1 7
                1 7 4
                1 5 5
                  1 9      Remainder
```

To check the division with a remainder present:

```
   2 7 5      Quotient
 ×   3 1      Divisor
   2 7 5
 8 2 5
 8 5 2 5      Product
 +   1 9      Remainder
 8 5 4 4      Dividend
```

SUMMARY REVIEW

Find the quotient for the following division problems. Carry answers three places to the right of the decimal point. Calculate these problems manually and then check all work.

1. 48 ÷ 12 = _____
2. 96 ÷ 3 = ________
3. 5)790
4. 8)1696
5. 46)2250

6. $58\overline{)896.74}$

7. $29\overline{)648.28}$

8. $344\overline{)988.42}$

9. A 480-pound side of beef is purchased costing $672.00. What is the cost per pound?

____

10. In one week the Prime Time Catering Company's delivery truck traveled 336 miles. They used 24 gallons of gasoline. How many miles did they average per gallon?

____

11. The chef at the Starlight Restaurant earns $38,400 per year. If this chef works 48 weeks per year, how much does she earn in one week?

____

12. The preparation cook at the Blue Star Restaurant works 5 days a week and earns $356.00 per week. How much does he earn in one day?

____

13. A restaurant orders 322 pounds of pork loins. Each loin weighs 14 pounds. How many loins are contained in the shipment?

____

14. The Deluxe Catering Company's delivery truck averages 13 miles per gallon of gasoline. During 30 days of operation, the truck travels 2,028 miles. How much gasoline is used?

____

15. One hundred twenty-eight ounces of orange juice are contained in one gallon. How many 4-ounce glasses of juice can be served?

____

Fractions, Decimals, Ratios, and Percents

OBJECTIVES

At the completion of this chapter, the student should be able to:

1. Simplify (or express) a fraction in lower terms without changing the value of the fraction.
2. Add, subtract, multiply, and divide fractions.
3. Change fractions to decimals.
4. Write decimals and mix decimal fractions in words.
5. Write numbers as decimals.
6. Find sums, differences, products, and quotients in decimal problems.
7. Solve problems by using given ratios.
8. Write common fractions as percents.
9. Write percents as common fractions, whole numbers, or mixed numbers.
10. Find the percents of meat cuts.

Now that you have learned about the roles that addition, subtraction, multiplication, and division play in food service operations, it is time to learn about the equally important roles played by fractions, decimals, ratios, and percents.

FRACTIONS

Fractions are not used extensively in a restaurant operation. They may play an important part when converting standard recipes, dealing with the contents of a scoop or dipper, and dividing certain items into serving portions, but compared to most other math operations, the use of fractions is limited. This does not mean, however, that the knowledge of fractions is unimportant. Situations will occur in your workplace and everyday life where knowledge of this subject will be required, so review this section just as intensely as the others.

Figure 4-1 *An example of a fractional part is shown when cutting a cake. Usually* $\frac{1}{8}$ *is a serving portion.*

A **fraction** indicates one or more equal parts of a unit. For example, a cake is usually divided into eight equal pieces. (See Figure 4-1.) If this is done, the following statements are true about the parts or slices of the cake:

One part is $\frac{1}{8}$ of the cake.

Three parts are $\frac{3}{8}$ of the cake.

Seven parts are $\frac{7}{8}$ of the cake.

Eight parts are $\frac{8}{8}$ of the cake or the whole cake.

Another example of this same teaching tool is the division of a 9-inch pie into slices. A 9-inch pie is usually cut into seven equal servings. In this case, the fractional parts would be a little different but the same theory shown for the sliced cake would hold true:

One part is $\frac{1}{7}$ of the pie.

Three parts are $\frac{3}{7}$ of the pie.

Six parts are $\frac{6}{7}$ of the pie.

Seven parts are $\frac{7}{7}$ of the pie or the whole pie.

T I P S . . . ***To Insure Perfect Solutions***

The parts of a fraction are the numerator (top number) and the denominator (bottom number). Think of the letter *d* in denominator as the *d* in down (in other words, the bottom number).

$$\frac{\text{Numerator}}{\text{Denominator}}$$

Since fractions indicate the division of a whole unit into equal parts, the numeral placed above the division or fraction bar indicates the number of fractional units taken and is called the **numerator.** The numeral below the bar represents the number of equal parts into which the unit is divided and is called the **denominator.** Thus, if a cantaloupe is cut into 8 equal wedges, but only 5 of those wedges are used on a fruit plate, the wedges used are represented by the fraction $\frac{5}{8}$.

A common fraction is written with a whole number above the division bar and a whole number below the bar. For example:

$\frac{5}{8}$ Numerator / Denominator

A **proper fraction** is a fraction whose numerator is smaller than its denominator. For example:

$\frac{5}{8}$ Numerator / Denominator

This type of fraction is in its lowest possible terms when the numerator and denominator contain no common factor. A **factor** refers to two or more numerals which, when multiplied together, yield a given product. For example: 3 and 4 are factors of 12. The fraction $\frac{5}{8}$ is in its lowest possible terms because there is no common number by which both can be divided. (See Simplification of Fractions.)

An **improper fraction** is a fraction whose numerator is larger than its denominator and whose value is greater than a whole unit. If, for instance, $1\frac{3}{4}$ hams are expressed as an improper fraction, it is expressed as $\frac{7}{4}$ since the one whole ham would be $\frac{4}{4}$ and the extra $\frac{3}{4}$ makes it $\frac{7}{4}$. Such fractions can be expressed as a mixed number by dividing the numerator by the denominator, as shown below:

$$\frac{7}{4} = 1\frac{3}{4} \text{ mixed number}$$

A **mixed number** is a whole number mixed with a fractional part. For example:

$$1\frac{1}{3},\ 3\frac{3}{4},\ \text{and } 8\frac{2}{3}$$

The Simplification of Fractions

Simplification is a method used to express a fraction in lower terms without changing the value of the fraction. This is achieved by dividing the numerator and denominator of a fraction by the greatest factor (number) common to both. For example:

$$\frac{12 \ (\div 4 \text{ greatest factor})}{28 \ (\div 4 \text{ greatest factor})} = \frac{3}{7}$$

$$\frac{16 \ (\div 8 \text{ greatest factor})}{24 \ (\div 8 \text{ greatest factor})} = \frac{2}{3}$$

The value of these fractions is unchanged, but they have been simplified or reduced to their lowest possible terms.

A mixed number is usually expressed as an improper fraction when it is to be multiplied by another mixed number, a whole number, or a fraction. The first step is to express the mixed number as an improper fraction. This is done by multiplying the whole number by the denominator of the fraction, and then adding the numerator to the result. The sum is written over the denominator of the fraction. For example:

$$1\tfrac{3}{4} \times 4\tfrac{1}{4} = \tfrac{7}{4} \times \tfrac{17}{4} = \tfrac{119}{16} = 7\tfrac{7}{16}$$

In this example, the whole number (1) is multiplied by the denominator of the fraction (4). To this result (4), the numerator (3) is added. The sum (7) is written over the denominator (4), creating the improper fraction $\frac{7}{4}$. The same procedure is followed in expressing the mixed number $4\frac{1}{4}$ as the improper fraction $\frac{17}{4}$. When the two mixed numbers are expressed as improper fractions, the product is found by multiplying the two numerators together and the two denominators together resulting in the improper fraction $\frac{119}{16}$ and simplifying (reducing) it to the lowest terms, $7\frac{7}{16}$.

Adding and Subtracting Fractions

Fractions are used most often to increase and decrease recipe ingredients. Ingredients such as herbs and spices generally appear in a recipe in fractional quantities. The addition and subtraction of fractions are used most often when adjusting recipes. However, all operations dealing with fractions will be required at some point on the job or in everyday activity. One example of the use of fractions in food service is illustrated in Figure 4-2.

Before fractions can be added or subtracted, they must have the same denominator. **Like fractions** are fractions that have the same denominator. To add or subtract like fractions, add or subtract the numerators and write the result over the common denominator. Examples of adding and subtracting like fractions are shown below:

$$\tfrac{2}{9} + \tfrac{5}{9} = \tfrac{7}{9} \qquad \tfrac{5}{9} - \tfrac{3}{9} = \tfrac{2}{9}$$

Note how simple it is to add and subtract like fractions. The next step, dealing with unlike fractions, becomes a little more difficult.

Figure 4-2 *A knowledge of fractions is important when dividing roll dough into units.*

Unlike fractions have different denominators. They are more difficult because only like things can be added or subtracted. Therefore, to add or subtract fractions that have unlike denominators, the fractions must first be expressed so the denominators are the same. To find this common denominator, multiply the two denominators together ($5 \times 4 = 20$). The product will, of course, be common to both. For example:

$$\frac{2}{5} + \frac{3}{4} = \frac{?}{20}$$

When a number is found that is a multiple of both denominators, the fractions are then expressed in terms of the common denominator, so $\frac{2}{5}$ is $\frac{8}{20}$ and $\frac{3}{4}$ is $\frac{15}{20}$. These fractions have now become like fractions that can be added or subtracted without too much difficulty, as shown below:

Add	Subtract
$\frac{2}{5} = \frac{8}{20}$	$\frac{3}{4} = \frac{15}{20}$
$+\frac{3}{4} = \frac{15}{20}$	$-\frac{2}{5} = \frac{8}{20}$
$\frac{23}{20} = 1\frac{3}{20}$ Sum	Difference $\frac{7}{20}$

In adding and subtracting unlike fractions, the common denominator may be any number that is a multiple of the original denominators. However, always use the least common denominator to simplify the work. The **least common denominator** is the smallest number that is a multiple of both denominators. For example: If $\frac{1}{3}$ and $\frac{2}{5}$ are to be added, the least common denominator is 15, since it is the smallest multiple of both 3 and 5.

$$\begin{array}{r} \frac{1}{3} = \frac{5}{15} \\ +\frac{1}{5} = \frac{3}{15} \\ \hline \frac{8}{15} \end{array}$$

Multiplying Fractions

Multiplying fractions is considered the simplest operation with fractions. When multiplying two fractions, multiply the two numerators and place the results over the result obtained by multiplying the two denominators. For example:

$$\frac{2}{3} \times \frac{7}{8} = \frac{14}{24} = \frac{7}{12}$$

If multiplying a whole number by a fraction, multiply the whole number by the numerator of the fraction, place the result over the denominator of the fraction, and divide the new numerator by the denominator. For example:

$$\frac{17}{1} \times \frac{3}{4} = \frac{51}{4} = 12\frac{3}{4}$$

Sometimes it is possible to simplify the problem before multiplying. In the example below, 6 is a factor of 24 because 24 contains 6 exactly 4 times. This step is commonly called *canceling:*

$$\frac{\overset{4}{24}}{1} \times \frac{5}{\underset{1}{6}} = 20$$

If the numerator and denominator can be divided evenly by the same number, simplify to lowest terms. For example:

$\frac{32}{48}$ Numerator and denominator can be divided evenly by the common factor 16 resulting in: $\frac{2}{3}$

If multiplying by one or two mixed numbers, express the mixed number or numbers as improper fractions and proceed to multiply as with two fractions. For example:

$$\frac{8}{1} \times 3\frac{5}{8} = \frac{8}{1} \times \frac{29}{8} = 29$$

$$2\frac{1}{3} \times 4\frac{3}{5} = \frac{7}{3} \times \frac{23}{5} = \frac{161}{15} = 10\frac{11}{15}$$

Dividing Fractions

Dividing fractions is perhaps the most difficult operation because it involves the process of inverting (turning over) the divisor. Always be careful to invert the correct fraction. Mistakes can be easily made when inverting takes place. After inverting the divisor, proceed to operate the same as you would when multiplying fractions.

Example A:

$$\frac{5}{8} \div \frac{1}{2} = \frac{5}{8} \times \frac{2}{1} = \frac{5}{4} \times \frac{1}{1} = \frac{5}{4} = 1\frac{1}{4}$$

Step 1: The divisor $\frac{1}{2}$ is inverted to $\frac{2}{1}$.

Step 2: Cancel a factor of 2 from the 8 and 2.

Step 3: Multiply $\frac{5}{4} \times \frac{1}{1}$ to get $\frac{5}{4}$.

Step 4: The result $\frac{5}{4}$ is an improper fraction and must be reduced to a mixed number, which would be $1\frac{1}{4}$.

Example B:

$$\frac{14}{1} \div \frac{1}{2} = \frac{14}{1} \times \frac{2}{1} = 28$$

Step 1: The divisor $\frac{1}{2}$ is inverted to $\frac{2}{1}$.

Step 2: Multiply $\frac{14}{1} \times \frac{2}{1} = 28$.

Example B results in a whole number so, of course, reducing is not necessary.

SUMMARY REVIEW

Find the sum in each of the following addition problems. Simplify all answers to lowest terms.

1. $\frac{3}{7} + \frac{2}{7}$
2. $\frac{4}{9} + \frac{2}{9}$
3. $\frac{7}{9} + \frac{1}{9}$
4. $\frac{1}{2} + \frac{1}{8}$
5. $\frac{7}{16} + \frac{1}{4}$
6. $\frac{3}{4} + \frac{1}{8}$
7. $1\frac{3}{16} + 3\frac{3}{4}$
8. $\frac{23}{32} + \frac{15}{16}$
9. $2\frac{1}{2} + 3\frac{3}{4} + 6\frac{1}{8}$
10. $\frac{4}{9}$, $\frac{5}{12}$, $+ \frac{5}{18}$
11. $\frac{1}{2}$, $\frac{1}{3}$, $+ \frac{1}{5}$
12. $6\frac{5}{6}$, $10\frac{5}{12}$, $+ 13\frac{2}{3}$
13. $20\frac{4}{5}$, $16\frac{3}{15}$, $+ 18\frac{3}{10}$
14. $12\frac{1}{6}$, $9\frac{1}{3}$, $+ 7\frac{1}{9}$
15. $12\frac{3}{8}$, $6\frac{1}{4}$, $+ 10\frac{1}{2}$

Find the difference in each of the following subtraction problems. Simplify all answers to lowest terms.

16. $\frac{3}{7} - \frac{2}{7}$

17. $\frac{4}{9} - \frac{2}{9}$

18. $\frac{7}{16} - \frac{5}{16}$

19. $\frac{3}{4} - \frac{2}{3}$

20. $3\frac{3}{4} - 1\frac{3}{16}$

21. $12\frac{1}{4} - 5\frac{5}{16}$

22. $14\frac{7}{24} - 6\frac{5}{16}$

23. $45\frac{5}{8} - 32\frac{7}{16}$

24. $18\frac{7}{16} - 13\frac{1}{4}$

25. $23\frac{5}{18} - 7\frac{5}{12}$

26. $42\frac{23}{32} - 23\frac{15}{16}$

27. $43\frac{5}{8} - 18\frac{1}{4}$

28. $21\frac{3}{16} - 16\frac{1}{8}$

29. $15\frac{5}{9} - 8\frac{2}{3}$

30. $20\frac{5}{12} - 12\frac{3}{16}$

Find the product in each of the following multiplication problems.

31. $\frac{5}{8} \times \frac{1}{2} =$ __________

32. $\frac{7}{8} \times \frac{1}{4} =$ __________

33. $5\frac{1}{2} \times 3\frac{1}{2} =$ __________

34. $1\frac{3}{4} \times 4\frac{3}{8} =$ __________

35. $36 \times 5\frac{3}{4} =$ __________

36. $45 \times 7\frac{1}{2} =$ __________

37. $4\frac{3}{4} \times 5\frac{1}{2} =$ __________

38. $18 \times 9\frac{5}{9} =$ __________

39. $\frac{2}{3} \times 12\frac{1}{3} =$ __________

40. $24\frac{1}{3} \times 7\frac{2}{3} =$ __________

41. $22\frac{5}{16} \times 4 =$ __________

42. $8\frac{2}{9} \times 3\frac{1}{2} =$ __________

43. $10\frac{3}{4} \times 3\frac{1}{2} =$ __________

44. $22 \times 5\frac{1}{4} =$ __________

45. $3\frac{5}{8} \times \frac{1}{2} =$ __________

Find the quotient in each of the following division problems:

46. $\frac{15}{16} \div \frac{3}{4} =$ ____________

47. $\frac{15}{16} \div 2 =$ ____________

48. $\frac{3}{4} \div \frac{3}{16} =$ ____________

49. $\frac{7}{16} \div \frac{3}{16} =$ ____________

50. $1\frac{1}{2} \div 6 =$ ____________

51. $2\frac{5}{8} \div 7 =$ ____________

52. $\frac{1}{4} \div 10 =$ ____________

53. $\frac{3}{4} \div 2 =$ ____________

54. $\frac{5}{16} \div 3 =$ ____________

55. $2\frac{1}{4} \div 1\frac{1}{2} =$ ____________

56. $7\frac{5}{8} \div 2\frac{1}{4} =$ ____________

57. $9\frac{3}{8} \div \frac{1}{4} =$ ____________

58. $10\frac{2}{3} \div \frac{1}{2} =$ ____________

59. $\frac{7}{8} \div \frac{1}{4} =$ ____________

60. $12\frac{3}{4} \div \frac{1}{3} =$ ____________

DECIMALS

A decimal is based on the number ten. The decimal system refers to counting by tens and powers of ten. The term **decimal** refers to decimal fractions. **Decimal fractions** are those fractions that are expressed with denominators of 10 or powers of 10. For example:

$$\frac{1}{10} \quad \frac{9}{100} \quad \frac{89}{1{,}000} \quad \frac{321}{10{,}000}$$

Instead of writing a fraction, a point (.) called a **decimal point** is used to indicate a decimal fraction. For example:

$$\frac{1}{10} = 0.1 \qquad \frac{9}{100} = 0.09$$

$$\frac{89}{1{,}000} = 0.089 \qquad \frac{321}{10{,}000} = 0.0321$$

Numbers go in both directions from the decimal point. The place value of the numbers to the left starts with the units or ones column, and each column (moving left) is an increasing multiple of 10.

Thousands	Hundreds	Tens	Units or Ones
1,000	100	10	1

To the right of the decimal point, each column is one-tenth of the number in the column immediately to its left. For example, one-tenth of one is $\frac{1}{10}$. Thus the decimals to the right of the decimal point are 0.1, 0.01,

0.001, 0.0001, and so on. These numbers stated as decimal fractions are $\frac{1}{10}$, $\frac{1}{100}$, $\frac{1}{1,000}$, and $\frac{1}{10,000}$.

Decimal fractions differ from common fractions because they have 10 or a power of 10 for a denominator, whereas common fractions can have any number for the denominator. To simplify writing a decimal fraction, the decimal point is used. For example, to express the decimal fraction $\frac{725}{1,000}$ as its equivalent using a decimal point:

1. Convert the decimal fraction to a decimal first by writing the numerator (725).
2. Count the number of zeros in the denominator and place the decimal point according to the number of zeros. There must always be as many decimal places as there are zeros in the denominator (0.725).

Often, when writing a decimal fraction as decimal, it is necessary to add zeros to the left of the numerator before placing the decimal point to indicate the value of the denominator. For example: $\frac{725}{10,000} = 0.0725$, which should be read as seven hundred twenty-five ten thousandths.

When a number is made up of a whole number and a decimal fraction, it is referred to as a **mixed decimal fraction.** To write a mixed decimal fraction, the whole number is written to the left of the decimal point and the fractional part to the right of the decimal point. For example: $7\frac{135}{1,000} =$ 7.135. The decimal point is read as "and" so to read this mixed decimal fraction, the whole number is read first, then the decimal point as "and." Next, read the fraction as a whole number and state the denominator. Following this procedure, 7.135 is read "seven and one-hundred thirty-five thousandths."

To add or subtract decimal fractions, keep all whole numbers in their proper column and all decimal fractions in their proper column. Remember that the decimal point separates whole numbers from fractional parts. It is therefore very important that decimal points are directly in line with each other. For example, in adding decimal fractions:

2.135	Addend
7.43	Addend
4.008	Addend
+ 1.125	Addend
14.698	Sum

Note that the decimal point in the sum goes under the decimal point of the other numbers.

When subtracting decimal fractions:

9.825	Minuend
− 5.450	Subtrahend
4.375	Difference

Note that the decimal point in the difference goes under the decimal point in the minuend and subtrahend.

To multiply decimal fractions, follow the same procedure as when multiplying whole numbers to find the product. To locate the decimal point in the product, count the number of decimal places in both the multiplicand and the multiplier. The number of decimal places counted in the product is equal to the sum of those in the multiplicand and multiplier. For example:

$$\begin{array}{rl} 4.32 & \text{Multiplicand} \\ \times\ 0.06 & \text{Multiplier} \\ \hline 0.2592 & \text{Product} \end{array}$$

There are four decimal places in the multiplicand and multiplier. Therefore, four decimal places are counted from right to left in the product.

In many cases, the total number of decimal places in the multiplicand and multiplier exceeds the number of numerals that appear in the product. In such cases, **ciphers** (zeros) are added to the left of the digits in the product to complete the decimal places needed:

$$\begin{array}{rl} 0.445 & \text{Multiplicand} \\ \times\ \ 0.16 & \text{Multiplier} \\ \hline 2670 & \\ 445\ & \\ \hline 0.07120 & \text{Product} \end{array}$$

Note that a cipher is added to the product to complete the five decimals places required.

To divide decimal fractions, proceed as if the numbers were whole numbers and place the decimal point as follows:

1. When dividing by whole numbers, place the decimal point in the answer directly above the decimal point in the dividend.

$$\begin{array}{rll} 0.06 & \text{Quotient} & \text{Use zeros as needed in the} \\ \text{Divisor } 6\overline{)0.36} & \text{Dividend} & \text{quotient to hold a place.} \\ \underline{0.36} & & \end{array}$$

$$\begin{array}{rll} 0.8 & \text{Quotient} & \text{Zeros are not needed in} \\ \text{Divisor } 5\overline{)4.0} & \text{Dividend} & \text{the quotient to hold a place.} \\ \underline{4.0} & & \end{array}$$

T I P S . . . ***To Insure Perfect Solutions***

Dividend divided by Divisor equals Quotient

$$\begin{array}{r} \text{Quotient} \\ \text{Divisor}\overline{)\text{Dividend}} \end{array}$$

T I P S . . . ***To Insure Perfect Solutions***

When dividing using the calculator, enter the dividend *first.*

2. When dividing a whole number or mixed decimal by a mixed decimal or decimal fraction, change the divisor and dividend so the divisor becomes a whole number. This is accomplished by multiplying both the dividend and divisor by the same power to ten. The divisor and dividend can be multiplied by the same power of ten without changing the value of the division.

```
                   12.     Quotient
Divisor 0.25)3.00.         Dividend
          ↪   ↪
           2 5
             50
             50
```

In the preceding example, the divisor 0.25 is made into the whole number 25 by multiplying by 100, moving the decimal point two places to the right. Since the dividend must also be multiplied by 100, the decimal point in the dividend is also moved two places to the right, so 3 becomes 300. The decimal point in the quotient is always placed directly over the decimal point in the dividend. The answer is 12, a whole number. Note that when moving a decimal point, an arrow is used to show where the decimal point is to be moved.

SUMMARY REVIEW

Change the following fractions to decimals.

1. $\frac{9}{10}$ = ____________
2. $\frac{3}{10}$ = ____________
3. $\frac{451}{1{,}000}$ = ____________
4. $\frac{7}{10}$ = ____________
5. $\frac{861}{100{,}000}$ = ____________
6. $\frac{429}{1{,}000}$ = ____________
7. $\frac{785}{10{,}000}$ = ____________
8. $\frac{843}{1{,}000}$ = ____________
9. $\frac{676}{10{,}000}$ = ____________
10. $\frac{39}{1{,}000}$ = ____________

Write the following decimals and mixed decimal fractions in words.

11. 0.6 ____________
12. 0.29 ____________
13. 0.85917 ____________
14. 0.002 ____________
15. 0.0578 ____________
16. 0.67187 ____________
17. 6.3 ____________
18. 7.42 ____________
19. 9.135 ____________
20. 3.41 ____________

Write each of the following numbers as decimals.

21. Five tenths ____________
22. Fourteen hundredths ____________
23. Sixteen hundredths ____________
24. Sixty-eight ten thousandths ____________
25. One hundred twenty-two thousandths ____________
26. Sixty-four hundred thousandths ____________
27. Three and five tenths ____________
28. Sixteen hundred thousandths ____________
29. One hundred thousandths ____________
30. Eight and nine hundredths ____________

Find the sum in each problem.

31. $0.45 + 0.062 + 8.169 + 0.046 =$ ____________
32. $0.58 + 0.675 + 6.225 + 9.323 =$ ____________
33. $0.015 + 0.702 + 10.318 + 12.962 =$ ____________
34. $0.056 + 0.015 + 0.711 + 6.25 + 16.37 =$ ____________
35. $0.046 + 0.002 + 643 + 6.1675 =$ ____________

Find the difference in each problem.

36. $9.765 - 0.046 =$ ____________
37. $8 - 0.123 =$ ____________
38. $1 - 0.685 =$ ____________
39. $0.0622 - 0.0421 =$ ____________
40. $139.371 - 123.218 =$ ____________

Find the product in each problem. Round the answers to the nearest ten thousandth when necessary.

41. $412 \times 0.52 =$ ____________
42. $0.922 \times 1.52 =$ ____________
43. $0.0524 \times 0.132 =$ ____________
44. $6.53 \times 0.38 =$ ____________
45. $7.323 \times 5.452 =$ ____________

Find the quotient in each problem. Give quotients three decimal places when necessary.

46. 0.49 ÷ 7 = __________
47. 15 ÷ 4.8 = __________
48. 945 ÷ 500 = __________
49. 0.0684 ÷ 24 = __________
50. 46.76 ÷ 400 = __________
51. 4 ÷ 0.25 = __________
52. 2.65 ÷ 1.5 = __________
53. 6.5 ÷ 2.45 = __________
54. 45.5 ÷ 3.5 = __________
55. 54.25 ÷ 4.8 = __________

RATIOS

The term *ratio* is used quite often in food service to express a comparison or rate. A **ratio** (proportion) is the relation between two numbers or quantities. The ratio between two quantities is the number of times one contains the other. For example, when preparing baked rice, the ratio is 2 to 1, that is, 2 parts liquid to 1 part rice. If you are preparing 1 quart of raw rice, you would use 2 quarts water or stock. As another example, when soaking navy beans overnight, to reduce cooking time, the ratio is 3 to 1. That is, for every amount of beans you are soaking you would use 3 times that amount of water. So if you are soaking 1 quart of navy beans, you would cover them with 3 quarts of water. The order in which the numbers are placed when expressing a ratio is important. If you would say that the ratio when cooking barley is 4 to 1, meaning 4 parts water to 1 part barley, it is not the same as saying 1 to 4, which would reverse the ratio and mean 1 part water to every 4 parts of barley (which would cause the barley to scorch and burn). An example of using a ratio as a comparison can be shown by stating the following: Last week we sold 3 times as many steaks as pork chops. You may also convey that fact by saying steaks outsold pork chops 3 to 1.

SUMMARY REVIEW

Solve the following problems using the ratios given.

1. How much water is needed to bake $\frac{3}{4}$ gallon of rice using a ratio of 2 to 1 liquid to rice?

   ____

2. How much water is required to soak $\frac{1}{2}$ gallon of navy beans using a ratio of 3 to 1 water to beans?

   ____

3. How much water should be used to cook 1 pint of barley using a ratio of 4 to 1 water to barley?

   ____

4. How much water is needed to prepare orange juice using $1\frac{1}{2}$ pints of orange concentrate and a ratio of 3 to 1 water to concentrate?

    ____

5. How much water is needed to prepare lemonade using $1\frac{3}{4}$ pints of frozen lemonade and a ratio of 4 to 1 water to lemonade?

    ____

6. How much chicken stock is needed to bake $1\frac{1}{4}$ quarts of rice using a ratio of 2 to 1 stock to rice?

    ____

7. How much water will it take to simmer $1\frac{3}{4}$ quarts of barley using a ratio of 4 to 1 water to barley?

    ____

8. How much water will it take to soak $\frac{3}{4}$ gallon of red beans using a ratio of 3 to 1 water to beans?

    ____

9. How much water is needed to prepare orange juice using $1\frac{3}{4}$ quarts of orange concentrate and a ratio of 4 to 1 water to concentrate?

    ____

10. How much water is required when making fruit punch if $1\frac{1}{4}$ pints of frozen punch concentrate is used and the ratio is 5 to 1 water to concentrate?

    ____

PERCENTS

Percent plays a big part in food service language. It is used to express a rate when dealing with important business matters such as food costs, labor costs, profits, and even that undesirable figure called loss. When management meets with food service employees and wishes to emphasize points that need improving, the message conveyed is usually done by expressing a percentage. For example: Last month our food cost was 45%. We must bring this figure under control.

Percent (%) means "of each hundred." Thus, 5 percent means 5 out of every 100. This same 5 percent can also be written 0.05 in decimal form. In fraction form it is $\frac{5}{100}$. The percent sign (%) is in reality a unique way of writing 100.

Figure 4-3 *An example of percent—Ten percent of the hot cross buns have been removed from the sheet pan (6 out of 60).*

Percents are a special tool used to express a rate of each hundred. If 50% of the customers in a restaurant select a seafood entree, a rate of a whole is being expressed. The whole is represented by 100 percent and all of the customers entering the restaurant would represent the whole or 100 percent. Another example of percent in food service is shown in Figure 4-3.

To find what percent one number is of another number, divide the number that represents the part by the number that represents the whole. For example: A hindquarter of beef weighs 240 pounds. The round cut weighs 52 pounds. What percent of the hindquarter is the round cut?

The 240-pound hindquarter represents the whole. The 52-pound round cut represents only a fractional part of the hindquarter. As a fraction it is written $\frac{52}{240}$. Simplified or reduced to lowest terms, it is $\frac{13}{60}$. To express a common fraction as a percent, the numerator is divided by the denominator. The division must be carried out two places (hundredth place) for the percent. Carrying the division three places behind the decimal gives the tenth of a percent, which makes the percent more accurate. The finished problem looks like this:

$$
\begin{array}{r}
0.2166 \text{ is equal to } 21.7\% \\
240\overline{)52.0000} \\
-48\,0 \\
\hline
4\,00 \\
-2\,40 \\
\hline
1\,600 \\
-1\,440 \\
\hline
1600 \\
-1440 \\
\hline
160
\end{array}
$$

Percent means hundredths, so the decimal is moved two places to the right when the percent sign is used.

This same percent could be obtained by converting the fraction $\frac{13}{60}$ into a percent by dividing the denominator into the numerator, as shown in the following example:

$$\begin{array}{r} 0.2166 \\ 60\overline{)13.0000} \\ -12\ 0 \\ \hline 1\ 00 \\ -\ 60 \\ \hline 400 \\ -\ 360 \\ \hline 400 \\ -\ 360 \\ \hline 40 \end{array} \quad \text{is equal to } 21.7\%$$

When a percent is expressed as a common fraction, the given percent is the numerator and 100 is the denominator. For example:

$$40\% = \frac{40}{100} \text{ or } \frac{2}{5};$$

$$20\% = \frac{20}{100} \text{ or } \frac{1}{5}.$$

When a percent is changed to a decimal fraction, the percent sign is removed and the decimal point is moved two places to the left. For example:

$$24.5\% = 0.245$$

$$75.7\% = 0.757$$

When a decimal fraction is expressed as a percent, move the decimal point two places to the right and place the percent sign to the right of the last figure. For example:

$$0.234 = 23.4\%$$

$$0.826 = 82.6\%$$

The preceding percents are read as twenty-three and four-tenths percent, and eighty-two and six-tenths percent.

Remember the following points when dealing with percents:

- When a number is compared with a number larger than itself, the result is always less than 100 percent. For example:
  72 is 80% of 90 since $\frac{72}{90} = \frac{4}{5} = 80\%$.
- When a number is compared with itself, the result is always 100 percent. For example:
  72 is 100% of 72 since $\frac{72}{72} = 1 = 100\%$.
- When taking a percent of a whole number, the method of operation is to multiply. For example:

If a restaurant takes in $9,462.00 in one week, but only 23 percent of that amount was profit, what is the profit?

```
  $ 9,462
  × 0.23
  -------
    28386
   18924
  -------
$2,176.26  Profit
```

Finding Percents of Meat Cuts

Since the use of percents in expressing a rate is a common practice in the food service business, this exercise is included for two reasons. First, to show the student how the sides of beef, veal, pork, and lamb are blocked out into wholesale or primal cuts, and second, to provide another opportunity to practice and understand percents.

A side is half of the complete carcass. A saddle, used in reference to the lamb carcass, is the front or hind half of the complete carcass that is cut between the twelfth and thirteenth ribs of lamb. The side or saddle is blocked out into wholesale or primal cuts at the meat processing plant.

Shown below is a blocked out side of beef and how the percentage of each wholesale cut is found. For the side of beef in Figure 4-4, find the percentage of each wholesale cut.

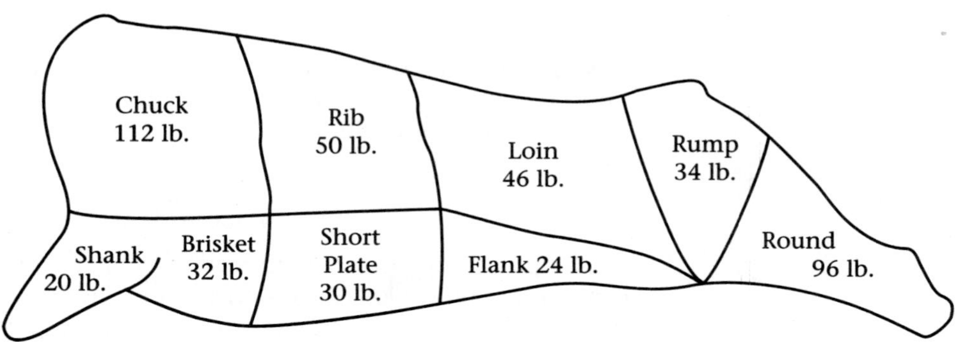

Figure 4-4 *A side of beef divided into cuts.*

To find a percentage, divide the whole into the part. In this case, the whole is represented by the total weight of the side of beef, 444 pounds. The part is represented by the weight of each individual wholesale cut. For example, the percentage of chuck is found as follows:

```
                                    0.252 is equal to 25.2%   Percentage of chuck
Total weight of side of beef 444)112.000                     Weight of chuck
                               − 88 8
                                 2320
                               − 2220
                                  1000
                                   888
                                   112
```

◆ *Chef Sez . . .*

"When developing a new Chef's Knife, the percentage of each raw material going into that item must be precisely calculated. If the metal alloys chromium, molybdenum and vanadium contained in the knife blade steel are not present in the correct amounts, the knife blade could be too soft, too hard or too brittle. If the percentages were incorrect, we'd end up with a poor quality knife that would be unacceptable for Culinary Professionals to use.

Peter Huebner
President and Owner of Canada Cutlery Inc.
Scarborough, Ontario, Canada

Canada Cutlery Inc. is a supplier of professional quality cutlery and kitchen tools. They have been marketing professional chef's knives and tools since 1954. They design their products to meet the demands of the professional chef. All products are made to their exacting specifications in leading cutlery manufacturing centers around the world. Originally, their cutlery was obtained from Solingen, Germany, and Sheffield, England. Today, they have products made to their demanding specifications in leading cutlery centers around the world.

The percentages of the other eight beef cuts are found by following the same procedure. Carry three places behind the decimal. When the exercise is completed and the percentages are totaled, the result should be 99% plus a figure representing a tenth of a percent. In the following example, the figure expressing the sum is 99.7%. A 100% will be unlikely since the individual percents will almost never figure out evenly.

25.2%	chuck
4.5%	shank
7.2%	brisket
6.7%	short plate
11.2%	rib
10.3%	sirloin
5.4%	flank
7.6%	rump
21.6%	round
99.7%	Total

SUMMARY REVIEW

Express the following common fractions as percents.

1. $\frac{3}{8}$ = ______	5. $\frac{3}{16}$ = ______	9. $\frac{2}{3}$ = ______
2. $\frac{5}{9}$ = ______	6. $\frac{5}{8}$ = ______	10. $\frac{4}{5}$ = ______
3. $\frac{3}{10}$ = ______	7. $\frac{5}{6}$ = ______	
4. $\frac{5}{12}$ = ______	8. $\frac{4}{9}$ = ______	

Express the following percents as common fractions, whole numbers, or mixed numbers. Reduce to the lowest common denominator.

11. 3% = _____	15. 100% = _____	19. 65% = _____
12. 40% = _____	16. 38% = _____	20. 140% = _____
13. 75% = _____	17. 68% = _____	
14. 60% = _____	18. 200% = _____	

Solve the following problems. Round answers to the nearest hundredth.

21.	5% of 85 = _____	26.	75% of $750.00 = _____
22.	30% of 678 = _____	27.	43% of $468.00 = _____
23.	42% of 500 = _____	28.	65% of $2,480.00 = _____
24.	14.5% of 92 = _____	29.	26% of $4,680.00 = _____
25.	39% of $38.20 = _____	30.	78% of $2,285.00 = _____

31. A 526-pound side of beef is ordered. The chuck cut weighs 76 pounds and the round cut weighs 58 pounds. What percent of the side is the chuck?_______________ What percent is the round?

____

32. A party for 225 people is booked. The cost of the party is $1,265.00. If they are given an 8 percent discount on their total bill, what is the cost of the party?

____

33. A party for 120 people is booked. The cost of the party is $960.00. If they are given a 12 percent discount on their total bill, what is the cost of the party?

____

34. If a restaurant takes in $25,680 in one week and 26 percent of that amount is profit, how much is profit?

____

35. Mrs. Hill purchased three new coffee urns at $1,586.00 each. For buying in quantity, she is given a $3\frac{1}{2}$ percent discount on the total bill. What is the amount she paid?

____

36. If a 48-pound beef round is roasted and 9 pounds are lost through shrinkage, what percent of the round is lost through shrinkage?

____

37. The food cost percentage for the month is 38%. If $26,485.00 was taken in that month, how much of that amount went for the cost of food?

____

38. If a restaurant's gross receipts for one week total $12,000.00 of which $8,000.00 is profit, what percent of the gross receipts is profit?

____

39. If a restaurant's gross receipts for one day total $18,500.00 of which $5,600.00 are expenses, what percent of the gross receipts is expenses?

____

40. If a 45-pound round of beef is roasted and 9 pounds are lost through shrinkage, what percent of the round is lost through shrinkage?

____

41. If a restaurant's gross receipts for one week total $22,080.00 but only 24 percent of that amount is profit, how much are expenses?

____

42. If a 52-pound round is roasted and 9 pounds are lost through shrinkage, what percent of the round roast is lost through shrinkage?

____

43. If a restaurant's gross receipts for one week is $42,682.00 and 26 percent of that amount is for labor, 37 percent for food cost, and 15 percent for miscellaneous items, how much is the profit?

____

Find the percentage of beef, pork, veal, and lamb wholesale cuts in the following problems.

44. Find the percentage of each cut of beef that makes up the side of beef shown in the figure.

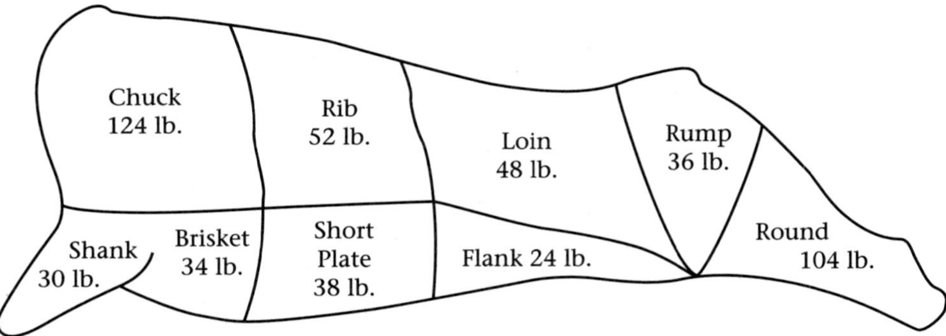

___________ % Chuck Total weight of the side ___________

___________ % Shank

___________ % Brisket

___________ % Short Plate

___________ % Rib

___________ % Loin

___________ % Flank

___________ % Rump

___________ % Round

45. Find the percentage of each cut of pork that makes up the side of pork shown in the figure.

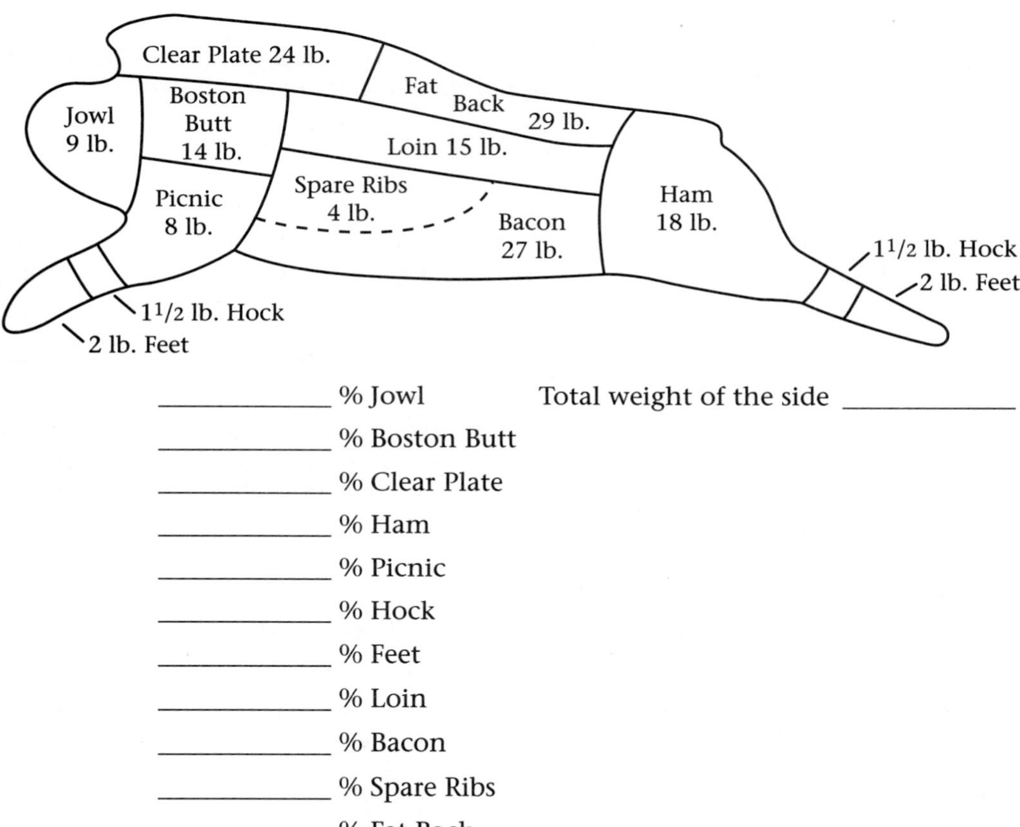

___________ % Jowl Total weight of the side ___________

___________ % Boston Butt

___________ % Clear Plate

___________ % Ham

___________ % Picnic

___________ % Hock

___________ % Feet

___________ % Loin

___________ % Bacon

___________ % Spare Ribs

___________ % Fat Back

PART III

MATH ESSENTIALS IN FOOD PREPARATION

Now that the review is completed and you have refreshed your math skills, it is time to approach the math functions used in kitchen production by the preparation crew.

In the past, the preparation crew was hired to perform individual production tasks such as broiling, sauteing, and roasting. Other details concerned with math skills were the responsibility of management. In addition, management set standards for controlling portions, converted recipes, and wrote food production reports. Today, controls in all areas of production have become everyone's job. Math skills must be learned and developed by all personnel. This is the only way management can control the high cost of food and labor as well as keep menu prices competitive. Developing math skills is also a step in moving up the ladder to a management position or from employee to employer.

There are a number of daily situations in the preparation area of a commercial kitchen where math skills are required for the operation to run efficiently. These situations require the attention of each member of the crew.

Kitchen personnel responsible for food preparation usually consist of the chef, sous chef, cooks, butcher, baker, and pantry or salad person. Every member of this crew should understand the math functions presented in this section of the text. Remember that the steps up the ladder of promotion and success are not difficult ones to climb if you are prepared when the opportunity arrives.

Weights and Measures

OBJECTIVES

At the completion of this chapter, the student should be able to:

1. Find equivalent measures.
2. Identify equipment (scoops, dippers, ladles, and the baker's balance scale) used for measurement.
3. Identify different types of portion scales (dial and digital).

The careful use of weights and measures is an essential part of a food service operation. It is a method used to obtain accuracy and consistent quality in all food products and to control cost. Uniform products mean repeat sales.

There are two essential kinds of measurement practiced in a food service operation. Both are extremely important for having and maintaining a successful operation. They are:

- Ingredient measurement
- Portion measurement

In this chapter the equipment used in weighing and measuring is discussed. The use of these devices is also explained and, on a lesser level, the two basic kinds of measurement are discussed. In the following chapter, portion control will be emphasized and clarified.

THE USE OF WEIGHTS AND MEASURES

Recipes or formulas used in commercial food establishments are stated in weights and measures. The more exact recipes or formulas are stated in weights and a balance baker's scale is used. In this way ingredient amounts can be found more accurately, and accuracy is of major importance—especially in baked products. An unbalanced baked product is sure failure. When measuring ingredients, one is very seldom exact; much depends on how firmly the ingredients are packed into the measuring device and what the individual considers a full measure. The common measures used are teaspoon, tablespoon, cups, pints, quarts, and gallons. These are usually abbreviated when stated in recipes. Figure 5-1 gives the common abbreviations used.

tsp. or small "t"	teaspoon
tbsp. or large "T"	tablespoon
C.	cup
pt.	pint
qt.	quart
gal.	gallon
oz.	ounce
lb.	pound
bch.	bunch
doz.	dozen
ea.	each
crt.	crate

Figure 5-1 *Common abbreviations of weights and measures.*

When weighing most ingredients in a bakery preparation, you can usually proceed without much concern. Just be sure you are using an accurate scale. When weighing ingredients that must be cleaned, peeled, or trimmed, however, you must be aware of the difference between **A.P. (as purchased) weight** and **E.P. (edible portion) weight.**

- A.P. is a term used to refer to the weight of a product as it was purchased.
- E.P. is a term used to refer to the weight of a product after it has been cleaned, trimmed, boned, etc. At this point all the nonedible parts have been removed.

A recipe or formula will usually indicate which weight is being referred to by using A.P. or E.P. when listing ingredients. If this step is neglected, you must attempt to judge from the instructions in the method of preparation. When the instructions state that the item must first be trimmed, peeled, and boned, then you can be certain that A.P. weight is stated. If the instructions indicate the item has already been cleaned, trimmed, and peeled, you know E.P. weight is called for.

Liquid measures are sometimes measured by volume. This practice is usually faster than weighing and just as accurate. As pointed out, volume measures are not recommended for measuring dry ingredients unless the amount is too small to weigh. An example of this would be a $\frac{1}{4}$ teaspoon of salt or a $\frac{1}{2}$ teaspoon of cinnamon.

The relationship of the various measures and weights is given in Figure 5-2. This figure can be used to convert from measures to weights or weights to measures, and can help save production time. For example, if 2 pounds of liquid milk are required in a recipe, this can be quickly measured by volume as 1 fluid quart since 2 pounds of liquid equals 1 fluid quart, or if 1 pound of whole eggs is needed, this can be measured as 1 fluid pint.

1 pinch	=	$\frac{1}{8}$ teaspoon (approx)
3 teaspoons	=	1 tablespoon
2 tablespoons	=	1 oz.
4 tablespoons	=	$\frac{1}{4}$ cup
8 tablespoons	=	$\frac{1}{2}$ cup
12 tablespoons	=	$\frac{3}{4}$ cup
16 tablespoons	=	1 cup
2 cups	=	1 pint
4 cups	=	1 quart
16 cups	=	1 gallon
2 pints	=	1 quart
4 quarts	=	1 gallon
5 fifths	=	1 gallon
2 quarts	=	1 magnum
8 quarts	=	1 peck
4 pecks	=	1 bushel
8 ounces	=	1 fluid cup
16 ounces	=	1 pound
1 pound	=	1 fluid pint
2 pounds	=	1 fluid quart
8 pounds	=	1 fluid gallon
12 dozen	=	1 gross
32 ounces	=	1 quart
64 ounces	=	$\frac{1}{2}$ gallon
128 ounces	=	1 gallon

Figure 5-2 *Equivalents of weights and measures.*

Measuring and Weighing Devices

There are many measuring and weighing instruments used in food service operations. They include an assortment of cups, spoons, ladles, dippers or scoops; baker's balance scales, digital platform scales, and portion scales; kitchen or serving spoons; and pints, quarts, and gallons that are used as a substitute for weighing liquid measures. Some of these are illustrated in Figure 5-3 and described in the following paragraphs.

Figure 5-3 *An assortment of measuring and weighing utensils used in food service operations.*

Summary Review

Fill in the correct measure.

1. 9 teaspoons equal _____ tablespoons
2. 8 tablespoons equal _____ cup
3. 2 pinches equal _____ teaspoon(s)
4. 16 tablespoons equal _____ cup(s)
5. 120 quarts equal _____ gallons
6. 1 magnum equal _____ quarts
7. 4 pounds equal _____ fluid quarts
8. 64 ounces equal _____ quarts
9. 20 gallons equal _____ quarts
10. 1 peck equal _____ quarts
11. 4 pints equal _____ quarts
12. 64 ounces equal _____ pounds
13. 8 cups equal _____ ounces
14. 1 bushel equal _____ pecks
15. 18 cups equal _____ pints

In food preparation and baking, a recipe or formula will call for so many pounds or ounces of liquid and a scale may not be available or it would be more convenient to measure the liquid. Assume this is the situation for the following problems. For each, state the amount of volume measure you would use.

16. The recipe calls for 1 pound 8 ounces of water. ________________
17. The recipe calls for 4 pounds of apple juice. ________________
18. The recipe calls for 5 pounds of apple juice. ________________
19. The recipe calls for 2 pounds of 12 oz. milk. ________________
20. The recipe calls for 6 pounds of skimmed milk. ________________

Scoops or Dippers

Scoops or **dippers** are used to serve many foods as well as to control the portion size. The various sizes are designated by a number that appears on the lever that mechanically releases the item from the scoop. The number that appears on the lever indicates the number of level scoops it will take to fill a quart. Figure 5-4 gives the relationship of the scoop number to the approximate capacity in ounces and volume content for both customary and metric measure.

Ladles

Ladles are used to serve stews, soups, sauces, gravies, dressings, cream dishes, and other liquids or semiliquids, when portioning and uniform servings are desired or required. (See Figure 5-5.) They come in assorted sizes holding from 2 to 8 ounces. The size, in ounces, is stamped on the handle. Figure 5-6 shows the ladle sizes most frequently used.

Scoop number	Volume customary	Approx metric	Approx weight	Approx metric
6	$\frac{2}{3}$ cup	160 ML	$5\frac{1}{3}$ oz.	140 g
8	$\frac{1}{2}$ cup	120 ML	4 oz.	110 g
10	$\frac{2}{5}$ cup	90 ML	$3\frac{1}{4}$ oz.	85-100 g
12	$\frac{1}{3}$ cup	80 ML	$2\frac{2}{3}$ oz.	75-85 g
16	$\frac{1}{4}$ cup	60 ML	2 oz.	60-65 g
20	$3\frac{1}{3}$ T	45 ML	$1\frac{2}{3}$ oz.	50 g
24	$2\frac{2}{3}$ T	40 ML	$1\frac{1}{3}$ oz.	40 g
30	$2\frac{1}{5}$ T	30 ML	$1\frac{1}{16}$ oz.	30 g
40	$1\frac{3}{4}$ T	24 ML	$\frac{3}{4}$ to 1 oz.	23 g

Figure 5-4 *Scoop and dipper sizes and approximate weights and measures in both customary and metric units.* Weights vary with different foods. This is only a guide and not exact.

Figure 5-5 *This chef is measuring a portion using a ladle.*

Size	Weight
$\frac{1}{4}$ cup	2 oz
$\frac{1}{2}$ cup	4 oz
$\frac{3}{4}$ cup	6 oz
1 cup	8 oz

Figure 5-6 *Ladle sizes.*

The Baker's Balance Scale

The **baker's balance scale** is the best type of scale to use because it ensures accuracy with the use of weight. The scale has a twin platform. (See Figure 5-7.) On the platform to the left is placed a metal scoop, in which the food to be weighed is placed. On the platform to the right is placed a special weight equal to the weight of the scoop. (See Figure 5-7.) If another container is used on the left platform, balance the scale by placing counterweights on the right side and/or by adjusting the ounce weight on the horizontal beam. This horizontal beam runs across the front of the scale. The beam has a weight attached to it and is graduated

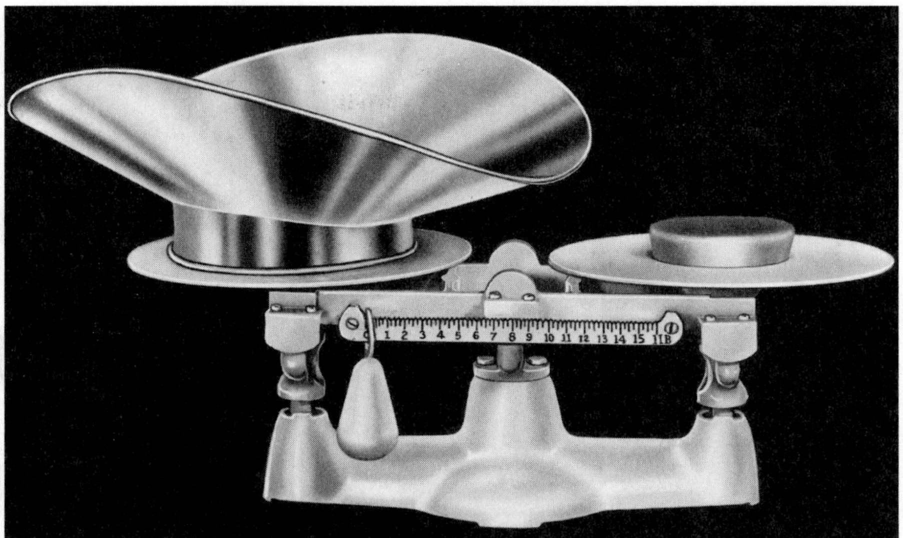

Figure 5-7 *Measuring scale.*

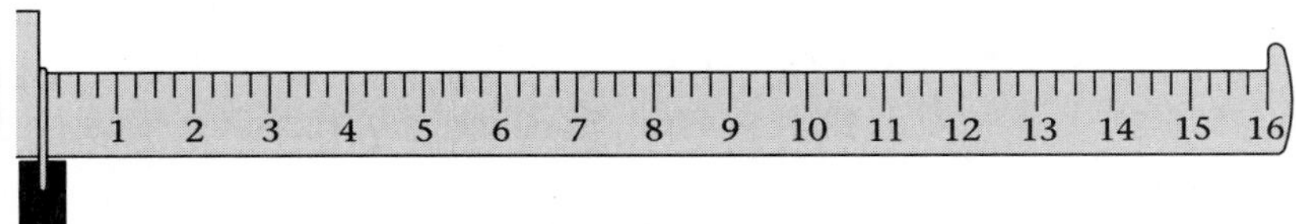

Figure 5-8 *Baker's scale beam graduated in $\frac{1}{4}$ ounces up to 16 ounces (1 pound).*

in $\frac{1}{4}$ ounces. The weight is placed on the number of ounces one wishes to weigh. The ounce weight can be graduated to 16 ounces (1 pound). (See Figure 5-8.) This scale can be used to weigh ingredients up to 10 pounds.

If a larger amount of food is to be weighed, additional metal weights of 1, 2, and 4 pounds are provided. When using this scale, always balance it before setting the weights for a given amount. It must balance again after the ingredients are placed on the scale.

When weighing 8 ounces of egg yolks, for example, place a container large enough to hold the yolks on the left platform and balance the scale. Move the weight on the horizontal beam 8 additional ounces. Then add the yolks to the container until the scale balances again.

If 1 pound $6\frac{1}{2}$ ounces of flour are to be weighed, place the metal scoop on the left-hand platform and the special balance weight on the right-hand platform. This brings the two platforms to a complete balance. The 1-pound weight is placed on the platform to the right and the weight on the scaling beam is set on $6\frac{1}{2}$ ounces. Flour is placed in the metal scoop until the two platforms balance a second time. For weighing small amounts, such as $1\frac{3}{4}$ ounces of baking powder, a piece of paper or a small paper plate should be placed on both platforms. To weigh the baking powder, slide the hanging weight (the weight on the horizontal beam attached to the scale) to $1\frac{3}{4}$ ounces. Pour the baking powder onto the paper on the left platform until it balances.

Figure 5-9 *This food service employee is using a scoop and a scale to determine quantities.*

Why the Baker's Balance Scale Is Important

Baking is fundamentally a science, so ingredients have to be accurate. A major challenge in baking is realizing that volume measures and measures of weights are different. For instance, if a recipe is written in **volume;** that is, the recipe states add 2 cups of flour, then the baker would measure 2 cups of flour by volume. But if the recipe calls for weighing out 16 ounces of flour, that may or may not be the same amount as the 2 cups of volume measure. The baker has to have the skill to use the balance scale accurately in order for the finished product to be a success.

To prove our point, obtain two 8-ounce measuring cups. Fill one with cotton balls and the other with crushed stone. Both of them measure 8 ounces of ingredients by volume, but do they both weigh the same amount? Of course not! To check our conclusion, practice by weighing both items using a baker's balance scale.

In the workplace, you will be expected to be able to use the baker's scale correctly. Practice is necessary to become competent, so whenever possible set the scale at various settings and weigh whatever items that are usually on hand. (See Figure 5-9.) Use items such as flour, salt, sugar, rice, and water.

Summary Review and Hands-on Activity

Total the amounts of each ingredient in the five formulas given and write the total below each formula.

For Example:

Ingredients	Pounds	Ounces
Sugar	1	8
Flour	4	6
Salt	—	1
Shortening	1	12
TOTAL	**6 lb.**	**27 oz. = 7 lb. 11 oz.**

(Note: There are 16 ounces in a pound, so for each 16 ounces, carry 1 pound to the pound column. Twenty-seven ounces equals 1 pound and 11 ounces, so 6 pounds 27 ounces equals 7 pounds 11 ounces.)

Then for hands-on practice, weigh each ingredient separately using sugar or rice to represent each ingredient. When this is done, weigh the total amount of all ingredients weighed. The amount should equal the sum of all the weights of ingredients listed.

Formula 1:

Ingredients	Pounds	Ounces
Shortening	1	6
Bread Flour	3	12
Salt	—	1
Sugar	2	10
Baking Powder	—	3
TOTAL		

Formula 2:

Ingredients	Pounds	Ounces
Shortening	1	8
Pastry Flour	2	10
Baking Powder	—	4
Baking Soda	—	$\frac{1}{2}$
Sugar	1	12
Salt	—	$2\frac{1}{4}$
TOTAL		

Formula 3:

Ingredients	Pounds	Ounces
Sugar	2	6
Baking Powder	—	$\frac{3}{4}$
Salt	—	$\frac{1}{2}$
Flour	4	10
Cornstarch	—	5
TOTAL		

Formula 4:

Ingredients	Pounds	Ounces
Butter	1	12
Pastry Flour	4	6
Dry Milk	—	$3\frac{1}{2}$
Shortening	1	6
Sugar	2	10
Salt	—	$\frac{3}{4}$
TOTAL		

Formula 5:

Ingredients	Pounds	Ounces
Butter	—	12
Cake Flour	—	10
Sugar	2	14
Baking Powder	1	$1\frac{3}{4}$
Dry Milk	—	6
Water	1	11
TOTAL		

◆ *Chef Sez . . .*

"In bread and roll production the student must weigh out ingredients. This is an important step because:

A. Balanced formula—varying the percent of ingredients will change the formula;
B. Consistent production of the required quantity—varying the ingredients may result in too large or too small a quantity;
C. Consistent production of quality;
D. Uniformity regardless of changes in mixing personnel;
E. Uniformity in fermentation times;
F. Control of costs."

Chef Noble Masi, Certified Master Baker,
Senior Chef Instructor
The Culinary Institute of America
Hyde Park, NY

Noble Masi was the 1999 American Culinary Chef of the Year. He is a professor of baking and pastry at The Culinary Institute of America. He was also the recipient of the 1996 ACF Chef Professionalism Award. He is an ACF-certified judge and a frequent speaker at seminars. He presented a seminar on signature breads at the 1998 American Culinary Federation National Convention held in Anaheim, California.

Portion Scale

Portion scales are used for measuring food servings, or **portions.** Sometimes ingredients are measured as well if a baker's balance scale is not available. A **portion scale** is operated by the use of a spring and can easily be unbalanced, so it is recommended that ingredients be weighed using the baker's balance scale if at all possible.

Portioning foods for service is a control method used in industry to ensure that the correct amount of an item or preparation is acquired and served. The scale would be used to portion a 3-ounce serving of baked ham, a $2\frac{1}{2}$-ounce serving of roast turkey, or for portioning a 5-ounce hamburger steak or a $4\frac{1}{2}$-ounce patty of pork sausage. If the exact cost of each item sold is to be determined, it is necessary to know the yield of each food. For example, if 15 pounds of beef round cost $27.75, the cost per serving cannot be determined until a serving portion and yield are established after the meat has been roasted.

Figure 5-10 *Portioning meat on a portion scale helps control serving size and cost.*

The portion scale shown in Figure 5-10 is used to weigh quantities up to 32 ounces (2 pounds). Each number on the movable dial represents 1 ounce. Each mark between the numbers represents $\frac{1}{4}$ ounce. For instance, the first mark past the pointer is $\frac{1}{4}$ ounce. The longer line next to it is $\frac{1}{2}$ ounce. The short line next in order is $\frac{3}{4}$ ounce and the long line that comes next is 1 full ounce.

The platform at the top of the portion scale is attached to a metal stem that fits into the scale. It is made of stainless steel and can be removed for washing, but care must be taken when replacing it to ensure that it fits properly and performs accurately. When the platform is properly placed, the pointer rests on 0, which also represents 32 ounces when weighing takes place. When weighing amounts that fit on the platform, first place waxed paper or some type of patty paper on the platform. Then, using the handle to move the scale dial, move the dial to the left until the pointer is again at zero. This action accounts for the weight of the paper. Place enough of the item being weighed on the paper until the pointer is exactly at the amount needed. For example, if portioning a 3-ounce salmon croquette, place enough of the mixture on the platform so that the pointer points directly at the 3, indicating that 3 ounces have been obtained. When weighing amounts that do not fit properly on the platform, use a light aluminum cake or pie pan to hold the item. Before weighing the item, however, be sure to balance the pan, using the same method as for balancing the paper.

Some approximate weights and measures of common foods are listed in Figure 5-11.

Food Product	Tbsp.	Cup	Pt.	Qt.
Allspice	$\frac{1}{4}$ oz.	4 oz.	8 oz.	1 lb.
Apples, Fresh, Diced	$\frac{1}{2}$ oz.	8 oz.	1 lb.	2 lb.
Bacon, Raw, Diced	$\frac{1}{2}$ oz.	8 oz.	1 lb.	2 lb.
Bacon, Cooked, Diced	$\frac{2}{3}$ oz.	$10\frac{1}{2}$ oz.	1 lb. 5 oz.	2 lb. 10 oz.
Baking Powder	$\frac{3}{8}$ oz.	6 oz.	12 oz.	1 lb. 8 oz.
Baking Soda	$\frac{3}{8}$ oz.	6 oz.	12 oz.	1 lb. 8 oz.
Bananas, Sliced	$\frac{1}{2}$ oz.	8 oz.	1 lb.	2 lb.
Barley	—	8 oz.	1 lb.	2 lb.
Beef, Cooked, Diced	$\frac{3}{8}$ oz.	$5\frac{1}{2}$ oz.	11 oz.	1 lb. 6 oz.
Beef, Raw, Ground	$\frac{1}{2}$ oz.	8 oz.	1 lb.	2 lb.
Bread Crumbs, Dry	$\frac{1}{4}$ oz.	4 oz.	8 oz.	1 lb.
Bread Crumbs, Fresh	$\frac{1}{8}$ oz.	2 oz.	4 oz.	8 oz.
Butter	$\frac{1}{2}$ oz.	8 oz.	1 lb.	2 lb.
Cabbage, Shredded	$\frac{1}{4}$ oz.	4 oz.	8 oz.	1 lb.
Carrots, Raw, Diced	$\frac{5}{16}$ oz.	5 oz.	10 oz.	1 lb. 4 oz.
Celery, Raw, Diced	$\frac{1}{4}$ oz.	4 oz.	8 oz.	1 lb.
Cheese, Diced	—	$5\frac{1}{2}$ oz.	11 oz.	1 lb. 6 oz.
Cheese, Grated	$\frac{1}{4}$ oz.	4 oz.	8 oz.	1 lb.
Cheese, Shredded	$\frac{1}{4}$ oz.	4 oz.	8 oz.	1 lb.
Chocolate, Grated	$\frac{1}{4}$ oz.	4 oz.	8 oz.	1 lb.
Chocolate, Melted	$\frac{1}{2}$ oz.	8 oz.	1 lb.	2 lb.
Cinnamon, Ground	$\frac{1}{4}$ oz.	$3\frac{1}{2}$ oz.	7 oz.	14 oz.
Cloves, Ground	$\frac{1}{4}$ oz.	4 oz.	8 oz.	1 lb.
Cloves, Whole	$\frac{3}{16}$ oz.	3 oz.	6 oz.	12 oz.
Cocoa	$\frac{3}{16}$ oz.	$3\frac{1}{2}$ oz.	7 oz.	14 oz.
Coconut, Macaroon, Packed	$\frac{3}{16}$ oz.	3 oz.	6 oz.	12 oz.
Coconut, Shredded, Packed	$\frac{3}{16}$ oz.	$3\frac{1}{2}$ oz.	7 oz.	14 oz.
Coffee, Ground	$\frac{3}{16}$ oz.	3 oz.	6 oz.	12 oz.
Cornmeal	$\frac{5}{16}$ oz.	$4\frac{3}{4}$ oz.	$9\frac{1}{2}$ oz.	1 lb. 3 oz.
Cornstarch	$\frac{1}{3}$ oz.	$5\frac{1}{3}$ oz.	$10\frac{1}{2}$ oz.	1 lb. 5 oz.
Corn Syrup	$\frac{3}{4}$ oz.	12 oz.	1 lb. 8 oz.	3 lb.
Cracker Crumbs	$\frac{1}{4}$ oz.	4 oz.	8 oz.	1 lb.
Cranberries, Raw	—	4 oz.	8 oz.	1 lb.

Figure 5-11 *Approximate weights and measures of common foods.* *(continued)*

Food Product	Tbsp.	Cup	Pt.	Qt.
Currants, Dried	$\frac{1}{3}$ oz.	$5\frac{1}{3}$ oz.	11 oz.	1 lb. 6 oz.
Curry Powder	$\frac{3}{16}$ oz.	$3\frac{1}{2}$ oz	—	—
Dates, Pitted	$\frac{5}{16}$ oz.	$5\frac{1}{2}$ oz.	11 oz.	1 lb. 6 oz.
Eggs, Whole	$\frac{1}{2}$ oz.	8 oz.	1 lb.	2 lb.
Egg Whites	$\frac{1}{2}$ oz.	8 oz.	1 lb.	2 lb.
Egg Yolks	$\frac{1}{2}$ oz.	8 oz.	1 lb.	2 lb.
Extracts	$\frac{1}{2}$ oz.	8 oz.	1 lb.	2 lb.
Flour, Bread	$\frac{5}{16}$ oz.	5 oz.	10 oz.	1 lb. 4 oz.
Flour, Cake	$\frac{1}{4}$ oz.	$4\frac{3}{4}$ oz.	$9\frac{1}{2}$ oz.	1 lb. 3 oz.
Flour, Pastry	$\frac{5}{16}$ oz.	5 oz.	10 oz.	1 lb. 4 oz.
Gelatin, Flavored	$\frac{3}{8}$ oz.	$6\frac{1}{2}$ oz.	13 oz.	1 lb. 10 oz.
Gelatin, Plain	$\frac{5}{16}$ oz.	5 oz.	10 oz.	1 lb. 4 oz.
Ginger	$\frac{3}{16}$ oz.	$3\frac{1}{4}$ oz.	$6\frac{1}{2}$ oz.	13 oz.
Glucose	$\frac{3}{4}$ oz.	12 oz.	1 lb. 8 oz.	3 lb.
Green Peppers, Diced	$\frac{1}{4}$ oz.	4 oz.	8 oz.	1 lb.
Ham, Cooked, Diced	$\frac{5}{16}$ oz.	$5\frac{1}{4}$ oz.	$10\frac{1}{2}$ oz.	1 lb. 5 oz.
Horseradish, Prepared	$\frac{1}{2}$ oz.	8 oz.	1 lb.	2 lb.
Jam	$\frac{5}{8}$ oz.	10 oz.	1 lb. 4 oz.	2 lb. 8 oz.
Lemon Juice	$\frac{1}{2}$ oz.	8 oz.	1 lb.	2 lb.
Lemon Rind	$\frac{1}{4}$ oz.	4 oz.	8 oz.	1 lb.
Mace	$\frac{1}{4}$ oz.	$3\frac{1}{4}$ oz.	$6\frac{1}{2}$ oz.	13 oz.
Mayonnaise	$\frac{1}{2}$ oz.	8 oz.	1 lb.	2 lb.
Milk, Liquid	$\frac{1}{2}$ oz.	8 oz.	1 lb.	2 lb.
Milk, Powdered	$\frac{5}{16}$ oz.	$5\frac{1}{4}$ oz.	$10\frac{1}{2}$ oz.	1 lb. 5 oz.
Molasses	$\frac{3}{4}$ oz.	12 oz.	1 lb.	3 lb.
Mustard, Ground	$\frac{1}{4}$ oz.	$3\frac{1}{4}$ oz.	$6\frac{1}{2}$ oz.	13 oz.
Mustard, Prepared	$\frac{1}{4}$ oz	4 oz.	8 oz.	1 lb.
Nutmeats	$\frac{1}{4}$ oz.	4 oz.	8 oz.	1 lb.
Nutmeg, Ground	$\frac{1}{4}$ oz.	$4\frac{1}{4}$ oz.	$8\frac{1}{2}$ oz.	1 lb. 1 oz.
Oats, Rolled	$\frac{3}{16}$ oz.	3 oz.	6 oz.	12 oz.
Oil, Salad	$\frac{1}{2}$ oz.	8 oz.	1 lb.	2 lb.
Onions	$\frac{1}{3}$ oz.	$5\frac{1}{2}$ oz.	11 oz.	1 lb. 6 oz.
Peaches, Canned	$\frac{1}{2}$ oz.	8 oz.	1 lb.	2 lb.

Figure 5-11 *Approximate weights and measures of common foods (continued).*

Food Product	Tbsp.	Cup	Pt.	Qt.
Peas, Dry, Split	$\frac{7}{16}$ oz.	7 oz.	14 oz.	1 lb. 12 oz.
Pickle Relish	$\frac{5}{16}$ oz.	$5\frac{1}{4}$ oz.	$10\frac{1}{2}$ oz.	1 lb. 5 oz.
Pickles, Chopped	$\frac{1}{4}$ oz.	$5\frac{1}{4}$ oz.	$10\frac{1}{2}$ oz.	1 lb. 5 oz.
Pimentos, Chopped	$\frac{1}{2}$ oz.	7 oz	14 oz.	1 lb 12 oz.
Pineapple, Diced	$\frac{1}{2}$ oz.	8 oz	1 lb.	2 lb.
Potatoes, Cooked, Diced	—	$6\frac{1}{2}$ oz	13 oz.	1 lb. 10 oz.
Prunes, Dry	—	$5\frac{1}{2}$ oz.	11 oz.	1 lb. 6 oz.
Raisins, Seedless	$\frac{1}{3}$ oz	$5\frac{1}{3}$ oz.	$10\frac{3}{4}$ oz.	1 lb. 5 oz.
Rice, Raw	$\frac{1}{2}$ oz	8 oz	1 lb.	2 lb.
Sage, Ground	$\frac{1}{8}$ oz	$2\frac{1}{4}$ oz	$4\frac{1}{2}$ oz.	9 oz.
Salmon, Flaked	$\frac{1}{2}$ oz	8 oz	1 lb.	2 lb.
Salt	$\frac{1}{2}$ oz	8 oz	1 lb.	2 lb.
Savory	$\frac{1}{8}$ oz	2 oz	4 oz.	8 oz.
Shortening	$\frac{1}{2}$ oz	8 oz	1 lb.	2 lb.
Soda	$\frac{7}{16}$ oz.	7 oz.	14 oz.	1 lb. 12 oz.
Sugar, Brown, Packed	$\frac{1}{2}$ oz.	8 oz.	1 lb.	2 lb.
Sugar, Granulated	$\frac{7}{16}$ oz.	$7\frac{1}{2}$ oz.	15 oz.	1 lb. 14 oz.
Sugar, Powdered	$\frac{5}{16}$ oz.	$4\frac{3}{4}$ oz.	$9\frac{1}{2}$ oz.	1 lb. 3 oz.
Tapioca, Pearl	$\frac{1}{4}$ oz.	4 oz.	8 oz.	1 lb.
Tea	$\frac{1}{6}$ oz.	$2\frac{1}{2}$ oz.	5 oz.	10 oz.
Tomatoes	$\frac{1}{2}$ oz.	8 oz.	1 lb.	2 lb.
Tuna Fish, Flaked	$\frac{1}{2}$ oz.	8 oz.	1 lb.	2 lb.
Vanilla, Imitation	$\frac{1}{2}$ oz.	8 oz.	1 lb.	2 lb.
Vinegar	$\frac{1}{2}$ oz.	8 oz.	1 lb.	2 lb.
Water	$\frac{1}{2}$ oz.	8 oz.	1 lb.	2 lb.

Figure 5-11 *Approximate weights and measures of common foods (continued).*

Summary Review

1. Determine the cost of a chop steak if the dial pointer on the portion scale points to the second mark beyond the 5 and the cost of 1 pound of lean ground beef is $1.78.

____

2. Determine the cost of a portion of corn beef if the dial on the portion scale points to the third mark beyond the 2 and the cost of 1 pound of cooked corn beef is $5.25.

____

3. Determine the cost of a portion of cooked ham if the dial pointer on the portion scale points to the first mark beyond the 3 and the cost of 1 pound of cooked ham is $3.45.

____

4. Determine the cost of a portion of roast loin of pork if the dial pointer on the portion scale points to the second mark beyond the 4 and the cost of 1 pound of cooked pork loin is $3.99.

____

5. Determine the cost of a filet mignon if the dial pointer on the portion scale points to the second mark beyond the 8 and the cost of 1 pound of beef tenderloin E.P. (edible portion) is $7.95.

____

Converting Decimal Weights into Ounces

As the food service industry moves toward using weights of ingredients based on the decimal system, the professional must know how to convert the amount of a decimal into weights. Many recipes state ingredients in ounces. For example, a soup recipe requires 5 ounces of pepperoni or a salad dressing requires 6 ounces of blue cheese. In the past, the food service professional used the ounce scale. It was, and still is, easy to weigh the ingredients on the scale. However, purveyors are selling and pricing ingredients based on the decimal system. It is common to have food products listed on invoices in pounds and the decimal of the pound. The blue cheese on the invoice may be listed as 5.637 pounds. How will the chef determine how many ounces has been received? The blue cheese must be converted to ounces. It is known that there are 16 ounces in a pound. Therefore, 5 pounds times 16 is equal to 80 ounces. That is the easy part. But how many ounces of blue cheese does the .637 represent? In order to find the answer, 16 must be multiplied by .637 ounces which equals 10.192 ounces.

How to calculate the math:

Decimal amount of ounces	
Multiplied by	.637
Number of ounces in a pound	× 16
Total ounces	10.192 ounces

The food service professional must realize that .5 on a digital scale is not 5 ounces, but is 8 ounces or half of a pound (16 × .5 = 8.0 ounces). Manufacturers are selling an increasing number of scales based on the decimal system.

SUMMARY REVIEW

Find the amount of ounces in the following problems based on a pound. Do not round off.

1. .45 lb. ________________
2. .75 lb. ________________
3. .25 lb. ________________
4. .333 lb. ________________
5. .618 lb. ________________
6. .737 lb. ________________
7. .921 lb. ________________
8. .279 lb. ________________
9. Chef Bhutta orders and receives 156.25 ounces of chicken. If each guest receives a 10-ounce portion of chicken, how many guests can be served?

   ____

10. The Merlot Restaurant receives 10 ribs of beef weighing 22.72 pounds each. How many ounces of beef does this represent?

   ____

Portion Control

OBJECTIVES

At the completion of this chapter, the student should be able to:

1. Identify methods of controlling portion size.
2. Identify portion sizes.
3. Find cost per serving.
4. Identify portion sizes using scoops or dippers.
5. Identify and find amounts of food to prepare.
6. Define and identify the terms E.P. (edible portion) and A.P. (as purchased).
7. Find the approximate number of serving portions.
8. Find the amount of food to order.
9. Find the amount of cost per portion.

There is a saying in food service that a good rich stock is the key to kitchen production. However, portion control is the key to profits.

Portion control is a term used in the food service industry to ensure that a specific or designated amount of an item is served to the guest. It is also the method used to acquire the correct number of servings from a standardized recipe, a ham roast, vegetable preparation, cake, or pie. In addition, portion control is helpful in controlling food production, pricing the menu, purchasing, and controlling food cost.

ACHIEVING PORTION CONTROL

The best way to control portions is to use standardized recipes that state the number of servings a preparation will produce. However, a standardized recipe gives only the stated number of portions if the servings are uniform in size. To ensure uniform servings or portions, the preparation crew and serving personnel must be instructed in the use of ladles, scoops, scales, spoons, and similar devices when dishing up food.

Another method of achieving a successful portion control program is intelligent buying. Buy foods in sizes that portion well. Work out buying specifications that suit the portion need. For example, cooked smoked ham can be purchased in many types and sizes. Purchase the kind that will produce a ham steak the diameter desired and one that produces little or no waste. Most link sausage such as wieners, pork links, and frank-

Figure 6-1 *Computerized scales can provide precise weight measurements.*

furters can be purchased at a certain number (6, 8, or 10) to each pound. Purchase the count per pound that best suits the portion requirement. Select veal, pork, lamb, and beef ribs and loins that provide the size chop or slice desired. You never want a slice or chop that will hang over or extend beyond the rim of the plate. Even when portioning, appearance is important. If the food does not look appetizing, the first bite may never be taken.

Many foods can be purchased ready-to-cook and are purchased for absolute portion control. This is another controlling device to consider. Fish fillets, steaks, chops, and cutlets are all cut to the exact ounce desired. (See Figure 6-1.) The cost per pound is much higher because the more labor involved in fabricating a product, the higher the cost. To many food service operators the final cost is, in reality, lower when considering the following factors:

- no leftovers,
- less storage required,
- no waste,
- no cutting equipment to purchase, and
- less labor cost.

T I P S . . . ***To Insure Perfect Solutions***

Always know the cost of the food that is placed on the plate in front of the guest.

Methods of Controlling Portion Size

There are five basic methods used in the food service industry to control portion size. They are listed in Figure 6-2 with a few examples of how each can be achieved.

Method	**Examples**
Weight	5 oz. pork cutlet $2\frac{1}{2}$ oz. roast beef 3 oz. roast pork
Count	8 fried scallops per order 2 Italian meatballs per order 3 corn fritters per order
Volume	2 oz. portion of Hollandaise over vegetables No. 12 scoop of baked rice 3 oz. kitchen spoonful of green beans
Equal Portions	Cake cut in 8 equal slices Pie cut into 7 equal wedges Pan of baked lasagna cut into 12 equal servings
Portioned Fill	8 oz. casserole of chicken pot pie 5 oz. glass of apple juice 4 oz. cup of chocolate pudding

Figure 6-2 *Methods of portion control.*

Portioning Food

When portioning food for a particular establishment, remember that portions can be too large as well as too small. Therefore, before a portion policy is established the manager as well as the chef should know their customers. This knowledge can be acquired by carefully observing the plates brought into the dishwashing area. Too much uneaten food left in a bowl or on a plate indicates that a portion is too large, or that the quality of the food does not satisfy the customer. In either case, the situation tells a story and must be corrected to improve customer satisfaction and to control food cost. Too small a portion is usually indicated by plates and bowls that are scraped entirely clean. A satisfied guest usually leaves a very small amount of food on the plate or in a bowl.

When portioning food by weight, it is easy to find how much raw food is needed and how much should be prepared for a specific number of people. (See Figure 6-3.) For example:

- **Number to be served × portion size = number of E.P. (edible portion) ounces needed.**
- **Number of ounces needed ÷ by 16 = number of E.P. pounds needed.**

Figure 6-3 *Precise portion control results in cost management.*

By finding the cost per ounce, a total cost is easy to calculate. Many chefs and managers become tired of hearing employees ask, *"How much should I prepare?"*. By observing portion control charts posted in the preparation area and by doing some simple figuring, employees can answer their own questions.

Once a portion policy is established, it should be posted in the kitchen. A typical portion chart is shown in Figure 6-4.

◆ *Chef Sez . . .*

"At Churchill Downs, the home of the Kentucky Derby, I am faced with the task of making certain that I have enough food to feed 56,000 guests over a seven day period. I also have to avoid ordering or cooking too much food, so I can meet my food costs guidelines.

For example, when a buffet meal is ordered I take many factors into consideration. First, I have to estimate the ounces of food each guest will eat. Second, the number of guests must be known. I multiply the ounces of food each guest will eat by the number of guests. I now have an estimate of how much food will be needed.

Next, I have to determine how many different selections are ordered for the buffet (for example, shrimp, beef, etc.). Now I determine the amount of chafing dishes that are needed for the buffet. I determine how many portions can be obtained from each chafing dish. Finally, I have to use my expertise to determine the amount of certain foods. This would depend on the popularity of the food and the make-up of the group.

Therefore, I must use addition, subtraction, multiplication and division to determine the amount of food needed to order and cook."

Chef John Harasty
Executive Chef
ARAMARK Corporation
Churchill Downs
Louisville, Kentucky

STEWS, BLANQUETTES, HASHES, ETC.	
Beef Goulash	7 oz.
Beef Stew	7 oz.
Veal Blanquette	6 oz.
Lamb Blanquette	7 oz.
Lamb Stew	7 oz.
Veal Stew	7 oz.
Oxtail Stew	10 oz.
Roast Beef Hash	6 oz.
Corned Beef Hash	6 oz.
Chicken Hash	6 oz.
Beef Stroganoff	7 oz.
Beef a la Deutsch	7 oz.

POTATO PREPARATIONS	
Baked	6 oz.
Au Gratin	4 oz.
Delmonico	4 oz.
French Fried	5 oz.
Mashed	5 oz.
Julienne	4 oz.
Lyonnaise	5 oz.
Croquette	5 oz.
Hash Brown	5 oz.
Escallop	4 oz.
Candied Sweet	5 oz.

VEGETABLES	
Asparagus, Spears	4 or 5 spears
Asparagus, Cut	4 oz.
Beans, Limas	4 oz.
Beans, String	4 oz.
Beans, Wax	4 oz.
Beets	4 oz.
Brussels Sprouts	5 oz.
Cabbage	5 oz.
Cauliflower	5 oz.
Carrots	4 oz.
Corn on the Cob	1 cob
Corn, Whole Kernel	4 oz.
Corn, Cream Style	5 oz.
Mushrooms, Whole	4 oz.
Onions	5 oz.
Peas	4 oz.
Rice	4 oz.
Squash	4 oz.
Succotash	3 oz.
Tomatoes, Stewed	4 oz.
Eggplant	4 oz.

DESSERTS	
Baked Alaska	1 slice—per Alaska
Compotes	5 oz.
Cake	1 slice—8 per cake
Ice Cream	4 oz.
Jubilee	5 oz. ice cream, 2 oz. cherries
Parfaits	5 oz. ice cream, 3 oz. sauce
Pie	1 slice—6 per pie
Pudding	5 oz.
Sherbets	4 oz.

SALADS	
Cole Slaw	4 oz.
Garden Salad	5 oz.
Ham Salad	5 oz.
Julienne	5 oz.
Macaroni	4 oz.
Potato	5 oz.
Toss	5 oz.
Waldorf	5 oz.

Figure 6-4 *Standardized portion chart (continued).*

STEAKS	
Chateaubriand	16 oz.
Filet Mignon	6 oz.
Minute	6 oz.
Sirloin	10 oz.
NY Strip Sirloin	16 oz.
T-bone	12 oz.
Club	10 oz.
Porterhouse	14 oz.
Baby T-bone	6 oz.
Beef Tenderloin	8 oz.
Salisbury	8 oz.
Ham	6 oz.
Veal Steak	6 oz.
Lamb Steak	7 oz.

CHOPS AND CUTLETS	
Pork Chops	2-3$\frac{1}{2}$ oz. each
Lamb Chops	2-3$\frac{1}{2}$ oz. each
Veal Chops	1-6 oz.
English Lamb Chop	6 oz.
Veal Cutlet	6 oz.
Pork Cutlet	6 oz.
Escallop of Veal	7 oz.
Noisette of Lamb	2-3$\frac{1}{2}$oz. each
Pork Tenderloin	7 oz.
Beef Tournedos	2-4 oz. each

POULTRY	
Fried Chicken	$\frac{1}{2}$ fryer—3$\frac{1}{2}$ lb. chicken
Broiled Chicken	$\frac{1}{2}$ broiler—2 lb. chicken
Roast Chicken	$\frac{1}{2}$ chicken—3 lb. chicken
Roast Turkey	2$\frac{1}{2}$ oz. white meat—3 oz. dark
Turkey Steak	5 oz. white meat
Boneless Turkey Wings	2 wings
Chicken a la King	6 oz.
Chicken Pot Pie	6 oz. plus crust
Chicken a la Maryland	$\frac{1}{2}$ fryer, 1 oz. bacon, 2 oz. cream sauce, 2 oz. corn fritters, 2 croquettes, 6 oz.
Chicken Cutlet	2 cutlets—6 oz.
Roast Duck	8 oz.
Roast Squab	1 bird
Roast Bnls Chicken Breast	5 oz. breast
Baked Stuffed Chicken Leg	1 leg, 3 oz. stuffing

Figure 6-4 *Standardized portion chart (continued).*

SEAFOOD	
Lobster, Broiled Whole	16 oz.
Lobster Newburg	5 oz. meat
Lobster Crab	5 oz. meat
Fried Shrimp	6 jumbo—8 medium
Shrimp Newburg	7 medium
Sauteed Shrimp	6 jumbo—8 medium
Softshell Crabs	2 crabs
Clam Roast	8 cherrystone
Steamed Clams	8 cherrystone
Fried Clams	8 cherrystone
Fried Oysters	7 select
Oyster Stews	6 select
Fried Scallops	8 small—6 large
Sauteed Scallops	8 small—6 large
Halibut	7 oz.
Cod	7 oz.
Spanish Mackerel	7 oz.
Pampano	7 oz.
Red Snapper	6 oz.
Frog Legs	8 oz.
White Fish	7 oz.
Lake Trout	7 oz.
Rainbow Trout	8 oz.
Brook Trout	8 oz.
Smelt	6 fish, about 7 oz.
Salmon	7 oz.
Shad Roe	4 oz.
English and Dover Sole	7 oz.

Figure 6-4 *Standardized portion chart (continued).*

ROASTED MEATS	
Roast Rib of Beef	8 oz.
Roast Tenderloin of Beef	6 oz.
Roast Sirloin of Beef	6 oz.
Roast Round of Beef	5 oz.
Roast Leg of Lamb	5 oz.
Roast Loin of Pork	6 oz.
Roast Leg of Veal	5 oz.
Roast Fresh Ham	6 oz.
Baked Ham	6 oz.

Figure 6-4 *Standardized portion chart (continued).*

Example:

Appetizer	4 oz.
Salad	4 oz.
Entree	8 oz.
Potato	4 oz.
Vegetable	4 oz.
Bread & Butter	3 oz.
Dessert	6 oz.
Beverage	7 oz.
	40 oz. = $2\frac{1}{2}$ pounds

Figure 6-5 *Ideal portion sizes for one meal.*

A point to remember when figuring portion sizes is that the average human stomach can only hold approximately $2\frac{1}{2}$ pounds of solid and liquid food comfortably. Therefore, oversized portions do not make customers satisfied, and usually create more waste. The intelligent restaurant operator figures portion sizes so that the customer has room left for dessert. An example of how the portion sizes for one meal should add up is given in Figure 6-5.

Cost Per Serving

To find the cost per serving, the total weight of the item is converted into ounces and divided into the total cost to find the cost of one ounce. The cost of one ounce is multiplied by the number of ounces being served. See the following formula to simplify this explanation.

Total weight × 16 = total ounces.
Total cost ÷ by total ounces = cost of 1 ounce.
Cost of 1 ounce × number of ounces served = cost per serving.

Example: A 5-pound box of frozen lima beans costs $6.24. How much does a 4-ounce serving cost?

Weight 5 lbs. × 16 = 80 ounces.
$6.24 (total cost) ÷ 80 (ounces) = 0.078 cost of 1 ounce.
0.078 (cost of 1 ounce) × 4 (ounces served) = 0.312 = $0.31
(cost of a 4-ounce serving).

The division is carried to three places to the right of the decimal point. Remember that the third digit is the mill, or $\frac{1}{10}$ of a cent.

Of course if a cost per pound is given rather than a total, the number of pounds given must be multiplied by the cost per pound to find a total cost.

Example: Find the cost of a 3-ounce serving of succotash (mixture of two vegetables) if the following ingredients are used.

5-pound box lima beans @ $1.23 per pound.
$2\frac{1}{2}$-pound box corn @ $0.58 per pound.
To state this function as a math formula, it would be expressed as:
Total weight × unit price = total cost.
5 pounds × $1.23 = $6.15 total cost of lima beans.
$2\frac{1}{2}$ pounds × $0.58 = $1.45 total cost of corn.
$7.60 total cost of succotash.

To complete the problem, follow the same steps explained in the previous example.

$7\frac{1}{2}$ pounds × 16 = 120 ounces.
$7.60 total cost ÷ 120 ounces = $0.063 cost of 1 ounce.
$.063 cost of 1 ounce × 3 ounces = $0.189 or $.019 cost of a 3-ounce serving.

SUMMARY REVIEW

Work each problem. Round answers to the nearest cent.

1. A $2\frac{1}{2}$-pound box of frozen corn costs $1.55. How much does a 4-ounce serving cost?

   ____

2. When preparing succotash, a $2\frac{1}{2}$-pound box of frozen corn costs $0.58 per pound and a 5-pound box of frozen lima beans costs $1.18 per pound. How much does a 3-ounce serving cost?

   ____

3. A $2\frac{1}{2}$-pound box of frozen peas and onions costs \$0.72 per pound. How much does a $3\frac{1}{2}$-ounce serving cost?

____

4. If frozen asparagus spears cost \$11.95 for a 5-pound box, how much does a 3-ounce serving cost?

____

5. If a $2\frac{1}{2}$-pound box of frozen cut broccoli costs \$1.70, what is the cost of a $3\frac{1}{2}$-ounce serving?

____

6. A 5-pound box of frozen asparagus spears costs \$2.39 per pound. How much does a $2\frac{1}{2}$-ounce serving cost?

____

7. A $2\frac{1}{2}$-pound bag of frozen oriental vegetable mix costs \$0.78 per pound. How much does a 4-ounce serving cost?

____

8. A 3-pound bag of frozen Scandinavian vegetable mix costs \$0.76 per pound. How much does a $3\frac{1}{2}$-ounce serving cost?

____

9. A 2-pound bag of frozen whole baby carrots costs \$0.82 per pound. How much does a 3-ounce serving cost?

____

10. Find the cost of a $5\frac{1}{2}$-ounce serving of a beef stir-fry if the following items were used:

    3-pound bag frozen stir-fry vegetables @ \$1.45 per pound.

    5 pounds of sliced fresh beef @ \$3.80 per pound.

    ____

PORTIONING WITH SCOOPS OR DIPPERS

Scoops or dippers, as mentioned in the previous chapter, are used to serve and portion such foods as bread dressing, rice, meat patties, croquette mixtures, ice cream, and muffin batters. Two examples of food scoops are shown in Figure 6-6. They have a metal bowl or cup of known capacity, an extended handle, and a thumb-operated lever to release the item being portioned or served. A movable strip of metal on the inside of the bowl releases its contents. This metal strip contains a number to indicate the size of the metal cup; the larger the number, the smaller the cup. The number indicates the number of scoops it will take to make a quart. Figure 6-7 relates each scoop number to its approximate capacity in ounces and also to the approximate content of each scoop size in cups or tablespoons. In the previous chapter, Figure 5-6 was shown with both their customary and metric weights and volume. Here they are repeated with only customary weights and volume for easy reference when working the summary review problems.

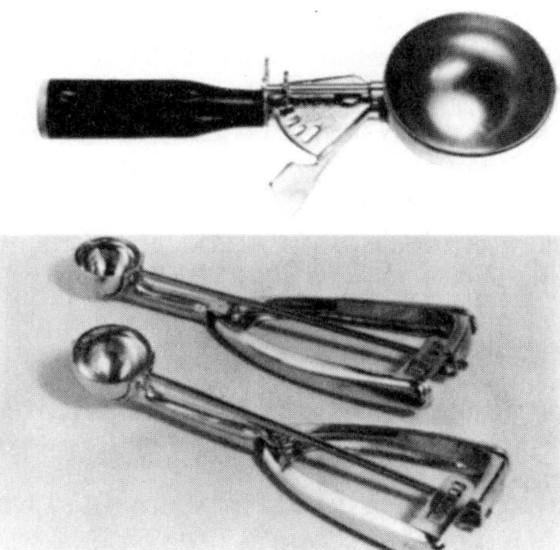

Figure 6-6 *Two examples of food scoops (Courtesy of Hamilton Beach).*

Scoop or dipper number	Approximate volume	Approximate weight
6	$\frac{2}{3}$ cup	5 oz.
8	$\frac{1}{2}$ cup	4 oz.
10	$\frac{2}{5}$ cup	$3\frac{1}{2}$ oz.
12	$\frac{1}{3}$ cup	3 oz.
16	$\frac{1}{4}$ cup	$2\frac{1}{2}$ oz.
20	$3\frac{1}{5}$ T	$1\frac{2}{3}$ oz.
24	$2\frac{2}{3}$ T	$1\frac{1}{2}$ oz.
30	$2\frac{1}{5}$ T	$1\frac{1}{4}$ oz.
40	$1\frac{3}{4}$ T	1 oz.

Figure 6-7 *Scoop volume and weight.* Weights vary with different foods. This is only a guide and not exact.

To find the number of servings a particular amount of food will produce when portioning with a scoop or dipper, divide the amount contained in the scoop or dipper into the amount being served. To state this function as a formula, it is as follows:

Amount portioned ÷ scoop content = number of servings.

Example: How many servings can be obtained from 4 gallons of ice cream if a No. 8 scoop is used to portion?

Convert 4 gallons to 64 cups (1 gallon contains 16 cups)
hence $16 \times 4 = 64$ cups.
This step is necessary because to divide, like things are required.

64 cups $\div \frac{1}{2}$ cup $= \frac{64}{1} \times \frac{2}{1} = 128$ servings
(amount portioned ÷ scoop content).

Example: How many individual salads can be obtained from 8 pounds of chicken salad if a No. 6 scoop is used to portion?

Convert 8 pounds to 128 ounces (1 pound contains 16 ounces) hence $16 \times 8 = 128$ ounces.
This step is necessary because to divide, like things are required.

128 ounces ÷ 5 ounces = $25\frac{3}{5}$ (or 25.6) servings = 25 servings
(amount portioned ÷ scoop content = total portions).

The remainder is dropped because it is not a complete portion.

Summary Review

In working the following problems, only record complete servings. Drop any remainder.

1. How many servings can be obtained from 3 gallons of mashed potatoes if a No. 12 scoop is used?

____

2. How many corn fritters can be obtained from 4 pounds of batter if a No. 24 scoop is used?

____

3. Determine how many servings can be obtained from 12 pounds of bread pudding if a No. 10 scoop is used to portion?

____

4. How many servings can be obtained from 5 quarts of strawberry mousse if a No. 6 scoop is used to portion?

____

5. How many individual salads can be obtained from 7 pounds of tuna fish salad if a No. 10 scoop is used to portion?

____

6. How many clam fritters can be obtained from 5 pounds of batter if a No. 24 scoop is used to portion?

____

7. How many blueberry muffins can be obtained from $2\frac{1}{2}$ gallons of batter if a No. 12 scoop is used to portion?

____

8. How many servings can be obtained from $\frac{1}{2}$ gallon of cold pack cheese if a No. 16 scoop is used to portion?

____

9. How many hush puppies can be obtained from $2\frac{1}{2}$ pounds of batter if a No. 30 scoop is used to portion?

____

10. How many servings can be obtained from 12 pounds of mashed potatoes if a No. 8 scoop is used to portion?

____

FIGURING AMOUNTS TO PREPARE

In any food service operation, it is constantly necessary to figure how many cans, boxes, or packages of certain food items are needed or must be opened in order to have enough food to serve a given number of people. This problem is solved by multiplying the number of people to be served by the portion size, giving the number of ounces needed. Next, the weight of the can, box, or package is converted into ounces and the given amount is divided into the number of ounces needed. If a remainder results from the division, an additional container must be opened. By utilizing mathematics in this situation, guesswork can be eliminated and food preparation can be controlled. Steps to simplify this function are as follows:

Number of people to be served × portion size = ounces needed.
Pounds in container × 16 + ounces = ounces in one container.
Ounces needed ÷ ounces in one container = containers needed.

Example: How many No. 10 cans of green beans are needed to serve a party of 260 people if each person is to receive a 3-ounce serving and each can contains 4 pounds 6 ounces?

Step 1:
260 × 3 ounces = 780 ounces
Number of people to be served × portion size
= ounces needed to serve 260 people.

Step 2:
4 pounds × 16 ounces per pound
= 64 ounces + 6 = 70 ounces.
Pounds in container × 16 + ounces in container
= content of 1 container.

Step 3:
780 ÷ 70 ounces = 11.14 cans.
Ounces needed to serve 260 people ÷ content of one container
= 12 No. 10 cans needed to serve 260 people.

The preceding example shows that 12 No. 10 cans are needed to serve each of the 260 people a 3-ounce serving. When dividing the content of the can into the number of ounces needed, a remainder resulted, so an additional can was required.

SUMMARY REVIEW

1. A 3-ounce serving of peas is to be served to each of 180 people. How many boxes of frozen peas should be cooked if each box weighs $2\frac{1}{2}$ pounds?

 ____

2. A 3-ounce serving of wax beans is served to each of 55 people. How many cans of wax beans are needed if each can weighs 14 ounces?

 ____

3. How many No. $2\frac{1}{2}$ cans of pork and beans are required to serve 84 people if each can weighs 1 pound 10 ounces and each serving is 5 ounces.

 ____

4. A 3-ounce serving of peas is to be served to each of 110 people. How many boxes of frozen peas are needed if each box weighs 5 pounds?

 ____

5. How many No. 10 cans of green beans are needed to serve a party of 270 people if each person is to receive a $3\frac{1}{2}$-ounce serving and each can weighs 4 pounds 4 ounces?

____

6. How many No. 5 cans of potato salad are required to serve 96 people if each can weighs 3 pounds 6 ounces and each serving is $5\frac{1}{2}$ ounces?

____

7. How many $2\frac{1}{2}$-pound bags of corn will be needed to serve 360 people if each person is to receive a $3\frac{1}{2}$-ounce serving?

____

8. How many boxes of frozen chopped spinach are needed to serve a party of 186 people if each person is to receive a 3-ounce serving and each box weighs 4 pounds?

____

9. How many 5-pound boxes of frozen lima beans are needed to serve a party of 350 people if each person is to receive a 4-ounce serving?

____

10. A $3\frac{1}{2}$-ounce serving of frozen peas and pearl onions is to be served to 145 people. How many 5-pound boxes will be needed?

____

11. How many No. 10 cans of cut green beans are needed to serve a party of 180 people if each person is to receive a 3-ounce serving and each can weighs 5 pounds 10 ounces?

____

12. How many 2-pound bags of Scandinavian vegetable mix will be required to serve a party of 85 people if each person is to receive a 4-ounce serving?

____

13. How many No. $2\frac{1}{2}$ cans of diced beets are needed to serve a party of 42 people if each person is to receive a $4\frac{1}{2}$-ounce serving and each can weighs 2 pounds 5 ounces?

____

14. How many No. 5 cans of tomato juice will be needed to serve 132 people if a person is to receive a 4-ounce serving and each can contains 48 fluid ounces?

____

15. How many No. $2\frac{1}{2}$ cans of diced carrots are needed to serve a party of 68 people if each person is to receive a 3-ounce serving and each can weighs 1 pound 12 ounces?

____

Finding the Approximate Number of Serving Portions

Finding approximately how many servings can be acquired from a given amount of food (as shown in Figure 6-8), or how much of a certain meat, fish, vegetable, or liquid food product should be ordered are additional portion control concerns. For example, how many 12-ounce strip steaks can be cut from a short loin? How many 2-ounce meatballs can be acquired from a certain amount of ground beef? How many pounds of fish steaks must be ordered for a party of 80 people? How many gallons of orange juice must be ordered to serve a party of 250 people?

The arithmetic involved in these problems is quite simple, and is an essential part of a food service operation. This arithmetic must be accurate to keep inventories at a minimum, to control waste, and to maintain an effective portion control program.

To find out how many servings can be obtained from a given amount, the E.P. (edible portion) must first be established (that is, waste must be eliminated). Waste such as bone, fat, and skin cannot be converted into serving portions so it must be subtracted from the original A.P. (as purchased) weight of the product. The size of the serving portion is then divided into the E.P. (edible portion) amount to give the approximate number of servings it will produce. Stating this function as a formula is shown as follows:

E.P. amount ÷ serving portion = number of servings.

Figure 6-8 *The top picture illustrates appropriate portion control. The bottom picture illustrates an unappealing presentation and inappropriate portion control.*

Example: An 18-pound short loin of beef is purchased, A.P. (amount purchased). 2 pounds 10 ounces are lost through boning and trimming. How many 12-ounce strip sirloin steaks can be cut from the short loin?

18 pounds (A.P. amount converted to ounces) × 16 = 288 ounces.
288 ounces − 42 ounces (lost through boning and trimming)
= 246 ounces E.P. amount.
246 ounces (E.P. amount) ÷ 12 ounces (amount of each steak)
= 20.5 or 20 12-ounce steaks.

Shown as long division:

$$
\begin{array}{r}
20.5 \\
12\overline{)246.0} \\
\underline{24} \\
60 \\
\underline{60}
\end{array}
\quad \text{E.P. Amount}
$$

Each steak is to weigh 12 ounces, so the weight of each steak is divided into 246 ounces E.P. amount. This shows that 20 steaks can be cut from the sirloin. It was necessary to convert the E.P. amount to ounces because you can only divide like things.

Summary Review

1. A 7-pound A.P. beef tenderloin is trimmed; 8 ounces are lost. How many 6-ounce filet mignons can be cut from the tenderloin?

   ____

2. How many 5-ounce pork chops can be cut from a pork loin weighing 15 pounds A.P. if the tenderloin, which is removed, weighed 9 ounces, and 3 pounds 5 ounces are lost through boning and trimming?

   ____

3. How many orders of meatballs can be obtained from 40 pounds E.P. of ground beef if each meatball is to weigh 2 ounces and two meatballs are served per order?

   ____

4. How many orders of Swedish meatballs can be obtained from 32 pounds E.P. of ground pork and veal if each meatball weighs $1\frac{1}{2}$ ounces and 4 meatballs are served with each order?

   ____

5. How many 5-ounce Swiss steaks can be cut from a beef round weighing 44 pounds A.P. if 4 pounds 3 ounces are lost in boning and trimming?

   ____

6. When preparing pork sausage, 16 pounds A.P. of pork picnic is purchased. One-fourth of the amount is lost through boning and trimming. How many 4-ounce patties can be obtained?

   ____

7. How many 5-ounce glasses of orange juice can be obtained from 2 gallons of orange juice? (1 quart = 32 ounces)

____

8. Forty-six pounds (A.P). of turkey breast are purchased. Four pounds 4 ounces are lost through boning and skinning. How many turkey steaks can be obtained if each steak is to weigh 5 ounces?

____

9. A 13-pound (E.P.) pork loin is roasted. One pound 2 ounces are lost through shrinkage. How many $2\frac{1}{2}$-ounce servings can be obtained from the cooked loin?

____

10. A 14-pound (A.P.) ham is trimmed. Twelve ounces are lost. How many ham steaks can be cut from the ham if each steak is to weigh 6 ounces?

____

11. A 19-pound (A.P.) rib eye is purchased. Two pounds 14 ounces are lost through trimming. How many rib steaks can be cut from the rib eye if each steak is to weigh 8 ounces?

____

12. A 12-pound (E.P.) pork loin is purchased. How many $4\frac{1}{2}$-ounce pork cutlets can be cut from the loin?

____

13. Eleven pounds of chicken croquette mixture is prepared. How many croquettes will the mixture produce if each croquette is to weigh $2\frac{1}{2}$ ounces?

____

14. A 20-pound (A.P.) leg of veal is purchased. Six pounds 6 ounces are lost through trimming and boning. How many 5-ounce veal cutlets can be obtained from the leg of veal?

____

15. How many $5\frac{1}{2}$-ounce chop steaks can be obtained from 18 pounds (E.P.) of ground chuck?

____

ORDERING FOOD

Controlling amounts to order is another important food service function. Ordering close to the proper amount needed will reduce inventories and help control food cost and waste. When ordering food for a specific number of people, the amount to order can be found by multiplying the amount of the serving portion by the number of people to be served. The result will be the number of ounces required. Next, convert the common purchasing quantity into ounces and divide this amount into the number of ounces needed. (Of course, in the case of meat, fish, etc., consideration must be given to the amount that may be lost through boning and trimming.) A suggested formula is as follows:

Amount of portion × number of people served
= number of ounces required.
Common purchase quantity × 16
= number of ounces in container.
Number of ounces required ÷ ounces in container
= number to order.

Example: How many pounds of ground chuck E.P. should be ordered if 42 people are to be served and each person is to receive a 5-ounce portion?

5 ounces × 42 = 210 ounces.
Amount of portion × number to be served
= number of ounces required to serve 42 people.
210 ounces ÷ 16 ounces = $13\frac{1}{8}$ = 14 pounds.
Number of ounces required ÷ 16 ounces in one pound
= Amount to order.

This example can also be shown as follows:

42	Number of people to be served
× 5	Serving portion 5 ounces
210	Number of ounces to serve 42 people

$$\begin{array}{r} 13\frac{1}{8} \\ 16\overline{)210 \text{ oz.}} \\ \underline{16\phantom{0 \text{ oz.}}} \\ 50\phantom{\text{ oz.}} \\ \underline{48\phantom{\text{ oz.}}} \\ 2\phantom{\text{ oz.}} \end{array}$$

14 pounds must be ordered

A total of 210 ounces will be required to serve 42 people. The common purchase quantity for meat is pounds. Since there are 16 ounces in a pound, 16 is divided into the number of ounces required. The result is 13 and $\frac{1}{8}$ remaining, so the actual number of pounds to be ordered must be 14 pounds. The remainder indicates that 13 pounds will not produce enough portions to serve 42 people.

Summary Review

1. For a wedding of 270 guests, an A.P. 8 oz. sirloin steak will be served. If each sirloin weighs 16 pounds, how many sirloins must be ordered?

   ____

2. Salisbury steak is to be served to a party of 195 people. Each portion is to weigh 7 ounces. How many E.P. pounds of ground beef must be ordered?

   ____

3. How many E.P. pounds of pork sausage should be ordered for 68 people, if each person is to receive two $2\frac{1}{2}$ ounce patties?

   ____

4. How many gallons of orange juice must be ordered for a party of 175 people if each person is to receive a 5-ounce glass?

   ____

5. How many pounds of bacon should be ordered when serving a breakfast party of 96 people if each person is to receive 3 sausages and there are 8 sausages to each pound?

   ____

6. When preparing a breakfast for 220 people, how many pounds of link sausage must be ordered if each person is to receive 3 sausages and there are 8 sausages to each pound?

   ____

7. How many E.P. pounds of short ribs should be ordered when preparing for 80 people if each person is to receive a 12-ounce portion?

   ____

8. How many pounds of ground beef must be ordered to serve spaghetti and meatballs to 130 people if each person is to receive two $2\frac{1}{2}$-ounce meatballs.

   ____

9. Pot roast of beef is being served to 110 people. Each person is to receive a 5-ounce serving. It is estimated that 3 pounds will be lost in shrinkage. How many E.P. pounds of beef brisket should be ordered?

____

10. When preparing a breakfast for 138 people, how many pounds of Canadian bacon must be ordered, if each person is to receive a $2\frac{1}{2}$-ounce portion?

____

11. How many pounds of ground beef must be ordered when preparing meat loaf for 76 people, if each person is to receive a $5\frac{1}{2}$-ounce serving?

____

12. How many gallons of apple juice must be ordered to serve a party of 115 people, if each person is to receive a 4-ounce glass of juice?

____

13. How many E.P. pounds of pork loin must be ordered when serving 4-ounce breaded pork chops to a party of 210 people?

____

14. How many E.P. pounds of spare ribs should be ordered when preparing for 65 people, if each person is to receive a 12-ounce portion?

____

15. How many A.P. pounds of beef tenderloin should be ordered to serve a party of 105 people, if each person is served a 6-ounce tenderloin steak and 1 pound 7 ounces are allowed for trimming?

____

PURCHASING FRESH FISH

The quantity of fresh fish to purchase depends on three things: the number of people being served, the portion size, and the market form desired. Figure 6-9 is a suggested guide associating the market form to the amount to purchase.

Market Form	**Amount per person**
Fish sticks, steaks & fillets (E.P.)	$\frac{1}{3}$ pound
Dressed fish (E.P.)	$\frac{1}{2}$ pound
Drawn fish (A.P.)	$\frac{3}{4}$ pound
Whole fish or fish in the round (just as it comes from the water) (A.P.)	1 pound

Figure 6-9 *Chart for purchasing fresh fish.*

The formula shown below will simplify the ordering procedure: Amount per person × number served = amount to order.

Example One: How many pounds of fish steaks must be ordered for serving a party of 84 people? (Use guide.)

$$\frac{1}{3} \times \frac{84}{1} = 28 \text{ pounds}$$

Example Two: How many pounds of dressed fish should be ordered when preparing for a group of 72 people? (Use guide.)

$$\frac{1}{2} \times \frac{72}{1} = 36 \text{ pounds}$$

Example Three: How many pounds of drawn fish should be ordered when preparing for a party of 56 people? (Use guide.)

$$\frac{3}{4} \times \frac{56}{1} = 42 \text{ pounds}$$

Summary Review

1. How many pounds of drawn fish should be ordered when preparing for a party of 88 people?

   ____

2. How many pounds of fish steaks should be ordered when preparing for a group of 78 people?

   ____

3. How many pounds of fish fillets should be ordered when preparing for a party of 75 people?

   ____

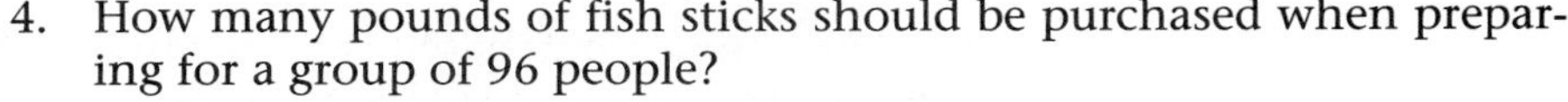

4. How many pounds of fish sticks should be purchased when preparing for a group of 96 people?

   ____

5. How many pounds of drawn fish should be purchased when preparing for a party of 140 people?

___

6. How many pounds of dressed fish should be purchased when preparing for a party of 94 people?

___

7. How many pounds of fish steaks should be ordered when preparing for a group of 135 people?

___

8. How many pounds of fish fillets should be ordered when preparing for a party of 114 people?

___

9. How many pounds of fish sticks should be purchased when preparing for a group of 123 people?

___

10. How many pounds of drawn fish should be ordered when preparing for a party of 64 people?

___

Costing Meat and Fish Portions

Meat and fish items are popular on a food service menu. They are also the most expensive. In fact, many food service establishments estimate that 25 to 35 percent of their food dollar goes for these two items. Therefore, the portion cost of these items must be controlled and reviewed from time to time because of fluctuating prices.

To find the cost of a portion, the total cost of the amount purchased must first be established. This is accomplished by multiplying the price per pound by the number of pounds purchased.

Price per pound × A.P. amount purchased = total cost.

The amount purchased is then converted into ounces by multiplying the number of pounds purchased by 16 (16 ounces to one pound).

A.P. amount purchased × 16 = total ounces.

The amount lost through boning, trimming, or shrinkage is converted into ounces and subtracted from the original amount.

Amount lost × 16 = total ounces lost.
Total ounces purchased − total ounces lost = E.P. ounces.

The actual usable amount (E.P.) is divided into the total cost (carry the division three places to the right of the decimal). This gives the cost of 1 ounce of cooked meat.

Total cost ÷ E.P. amount = cost of 1 ounce.

The cost of 1 ounce is multiplied by the number of ounces contained in one portion.

Cost of 1 ounce × serving portion = cost of one portion.

Example: A 9-pound leg of lamb costs $4.85 per pound. A total of 15 ounces is lost in boning and trimming and 1 pound 8 ounces through shrinkage during the roasting period. How much does a 3-ounce serving cost?

$ 4.85	Price per pound
× 9	Pounds purchased (A.P.)
$43.65	Total cost

16	Ounces in 1 pound
× 9	Number of pounds purchased
144	Number of ounces purchased

144	Number of ounces purchased
− 39	Number of ounces lost
105	Number of E.P. ounces

```
                 0.415      Cost of 1 ounce of cooked meat
E.P. ounces 105)43.650      Total cost
                420
                 165
                 105
                  600
                  525
```

$0.415	Cost of 1 ounce
× 3	Ounce serving portion
$1.245	Cost of each 3-ounce serving of roast lamb
$ 1.25	Cost of each 3-ounce serving of roast lamb

Once the actual cost of a serving is established, it is easy to determine a selling price by adding on the amount of markup.

TIPS . . . ***To Insure Perfect Solutions***

It would be advantageous for the chef or manager to round up when calculating food cost.

Summary Review

Round to the nearest cent.

1. If a 24-pound (A.P.) leg of veal costs $8.50 per pound and 5 pounds 6 ounces are lost through trimming and boning, how much does a 5-ounce veal cutlet cost?

 ____

2. A 24-pound (A.P.) rib of beef costs $2.85 per pound. Four pounds are lost through trimming and $\frac{1}{4}$ of the remaining weight is lost through shrinkage when it is roasted. How much does a 6-ounce serving cost?

 ____

3. A 50-pound (A.P.) round roast costs $92.50. Five pounds are lost through trimming and 5 pounds through shrinkage when it is roasted. How much does 1 pound of cooked meat cost?

 ____

4. A 6-pound 6-ounce (A.P.) beef tenderloin costs $90.00. One pound 5 ounces are lost through trimming. How much does an 8-ounce filet mignon cost?

 ____

5. If a 20-pound (E.P.) rib of beef costing $45.00 is purchased oven-ready and one-fourth of it is lost during roasting, how much does a 6-ounce serving cost?

 ____

6. A 9-pound (E.P.) leg of lamb costing $4.85 per pound is roasted. When the roast is removed from the oven, only $\frac{2}{3}$ of the original amount is left. How much does a $3\frac{1}{2}$-ounce serving cost?

 ____

7. Roast sirloin of beef is served to a party. Each sirloin weighs 16 pounds (E.P.) and costs $5.90 per pound. If 17 portions are cut from the sirloin, what is the cost per serving?

 ____

8. A 10-pound (E.P.) box of halibut steaks is ordered costing $4.65 per pound. If each steak weighs 5 ounces, what is the cost of each steak?

____

9. A 13-pound pork loin costs $2.92 per pound. A 10-ounce tenderloin is removed from the loin and 2 pounds 2 ounces are lost through boning and trimming. How much does a 4-ounce chop cost?

____

10. A 9-pound (A.P.) saddle of lamb costs $5.62 per pound. Twelve ounces are lost through trimming. How much does a 4-ounce chop cost?

____

Converting and Yielding Recipes

OBJECTIVES

At the completion of this chapter, the student should be able to:

1. Convert standard recipes from larger to smaller amounts, or from smaller to larger amounts.
2. Find approximate recipe yields.

During your food service career, occasions will frequently occur when you will be required to convert recipes to amounts that will differ from the original recipe. These amounts may be more or less than the recipe yield. For example, the recipe you have may yield 50 portions, but the need is for 25 or 100 portions.

Some food service establishments produce food from what is referred to as a **standardized recipe.** This is a recipe that will produce the same quality and quantity each and every time. Standardized recipes are ideal for certain food service operations such as nursing homes, retirement villages, and some school cafeterias. However, food production will vary in most food service operations so converting recipes is a very important technique to master. (See Figure 7-1.)

Figure 7-1 *The chef is converting a recipe to determine the amounts needed to produce the required number of servings.*

Converting Standard Recipes

It is a simple matter to double or cut a recipe in half. Many times this can be done mentally with little or no effort. However, when it becomes necessary to change a recipe from 12 to 20 portions or from 50 to 28 it appears to be more complicated. Actually, the procedure is the same for both and involves a fairly simple function of finding a working factor and multiplying each ingredient quantity by the working factor.

The first step in converting a recipe is to find the working factor. This is done as follows:

Step 1:
Divide the yield desired by original recipe yield.

$$\frac{\text{New yield}}{\text{Old yield}} = \text{Working factor}$$

Step 2:
Multiply each ingredient in the original recipe by the working factor.
Working factor × old quantity = new quantity (desired quantity).

To simplify this procedure, change ingredient pounds to ounces before starting to multiply. In this way, it is only necessary to multiply ounces. After multiplying, convert the product back to pounds and ounces. If for some reason you would be using the metric system, this step is not necessary.

Example: A standardized recipe yields 40 portions. Only 30 portions are desired.

First, you must find the working factor by following the formula given in Step 1.

$$\frac{30 \text{ New yield}}{40 \text{ Old yield}} = \frac{3}{4} \text{ Working factor}$$

Next, convert the quantity of each ingredient in the original recipe to ounces and multiply each ingredient by $\frac{3}{4}$, the working factor, as stated in Step No. 2. Convert new amounts back to pounds and ounces.

Example: A standardized recipe yields 75 portions. A large party is booked, and 225 portions are required.

First, you must find the working factor by following the formula given in Step 1:

$$\frac{225 \text{ New yield}}{75 \text{ Old yield}} = 3 \text{ Working factor}$$

Next, convert the quantity of each ingredient in the original recipe to ounces and multiply each ingredient by 3, the working factor, as stated in Step No. 2. Convert new amounts back to pounds and ounces.

T I P S . . . ***To Insure Perfect Solutions***

When converting recipes to **more portions,** realize that the working factor will be **greater than one.**

When converting recipes to **fewer portions,** realize that the working factor will be **less than one.**

When working a recipe after a conversion has taken place, some common sense must also be applied. You might think of this common sense or judgment as an extra ingredient. For instance, the recipe may not account for how fresh or old the spices or herbs are or how hot the kitchen or bakeshop is when mixing a yeast dough. Common sense or judgment must be applied when converting any recipe because it may not be practical to increase or decrease the quantity of each ingredient by the exact same rate. Many spices and herbs cannot be increased or decreased at the same rate as other ingredients. This may also be true of salt, garlic, and sugar in certain situations. Use good judgment in these situations and carry out tests before deciding on amounts.

Example: The following recipe yields 12 dozen hard rolls. It must be converted to yield 9 dozen rolls.

Ingredients for 12 dozen rolls	Amount of conversion	Amount needed to yield 9 dozen rolls
7 lb. 8 oz. bread flour	$\frac{3}{4}$	5 lb. 10 oz.
3 oz. salt		$2\frac{1}{4}$ oz.
$3\frac{1}{2}$ oz. granulated sugar		$2\frac{5}{8}$ oz.
3 oz. shortening		$2\frac{1}{4}$ oz.
3 oz. egg whites		$2\frac{1}{4}$ oz.
4 lb. 8 oz. water (variable)		3 lb. 6 oz.
$4\frac{1}{2}$ oz. yeast, compressed		$3\frac{3}{8}$ oz.

Step 1: Find the working factor.

$$\frac{\text{9 dozen new yield}}{\text{12 dozen old yield}} = \frac{3}{4} \text{ Is the working factor}$$

The quantity of each ingredient in the original recipe is multiplied by $\frac{3}{4}$ (working factor).

Step 2: Convert all ingredients.

Example 7 pounds 8 ounces of bread flour
$(7 \times 16) + 8 = 120$ ounces

Example $3\frac{1}{2}$ ounces of granulated sugar $= \frac{7}{2}$ ounces

Step 3: Multiply all ingredients by the working factor ($\frac{3}{4}$).

Example bread flour—120 ounces $\times \frac{3}{4} = 90$ ounces

Example granulated sugar—$\frac{7}{2}$ ounces $\times \frac{3}{4} = \frac{21}{8}$

Step 4: Convert new amounts back to pounds and ounces

Example bread flour—90 ounces divided by 16 = 5 pounds and 10 ounces

Example granulated sugar—$\frac{21}{8} = 2\frac{5}{8}$ ounces

SUMMARY REVIEW

1. The following recipe yields 50 portions of curried lamb. Convert it to yield 150 portions.

Ingredients for 50 Portions	Amount of Conversion	Amount Needed to Yield 150 Portions
18 lb. lamb shoulder, boneless, cut into 1-inch cubes		
$2\frac{1}{2}$ gallons water		
2 lb. butter or shortening		
1 lb. 8 oz. flour		
$\frac{1}{3}$ cup curry powder		
2 qt. tart apples, diced		
2 lb. onions, diced		
$\frac{1}{2}$ tsp. ground cloves		
2 bay leaves		
1 tsp. marjoram		
salt and pepper to taste		

2. The following recipe yields 100 portions of Hungarian goulash. Convert it to yield 75 portions.

Ingredients for 100 Portions	Amount of Conversion	Amount Needed to Yield 75 Portions
36 lb. beef chuck or shoulder, diced 1-inch cubes		
$1\frac{1}{4}$ oz. garlic, minced		
1 lb. 4 oz. flour		
$1\frac{1}{4}$ oz. chili powder		
10 oz. paprika		
2 lb. tomato puree		
2 gal. brown stock		
4 bay leaves		
$\frac{3}{4}$ oz. caraway seeds		
3 lb. 8 oz. onions, minced		
salt and pepper to taste		

3. The following recipe yields nine 8-inch lemon pies. Convert it to yield six 8-inch pies.

Ingredients for 9 Pies	Amount of Conversion	Amount Needed to Yield 6 Pies
4 lb. water		
3 lb. 6 oz. granulated sugar		
$\frac{1}{2}$ oz. salt		
3 oz. lemon gratings		
1 lb. water		
8 oz. corn starch		
12 oz. egg yolks		
1 lb. 6 oz. lemon juice		
4 oz. butter, melted		
yellow color, as needed		

4. The following recipe yields 12 dozen hard rolls. Convert it to yield 48 dozen rolls.

Ingredients for 12 Dozen Rolls	Amount of Conversion	Amount Needed to Yield 48 Dozen Rolls
7 lb. 8 oz. bread flour		
3 oz. salt		
$3\frac{1}{2}$ oz. granulated sugar		
3 oz. shortening		
3 oz. egg whites		
4 lb. 8 oz. water (variable)		
$4\frac{1}{2}$ oz. yeast, compressed		

5. The following recipe yields 8 dozen soft dinner rolls. Convert it to yield 5 dozen rolls.

Ingredients for 8 Dozen Rolls	Amount of Conversion	Amount Needed to Yield 5 Dozen Rolls
10 oz. granulated sugar		
10 oz. hydrogenated shortening		
1 oz. salt		
3 oz. dry milk		
4 oz. whole eggs		
3 lb. 12 oz. bread flour		
2 lb. water		
5 oz. yeast, compressed		

◆ *Chef Sez . . .*

"If you are the chef owner of a restaurant, you must have a knowledge of math and how to use it or else you will go under (bankrupt). When you are the head chef, if you are not good at math you lose your job."

Andre Soltner
Founder and former owner of Lutece
Master Chef, Senior Lecturer
The French Culinary Institute
New York City

To fully understand Chef Soltner's remarks and to discover why Lutece has been called the finest French restaurant in America, the authors recommend the book, *Lutece, A Day in the Life Of America's Greatest Restaurant,* by Irene Daria. The book is published by Random House, copyright 1993.

FINDING APPROXIMATE RECIPE YIELD

Yield is defined as the amount of portions, servings, or units a particular recipe or formula will produce. It is one of the most important features of a recipe or formula. Yield is probably one of the first items a cook will look at when selecting a certain recipe for preparation. By observing a recipe or formula yield, it provides the preparer with an approximate guide to the numbers the recipe or formula will produce. The yield must also be known before conversion can take place.

Most recipes provide an approximate guide as to the number or amounts the recipe will produce. However, occasions arise when you will want to determine your own yield because the suggested recipe or formula portion size is too large or small for your need.

You may also wish to work out your own recipe for a preparation—a recipe you have used many times, but have never determined an approximate yield.

Suggested recipe or formula yields will fluctuate if you determine a larger or smaller portion is required. To show how this situation could happen, let us assume a yellow cake batter is prepared from a recipe that states the approximate yield is 20 14-ounce cakes (14 ounces of batter used in each cake). You wish to use a smaller pan that will only hold 10 ounces. The yield will, of course, fluctuate and produce a larger amount of yellow cakes.

It is for these reasons that the student cook or baker must understand how a yield can be determined by applying some simple mathematics. The chef can approximate the serving size by determining a formula yield (see Figure 7-2).

The yield for some recipes or formulas is found by preparing a certain amount, determining a serving portion, and measuring it to see what it will produce. The yield for other recipes—such as cake or muffin batters, roll or sweet doughs, pie filling and some cookie doughs—can be determined by taking the total weight of all ingredients used in the preparation and dividing that figure by the weight of an individual portion or unit. Let us take the formula of a white cake and of a roll dough to show how an approximate yield can be obtained by this method.

Figure 7-2 *By determining a formula yield, the chef can approximate the serving size.*

The formula is:

Total weight of preparation ÷ weight of portion = recipe yield.

Example:

White Cake

Ingredients:

Find the approximate yield ______

2 lb. 8 oz. cake flour

1 lb. 12 oz. shortening

3 lb. 2 oz. granulated sugar

$1\frac{1}{2}$ oz. salt

$2\frac{1}{2}$ oz. baking powder

14 oz. water

$2\frac{1}{2}$ oz. dry milk

10 oz. whole eggs

1 lb. egg whites

1 lb. water

vanilla to taste

The total weight of all ingredients is 11 pounds $4\frac{1}{2}$ ounces. Each cake is to contain 14 ounces of batter. The first step is to convert the weight of all ingredients to ounces since only like things can be divided: 11 pounds $4\frac{1}{2}$ ounces contains $180\frac{1}{2}$ ounces. The second step is to divide the weight of one cake (14 ounces) into the total weight of all ingredients:

$$\begin{array}{r} 12 \\ 14\overline{)180.5} \\ \underline{14} \\ 40 \\ \underline{28} \\ 12 \end{array}$$

When preparing a cake from scratch—that is, step-by-step preparation—the baker must first determine the size of each pan to be used and the amount of batter each pan is to contain. He or she may determine an 8-inch cake pan will be used and each pan is to contain 14 ounces of batter to produce the size of cake desired. Many times the cake recipe will state, in the method of preparation, the amount of batter to place in a certain size pan. Usually the type of cake prepared will have a bearing on the amount of batter placed in each pan. For example, light semi-sponge cake batters will not require as much batter as a pound cake.

There is no reason to carry the division any further because only figures on the left side of the decimal point are whole numbers. So 12 cakes, each containing 14 ounces of batter, were realized from this recipe.

When preparing a roll dough, the baker must determine how much each roll will weigh. Some bakers like a larger roll than others. The usual size is $1\frac{1}{4}$ to 2 ounces. Once the size is determined an approximate yield is easy to find.

Example:

Soft Dinner Roll Dough

Ingredients: Find the approximate yield ______

1 lb. 4 oz. granulated sugar

1 lb. 4 oz. shortening

2 oz. salt

6 oz. dry milk

6 oz. whole eggs

7 lb. 8 oz. bread flour

4 lb. water

10 oz. compressed yeast

The total weight of all ingredients is 15 pounds 8 ounces. Each roll is to weigh $1\frac{1}{2}$ ounces. The first step is to convert the weight of all ingredients to ounces, since only like things can be divided; 15 pounds 8 ounces contain 248 ounces. Now, dividing the total weight by the weight of one roll gives the recipe yield:

```
         165.
 1.5 )248.0.
       15
       98
       90
        80
        75
         5
```

Thus, the yield is 165 rolls or $13\frac{3}{4}$ dozen rolls, or 13 dozen and 9 rolls, when yielding a 1.5-ounce roll.

Most recipes used in the commercial kitchen will be stated in weights and an approximate yield is easier to determine when ingredients are listed in weights. Weights will also produce a more accurate preparation. There are occasions when recipes will be stated in measures. In this case the formula used to determine a yield will be the same, but the measuring units in finding an approximate yield will differ.

Example:

Honey Cream Dressing

Ingredients: Find the approximate yield ______

3 cups cream cheese

2 cups honey

$\frac{1}{2}$ cup pineapple juice (variable)

$\frac{1}{4}$ tsp. salt

$2\frac{1}{2}$ qt. mayonnaise

In this example, total cups must be determined. There are $15\frac{1}{2}$ cups in the preparation. A 2-ounce ladle is used to portion. Referring to the chapter on weights and measures, we find that a 2-ounce ladle contains $\frac{1}{4}$ cup so following the formula given to determine an approximate yield, the math involved would be as follows:

$15\frac{1}{2}$ cups (total measure of preparation) $\div \frac{1}{4}$ cup (portion measure)

$= \frac{31}{2} \times \frac{4}{1} = 62$ portions (yield).

Summary Review

1. Determine the approximate yield of the following formula if each coffee cake is to contain a 12-ounce unit of sweet dough.

Coffee Cake Ingredients Find the approximate yield ______

1 lb. granulated sugar

1 lb. golden shortening

1 oz. salt

3 lb. bread flour

1 lb. 8 oz. pastry flour

12 oz. whole eggs

4 oz. dry milk

2 lb. water

8 oz. compressed yeast

mace to taste

vanilla to taste

2. Determine the approximate yield of the following formula if each cookie is to contain $1\frac{1}{2}$ ounces of dough.

Fruit Tea Cookies Find the approximate yield ______

1 lb. 6 oz. shortening

1 lb. 6 oz. powdered sugar

2 lb. 8 oz. pastry flour

2 oz. liquid milk

6 oz. raisins, chopped

2 oz. pecans, chopped

3 oz. pineapple, chopped

2 oz. peaches, chopped

8 oz. whole eggs

$\frac{1}{4}$ oz. baking soda

$\frac{1}{4}$ oz. vanilla

$\frac{1}{2}$ oz. salt

3. Determine the approximate yield of the following formula if each cake is to contain 11 ounces of batter.

Yellow Cake Ingredients Find the approximate yield _____

2 lb. 8 oz. cake flour

1 lb. 6 oz. shortening

3 lb. 2 oz. granulated sugar

1 oz. salt

$1\frac{3}{4}$ oz. baking powder

4 oz. dry milk

1 lb. 4 oz. water

1 lb. 10 oz. whole eggs

12 oz. water

$\frac{1}{4}$ oz. vanilla

4. Determine the approximate yield of the following recipe if each gelatin mold is to hold $\frac{3}{4}$ cup of liquid gelatin mix.

Sunshine Salad Find the approximate yield _____

1 pt. lemon flavored gelatin

1 qt. hot water

1 qt. cold water

$\frac{1}{4}$ cup cider vinegar

1 qt. grated carrots

1 pt. pineapple, crushed

5. Determine the approximate yield of the following recipe if a 6-ounce ladle ($\frac{3}{4}$ cup) is used to portion.

Beef Stroganoff Find the approximate yield _____

2 gal. beef tenderloin, cut into thin strips

1 cup flour

$\frac{1}{2}$ cup shortening

3 qt. water

$\frac{1}{2}$ cup tomato puree

$\frac{1}{2}$ cup cider vinegar

1 lb. onions, minced

1 qt. mushrooms, sliced

1 qt. sour cream

1 tbsp. salt

3 bay leaves

Production and Baking Formulas

OBJECTIVES

At the completion of this chapter, the student should be able to:

1. Use formulas to produce basic foods.
2. Find percents for bakers' formulas.

Production formulas are used in the food service industry to increase productivity, save valuable preparation time, and increase the production workers' knowledge of food. Knowing a few basic formulas, the production worker will be able to produce a preparation with little or no hesitation. He or she will not have to stop to look up important ratios or amounts and consequently can become a more valuable employee.

The formulas presented in this chapter are those that have been found to be the most helpful to production workers. They also put into practice the usage of ratios, discussed earlier in this text. Students should familiarize themselves with each and every formula in this chapter and learn how they are applied by the use of very simple mathematics. Some of the amounts suggested in these formulas may vary slightly depending on the quality of the product used. For example, when using a chicken, beef, or ham base, we have suggested that $\frac{1}{2}$ cup or 4 ounces of base be used for each gallon of water. There are products on the market that suggest using only 3 ounces. In all probability, this product is a richer concentrate and carries a higher price. Exercise a little common sense when using production formulas. If in doubt, read and follow the label directions.

◆ *Chef Sez . . .*

"One of the keys to being a successful chef is having the understanding of business mathematics; unless you are going to start giving the food away. The industry is built on great food and hospitality, but survives by making money."

Michael Thompson
Professional Culinary Recruiter
Walt Disney World
Disney Worldwide Services
Lake Buena Vista, Florida

Walt Disney World has 250 different types of restaurant and dining operations for the guests. Chef Thompson is responsible for the hiring of 1,856 hourly and 248 salaried cast members to staff the 250 dining operations. The challenge for Chef Thompson is to find culinary professionals who can prepare food and use math to make money in the food service industry.

Basic Production Formulas

In kitchen production you constantly hear the question, *"How much should I use?"* By learning the following twenty-two production formulas you will not have to direct this question to a supervisor. In fact, you will most likely be able to supply an answer if the question is ever directed to you.

1. *A pint of liquid is a pound the world around.* This formula is applied when the liquid amount is expressed in weights. It eliminates the time-consuming task of actually weighing the item. For example, if the recipe requires 2 pounds of milk, fill a quart container with milk to get the required 2 pounds. If the recipe requires 4 pounds of water, fill a half-gallon container to get the required 4 pounds. This formula also applies to whole eggs, egg whites, and egg yolks.
2. *Four ounces of* **powdered milk** *(dry milk solids) added to 1 quart of water produces 1 quart of liquid milk.* Powdered milk (dry milk solids) is cheaper to buy than whole milk. Therefore, it is often used as a substitute for whole milk in food service production. For example, a vanilla pie filling recipe may require 6 quarts of milk. The chef may instruct that 4 quarts of fresh whole milk be used with 2 quarts of reconstituted dry milk. In this case, 8 ounces of dry milk are dissolved in 2 quarts of water. The quality of the product remains the same, but the food cost is reduced. When purchasing dry milk (dry milk solids), purchase the kind that has a high degree of solubility (ability to dissolve) so it blends quickly when mixed with water.
3. *To prepare* **flavored gelatin,** *use 1 cup of gelatin powder to each quart of liquid (water or fruit juice).* This formula provides a gelatin that is stiff enough to keep its shape if unmolded properly. It also provides excellent eating qualities. If the gelatin mold is to be displayed in a slightly warm room, a little more gelatin should be added. When preparing the gelatin, half the liquid should be hot and the other half ice cold. Thoroughly dissolve the gelatin powder in the hot liquid before adding the cold liquid.
4. *To prepare* **aspic** *(clear meat, fish, or poultry jelly) or chaud-froid (jellied white meat, or poultry sauce) use 6 ounces of* **unflavored gelatin** *to each gallon of liquid.* This produces an aspic or chaud-froid that adheres tightly to the product it covers. To determine the amount of gelatin needed, use 6 times the number of gallons required. For example, if 3 gallons of aspic are needed, $6 \times 3 = 18$ ounces (1 pound 2 ounces) of gelatin are required.
5. *To prepare* **baked rice,** *use a ratio of 2 parts liquid to every 1 part raw rice by volume.* If the rice is baked properly (approximately 20 minutes in a 400°F oven), this produces an excellent finished product. To determine the amount of liquid needed when preparing a specific amount of rice, multiply the amount of rice by 2. For example, if 2 quarts of rice are to be baked, 4 quarts (1 gallon) of liquid would be needed ($2 \times 2 = 4$).
6. *To boil* **barley,** *use a ratio of 4 parts liquid to every 1 part raw barley by volume.* For example, if it is desired to boil 2 quarts of barley, 8 quarts (2 gallons) of liquid are required ($2 \times 4 = 8$).

7. *To prepare chicken, beef, or ham stock using the flavored* **soup bases,** *use $\frac{1}{2}$ cup (or 4 ounces) of the base for every gallon of water.* For example, if 3 gallons of stock are needed, 12 ounces of base ($4 \times 3 = 12$) or $1\frac{1}{2}$ cups ($\frac{1}{2} \times 3 = 1\frac{1}{2}$) are dissolved into 3 gallons of water.
8. *To prepare a* **meringue** *using meringue powder, whip together 5 ounces of meringue powder, 1 quart of water, and 3 pounds of granulated sugar.* This mixture produces approximately 3 gallons of meringue.
9. *To prepare* **pudding** *using the pudding powder mix, use $3\frac{1}{4}$ ounces of powder for every pint of milk.* For example, if 2 quarts of pudding are required, $3\frac{1}{4}$ is multiplied by 4 (4 pints are contained in 2 quarts).

$$3\tfrac{1}{4} \times \tfrac{4}{1} = \tfrac{13}{4} \times \tfrac{4}{1} = 13$$

10. *To thicken* **fruit pie filling,** *use 4 to 5 ounces of* **starch** *for every quart of fruit juice.*
11. *To convert* **dry nondairy creamer** *to liquid, mix 1 pint of dry creamer to 1 quart of hot water.*
12. *To cook* **pasta** *(spaghetti, mostaccioli, macaroni, etc.), use 1 gallon of boiling water for every 1 pound of pasta.* For example, if cooking $3\frac{1}{2}$ pounds of spaghetti, $3\frac{1}{2}$ gallons of boiling water are required. This formula can also be used for egg noodles.
13. *To every 1 pound of* **coffee,** *use $2\frac{1}{2}$ gallons of water.* For example, $2\frac{1}{2}$ gallons of liquid coffee equals approximately 60 to 65 cups of coffee.
14. *To prepare mashed potatoes using the dry* **instant potato powder,** *use 1 pound 13 ounces of the powder for each gallon of water, milk, or water-milk mixture.* For example, if 4 gallons of mashed potatoes are to be prepared, multiply 4×1 pound 13 ounces to determine the amount of instant potato powder needed. First, the pounds must be converted into ounces before multiplication can take place. 1 pound 13 ounces = 29 ounces. $4 \times 29 = 116$ ounces. The 116 ounces needed must then be divided by 16 to determine pounds and ounces. $116 \div 16 = 7\frac{1}{4}$ pounds or 7 pounds 4 ounces.
15. *If* **dry yeast** *must be substituted for compressed yeast, 40 percent of the compressed yeast amount is dry yeast. (See Figure 8-1.) The remaining 60 percent is made up of water.* For example, a recipe may require the use of 1 pound of compressed yeast (16 ounces). 40 percent of 16 = 6.4 ounces. 6.4 is equal to $6\frac{4}{10}$ or $6\frac{2}{5}$. A baker's scale is graduated in $\frac{1}{4}$ ounces. Therefore, $6\frac{2}{5}$ is more than $6\frac{1}{4}$ but less than $6\frac{1}{2}$. This very slight difference in weight has no effect on the recipe. Use $6\frac{1}{2}$ ounces of dry yeast. The remaining 60 percent is water. 60 percent of 16 = 9.6 ounces. Use $9\frac{1}{2}$ ounces of water.
16. *To prepare* **iced tea** *using large 1-ounce tea bags, use the 1-2-3 method.* (See Figure 8-2.) That is, steep 2 ounces of tea (two bags) in 1 quart of scalding hot water. Steep for approximately 6 minutes. Remove bags and add 3 quarts of cold water. If using instant tea, use 1 ounce of instant tea for every gallon of cold water.

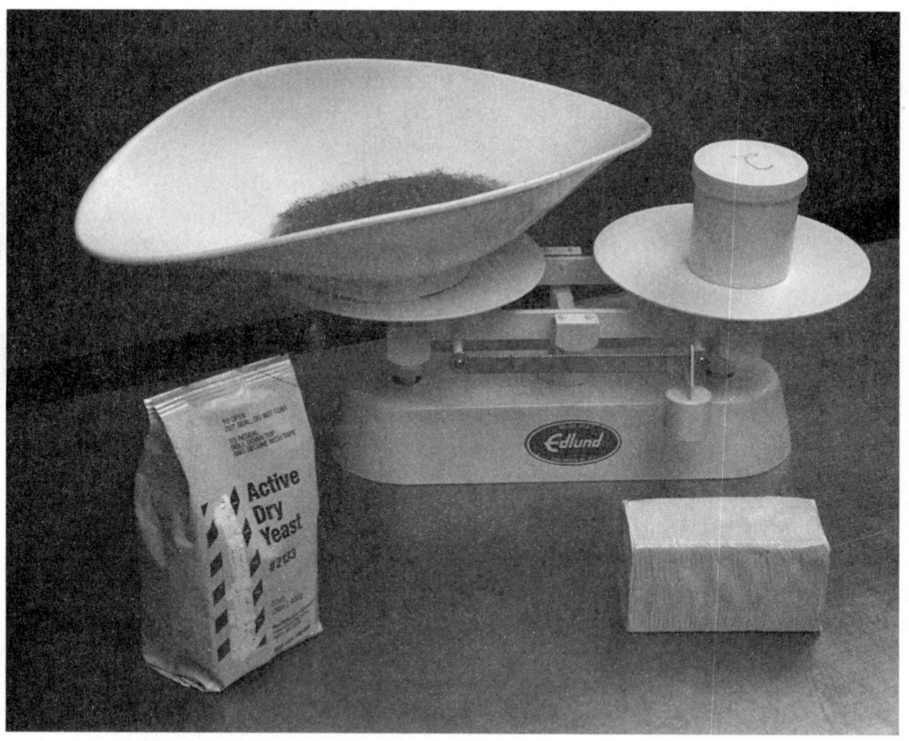

Figure 8-1 *This photo shows the amount of dry yeast needed to replace 1 pound of compressed yeast.*

Figure 8-2 *Preparing smaller quantities of iced tea.*

Figure 8-3 *Roux is equal measures of fat and flour.*

17. *To prepare a proper* **roux** *(thickening agent consisting of melted fat and flour), use equal amounts of fat and flour.* (See Figure 8-3.) For example, if using 8 ounces of melted shortening, then 8 ounces of flour must be added to prepare a proper roux. Roux is used to thicken most soups and sauces because it does not break, or separate, when excessive heat is applied to the product.
18. *When cooking* **dried legumes** *(dried vegetables), use a ratio of 4 to 1, or 1 gallon of water to every 1 quart of legumes.* For best results, soak the legumes overnight before cooking. Cook by simmering.
19. *To prepare* **pan grease,** *thoroughly mix together 8 ounces of flour to every 1 pound of shortening.* Pan grease is used to prepare pans for certain baked goods, which require that pans be greased and dusted with flour.
20. *To prepare a fairly rich* **egg wash,** *mix together 4 whole eggs to every quart of milk.* (See Figure 8-4.) Egg wash is used quite often in the commercial kitchen. Its most popular use is in the breading procedure. The procedure for breading is to pass an item through seasoned flour, egg wash, and then bread crumbs. Most fried items are breaded.
21. *The suggested amount of liquid to use in the preparation of* **pie dough** *is 1 quart of liquid to every 4 pounds of flour.* For example, if 6 pounds of flour are used in a formula, approximately $1\frac{1}{2}$ quarts of liquid should be used.

$$\begin{array}{r} 1.5 = 1\tfrac{1}{2}\text{ quarts} \\ 4\overline{)6.0} \\ \underline{4} \\ 2\,0 \\ \underline{2\,0} \end{array}$$

Figure 8-4 *Cook preparing an egg wash.*

22. *To prepare a* **pie filling using fresh fruit,** *the amount of liquid used is based on the amount of fresh fruit contained in the formula.* Usually 65 percent of the fresh fruit amount will provide a sufficient amount of liquid. For example, if 10 pounds of fresh fruit are being used, convert the 10 pounds to 160 ounces (16 × 10 = 160). Take 65 percent of 160 ounces to determine the amount of liquid to use.

$$\begin{array}{r} 160 \\ \times\ 0.65 \\ \hline 800 \\ 960 \\ \hline 104.00 \end{array}$$

104.00 ounces, or 6 pounds 8 ounces of liquid.

Summary Review

1. Determine the amounts of liquid required if a pie dough formula contains the following amounts of flour.
   a. 10 pounds ________
   b. 12 pounds ________
   c. 16 pounds ________
   d. 18 pounds ________

2. Determine the amount of dry milk required to produce the following amounts of liquid milk.

   a. $1\frac{1}{2}$ gallons liquid milk ________________

   b. 3 gallons liquid milk ________________

   c. $3\frac{1}{2}$ quarts liquid milk ________________

   d. $4\frac{3}{4}$ gallons liquid milk ________________

3. Determine the amount of unflavored gelatin required to jell the following amounts of aspic.

   a. 6 quarts aspic ________________

   b. $1\frac{3}{4}$ gallons aspic ________________

   c. $3\frac{1}{2}$ gallons aspic ________________

   d. $2\frac{1}{2}$ gallons aspic ________________

4. Determine the amount of liquid needed to prepare the following amounts of raw barley.

   a. 1 pint raw barley ________________

   b. 3 pints raw barley ________________

   c. 3 quarts raw barley ________________

   d. 1 cup raw barley ________________

5. Determine the amount of pudding powder needed to prepare the following amounts of pudding.

   a. 3 quarts pudding ________________

   b. $2\frac{1}{2}$ quarts pudding ________________

   c. 6 quarts pudding ________________

   d. $1\frac{1}{2}$ quarts pudding ________________

6. Determine the amount of dry nondairy creamer required to produce the following amounts of liquid cream.

   a. 2 gallons liquid cream ________________

   b. $1\frac{1}{2}$ gallons liquid cream ________________

   c. $\frac{1}{2}$ gallon liquid cream ________________

   d. $3\frac{1}{2}$ gallons liquid cream ________________

7. Determine the amount of dry instant potato powder needed to prepare the following amounts of mashed potatoes.

   a. 2 gallons mashed potatoes ________________

   b. 6 gallons mashed potatoes ________________

   c. $2\frac{1}{2}$ gallons mashed potatoes ________________

   d. $4\frac{1}{2}$ gallons mashed potatoes ________________

8. Determine how many pounds are contained in the following amounts of liquid.

   a. $1\frac{1}{2}$ gallons __________

   b. 3 gallons __________

   c. $2\frac{3}{4}$ gallons __________

   d. $4\frac{1}{4}$ gallons __________

9. When preparing egg wash, how many eggs will be needed when preparing the following amounts?

   a. 1 cup __________

   b. 1 pint __________

   c. 2 quarts __________

   d. 3 quarts __________

10. Determine the amount of flour needed if the following amounts of shortening are used when preparing pan grease.

    a. $1\frac{1}{2}$ pounds of shortening __________

    b. 8 ounces of shortening __________

    c. 12 ounces of shortening __________

    d. $2\frac{3}{4}$ pounds of shortening __________

FINDING PERCENTS

In cooking, if a recipe or formula should become unbalanced or if a mistake should occur when adding ingredients, the situation might easily be corrected by making a few adjustments. This is not the case when working with baking formulas. Bakers use a simple yet versatile system designed to balance all formulas with flour as the main ingredient. Each minor ingredient is a percentage of the main (flour) ingredient. Industry standards determine the percentages of each ingredient in most of the popular formulas to ensure that the formula is balanced.

The ingredients in baking formulas must be balanced if the finished product is to possess all the qualities necessary to please the customer and to warrant return sales. Most formulas used in bakeshops today have been developed in research laboratories operated by the companies that manufacture the products bakers use. The formulas are used to test the manufacturer's products and are passed on to bakers in the hope that they will use the manufacturer's products.

Keeping in mind that flour is the main ingredient, bakers' percentages designate the amount of each ingredient that would be required if 100 pounds of flour were used. Thus, flour is always 100 percent. If, for instance, two kinds of flour were used in a preparation, the total amounts of the two would represent 100 percent and any other ingredient that weighs the same as the flour is also listed at 100 percent. To find ingredient percentages, divide the total weight of the ingredient by the weight of the flour, then multiply by 100 percent.

$$\frac{\textbf{Weight of ingredient}}{\textbf{Weight of flour}} \times \textbf{100\%} = \textbf{\% of ingredient}.$$

Example:

The following ingredients for a yellow pound cake illustrate how these percentages are found.

Yellow Pound Cake

Ingredients	**Weights**	**Percentage**
Cake flour	2 lb. 8 oz.	100%
Vegetable shortening	1 lb. 12 oz.	70%
Granulated sugar	2 lb. 8 oz.	100%
Salt	$1\frac{1}{2}$ oz.	$3\frac{3}{4}$% or 3.75%
Water	1 lb. 4 oz.	50%
Dry milk	$2\frac{1}{2}$ oz.	$6\frac{1}{4}$% or 6.25%
Whole eggs	1 lb. 12 oz.	70%
Vanilla to taste	—	—

The following steps illustrate the method used in finding ingredient percentages:

Step 1: Convert 2 lb. 8 oz. cake flour to 40 ounces.
Step 2: $\frac{40}{40} \times \frac{100}{1} = \frac{4000}{40} = 100\%$

Step 1: Convert 1 lb. 12 oz. vegetable shortening to 28 ounces.
Step 2: $\frac{28}{40} \times \frac{100}{1} = \frac{2800}{40} = 70\%$

Step 1: Convert 2 lb. 8 oz. granulated sugar to 40 ounces. The weight of the sugar is the same as the flour, so it, too, will equal 100%.

Step 1: Salt does not have to be converted to ounces because it is already given in ounces ($1\frac{1}{2}$ ounces or 1.5 ounces).
Step 2: $\frac{1.5}{40} \times \frac{100}{1} = \frac{150}{40} = 3\frac{3}{4}\%$ or 3.7%

Step 1: Convert 1 lb. 4 oz. water to 20 ounces.
Step 2: $\frac{20}{40} \times \frac{100}{1} = \frac{2000}{40} = 50\%$

Step 1: Dry milk does not have to be converted to ounces because it is already given in ounces ($2\frac{1}{2}$ ounces or 2.5 ounces).
Step 2: $\frac{2.5}{40} \times \frac{100}{1} = \frac{250}{40} = 6\frac{1}{4}\%$ or 6.25%

Step 1: Convert 1 lb. 12 oz. whole eggs to 28 ounces. This is the same total ounces as the vegetable shortening, so the percentage is the same (70%).

The advantage of finding and using these percentages, when flour is the main ingredient, is that the formula can be changed easily to any yield and, if a single ingredient needs to be altered, it can be done without changing the complete formula.

Example:

If you wish to change recipe amounts to provide a higher or lower yield, simply multiply its percentage, in the original formula, by the weight of the flour. Assume that the original recipe calls for 25 percent sugar and you are using 10 pounds of flour. You multiply 0.25×10 lb. = 2.5 lb. or 2 pounds 8 ounces sugar.

SUMMARY REVIEW

Find the percent of each ingredient used in the following formulas. Remember that flour is always 100 percent. Round to the tenth place.

1. **Pie dough**

(a)

Ingredients	**Weight**	**Percentage**
Pastry flour	10 lb.	________
Shortening	7 lb. 8 oz.	________
Salt	5 oz.	________
Sugar	3 oz.	________
Cold water	2 lb. 8 oz.	________
Dry milk	3 oz.	________

Using the percentage found for each ingredient, determine the amount of each ingredient if the flour amount is changed to 12 pounds.

(b)

Ingredients	**Weight**
Pastry flour	12 lb.
Shortening	________
Salt	________
Sugar	________
Cold water	________
Dry milk	________

2. **Golden Dinner Roll Dough**

(a)

Ingredients	**Weight**	**Percentage**
Bread flour	9 lb.	________
Pastry flour	1 lb.	________
Shortening	1 lb.	________
Sugar	18 oz.	________
Eggs	13 oz.	________
Salt	5 oz.	________
Dry milk	8 oz.	________
Compressed yeast	10 oz	________
Cold water	5 lb.	________

Using the percentage found for each ingredient, determine the amount of each ingredient if the flour amount is changed to: Bread flour 10 lb., pastry flour 2 lb.

(b) **Ingredients**	**Weight**
Bread flour	__________
Pastry flour	__________
Shortening	__________
Sugar	__________
Eggs	__________
Salt	__________
Dry milk	__________
Compressed yeast	__________
Cold water	__________

3. **Brown Sugar Cookies**

(a) **Ingredients**	**Weight**	**Percentage**
Pastry flour	4 lb. 8 oz.	__________
Hydrogenated shortening	2 lb. 4 oz.	__________
Whole eggs	1 lb.	__________
Brown sugar	3 lb. 2 oz.	__________
Salt	1 oz.	__________
Baking soda	$\frac{1}{2}$ oz.	__________
Vanilla	to taste	__________

Using the percentage found for each ingredient, determine the amount of each ingredient if the flour amount is changed to 6 lb. 10 oz.

(b) **Ingredients**	**Weight**
Pastry flour	__________
Hydrogenated shortening	__________
Whole eggs	__________
Brown sugar	__________
Salt	__________
Baking soda	__________
Vanilla	__________

Using the Metric System of Measure

OBJECTIVES

At the completion of this chapter, the student should be able to:

1. Measure length, volume, capacity, and mass.

It is difficult to understand why the **metric system** of measure, a decimal system which counts by tens and is based on the meter, a length about $39\frac{1}{2}$ inches long, has never been adopted for exclusive use in the United States. It has been used in a limited capacity over the last twenty-five years, but never to its fullest extent. Perhaps it can be blamed on the fact that most people resist change. There have been attempts over the years to bring about the change. In 1971, the Department of Commerce recommended that the United States adopt the system in a report made to Congress. The report stated that the question was not whether the United States should go metric, but how the switch should take place. It proposed that the switch be made over a ten-year period, as done in Great Britain and Canada. A key element in the Great Britain and Canadian conversion was education. It became the only system taught in the primary schools. The general public was taught the metric system and language by means of magazines, posters, television, newspapers, radio, etc. A demonstration center was even set up so that the public could practice purchasing food using the metric system. In the United States, little action was taken on this report until December 23, 1975. At that time, President Ford signed into law the Metric Conversion Act, establishing a national policy in support of the metric system and supposedly ending the dilemma that had continued for so long.

With the signing of the new law it was understood that, through a national policy of coordinating the increasing use of metrics in the United States, the conversion to the metric system would be done on a voluntary basis. The government also created a metric board, appointed by the president with the advice and consent of the Senate. The board was made up of individuals from the various economic sectors that would be influenced most by the metric changeover. Included were people representing labor, science, consumers, manufacturing, construction, and so forth. The function of this board was to create and carry out a program that would allow the development of a sensible plan for a voluntary changeover. This all took place in the 1970s. Today little is heard of this law or program, although slowly some progress is being made. In 1988, President Bush ordered every federal agency to go metric. However, again the president was not specific as to when the change should occur. No timetable was set. The president left it to each individual federal agency. Some of these agencies have set a date for the change, while others have not. The Federal Highway Administration, for example, moved forward and ordered states to use the metric system in designing all roads that were built after September 30, 1996. If states did not comply, a penalty was assessed.

Some industries, notably science, pharmaceutical, engineering, and automotive, have found it necessary to go metric in order to participate in world trade. The medical field has also joined in the use of metric language. Doctors learn early in their training to specify drug dosage in metric units.

Today, over *90 percent* of the world's population uses the metric system. It is also used by over *nine-tenths* of the world's *nations.*

If and when a change to the metric system becomes reality, the people who will be affected most are those whose jobs are concerned with weights and measures. This is certainly the case for food service workers. Instead of pints, quarts, and gallons, they will have to adjust to liters. Instead of pounds and ounces, they will use kilograms and grams; and instead of degrees Fahrenheit, temperature will be in degrees *Celsius* (previously known as *Centigrade*). The purpose of this chapter, therefore, is to make these terms and others dealing with the metric system more familiar to the food service student.

In recent years, food service students in the United States have been exchanged with students from foreign countries in similar programs. When an exchange like this takes place, certainly recipes and formulas are exchanged, making knowledge of the metric system an asset. The student should be able to convert recipes and formulas both ways. That is, from customary to metric and vice versa.

The metric system was introduced to the world by France during the French Revolution. France's lawmakers, during that period of history, asked their scientists to develop a system of measurement based on science rather than custom. They developed a system of measurement which was based upon a length called the meter. A metal bar was used to represent a standard meter of measurement. The *meter* is slightly longer than one yard.

The metric system is a decimal system based on the number ten. For example, when the meter is divided by ten, it produces 10 *decimeters;* a decimeter divided by ten produces 10 *centimeters;* and a centimeter divided by 10 produces 10 *millimeters.* To put it another way, one meter equals 1000 millimeters, or 100 centimeters, or 10 decimeters. (Note: The comma is not used in metric notation; instead, a space is left. Example: 1000 millimeters.) This system of measure seems more practical when compared to our customary units of measure—the yard, which is divided into 3 feet (or 36 inches); and the foot, which is divided into 12 inches.

The metric system also provides standard rules for amounts of its units through prefixes. For example, a *milligram* is one thousandth of a gram (weight), a *milliliter* is one thousandth of a liter (volume), and a *millimeter* is one thousandth of a meter (length). When the unit is increased and the prefix kilo is added, a *kilogram* is 1000 grams and a *kilometer* is 1000 meters. The American and English systems lack this kind of uniformity.

Chef Sez . . .

"I work with metric units daily. Wine and spirits packaging is always in metric units to meet international standards. However, in America, serving sizes are measured in customary units, specifically ounces.

One part of my job is to determine how much wine is needed for banquets. I must calculate how many bottles of red and white wine should be bought and issued from the wine cellar. We supply enough wine to give each guest 1 and $\frac{1}{2}$ glasses of each type of wine ordered (just in case they're thirsty). I also have to determine how many 750 ml bottles of the bubbly (champagne) for the toast, allowing four ounces per flute. Metric conversion is simple multiplication or division and memorization of the conversion factor (or knowledge of where to find the conversion factor). Fortunately, it's not integral calculus!"

Rick Schofield
Manager Beverage Operations
The Culinary Institute of America
Hyde Park, NY

The Culinary Institute of America has been America's Center for Culinary Education since 1946. In addition to serving banquets, the Culinary Institute of America has four restaurants that are open to the public.

Units of Measure in the Metric System

The best way to learn the metric system is to forget all about the customary measurements and simply think metric. To think metric is to think in terms of *ten* and to understand the following basics: the **meter** represents *length;* **grams,** or in most cases, **kilograms** represent *mass;* **liters** or **cubic meters,** represent *volume;* and **degrees Celsius** deals with *temperature.* To compare these new units of measure with familiar ones, a meter is about 39 inches, which is slightly longer than the yard. The gram is such a small unit of mass, approximately 0.035 of an ounce, that to make a comparison it is necessary to take 1,000 grams or 1 kilogram, which is equal to 2.2 pounds. The liter is equal to about 1.0567 quarts, which means it is about 5 percent larger than a quart. There are other units of measure in the metric system, but the ones mentioned are those that will be of most concern to the people involved in food service.

Lengths

It was stated that to think metric is to think in terms of 10. To show how this is done, take the base unit of length (the *meter*), and multiply or divide it by 10. Each time the meter is multiplied or divided by 10, special names are attached on the front of the word to indicate the value. These names are called **prefixes.** For lengths smaller than a meter, it is divided by ten and the result is called a **decimeter.** Dividing a decimeter by ten gives a **centimeter.** When the centimeter is divided by ten, it is called a **millimeter.**

1 decimeter = 0.1 meter
1 centimeter = 0.01 meter
1 millimeter = 0.001 meter

TIPS . . . *To Insure Perfect Solutions*

The length of a *meter* is about *one giant step.*

So for the units smaller than a meter, the prefixes are *deci* (a tenth of a meter), *centi* (a hundredth of a meter), and *milli* (a thousandth of a meter).

For lengths larger than a meter, multiply by 10. For 10 meters the prefix *deka* is used. For 100 meters, the prefix is *hecto*. The prefix for 1,000 is *kilo*. So 10 meters are called a **dekameter,** 100 meters a **hectometer,** and 1000 a **kilometer.** Kilo is a very popular prefix because most distances on roadways are given in kilometers.

1 kilometer = 1000 meters
1 hectometer = 100 meters
1 dekameter = 10 meters

Volume and Capacity

When measuring volume and capacity, it is first necessary to understand what a cubic meter is before learning what a liter represents. A **cubic meter** is a cube with the sides each one meter long. In other words, a cubic meter equals the length of one meter, the width of one meter, and the height of one meter. If a metal container is $\frac{1}{10}$ of a meter (one decimeter) on each side, it is referred to as one *liter.* It would contain one liter of liquid and the liquid would weigh one kilogram. When measuring liquid by the American customary system, it is said that *"A pint is the pound the world around."* In the metric system, it can be changed to *"A liter is a kilogram the world around,"* meaning that every liter of liquid weighs one kilogram, or 2.2 pounds. For units smaller than a liter, a container that has sides one centimeter long is called a **cubic centimeter.** It would hold one milliliter of water and one milliliter weighs one gram. From this, of course, it can be seen that in the metric system there is a very direct relationship among length, volume, and mass.

Mass

The base unit for mass is the gram, but (as stated before), the gram is such a small unit of weight it did not prove practical for application, so the kilogram (1000 grams) is used as the base unit. It is the only base unit that contains a prefix. When the metric system is adopted, all weights will be given in grams or kilograms. Since the kilogram is a fairly large unit, it may be too large to be a convenient unit for packing most foodstuffs, so the half-kilo (500 grams) may become a more familiar unit. Prefixes such as deci, centi, milli, hecto, and deka may be used with the gram, but they are not practical in everyday life, so the gram and kilogram are the common terms used.

T I P S . . . ***To Insure Perfect Solutions***

One **gram** is about the **weight** of a **paper clip.** One **kilogram** is about the **weight** of a **large book or dictionary.**

Quantity	Unit	Symbol
Length	meter decimeter centimeter millimeter kilometer hectometer dekameter	m dm cm mm km hm dam
Volume	cubic centimeter cubic meter	cm^3 m^3
Capacity	milliliter liter	ml l
Mass	gram kilogram	g kg
Temperature	degrees Celsius	°C

Figure 9-1 *Metric units and their symbols.*

When using the metric system, it has proven difficult to remember the names of all the units and terms, so abbreviations are used. (See Figure 9-1.)

In the metric system temperature is measured in degrees Celsius (°C). On the Celsius scale, the boiling point of water is 100 degrees and the freezing point is at 0 degrees. On the Fahrenheit (F) scale, the boiling point is 212°F and the freezing point is 32°F. (See Figure 9-2.) Actually, the official metric temperature scale is the Kelvin scale, which has its zero point at absolute zero. Absolute zero is the coldest possible temperature in the universe. The Kelvin scale is used often by scientists and very seldom, if ever, used in everyday life.

To convert Fahrenheit temperature to degrees Celsius: Subtract 32 from the given Fahrenheit temperature and multiply the result by $\frac{5}{9}$.

Example:

$$212°F - 32° = 180°$$
$$\frac{5}{9} \times \frac{180°}{1} = 100°C$$

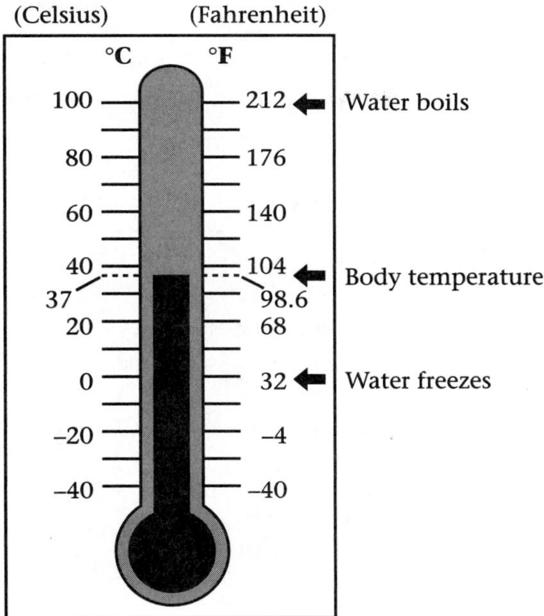

Figure 9-2 *Some common temperatures expressed in Fahrenheit and Celsius.*

To convert Celsius degrees to Fahrenheit: Multiply the Celsius temperature by $\frac{9}{5}$ and add 32 to the result.

Example:

$$\frac{9}{5} \times \frac{100°}{1} = 180°$$
$$180° + 32° = 212°\text{F}$$

Figure 9-3 is a table of approximate metric conversions. Figure 9-4 is an example of how to use this table to convert a recipe from the customary system to the metric system.

The first ingredient is 18 pounds of veal shoulder. Look at Figure 9-3 and find the pounds line in the mass section. The chart shows the reader that in order to convert pounds to kilograms, pounds must be multiplied by 0.45. Therefore, multiply 18 times 0.45 which equals 8.10 kilograms, the metric equivalent. Follow this same procedure to convert a recipe from the customary system to the metric system.

	When you know...	Multiply by	To find	Symbol
Length	inches	2.5	centimeters	cm
	feet	30	centimeters	cm
	yards	0.9	meters	m
	miles	1.6	kilometers	km
Capacity	teaspoons	5	milliliters	ml
	tablespoons	15	milliliters	ml
	fluid ounces	30	milliliters	ml
	ounces	0.03	liters	l
	cups	0.25	liters	l
	pints	0.47	liters	l
	quarts	0.95	liters	l
Volume	cubic feet	0.03	cubic meters	m3
	cubic yards	0.76	cubic meters	m3
Mass	ounces	28	grams	g
	pounds	0.45	kilograms	kg
Temperature	degrees Fahrenheit	subtract 32 and $\times \frac{5}{9}$	degrees Celsius	°C

Figure 9-3 *Conversion from customary to metric units.*

Fricassee of Veal Ingredients	
Customary	**Metric**
18 pounds—Veal shoulder, cut into 1-inch cubes	8.10 kilograms
3 gallons—Water	11.4 liters
2 pounds—Shortening	0.90 kilogram
1 pound 8 ounces—Flour	672 grams
Yellow color as desired	
Salt and pepper to taste	

Figure 9-4 *Converting a recipe from customary measures to metric measures.*

Figure 9-5 is a table for converting metric measure to customary measure. Figure 9-6 is an example of how to use this table to convert a recipe from metric measure to customary measure. Figure 9-7 provides equivalents that may prove helpful.

	When you know...	**Multiply by**	**To find**	**Symbol**
Length	millimeters	0.04	inches	in.
	centimeters	0.4	inches	in.
	meters	3.3	feet	ft.
	meters	1.1	yards	yd.
	kilometers	0.6	miles	mi.
Capacity	milliliters	0.2	teaspoons	tsp.
	milliliters	0.07	tablespoons	tbsp.
	milliliters	0.03	fluid ounces	fl. oz.
	liters	30	ounces	oz.
	liters	4.2	cups	C.
	liters	2.1	pints	pt.
	liters	1.06	quarts	qt.
	liters	.026	gallons	gal.
Volume	cubic meters	35	cubic feet	ft^3
	cubic meters	1.3	cubic yards	yd^3
Mass	grams	0.035	ounces	oz.
	kilograms	2.2	pounds	lb.
Temperature	Celsius temperature	$\frac{9}{5}$, then add 32	Fahrenheit temperature	°F

Figure 9-5 *Conversion from metric to customary measures.*

Metric	**Eclair Dough Ingredients**	**Customary**
500 ml	water	15 fl. oz., 1 pint
5 ml	salt	1 teaspoon
22 ml	sugar	$1\frac{1}{2}$ tablespoon
450 g	butter or margarine	15.75 oz. or 1 pound
450 g	bread flour	15.75 oz. or 1 pound
16	eggs	16

Figure 9-6 *Converting a recipe from metric to customary measure.*

Weights and Measure U.S. Customary and Metric Systems Equivalents that May Prove Helpful		
1 gram	=	0.035 ounce
1 kilogram	=	2.2 pounds
28 grams	=	1 ounce
454 grams or 0.45 kg	=	1 pound
5 milliliters	=	1 teaspoon
15 milliliters	=	1 tablespoon
240 milliliters or 0.24 liters	=	1 cup
0.47 liters	=	1 pint
0.95 liters	=	1 quart
1 liter	=	1.06 quarts

Figure 9-7 *Weights and measures equivalents.*

Summary Review

1. Convert recipes (a) through (e) from the American Customary System to the metric system. Use the conversion table shown in Figure 9-3.

   (a) **White cream icing ingredients**

1 lb. 4 oz. shortening	______ g
$\frac{1}{4}$ oz. salt	______ g
5 oz. dry milk	______ g
14 oz. water	______ ml
5 lb. powdered sugar	______ kg
vanilla to taste	______ to taste

   (b) **Yellow cake ingredients**

2 lb. 8 oz. cake flour	______ kg
1 lb. 6 oz. shortening	______ g
3 lb. 2 oz. granulated sugar	______ kg
1 oz. salt	______ g
$1\frac{3}{4}$ oz. baking powder	______ g
4 oz. dry milk	______ g
1 lb. 4 oz. water	______ g
1 lb. 10 oz. whole eggs	______ g
12 oz. water	______ ml
vanilla to taste	______ to taste

(c) **Italian meringue ingredients**

1 lb. egg whites	________ g
1 lb. 8 oz. water	________ ml
1 lb. 12 oz. sugar	________ g
$1\frac{1}{2}$ oz. egg white stabilizer	________ ml
$\frac{1}{8}$ oz. vanilla	________ ml

(d) **Vanilla pie filling ingredients**

12 lb. liquid milk	________ kg
4 lb. granulated sugar	________ kg
1 lb. cornstarch	________ g
$\frac{1}{4}$ oz. salt	________ g
2 lb. whole eggs	________ g
6 oz. butter	________ g
vanilla to taste	________ to taste

(e) **Fruit glaze ingredients**

2 lb. water	________ g
2 lb. 8 oz. granulated sugar	________ kg
8 oz. water	________ ml
4 oz. modified starch	________ g
4 oz. corn syrup	________ ml
1 oz. lemon juice	________ ml
food color as desired	

2. Convert the following Fahrenheit temperatures to Celsius temperatures. Use the formulas given in this unit.

   1. 180°F
   2. 140°F
   3. 98°F
   4. 210°F
   5. 45°F

3. Convert the following Celsius temperatures to Fahrenheit temperatures. Use the formula given in this unit.

   1. 32°C
   2. 204°C
   3. 60°C
   4. 120°C
   5. 20°C

4. Convert recipes (a) through (e) from the metric system to the American Customary System. Use the conversion table shown in Figure 9-5.

(a) **Chicken a la king ingredients**

4.5 kilograms boiled chicken or turkey, diced	________ lb.
0.45 kilograms green peppers, diced	________ lb.
227 grams pimentos, diced	________ oz.
0.9 kilograms mushrooms, diced	________ lb.
2.8 liters chicken stock	________ qt.
0.74 kilograms flour	________ lb.
0.9 kilograms shortening	________ lb.
2.8 liters milk	________ qt.
240 milliliters sherry wine	________ C.

(b) **Tartar sauce ingredients**

110 grams dill pickles, chopped fine	________ oz.
60 grams onions, chopped fine	________ oz.
0.14 grams parsley, chopped fine	________ oz.
1 liter mayonnaise	________ qt.
5 milliliters lemon juice	________ tsp.

(c) **Cocktail sauce ingredients**

0.95 liters catsup	________ qt.
0.6 liters chili sauce	________ oz.
0.24 liters prepared horseradish	________ oz.
120 milliliters lemon juice	________ oz.
30 milliliters Worcestershire sauce	________ oz.
hot sauce to taste	

(d) **Spicy peach mold ingredients**

0.95 liters peaches, canned, sliced, drained	________ qt.
0.45 liters peach syrup	________ oz.
0.45 liters hot water	________ oz.
0.95 liters cold water	________ oz.
0.24 liters vinegar	________ oz.
0.36 liters sugar	________ C.
28 grams cinnamon stick	________ oz.
15 milliliters whole cloves	________ tsp.
392 grams orange gelatin	________ oz.

(e) **Brussels sprouts and sour cream ingredients**

2.7 kilograms brussels sprouts	________ lb.
30 milliliters salt	________ tsp.
112 grams onions, minced	________ oz.
140 grams butter	________ oz.
0.90 kilograms sour cream	________ oz.
water to cover, boiling	

PART IV

MATH ESSENTIALS IN FOOD SERVICE RECORDKEEPING

Every business, small and large must keep accurate, up-to-date, and detailed records if it is to survive in today's very competitive world. Most businesses depend on the computer to record and store their records either at the source of the operation or sent over telephone wires, using a modem, to a remote location that allows monitoring several business operations from one location (an ideal situation for chain food service operations).

Chapters 10 through 13 will focus on food service recordkeeping. The material will be presented in the simplest form to convey how these records are acquired and how they can be recorded if there is no computer available. Most food service operations have a computer on the premises; however, they do not use it for all reports and even if they do, the data must first be acquired before it can be input and stored in the computer.

The chapters in this part explain how and why functions such as purchasing and receiving and the proper preparation of daily production reports, guest checks, and cashier reports are vital to the success of a food service operation. The chapter concerned with using computer applications introduces the tools that can be used to calculate and store this vital information for present and future use.

The functions presented in this part are usually the responsibility of the production or service crew with the exception of bank deposits and purchasing. Those are the responsibility of management.

Part Five of this text will consist of more recordkeeping reports, but will focus on those that are the responsibility of management.

Daily Production Reports

OBJECTIVES

At the completion of this chapter, the student should be able to:

1. Complete the cook's production report.
2. Complete the baker's production report.
3. Complete the salad production report.
4. Complete the counter production report.

There are a number of production departments in a commercial kitchen. The number and size depends on the size of the food service operation. Each department produces its own special kind of food to meet the needs required for serving breakfast, luncheon, and dinner menus. The production departments will include *cooking, salad, pastry, baking,* and *butchering.* The production that goes on in these departments must be *controlled.* The device used is called a **food production report.** These reports are probably more important in large operations because they help the chef or manager control production situations that can become out of control. (See Figure 10-1.) In small operations, with a smaller production crew and work areas, it is easier to observe all that is taking place, so these production reports become less important.

Chef Sez . . .

Chef Greg has a lot of sayings:

"Little things mean a lot."

"Being organized and accurate are two of the most important keys to a successful operation."

"In higher volume establishments, even items dropped or damaged should be counted."

"When calculating food wastage (or food harvest that goes to a shelter which is common now) everything should be accounted for, because it is here where your profits and losses will occur."

"In accordance with daily reports, accuracy is essential in completing food production sheets and annual forecasts."

Greg Benamati
50's Prime Time Restaurant
M.G.M. Studios at Walt Disney World
Lake Buena Vista, Florida

Chef Greg Benamati is the Restaurant Chef in the 257-seat Prime Time Cafe Restaurant, which is open for lunch and dinner in the M.G.M. Studios Theme Park at Walt Disney World. The kitchen staff has about 20 cast members (Walt Disney World's name for employees) that are influenced by Chef Greg's sayings.

Figure 10-1 *Cook completing a daily production report.*

USES OF DAILY PRODUCTION REPORTS

Production reports help to control such essentials as:

- Over or under production
- Leftovers
- Purchasing
- Labor cost
- Waste
- Theft

They will also inform the manager of popular preparations that are selling out, menu items that are not selling, and, to a degree, whether portion sizes should be adjusted. In addition, the report is used in predicting future sales, sometimes referred to as *forecasting*. Predicting future sales assists management in the purchasing of food and hiring of future food service employees. If a rotating menu is being used on a monthly, biannual, or annual basis, these reports become even more valuable. Management can check back and see which items sold best and how many of each item was sold the last time the menu was used. If these reports are used properly, management can improve the food cost percentage.

FOOD PRODUCTION REPORTS

The forms used in compiling the daily food production reports vary depending on the individual food service operation. Each establishment has its own ideas about control and the information it would like to have listed on the report. Most establishments do, however, request reports from cooks, pastry cooks, bakers, and the salad and counter service departments. The report forms are usually quite simple to fill out so they do not take up too much of an employee's time to complete. Some forms, such as the one used in the counter report, show unit price, total price, and total sales.

Examples of four different daily food production reports are shown in Figures 10-2 through 10-6. These forms are typical of those used in the food service industry. Although these examples are easy to follow, a few comments on each can help you to become more competent when filling them out.

Unit: First National Bank | Meal: Luncheon | Customers: 150
Day: Thursday | Date: June 23, 20___

Item	Recipe File Number	Size of Portion	Raw Quantity Required	Portions to Prepare	Portions Left or Time Out	Portions Served
Roast Round of Beef	15	3 oz.	25 lb.	80	out 8:15	80
Roast Loin of Pork	20	$4\frac{1}{2}$ oz.	12 lb.	30	8	22
Filet of Sole	8	5 oz.	14 lb.	42	2	40
Veal Goulash	18	6 oz.	10 lb.	24	9	15
Swiss Steak	14	5 oz.	15 lb.	48	12	36
Mashed Potatoes	42	4 oz.	20 lb.	60	5	55
Peas and Carrots	51	3 oz.	9 lb.	48	18	30
Succotash	52	3 oz.	5 lb.	26	1	25

Figure 10-2 *Cook's production report.*

Day: Monday | Date: June 27, 20___ | Unit: Leo's Cafeteria

Item	Order	On Hand	Prepare	Left	Sold	Comment
Rolls						
Soft Rye	20 doz.	3 doz.	17 doz.	2 doz.	18 doz.	
Soft White	35 doz.	4 doz.	31 doz.	6 doz.	29 doz.	
Hard White	26 doz.	5 doz.	21 doz.	4 doz.	22 doz.	
Cinnamon	18 doz.	2 doz.	16 doz.	1 doz.	17 doz.	
Rye Sticks	15 doz.	6 doz.	9 doz.	0	15 doz.	Out 7 p.m.
Quick Breads						
Biscuits	12 doz.	1 doz.	11 doz.	3 doz.	9 doz.	Biscuits left unbaked in freezer
Raisin Muffins	24 doz.	5 doz.	19 doz.	5 doz.	19 doz.	
Pies						
Cherry	22	6	16	0	22	Out 8 p.m.
Apple	25	4	21	2	23	
Chocolate	15	3	12	0	15	Out 7:30 p.m.
Banana	12	1	11	8	4	
Cakes						
Bar	6	2	4	3	3	These left in freezer
899 White	10	4	6	6	4	
Mocha	8	1	7	0	8	Out 7 p.m.

Figure 10-3 *Baker's production report.*

Figure 10-4 *Baker completing a production report.*

Day: Tuesday	Date: June 29, 20___		Unit: First National Bank		
Item	**Order**	**On Hand**	**Prepare**	**Left**	**Sold**
Toss	23	8	15	3	20
Italian	12	0	12	0	12
Garden	22	9	13	7	15
Waldorf	16	2	14	6	10
Potato	25	10	15	6	19
Cole Slaw	32	8	24	1	31
Sliced Tomato	26	0	26	3	23
Fruited Gelatin	28	12	16	2	26
Sunshine	14	3	11	4	10
Green Island	25	5	20	5	20
Mixed Fruit	35	6	29	3	32
Chef	46	7	39	12	34
Cucumber	12	1	11	10	2

Figure 10-5 *Salad production report.*

Unit: Latonia Race Track — Customer Count: 405
Day: Tuesday — Date: June 28, 20___

Item	Number of Portions for Sale	Number of Portions Not Sold	Number of Portions Sold	Unit Price	Value Sold
Hot Dogs	135	26	109	$3.25	$354.25
Chicken Patty	75	15	60	4.75	285.00
Hamburgers	150	23	127	4.75	603.25
Barbecue	50	5	45	4.75	213.75
Cube Steaks	70	6	64	5.25	336.00
Milk	125	18	107	1.00	107.00
Shakes	80	7	73	2.50	182.50
Soda	225	28	197	2.00	394.00
Cake	15	2	13	2.75	35.75
Pie	35	8	27	2.75	74.25
Ice Cream	65	9	56	2.25	126.00
Potato Chips	85	13	72	1.50	108.00
Pretzels	45	11	34	1.50	51.00

Name: Bill Thompson — Total $2870.75

Figure 10-6 *Counter production report.*

Cook's Production Report (See Figure 10-2)

Recipe File Number. This number is placed on the recipe for easy access when it is filed. Standard recipes are used in some food service establishments to control the cost, taste, texture, quality, and amount of food being prepared.

Size of Portion. The manager or chef fills in this column to let the cook and perhaps the waitperson know the portion size they are serving or dishing up. In most establishments, the portion size is a set policy and is indicated on the portion charts on display in the production area.

Raw Quantity Required. This is usually designated by the chef or cook. Sometimes the manager lists this figure, but it must be done by a person familiar with production and with the policy of the establishment. The chef, manager, or purchasing agent is responsible for ordering the raw quantity required from a vendor and seeing that it is on hand when needed.

Portions to Prepare. This decision is made by the manager or chef and is based on previous production reports and sales history. It is important to know how much of a particular item was sold the last time it appeared on the menu. Also, consideration must be given to other external factors. For example, cold weather could have resulted in an increase of soup sales.

Portions Left or Time Out. This figure is recorded by the cook and is found by counting the number of portions left after the meal is over. Time out is recorded when the number of a certain item is completely sold out. The time an item sold out is important because it affects the number of items prepared the next time the item appears on the menu.

Portions Served. This is recorded by the cook and is found by subtracting the number left from the number prepared. It is an important figure because this number influences the number of portions prepared when the item appears again on the menu.

SUMMARY REVIEW

Complete the following cook's production reports. Use the present day and date.

1. Unit: Mason Art Co.

   Day: ____________

   Date: ____________

   Meal: Luncheon

   Customers: 50

Item	Recipe Number	Size of Portion	Raw Quantity Required	Portions to Prepare	Portions Left or Time Out	Portions Served
Spanish Steak	18	5 oz.	8 lb.	25	7	________
Salisbury Steak	19	5 oz.	7 lb.	22	9	________
Beef Pot Roast	20	3 oz.	8 lb.	32	13	________
Au Gratin Potatoes	2	4 oz.	10 lb.	35	6	________
KY Succotash	10	3 oz.	5 lb.	30	4	________
Mashed Potatoes	3	4 oz.	20 lb.	60	13	________
Lima Beans	12	3 oz.	$2\frac{1}{2}$ lb.	15	2	________

2. Unit: 2nd National Bank

   Day: ____________

   Date: ____________

   Meal: Luncheon

   Customers: 131

Item	Recipe Number	Size of Portion	Raw Quantity Required	Portions to Prepare	Portions Left or Time Out	Portions Served
Sautéed Pork Chop	32	4 oz.	6 lb.	22	8	________
Turkey Steaks	45	4 oz.	12 lb.	45	7	________
Baked Halibut	54	5 oz.	10 lb.	32	12	________
Roast Veal	30	3 oz.	10 lb.	38	13	________
Parsley Potatoes	4	4 oz.	15 lb.	50	6	________
Hash in Cream Potatoes	5	4 oz.	14 lb.	45	11	________
Peas and Celery	13	3 oz.	$7\frac{1}{2}$ lb.	44	9	________
Cut Green Beans	16	3 oz.	5 lb.	30	5	________

3. Unit: Chase Machine Tool Co.

   Day: ___________________

   Date: ___________________

   Meal: Luncheon

   Customers: 155

Item	Recipe Number	Size of Portion	Raw Quantity Required	Portions to Prepare	Portions Left or Time Out	Portions Served
Sautéed Veal Steak	31	4 oz.	5 lb.	26	3	________
Beef Sauerbraten	21	3 oz.	8 lb.	32	6	________
Beef Goulash	26	6 oz.	15 lb.	54	2	________
Swiss Steak	22	5 oz.	20 lb.	62	8	________
Rissel Potatoes	1	4 oz.	12 lb.	36	9	________
Escallop Potatoes	6	4 oz.	8 lb.	26	11	________
Stewed Tomatoes	14	3 oz.	1 #10 can	22	5	________
Corn	15	3 oz.	$7\frac{1}{2}$ lb.	44	12	________

4. Unit: Norwood High School

   Day: ___________________

   Date: ___________________

   Meal: Luncheon

   Customers: 100

Item	Recipe Number	Size of Portion	Raw Quantity Required	Portions to Prepare	Portions Left or Time Out	Portions Served
Ham Steak	34	4 oz.	7 lb.	28	6	________
Roast Turkey	37	3 oz.	15 lb.	36	8	________
Hamburger Steak	23	5 oz.	13 lb.	42	7	________
Beef Stroganoff	25	6 oz.	7 lb.	20	5	________
Macaroni Au Gratin	74	4 oz.	4 lb.	45	11	________
Mashed Potatoes	3	4 oz.	12 lb.	40	9	________
Mixed Greens	9	3 oz.	10 lb.	58	13	________
Carrots Vichy	17	3 oz.	5 lb.	29	16	________

Baker's Production Report (See Figure 10-3)

Order. The order is recorded by the manager, chef, or pastry chef, and this represents the amount of bakery and pastry items needed for service throughout the day in all departments of the food service operation. If the operation is a catering company, it represents the amount needed in all units served.

On Hand. This figure is recorded by the baker and represents the amount of each item that was left by the previous shift or from the previous day and is still in a usable condition. It may be in a raw or cooked state, frozen or unfrozen.

Prepare. The number to prepare is found by subtracting the amount on hand from the amount ordered. The remainder is the amount to prepare and is recorded by the baker or pastry chef.

Left. The number left is found by counting the number of pieces remaining after the day's service is over. This figure is recorded by the baker or pastry chef.

Sold. The number sold is found by subtracting the number left from the number ordered. This figure is recorded by the cook or pastry chef.

Comments. This space is provided for any information that may be valuable to management. Examples: the time a product is sold out and the disposition of leftover items.

SUMMARY REVIEW

Complete the following bakery production reports. Use the present day and date.

1. Unit: Norwood High School

   Day: ____________

   Date: ____________

Item	Order	On Hand	Left	Sold
Seed Rolls	25 doz.	6 doz.	4 doz.	________
Rye Rolls	36 doz.	3 doz.	5 doz.	________
Hard Rolls	28 doz.	6 doz.	2 doz.	________
Rye Sticks	22 doz.	4 doz.	3 doz.	________
Biscuits	12 doz.	0	3 doz.	________
Banana Muffins	10 doz.	0	$1\frac{1}{2}$ doz.	________
Cherry Pies	18	5	2	________
Banana Pies	16	2	4	________
Boston Cream Pies	22	7	6	________
Devil's Food Cake	13	5	2	________

2. Unit: Deluxe Shoe Co.

   Day: ___________________

   Date: ___________________

Item	**Order**	**On Hand**	**Left**	**Sold**
Soft Rolls	30 doz.	4 doz.	2 doz.	________
Hard Rolls	28 doz.	6 doz.	5 doz.	________
Rye Sticks	22 doz.	4 doz.	1 doz.	________
Pecan Rolls	16 doz.	2 doz.	$\frac{1}{2}$ doz.	________
Raisin Muffins	9 doz.	1 doz.	$\frac{3}{4}$ doz.	________
Apple Pies	18	3	1	________
Peach Pies	14	2	2	________
Chocolate Pies	22	4	3	________
Lemon Cake	9	2	4	________
Chocolate Bar Cake	12	5	3	________
Fudge Cake	14	1	5	________

3. Unit: Joe's Cafeteria

   Day: ___________________

   Date: ___________________

Item	**Order**	**On Hand**	**Left**	**Sold**
Cloverleaf Rolls	40 doz.	7 doz.	3 doz.	________
Caramel Rolls	26 doz.	3 doz.	1 doz.	________
Seed Rolls	35 doz.	4 doz.	2 doz.	________
Biscuits	22 doz.	5 doz.	$\frac{1}{2}$ doz.	________
Corn Muffins	18 doz.	2 doz.	$\frac{3}{4}$ doz.	________
Pecan Pie	12	3	5	________
Pumpkin Pie	15	2	4	________
Custard Pie	10	4	3	________
Eclair	48	0	8	________
Cherry Tarts	54	5	7	________

4. Unit: Wine & Dine Restaurant

Day: ___________________

Date: ___________________

Item	Order	On Hand	Left	Sold
Soft Rolls	68 doz.	9 doz.	$4\frac{3}{4}$ doz.	________
Rye Rolls	38 doz.	4 doz.	$5\frac{1}{2}$ doz.	________
Split Rolls	26 doz.	7 doz.	$2\frac{1}{4}$ doz.	________
Cinnamon Rolls	32 doz.	6 doz.	$7\frac{3}{4}$ doz.	________
Apple Muffins	18 doz.	4 doz.	$4\frac{1}{2}$ doz.	________
Corn Sticks	16 doz.	3 doz.	$2\frac{1}{4}$ doz.	________
Blueberry Pie	12	4	2	________
Coconut Cream Pie	14	3	4	________
White Cake, 8″	9	2	1	________
Apple Cake, 8″	8	1	0	________
Yellow Cake, 8″	6	0	3	________

Salad Production Report (See Figure 10-5)

Order. The order is recorded by the manager, chef, or head salad person, and this represents the amount of each salad to be prepared. It is an estimate of the number or kind of salad needed for serving one meal or for the complete day. Cafeterias and buffet style restaurants provide an array of assorted salads. The order is very helpful in this type of operation.

On Hand. This figure is recorded by the salad person and represents the amount of each salad that was left by the previous shift or from the previous day and is still in a usable condition.

Prepare. The number to prepare is found by subtracting the amount on hand from the amount ordered. This figure is recorded by the salad person.

Left. The number left is found by counting the number of each kind of salad remaining after the meal or day's service is concluded. The salad person records this figure.

Sold. The number sold is found by subtracting the number left from the number ordered. This figure is recorded by the salad person.

Comments. This space is provided for information that may be valuable to the head salad person or management. Examples: weather conditions that day, the time a certain salad is sold out, production information or mistakes, and the disposition of leftover salads.

SUMMARY REVIEW

Complete the following salad production reports. Use the present day and date.

1. Unit: 1st Federal Bank

   Day: ____________________

   Date: ____________________

Item	Order	On Hand	Left	Sold
Toss	24	4	4	________
Chef	20	3	2	________
Garden	16	6	6	________
Slaw	12	2	3	________
Gelatin	9	1	7	________
Fruit	15	9	5	________
Sliced Tomato	18	4	1	________
Waldorf	8	5	0	________

2. Unit: 2nd Federal Bank

   Day: ____________________

   Date: ____________________

Item	Order	On Hand	Left	Sold
Italian	22	5	1	________
Cucumber	24	4	4	________
Jellied Slaw	18	2	5	________
Green Island	16	1	2	________
Macaroni	12	3	6	________
Carrots	15	6	3	________
Mixed Greens	14	4	0	________
Sunshine	26	2	1	________

3. Unit: Western Insurance Co.

   Day: ________________

   Date: ________________

Item	Order	On Hand	Left	Sold
Chef	32	6	7	________
Waldorf	18	7	6	________
Fruited Slaw	14	8	5	________
Fruited Gelatin	16	4	1	________
Sliced Tomato	25	3	0	________
Garden	28	2	2	________
Italian	35	0	3	________
Mixed Green	40	1	4	________

4. Unit: Garrison Greeting Card Co.

   Day: ________________

   Date: ________________

Item	Order	On Hand	Left	Sold
Toss	35	4	0	________
Mixed Green	25	8	2	________
Garden	20	6	4	________
Spring	22	2	7	________
Cottage Cheese	18	0	6	________
Waldorf	16	3	3	________
Sunshine	14	0	2	________
Hawaiian	12	1	0	________
Macaroni	10	7	1	________

Counter Production Report (See Figure 10-6)

Number of Portions for Sale. This figure may be recorded by management or the person working the counter. It represents the number of on-hand items that are for sale.

Number of Portions Not Sold. This figure is recorded by the person working the counter. It is found by counting the remaining pieces of each item left after the day's service is concluded.

Number of Portions Sold. This is found by subtracting the number of portions not sold from the number of portions for sale. It is recorded by the person working the counter.

Value Sold. This is found by multiplying the number of portions sold by the unit price. It is found and recorded by the person working the counter.

Total. This is found by adding the figures in the value sold column.

It is found and recorded by the person working the counter.
Customer Count. This figure is recorded on the register.

SUMMARY REVIEW

Complete the following counter production reports. Use the present day and date.

1. Unit: Stevens Processing Co.

   Customer Count: 305

   Day: ________________

   Date: ________________

Item	Number of Portions for Sale	Number of Portions Sold	Unit Price	Value Sold
Hot Dogs	85	80	$3.25	________
Hamburgers	95	75	4.75	________
Chicken Patty	65	63	4.75	________
Barbecue	55	53	4.75	________
Cube Steak	40	32	5.25	________
Soda	120	109	2.00	________
Shakes	60	56	2.50	________
Milk	110	107	1.00	________
Pie	48	42	2.75	________
Ice Cream	60	38	2.25	________

2. Unit: Wall Manufacturing Plant

   Customer Count: 435

   Day: ________________

   Date: ________________

Item	Number of Portions for Sale	Number of Portions Sold	Unit Price	Value Sold
Hot Dogs	120	89	$3.25	________
Hamburgers	115	106	4.75	________
Chicken Patty	112	98	4.75	________
Barbecue	75	58	4.75	________
Cube Steak	85	81	5.25	________
Soda	125	106	2.00	________
Shakes	90	79	2.50	________
Milk	120	99	1.00	________
Pie	90	83	2.75	________
Ice Cream	90	82	2.25	________

3. Unit: Deluxe Playing Card Co.

Customer Count: 308

Day: ____________________

Date: ____________________

Item	Number of Portions for Sale	Number of Portions Sold	Unit Price	Value Sold
Hamburgers	90	82	$4.75	________
Hot Dogs	85	73	3.25	________
Chicken Patty	70	68	4.75	________
Barbecue	50	43	4.75	________
Cube Steaks	45	38	5.25	________
Soda	95	87	2.00	________
Shakes	45	41	2.50	________
Milk	85	76	1.00	________
Pie	54	39	2.75	________
Cake	60	42	2.25	________

4. Unit: United Shoe Co.

Customer Count: 390

Day: ____________________

Date: ____________________

Item	Number of Portions for Sale	Number of Portions Sold	Unit Price	Value Sold
Hamburgers	110	102	$4.75	________
Hot Dogs	105	96	3.25	________
Chicken Patty	80	74	4.75	________
Barbecue	75	66	4.75	________
Cube Steaks	65	52	5.25	________
Soda	100	89	2.00	________
Shakes	85	72	2.50	________
Milk	95	69	1.00	________
Pie	66	58	2.75	________
Cake	40	36	2.25	________

Purchasing and Receiving

OBJECTIVES

At the completion of this chapter, the student should be able to:

1. Prepare requisitions.
2. Prepare invoice forms and find extension prices.
3. Prepare purchase specifications and purchase orders.
4. Identify the fax machine as a means of communication.

The introduction to Part Four of this text explains the need and importance of keeping accurate, up-to-date, and detailed records. Records must be kept of all business transactions that are carried on within an organization. In this chapter, we will discuss three vital business forms that are used in the food service industry. Invoices, requisitions, and purchase orders are familiar forms to managers that buy and sell a product.

VITAL BUSINESS FORMS

Business forms used in food service operations vary depending on the accounting system. The accountant may be a full-time employee or hired on a part-time basis. He or she provides the operation with forms that must be kept up to date and which reflect the daily business operation. It is important to keep a daily record of such items as the cash register readings, cash on hand, bank deposits, cash paid out, checks issued, invoices, requisitions, and purchase orders.

It can be said, without hesitation, that behind every successful business is usually a good record keeper. In a restaurant operation, that person might be the manager, assistant manager, or someone designated for this specific duty.

Requisitions

In a food service operation, all supplies (food, cleaning products, paper products, etc.) are kept in the storeroom. The storeroom may be located on the same floor as the kitchen for easy access, or on another floor or basement area making it a little difficult to reach. A cook in the kitchen needs certain supplies from the storeroom to carry out the day's production. To obtain these supplies, the cook fills out a storeroom **requisition.** (See Figure 11-1.) A requisition is a demand made, usually in written form, for something that is required. On the form, the cook states the quantity needed, the unit, and a description or name of each item. The

Storeroom Requisition

Date: October 23, 20 ___ Charge to Kitchen

Quantity	Unit	Item	Unit Price	Extension Price
6	#10 cans	Sliced Apples	$3.55	$21.30
4	#10 cans	Tomato Juice	1.97	7.88
1	lb.	Fresh Mushrooms	1.55	1.55
2	lb.	Beef Base	5.21	10.42
4	lb.	Cornstarch	.46	1.84
			TOTAL	$42.99

Approved by ______________

Signed ______________

Figure 11-1 *Storeroom requisition form.*

requisition must be approved by a superior. The cook who is going to use the items must also sign the requisition. This requisition is then taken to the storeroom and the supplies are issued. If the storeroom is a distance from the cook's station, the requisition may be given to a pot washer or a person called a runner who acquires the supplies for the cook. The person in charge of the storeroom, usually referred to as the steward, marks the unit price and extension price on each item. The steward also finds the total price of the food items issued. The requisition is then filed and used for the following purposes:

1. Accounts for all items issued from the storeroom each day.
2. Controls theft and waste.
3. Provides the figures necessary for the daily food cost report.
4. Ensures that all items are issued only to the proper personnel.
5. Assists in controlling purchasing and eliminating large inventories.

◆ *Chef Sez . . .*

"We have three and a half hours to feed a small city; potentially 78,000 guests. When a popular team or a popular player is scheduled, we have a capacity crowd. The next day we may only have 11,000 fans. A chef or food service manager needs to use math to figure out how much food to order and how much to cook in order to have enough food for our guests, but not too much where we have waste."

Matthew J. Kaperka
Division Manager, Concessions
Sports & Entertainment, ARAMARK Corporation

Matt Kaperka is the concessions manager at Shea Stadium in New York, home of the New York Mets professional baseball team. He has had a wealth of experience in sports and entertainment food service. Previously, he worked in Houston, Texas, at the Astrodome. The tenants at the Astrodome included the Houston Astros baseball team and the Houston Oilers football team. In addition, there were many special events such as the rodeo, for which ARAMARK and Mr. Kaperka had to provide the concessions. He must use his math skills daily to accomplish his goals.

T I P S . . . ***To Insure Perfect Solutions***

Multiply the quantity times the unit price to find the extension price.

Summary Review

Prepare four storeroom requisition forms using the example shown in this section. Work the following problems by finding the extension price and the total.

1. 8—#10 cans sliced peaches @ $3.71 per can
   7—#10 cans whole tomatoes @ $2.83 per can
   12 heads iceberg lettuce @ $0.79 per head
   3 dozen eating apples @ $3.50 per dozen
   5 pounds corn starch @ $.56 per pound
   4 pounds margarine @ 4.76 per pound

2. 5—#10 cans sliced pineapple @ $3.50 per can
   4—#10 cans cherries @ $7.21 per can
   3 bunches celery @ $0.89 per bunch
   6 pounds tomatoes @ $0.76 per pound
   2 bunches carrots @ $0.59 per bunch
   9 dozen eggs @ $0.92 per dozen

3. 8—13-ounce cans tuna fish @ $1.79 per can
   5 dozen eggs @ $0.92 per dozen
   9—1-pound cans salmon @ $2.25 per can
   6—$2\frac{1}{2}$-pound boxes frozen peas @ $0.56 per pound
   8—$2\frac{1}{2}$-pound boxes frozen corn @ $0.58 per pound
   7 heads iceberg lettuce @ $0.79 per head

4. 3—#10 cans tomato puree @ $2.65 per can
   4—1-pound boxes cornstarch @ $0.56 per pound
   $2\frac{1}{2}$ pounds leaf lettuce @ $0.89 per pound
   5—$2\frac{1}{2}$-pound boxes lima beans @ $1.23 per pound
   $2\frac{1}{2}$ pounds fresh mushrooms @ $1.26 per pound
   4 bunches green onions @ $0.95 per bunch
   3 bunches parsley @ $0.49 per bunch
   5 heads iceberg lettuce @ $0.79 per head

Invoices

An **invoice** is a written document listing goods sent to a purchaser by a vendor with their prices, quantity, and charges. (See Figure 11-2.) Individual companies have their own types of invoices depending upon

Distributor:	Haines Foods, Inc.		Phone: ____________ Date: October 20, 20___		
Address:	70 Greenbrier Avenue Ft. Mitchell, KY 41017				
Distributors of Fine Food Products — Wholesale Only					
No. of Pieces 5	Salesperson Joe Jones		Order No. 2860		Invoice # J 2479
Packed by: G.C. City:	Sold To: Mr. John Doe Street: 120 Elm Avenue Covington, KY				
Case	**Pack**	**Size**	**Canned Foods**	**Price**	**Amount**
4	6	#10 can	Sliced Apples	20.87	83.48
3	6	#10 can	Pitted Cherries	43.85	131.55
2	12	#5 can	Apple Juice	11.97	23.94
1	24	1 lb.	Cornstarch	11.04	11.04
2	24	#2$\frac{1}{2}$ can	Asparagus	25.73	51.46
				Total Amount	$301.47

Figure 11-2 *Invoice form.*

what they feel is necessary to list. Some invoices are simple, while others are more complex. Most invoices today, in our computerized world, are computer printouts. An invoice accompanies each shipment or delivery of food brought into a food service operation. Before signing for a shipment, the person receiving the delivery must check the items delivered with those listed on the invoice to ensure all items listed have been received.

The invoice is important to the food service operator or manager because it provides the figures for the food purchased during the month. These figures are necessary when computing the monthly food cost percent. The invoice is also important when checking the charges listed on the monthly bill or statement sent by the vendor. Some business people opt to pay cash for the delivery or must pay cash on delivery because of a poor credit rating. Most wait for a monthly bill or statement and check all charges against the invoices received with each delivery. This is a good business practice.

If an establishment has a policy of using purchase orders, then the invoice can be used by the bookkeeper to check against a copy of the purchase order before the bill is paid.

TIPS . . . ***To Insure Perfect Solutions***

To find the amount column, multiply the number of cases times the price.

Summary Review

Prepare four invoice forms using the example shown in this section. Work the following problems by finding the extension price and the total. Assume that you work for Curran Foods, Inc. Use today's date and your own name as salesperson.

1. Order No. 2861; Invoice No. J2480; packed by R.G.;
   sold to Manor Restaurant, 590 Walnut Street,
   Cincinnati, Ohio 45202.
   4 cases 6—#10 cans whole tomatoes @ $16.98 per case
   6 cases 12—50-ounce cans tomato soup @ $16.40 per case
   2 cases 20 pounds spaghetti @ $9.77 per case
   $4\frac{1}{2}$ cases 4—1-gallon jars mayonnaise @ $14.84 per case
   2 boxes—15 pounds sliced bacon @ $24.30 per box
   2 cases 24—1-pound cans coffee @ $68.17 per case

2. Order No. 2862; Invoice No. J2481; packed by R.H.;
   sold to Sinton Hotel, 278 Vine Street,
   Cincinnati, Ohio 45202.
   3 cases 4—1-gallon whole dill pickles @ $16.10 per case
   6 cases 12—15-ounce chicken rice soup @ $27.37 per case
   4 cases 4—1-gallon sweet pickle relish @ $18.40 per case
   6 cases 6—#10 cans tomatoes diced @ $13.97 per case
   5 cases 6—#10 cans sliced pineapple @ $22.70 per case
   3 cases 4—5-pound American cheese, sliced @ $33.98 per case

3. Order No. 2863; Invoice No. J2482; packed by B.B.;
   sold to Cincinnati Businessmen's Club, 529 Plum Street,
   Cincinnati, Ohio 45202.
   3 cases 6—#10 cans catsup @ $19.51 per case
   2 cases 6—#10 cans chili sauce @ $22.49 per case
   1 case 6—1-gallon cider vinegar @ $10.41 per case
   3 boxes 10 pounds lasagna @ $6.84 per box
   9 cases 6—#10 cans sliced peaches @ $22.26 per case
   2 pack 16-ounce cracked black pepper @ $5.30 per pack

4. Order No. 2864; Invoice No. J2482; packed by J.M.;
   sold to Norwood High School Cafeteria,
   2078 Elm Avenue, Norwood, Ohio 45212.
   7 cases 6—#10 cans sliced apples @ $20.87 case
   6 boxes 10 pounds medium egg noodles @ $8.86 per box
   2 cases 6—#10 cans bean sprouts @ $16.72 per case
   3 bags 50 pounds granulated sugar @ $16.70 per bag
   2 cases 12—2-pound brown sugar @ $12.67 per case
   2 cases 30—1-pound margarine @ $10.77 per case

PURCHASE SPECIFICATIONS

Purchase specifications are an important part of a successful food service operation. They provide a detailed description of the items being purchased.

Most restaurants use purchase specifications when purchasing meat, seafood, and produce (fruit and vegetables). For example, when purchasing ribs of beef, the specifications may be:

1. Grade—choice.
2. Weight—20 to 22 pounds.
3. Short ribs removed after measuring $1\frac{1}{2}$ inches from the "eye" of the rib.
4. The back should not have a heavy covering of fat.
5. Ribs should be aged 15 to 20 days.
6. Back bones should be separated from the seven rib bones.
7. Rib tied—Oven ready.

When purchasing fruit, the specifications usually list the size, weight, softness, brand, number desired, and, when appropriate, the color. A copy of purchase specifications is mailed, given, or faxed to the vendor before the food service establishment begins buying. In some cases, however, the purchase specifications are sent with the purchase order or written on the purchase order.

Purchase Orders

Purchase orders are used often in certain business operations, but only occasionally in the food service business. Large restaurant chains are more likely to use them than small or independent operators.

A **purchase order** is a written form that indicates to the vendor how many items are to be delivered to an establishment, and lists the prices for each item. (See Figure 11-3.) The order is usually signed by two of the following people: the owner, manager, purchasing agent, or chef. This form tells the vendor that if the items delivered compare favorably with the items and prices listed on the order, then payment will be made.

In most food service operations, one person is designated to do the purchasing. This person is usually called the *purchasing agent.* In small operations, this duty is often performed by the manager, assistant manager, or chef. In any case, the person doing the buying checks prices and quality with about three different vendors before the purchase order is sent to the one offering the best deal. Recently, the trend has been to compare vendor prices at the beginning of the year and purchase from one vendor throughout the year. This vendor is referred to as the primary vendor.

The purchase order is usually made out in triplicate (three copies). An original copy is sent to the vendor or, if both have fax (facsimile) machines, it is faxed to them. Copies are kept by the steward and the bookkeeper. The steward uses a copy of the purchase order to check the mer-

Hasenours Restaurant Barret and Oak Streets Louisville, KY 40222				Purchase Order No. 1492 Date: October 20, 20___
To: Jefferson Meat Co. 2868 Baster Avenue Louisville, KY 40222				
Ship To: Hasenours Restaurant Barrett and Oak Streets Louisville, KY 40222				
Date of Delivery: January 10, 20___ Deliver the items listed below, which are being purchased in accordance with descriptions and prices stated.				
Description	**Unit**	**Quantity**	**Unit Price**	**Amount**
Ribs of Beef — choice 20 to 22 lbs. Aged 15 to 20 days Short ribs removed	lb.	132 lb.	$2.95	$389.40
12 oz. Sirloin Steaks — choice $1\frac{1}{2}$-inch thick Packed for storage	lb.	288 lb.	$3.75	$1,080.00
Beef Chuck for Stew Cut into 1-inch cubes Grade Choice	lb.	40 lb.	$2.28	$91.20
			Total Cost	$1,560.60
				____________________ Purchasing Agent

Figure 11-3 *Purchase order form.*

chandise when it is delivered by the vendor. A bookkeeper uses a copy to check what was ordered against invoices and statements. Purchase orders eliminate controversy over what was ordered, how much was ordered, who ordered it, and when it was ordered. It is another tool used to exercise good business practices. The memory sometimes fails, which is why records are essential.

T I P S . . . ***To Insure Perfect Solutions***

To find the amount on the purchase order form, multiply the quantity times the unit price.

SUMMARY REVIEW

Prepare four purchase order forms as shown in this section. Work the following problems by finding the amount and total cost for all items. Assume that you are purchasing for Scarlet Oaks Vocational School, 3254 East Kemper Road, Cincinnati, Ohio. Use today's date and show the date of delivery as one week from that date.

1. Purchase Order No. 1493; To: Hands Packing Co., 8567 Spring Grove Avenue, Cincinnati, Ohio.

   Description: Ground Beef—Chuck
85% lean 15% suet
Medium grind
Quantity: 165 pounds
Unit Price: $2.10 per pound

   Description: 10-ounce Sirloin Steaks—Choice
$1\frac{1}{2}$-inch tail
Frozen
Quantity: 260 pounds
Unit Price: $3.96 per pound

   Description: 14 pounds pork loins—spine bones removed; rib and loin end are separated leaving 2 ribs on loin end. Tenderloin left on loin end.
Quantity: 84 pounds
Unit Price: $2.85 per pound

2. Purchase Order No. 1494; To: Ideal Bakers Supply, 458 Ross Avenue, Cincinnati, Ohio.

   Description: Cake Flour, 100 pounds
Quantity: 9
Unit Price: $24.58 per 100 pounds

   Description: Pastry flour, 100 pounds
Quantity: 9
Unit Price: $17.52 per 100 pounds

   Description: Powdered sugar, 10X, 25-pound bag
Quantity: 5
Unit Price: $9.01 per bag

   Description: Meringue powder, 10-pound box
Quantity: 3
Unit Price: $21.20 per box

3. Purchase Order No. 1495; To: Deluxe Foods, 6870 High Street, Hamilton, Ohio.

   Description: Tuna fish, light meat, chunk 24—13-ounce cans
   Quantity: 12 cases
   Unit Price: $42.89 per case

   Description: Coffee, drip grind, 12—2-pound cans
   Quantity: 5 cases
   Unit Price: $32.16 per case

   Description: Sliced pineapple, 50 count, 6—#10 cans
   Quantity: 13 cases
   Unit Price: $22.70 per case

   Description: Pear halves, 50 count, 6—#10 cans
   Quantity: 7 cases
   Unit Price: $21.50 per case

4. Purchase Order No. 1496; To: Surk's Meat Packing Co., 1520 Eastern Avenue, Covington, Kentucky.

   Description: Boston Butt, average, 4 pounds, cottage butt and blade bone removed.
   Quantity: 48 pounds
   Unit Price: $1.92 per pound

   Description: Ham, average, 12 pounds, shank bone removed
   Quantity: 36 pounds
   Unit Price: $2.12 per pound

   Description: Sausage, 6 to 1 pound
   Quantity: 26 pounds
   Unit Price: $1.79 per pound

   Description: Bacon, lean, 28 slices to 1 pound
   Quantity: 28 pounds
   Unit Price: $1.72 per pound

FAXING OR FACSIMILE

Information concerning *faxing* is being introduced in this chapter to make the food service student aware of this rapid communication system that is being used more and more in the food service industry. Purchase orders and specifications are examples of documents that are ideal for faxing.

Facsimile or the more popular term *fax machine* is a rapid way to communicate. It is a fairly old form of communicating that in recent years has been perfected to the point that it rivals the telephone and overnight delivery services. Years ago the machine was used by international companies, but at the time it did not become popular because it was slow in transmitting, and it was expensive and noisy.

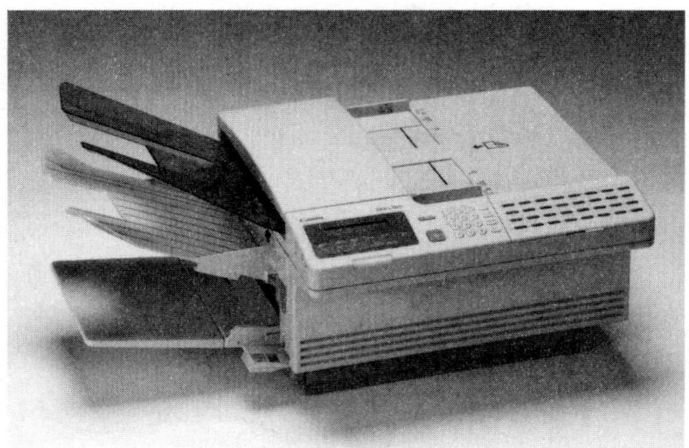

Figure 11-4 *Fax machine (Courtesy of Canon USA Inc.).*

Faxing equipment allows one to send and receive any type of text or graphic information over telephone lines. When transmitting the information, the machine scans the item being sent and converts it into electronic data. The data is sent by regular telephone lines to a receiving machine at a location selected by the sender. When received, the data is decoded and printed at the receiving fax. A fax machine is pictured in Figure 11-4.

To explain the process in simplified form, to send a fax you place the document being sent into the fax machine and dial the fax telephone number of the vendor. The document will pass through telephone lines and appear on the fax at the other end of the line. This unique communication device not only duplicates original documents at another location, it does so unattended. Faxes are ideal for ensuring important business transactions get to the right person at the right time. Remember that—in any business venture—receiving the right information at the proper time can translate into profits.

With most things, there are advantages and disadvantages. The advantages of faxing are:

1. Usually saves time and money.
2. Can transmit both text and graphic information of any length.
3. The information sent demands attention at the receiving end.
4. Most fax machines are simple to operate. Little or no training is required. It is just like dialing a telephone.
5. Messages received are easy to file.
6. The person for whom the message is intended need not be present.
7. The sender is informed that a message has been received or if there was a problem.
8. Simple or complicated information can be sent.

The disadvantages to faxing are:

1. Basic fax machines are simple to operate, but the more expensive ones with modern advanced features can be complicated and require training.

2. Because faxing has found new popularity in this country and the transmitting process is unique, curiosity may cause improper use.
3. With a fax machine, you may receive unsolicited transmissions.
4. Sometimes the messages received are of uneven quality. This will improve as technology improves.
5. Except for more expensive plain-paper faxes, paper quality is poor, often curly, and does not hold up for long-term filing.

Serious thought must go into making the decision as to whether a fax machine would be an asset in your food service operation. Consider the following questions: Do you exchange written information with the main office and your suppliers? Do you frequently request price quotes and need purchase orders immediately? Must weekly or biweekly inventories be sent to the home office? Would it be more convenient to fax your food orders to a vendor?

The more advanced models are multi-purpose and produce clearer and sharper text and graphic material. Keep in mind that now and in the future, speed of communication will be an asset for any business. Even though the telephone is fast and communication is instantaneous, all that is conveyed is not remembered. When faxing, you have written verification of all information conveyed.

Using today's technology, food service operations may order their purchases directly from the vendor via the computer and a modem. This method of ordering will be explained in detail in Chapter 12 (Computer Applications in Food Service Occupations).

Computer Applications in Food Service Occupations

OBJECTIVES

At the completion of this chapter, the student should be able to:

1. Identify computer hardware and software.
2. Write formulas and use them in spreadsheets.

The food service business is complex, competitive, fast-paced, and constantly changing. Escalating food and labor costs are always a major concern. With all of these variables confronting management, the need for quick, accurate information is essential. To obtain this information a computer is necessary in the food service operation.

The computer can be put to use in producing swift and precise results for most food service operational procedures. Procedures that used to take hours when done manually can now be done in minutes and stored for future reference with the help of the computer. This equipment will almost pay for itself with the hours of work saved.

Computers can assist management in calculating unit cost, extension figures, and totals when preparing the monthly inventory and daily food cost reports. They can record all necessary information for present and future use. Using a spreadsheet, management can view vital information with no more than a glance when filling out daily production reports or figuring standard recipe cost. Computers can also assist in pricing the menu by eliminating manual figuring. In addition, when financial statements such as profit and loss sheets, balance sheets, and budgeting are due, computers, with the help of a special software program, can assist in producing reports that are precise, accurate, and very easy to follow. Software programs have been developed and designed to assist the chef in calculating nutritional analyses in order to determine fat content, calories, and other factors. This allows a chef to create special menus for guests who have specific dietary concerns.

Business software can prove invaluable to the food service operator. There are large selections of programs, which include management programs, accounting packages, and developing manipulative skills programs to help the food service operator with just about any task. For many reasons, it is difficult to imagine a food service operator running a business without a computer. Today it would be unthinkable for someone to try to organize and analyze the endless amounts of paperwork without a computer to assist.

COMPUTER OPERATIONS IN THE FOOD SERVICE INDUSTRY

Computer companies can set up a food service management system using a personal computer, a desktop or laptop computer used at home and in business. Specially designed software programs can be installed that will provide management with up-to-date, easily accessible, and accurate information in all areas of a food service operation. The system will automate many functions that you now do manually such as those mentioned previously. It also assists in collecting specific information that will help in forecasting and other management decision making.

A computerized system can be set up in two ways: with data remaining within a food service establishment or sent to a centrally located office.

If the operation is individually owned and doing a large volume of business, the computerized system will produce printed reports or spreadsheets at the establishment. This convenience frees the manager to perform other important tasks.

If, on the other hand, the operation consists of a number of food service establishments in remote areas, such as a chain operation with one centrally located office, reports can be sent to that office over telephone wires using a **modem,** an instrument that will send information from one location to a remote location provided the other location has a modem as well. This type of computerized system allows operators to monitor several food service establishments from one office. (See Figure 12-1.)

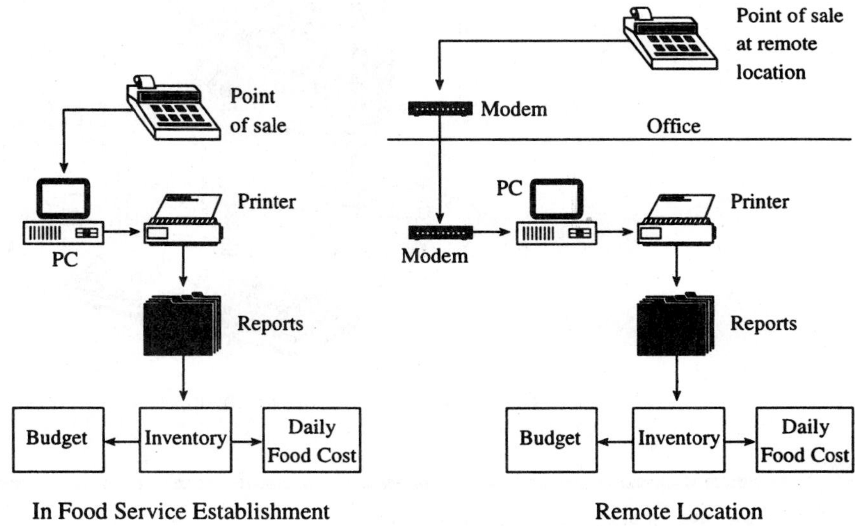

Figure 12-1 *Diagram of data flow.*

Computer Hardware

There are many types of computers and computerized registers available for the foodservice professional. All computers, regardless of their brand, contain hardware. Hardware is what makes up the physical part of the computer. Examples of hardware are the monitor, keyboard, central processing unit and printer.

- Central Processing Unit (System Unit)—a microchip that is the computer's brain.
- Monitor—Viewing screen (looks like a TV screen).
- Keyboard—input device.
- Touch screen—input device for point of sale.
- Disk and diskette drives—to copy and store information.
- Communications ports—to send and receive information.
- Printer—copies information on paper.

(See Figure 12-2)

For more specific explanation of the purpose of each piece of hardware the authors recommend that the student consult a textbook or take a course dedicated to computers. For the purpose of this book, we will concentrate on how computer software will assist the food service professional.

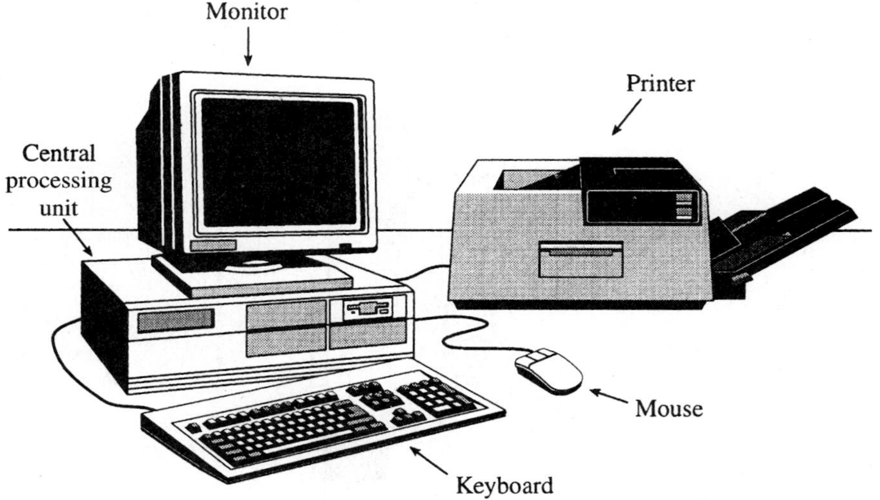

Figure 12-2 *Computer hardware.*

Computer Software

Computer software is the magic that gives the computer its countless personalities and makes it so versatile. **Software** is programs of instructions encoded on a disc or CD that resembles a very small record. The software instructs the computer how to perform. It takes the data (collection of information, facts, statistics, instructions, etc.) that is typed in and translates it into something the computer hardware components can understand. There are many different kinds of software available on the market. You purchase a diskette and load the instructions onto the computer for performing a specific task. The computer may be instructed to help in areas of writing, storing, communicating, retrieving information, etc. Each software program does a specific task on the computer, such as word processing, database management, and the construction of a spreadsheet.

Word processing is the system of recording, storing, and retrieving typewritten information. It can create almost any type of written document, from a routine memo to a manual that assists a new employee in the operation of the establishment. A big advantage to a word processor is that it allows you to make changes in your text quickly, accurately, and easily. It will also tell you when you have made spelling and grammatical errors. Some of the more popular word processors are WordPerfect and Microsoft Word.

Data base management is the sorting and categorizing of information or data. It can be looked upon as a computerized filing cabinet; keeping track of purchase orders, storeroom requisitions, invoices, and even the inventory. Within seconds you can determine what accounts still need to be paid, and determine what supplies are low and need to be ordered. Some of the more popular data base management software are ChefTec and ExecuChef.

ChefTec and ExecuChef combine data base management and spreadsheet for cost analysis and controls. The authors suggest that you contact them or other software companies to determine if their products will be beneficial. ChefTec can be contacted at *www.culinarysoftware.com* and ExecuChef at *www.execuchef.com.*

A **spreadsheet** is, for the most part, an electronic ledger. It is made up of rows and columns of boxes (referred to as *cells)* that you use in creating tables and graphs that help you run your business. Within the spreadsheet, you can tell the computer when you want specific numbers added, subtracted, multiplied, or divided. The number crunching capabilities of the spreadsheet makes it great for lists that involve a lot of numbers such as inventory, production reports, and budgets. Some of the more popular spreadsheets on the market today are 1-2-3 (Lotus) and Excel (Microsoft).

An **operating system** directs the flow of information to and from various parts of your computer, and is needed by your computer to run programs. A widely used operating system is called the Disc Operating System or DOS.

Many of the programs you will encounter will be found on a diskette or on the hard disc drive.

Spreadsheets

Spreadsheet programs such as Lotus and Microsoft Excel require that individuals have an understanding and working knowledge of math concepts and techniques because formulas must be devised and entered to make the software function correctly.

As mentioned before, a computer spreadsheet is made up of rows and columns. The columns are identified by letters at the top of the screen, and the rows by numbers along the left side of the screen. There will always be a highlighted cell identifying your location. (See Figure 12-3.)

	Column A	Column B	Column C	Column D	Column E
Row 1					
Row 2					
Row 3					
Row 4					
Row 5					

Figure 12-3 *Computer spreadsheet with highlighted cell D3.*

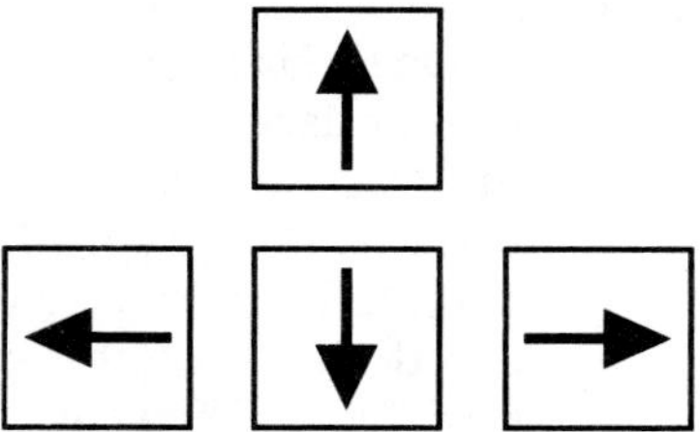

Figure 12-4 *Direction keys on a computer keyboard.*

In Figure 12-3, the shaded cell is the column labeled with D, and it is in the third row. We refer to this location as D3. When identifying a particular cell location, always put the column letter first and then the row number. It is within these cells that words and data are entered to create the tables to help in the running of the establishment. In order to move from one cell to the next, use the arrow keys on your keyboard. The direction the arrow is pointing is the direction that the highlighting will move. (See Figure 12-4.)

The counter production report, as discussed in Chapter 10, is one example of a spreadsheet. (See Figure 12-5.)

Entering information on a spreadsheet is much like entering it by hand. Figure 12-6 provides an example of a blank counter production report.

Now let us fill in the spreadsheet shown in Figure 12-6 using the following information: You are serving 340 people from Reeves Tire Company on Tuesday, January 10. There are 90 hot dogs for sale at $0.75 per hot dog and 76 are sold; there are 105 hamburgers for sale at $1.05 per hamburger and 91 are sold; there are 55 sausages for sale at $0.95 per sausage and 35 are sold.

	A	B	C	D	E
1	Unit ______________			Customer Count ______	
2	Day ______________			Date ______________	
3					
4 5 6	Item	Number of Portions For Sale	Number of Portions Sold	Unit Price	Value Sold
7					
8					
9					
10					
11					
12					
13					
14					
15					
16				Total	

Figure 12-5 *Counter production report, example of a spreadsheet.*

	A	B	C	D	E
1	Unit ______________			Customer Count ______	
2	Day ______________			Date ______________	
3					
4 5 6	Item	Number of Portions For Sale	Number of Portions Sold	Unit Price	Value Sold
7					
8					
9					
10					
11					
12					
13					
14					
15					
16					

Figure 12-6 *Blank counter production report.*

We will begin by typing in the company name, unit, the day of the week, the customer count, and the date. Your production report should now look like the one shown in Figure 12-7.

We will now enter the items for the report. Move the highlighted cell to A7 and type in Hamburgers. Now move the highlighted cell to A8 and type in Hot Dogs. Finally, move the highlighted cell to A9 and type in sausages. Your production report should look like the one shown in Figure 12-8.

	A	B	C	D	E
1	Unit Reeves Tire Company			Customer Count 340	
2	Day Tuesday			Date Jan 10, 20__	
3					
4–6	Item	Number of Portions For Sale	Number of Portions Sold	Unit Price	Value Sold
7					
8					
9					
10					
11					
12					
13					
14					
15					
16					

Figure 12-7 *Counter production report, step 1.*

	A	B	C	D	E
1	Unit Reeves Tire Company			Customer Count 340	
2	Day Tuesday			Date Jan 10, 20__	
3					
4–6	Item	Number of Portions For Sale	Number of Portions Sold	Unit Price	Value Sold
7	Hamburgers				
8	Hot Dogs				
9	Sausages				
10					
11					
12					
13					
14					
15					
16					

Figure 12-8 *Counter production report, step 2.*

We will now enter the number of portions for sale. Move the highlighted cell to B7 and type in 90. Now move the highlighted cell to B8 and type in 105. Finally, move the highlighted cell to B9 and type in 55. Your production report should look like the one shown in Figure 12-9.

Now we will enter the number of portions sold. Move the highlighted cell to C7 and type in 76. Now move the highlighted cell to C8 and type in 91. Finally, move the highlighted cell to C9 and type in 35. Your production report should look like the one shown in Figure 12-10.

	A	B	C	D	E
1	Unit Reeves Tire Company			Customer Count 340	
2	Day Tuesday			Date Jan 10, 20 ___	
3					
4–6	Item	Number of Portions For Sale	Number of Portions Sold	Unit Price	Value Sold
7	Hamburgers	90			
8	Hot Dogs	105			
9	Sausages	55			
10					
11					
12					
13					
14					
15					
16					

Figure 12-9 *Counter production report, step 3.*

	A	B	C	D	E
1	Unit Reeves Tire Company			Customer Count 340	
2	Day Tuesday			Date Jan 10, 20 ___	
3					
4–6	Item	Number of Portions For Sale	Number of Portions Sold	Unit Price	Value Sold
7	Hamburgers	90	76		
8	Hot Dogs	105	91		
9	Sausages	55	35		
10					
11					
12					
13					
14					
15					
16					

Figure 12-10 *Counter production report, step 4.*

	A	B	C	D	E
1	Unit Reeves Tire Company			Customer Count 340	
2	Day Tuesday			Date Jan 10, 20 __	
3					
4–6	Item	Number of Portions For Sale	Number of Portions Sold	Unit Price	Value Sold
7	Hamburgers	90	76	$ .75	
8	Hot Dogs	105	91	1.05	
9	Sausages	55	35	.95	
10					
11					
12					
13					
14					
15					
16				Total	

Figure 12-11 *Counter production report, step 5.*

Next, we will enter the unit price. First move the highlighted cell to D7 and type in .75. Now move the highlighted cell to D8 and type in 1.05. Then, move the highlighted cell to D9 and type in .95. Your production report should look like the one shown in Figure 12-11.

The key factor in making spreadsheets effective is the entering of formulas. The software program has to be instructed to multiply the number of portions sold (the C column) by the unit price (the D column) in order to equal the value sold (the E column). To do this correctly, a formula is entered using cell locations rather than the actual numbers of 76 (in cell C7) and $.75 (in cell D7). Figure 12-12 illustrates the formulas that must be entered to determine the amount of value sold that will be calculated in the E column. The formula that is in cell E7 (+C7*D7) commands the program to multiply the information in cell C7 by the information in cell D7. Notice the plus (+) sign before the first cell location address (+C7). This plus sign instructs the software to go to cell C7 and take whatever number is in that cell. If a plus sign is not used the letter C and number 7 will appear in cell E7 and the software program will not do the math. To inform the software to multiply, the star or asterisk (*) is placed between the two cell locations.

TIPS . . . ***To Insure Perfect Solutions***

In Lotus 1-2-3,

+ means **add;** – means **subtract;** * means **multiply;** / means **divide**

@Sum means **add up all the items specified in the cell address**

	A	B	C	D	E
1	Unit	Reeves Tire Company		Customer Count	340
2	Day	Tuesday		Date	Jan 10, 20 ___
3	Item	Number of Portions For Sale	Number of Portions Sold	Unit Price	Value Sold
4					
5					
6					
7	Hamburgers	90	76	.75	+C7*D7
8	Hot Dogs	105	91	1.05	+C8*D8
9	Sausages	55	35	.95	+C9*D9
10					
11	Total				@Sum(E7..E9)
12					
13					
14					
15					
16					
17					

Figure 12-12 *In this program + sign informs the computer program that a math formula is entered.*

Therefore, the formula in cell E7 means to take the number in cell C7 which is 76 and multiply it by the number in D7 which is .75. The formulas are shown for cells E8 and E9. In cell E11 the computer is being told to total the numbers (@sum) in cells E7 through E9 (E7..E9).

Figure 12-13 illustrates how the computer has calculated the value sold and the total sum of the sales for the day. Without having to do the calculations yourself, you will have more time to work on other aspects of the business.

In the event that you make a mistake, the computer can also save you time in correcting. In the spreadsheet shown in Figure 12-12, the price of a hot dog is $1.05. What if hot dogs were actually sold at $1.15?

If you were calculating it by hand you would have to go back and recalculate the value and then recalculate the total. Depending on the number of items, this could take quite some time. With the computer spreadsheet all you need to do is move the highlighted cell back to D8, and type in 1.15 in place of the 1.05 and the computer will automatically do all the recalculations for you. (See Figure 12-14.)

Computers are a time- and cost-saving invention. The description above illustrates why the food service professional must know math in order to develop and use a spreadsheet program.

If the professional does not want to develop a software program for his or her specific food service location, there are many software programs available that have been designed for the food service industry. Recipe and menu costing, as well as inventory control and nutritional analysis software can be purchased. Most of these software programs are easy to use and they have been developed by chefs. More restaurant executives

	A	B	C	D	E
1	Unit Reeves Tire Company			Customer Count 340	
2	Day Tuesday			Date Jan 10, 20 __	
3	Item	Number of Portions For Sale	Number of Portions Sold	Unit Price	Value Sold
4					
5					
6					
7	Hamburgers	90	76	.75	$ 57.00
8	Hot Dogs	105	91	1.05	$ 95.55
9	Sausages	55	35	.95	$ 33.25
10					
11	Total				$185.80
12					
13					
14					
15					
16				Total	
17					

Figure 12-13 *The computer has calculated the value sold and the total.*

	A	B	C	D	E
1	Unit Reeves Tire Company			Customer Count 340	
2	Day Tuesday			Date Jan 10, 20 __	
3					
4–6	Item	Number of Portions For Sale	Number of Portions Sold	Unit Price	Value Sold
7	Hamburgers	90	76	.75	$ 57.00
8	Hot Dogs	105	91	1.15	104.65
9	Sausages	55	35	.95	33.25
10					
11					
12					
13					
14					
15					
16				Total	$194.90

Figure 12-14 *Counter production report, recalculated.*

are discovering the benefits of using software programs such as ChefTec and ExecuChef. For example, in 1999 Marriott International signed an agreement with ChefTec to provide the recipe-costing and inventory-control system software for Marriott's hotels worldwide. ExecuChef has developed a student software program for the chef in training, which is called Chef Apprentice. Some of the tasks that Chef Apprentice will provide are food cost analysis, metric conversions, and A.P. to E.P. cost conversions, plus a variety of other functions.

Point of Sale Computers

Computers have also revolutionized the dining experience. In many restaurants, the waitstaff enters the order of the guest into a computer called Point of Sales (POS) either via a touch screen or a handheld terminal. The order is then transmitted to printers in the kitchen. The culinary staff prepares the orders as they are printed in the kitchen. These computerized POS systems save time for food service professionals in many ways—in taking inventory, making reports, handling accounting, etc. The systems will calculate the total amount of meals served, the individual items ordered, and numerous other reports that enable a chef to manage the kitchen effectively. Some point of sale computers are integrated with inventory programs; when an item is ordered the inventory is updated instantaneously. The computer has been programmed to know the ingredients in each item ordered. Every time an item is ordered, the computer program subtracts the amount from its inventory data base. The chef must know math basics in order to eyeball the reports and determine if the computer is programmed incorrectly.

Purchasing Food Using the Computer

Most major food purveyors (SYSCO, Alliant, USFoodservice) have a software program that enables a food service professional to place orders using the computer and a modem. This allows information to be transmitted directly (See Figure 12-15).

Each purveyor has developed a software program that lists all of their products offered for sale. The products are categorized (e.g., fish, meat, poultry), or they may be looked up alphabetically. Each product lists information concerning quality, pack, size, and pricing. Many programs also give the buyer nutritional information about the product. Once the purchaser decides how much food to order, the food order is entered into the computer and transmitted to the purveyor. The food company delivers the order at the next scheduled delivery. The food service professional can print the order, invoice, and the receiver's copy with or without prices before it arrives at the establishment. The purveyor can also give the food service professional a list of products and amounts purchased during a specific time period.

In this chapter, our purpose has been to introduce you to the computer and how it might be used in one simple food service function, hoping to impress upon you the importance this very versatile tool plays in a present-day food service operation and how it will continue to become

Figure 12-15 *Computer operator at work*

◆ *Chef Sez . . .*

"Computers are an important tool for me to do my job at HersheyPark. In preparing over 26,000 meals daily in our 51 food service units, we have to have the correct amount of food available and prepared for our guests. Each night our inventory is counted and entered into the computer. We are then able to replenish our food. Our point of sale computers are linked up with our main frame, so at any time I can determine our food and labor cost. We are able to forecast and prepare the correct amount of food, because we can determine the attendance at the park at any time."

Charlie Gipe
Executive Chef/Pippins Manager
HERSHEYPARK
Hershey, Pennsylvania

Chef Grip manages three of the 51 food units at the 110-acre HersheyPark. The park opened on April 24, 1907, and was made a regional entertainment complex in 1971 with a one price admission charge. In addition to the shows, rides, and entertainment, the park has six roller coasters and a zoo that was opened in 1916.

more important in the future. In any new venture, in your attempt to develop a skill, whether it be driving a car, learning to type, or using a French knife properly, confidence is developed by practice . . . constant practice. If you have access to a computer at home or school, practice when the opportunity presents itself. If a computer course is offered at your school or elsewhere, take advantage of the opportunity. It is a skill that will be needed for future employment in most fields of endeavor.

SUMMARY REVIEW

Enter the computer formula to determine the amount of food served for each item. Use today's day and date.

1. Unit—2nd National Bank

   Meal—Luncheon Day of week _______

   Customers—177 Date ______________

	A	B	C	D
	Item	Portion Prepared	Portion's Left	Formula
1	Sautéed Pork Chops	63	5	
2	Salisbury Steak	57	2	
3	Beef Pot Roast	67	3	
4	Au Gratin Potatoes	112	1	
5	Succotash	128	6	
6	Escallop Potatoes	75	9	
7	Cut Green Beans	57	2	
8	Total of Pork, Beef and Steak			
9	Total of Potatoes			
10	Total of Succotash and Beans			

2. Unit—Harold Steel Mill

   Meal—Luncheon Day of week _______

   Customers—132 Date ______________

	A	B	C	D
1	Item	Portion Prepared	Portions Left Over	Formula
2	Ham Steak	27	2	
3	Roast Turkey	43	5	
4	Flank Steak	39	2	
5	Hamburger	35	3	
6	Mashed Potatoes	167	35	
7	Mixed Greens	39	4	
8	Corn O'Brien	26	2	
9	Peas and Onions	78	5	
10	Total of Meat Items			
11	Total of Potatoes			
12	Total of Vegetables			

Waiting Tables, Guest Checks, and Tipping

OBJECTIVES

At the completion of this chapter, the student should be able to:

1. Identify the different methods of taking guest orders.
2. Identify how to place an order in the kitchen.
3. Identify the different types of guest checks that are used to charge guests for their food and/or beverage.
4. Identify the terms *minimum* and *cover charge.*
5. Calculate sales tax.
6. Calculate the amount of tip.
7. Find the total amount of a guest check.

DINING ROOM STATIONS

The dining room of a food service establishment is usually divided into serving sections called **stations.** The individual in charge of these serving sections may be the **host/hostess, captain,** or **maitre d'.** Each station consists of a number of tables and chairs, booths, or section of a counter. Either the stations are numbered, the tables are numbered on the floor, or a floor plan is posted in the kitchen area outlining the arrangement of the dining room. It is the responsibility of the serving crew (waitperson and bus person) to learn the location of each service station and the number of customers that can be seated in their area of responsibility.

Each waitperson is assigned a station by the individual in charge of the dining area. Figure 13–1 shows a waitperson setting a table. This is their primary area of responsibility. All the guests seated in the area are greeted and served by the person assigned to the area. The table number (or numbers) assigned to a station is placed on the guest check to eliminate confusion if there is a problem or when the serving person is relieved or assisted by another member of the service crew. These stations may be assigned to a waitperson each day or once a week. Station assignments are changed frequently because some stations are more desirable than others. Guests generally tip greater amounts in the desirable areas. This is particularly true in establishments that have entertainment or provide a scenic view.

Figure 13-1 *Wait-person setting table.*

Greeting Guests and Taking the Order

As guests approach a service area, they should be greeted in an appropriate manner. Most establishments have their own standard procedure for greeting guests. Always smile and be cheerful. Assist the host/hostess or captain in seating the guests; never stand with arms folded. Check the table to be sure all necessary equipment is present and in its proper place. Fill the glasses with ice water while the host/hostess or captain presents the menu.

The waitperson stands to the left of the guest with an order form or a handheld computerized order pad and begins to fill in the required information. Then the waitperson takes the order according to the following steps:

1. Entree selection is taken first. Ask how the item is to be cooked if this information applies to the selected item. Examples: roast beef, steaks, or chops—well done, medium, or rare. Notice whether the guests are ordering a la carte or table d'hote, since pricing will be different.
2. Appetizer selection. There may be an extra charge for this.
3. Salad selection and dressing desired. Name the dressings that are available.
4. Vegetable, if one is included, and potato selection. If a baked potato is selected, do they prefer butter or sour cream?
5. Beverage selection. If coffee is selected, would they like it served with the meal or with dessert?
6. Dessert selection. If this is not included on the table d'hote menu, an extra charge must be made.

Med	Medium	Din.	Dinner
R.	Rare	Cof.	Coffee
W.D.	Well Done	Choc.	Chocolate
N.Y.	New York	Fr.Fr.	French Fries
T.I.	Thousand Island Dressing	Van.	Vanilla
Fr.D.	French Dressing	Tom.	Tomato
Sm.	Small	Ch.	Cheese
Lg.	Large	St. B.	String Beans

Figure 13-2 *Common abbreviations for taking orders.*

Certain abbreviations are used by the waitperson when taking an order to speed up the process. Some of the common abbreviations are given in Figure 13-2.

Systems of Taking Food Orders

There are two systems used for taking the food orders and filling out the check:

1. The guest writes the order; or
2. The waitperson takes a verbal order from the guest.

Guest Writes Own Order

System No. 1 is usually used in private clubs, on trains, or in some in-plant food service operations. The guest is given a check and a pencil and is instructed to write the desired order. This is not a very popular system. When it is used, the following procedure is recommended:

1. Present the menu to the guest.
2. Make sure the information at the top of each check is completed.
3. Provide the guest with a check and a sharp pencil.
4. If the guest is hesitant to make out the check, offer assistance.
5. Your approach should be, "Would you please write your own order? I will return for it shortly."
6. Collect the checks and go to the kitchen to place and assemble the orders.
7. When the food is served, enter the proper prices for each item listed. Extend the prices if there are two or more orders of the same item.
8. Total the check carefully to find the correct subtotal.
9. Enter the proper amount of tax. This is usually found by consulting a tax table.
10. Calculate the total and check all figures. Steps 7 through 10 may not be necessary if a computerized cash register is used.

Taking Verbal Orders

In System No. 2, the waitperson takes a verbal order from the guest, and either writes the order on a scratch pad later transferring the order to a sales check, writes the order directly on the sales check, or enters the order into a computer terminal. Taking the order on a scratch pad first will usually produce a clearer, neater check. This system is by far the most popular because the guests feel they are getting more service. When this system is used the following procedure is recommended:

1. Present the menu to the guest.
2. Fill out the required information at the top of the check.
3. Enter on the check all items requested or make a list of all items for entry into the computer.
4. Take checks to the kitchen to place and assemble the order.
5. Enter the proper prices for each item listed. Extend prices correctly. Find subtotals. Steps 4-7 are not necessary if a computerized cash register is used.
6. Enter the proper amount of tax. This is usually found by consulting a tax table. (See Figure 13-10.)
7. Calculate the total and check all figures.

◆ *Chef Sez . . .*

"Chefs need to learn the books, the Profit and Loss statement. You might be very talented, but if you can't control the numbers, you can't make any money. You've got to know the cost of food, when products are out of season and costly, and when they are in season and are a good buy. So, you see, you can be talented, but you also need to think like a business owner."

Rodney Renshaw
Executive Chef
The Savoy
Washington, DC

Chef Renshaw was featured in the May 10, 1999, Culinary Currents of *Nation's Restaurant News,* written by Milford Prewitt. Besides the above quote, Prewitt also writes that "Renshaw is one of a growing number of black chefs, striving to catapult African-American cuisine into the realm of fine dining." The Savoy is a supper club that features live jazz and true Southern fine dining in Washington, D.C.

A La Carte

Some quality or gourmet restaurants feature an **a la carte** menu (items priced separately) as well as a **table d'hote** menu (complete dinner). For a la carte orders, each item is priced separately. If the guest orders a crabmeat cocktail, the price of the crabmeat cocktail shown on the a la carte menu is recorded on the check. The guest may proceed to order a broiled sirloin steak, hash brown potatoes, side salad and coffee, and in each case a price for that particular item is recorded on the guest check.

A la carte menus are preferred by certain guests such as those who do not like the selections offered on the table d'hote menu, those who are on diets, or those who wish to order only one or two courses.

Ordering from the table d'hote menu is the simplest and most economical way of dining out. The total price is usually shown opposite the entree (main course). The price usually includes salad, potato or starch food item, vegetable, entree, bread and butter, beverage, and, in some cases, dessert. From restaurant to restaurant you will find variations of the table d'hote menu. Some offer more than others. Selections on this type of menu are fairly extensive. The intent is to present items that will satisfy most appetites. This is why the selections include fish or shellfish, beef, pork, chicken, turkey, and sometimes veal and pasta.

Placing the Order in the Kitchen

After the orders are taken, the waitperson gathers the menus and goes to the preparation or kitchen area. The waitperson is responsible for assembling juices, relishes, crackers, soups, bread, butter, condiments, and beverages. The **entree** is ordered from the cooking station responsible for that particular preparation. For example, broiled foods are ordered from the broiler cook; fried foods from the fry cook; stews, potted meats, and sautéed foods from the second cook; and so on. In smaller restaurants, all foods can be ordered and picked up in one area. When the foods are ready, it may be the responsibility of the waitperson to pick them up and garnish them for service. Remember that food must first be ordered before it can be picked up. At times, the waitperson will forget to place the orders resulting in the start of arguments and general confusion.

After all foods are assembled and placed on a waitperson's tray, the tray is taken to the expediter (food checker) who checks to see that only those items ordered by the guests are on the tray. This is done to control portions and food cost. The foods are then served to the guests in the proper order and fashion.

Presenting the Check

At the conclusion of the meal, take the check to the cashier with all the necessary information required so that the cashier can process the check according to the proper accounting procedures. The register will print out most of the necessary information automatically, neatly, and legibly letting the guest know just what he or she is paying for and, usually with great concern, how much each item cost. Before presenting the check to the guest, check to see that all information is correct.

The check may be presented to the guest in a number of ways. You may place the check under the edge of the guest's plate if single checks are given or under the host's plate if only one check for a group is given. The check can also be placed on a small tray, usually to the left of the guest. In any case, the check is presented face down if payment is to be made to a cashier when the guest leaves (see Figure 13-3), or is collected by the waitperson at the end of the meal. If collection is to be made at the time the check is presented, it is then placed face up. Another popular practice, especially in the finer gourmet restaurants, is to present the check in a special book-type folder. The guest will check the bill and place the payment or credit card in the folder. The waitperson will return and take the folder to the cashier for payment. If a credit card is used, they will return for a signature.

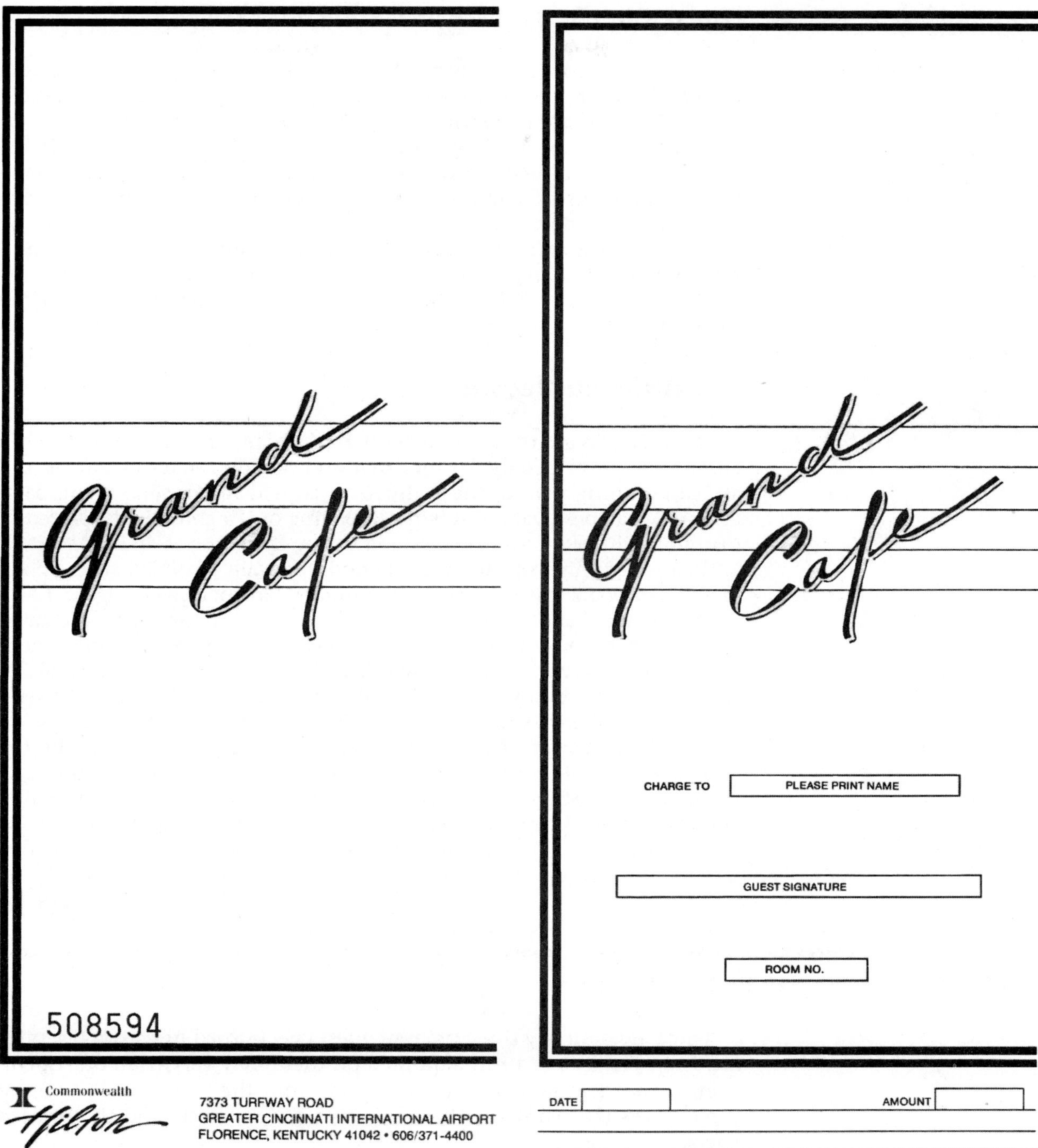

Grand Cafe

508594

Commonwealth Hilton

7373 TURFWAY ROAD
GREATER CINCINNATI INTERNATIONAL AIRPORT
FLORENCE, KENTUCKY 41042 • 606/371-4400

Grand Cafe

CHARGE TO | PLEASE PRINT NAME

GUEST SIGNATURE

ROOM NO.

DATE | AMOUNT

Figure 13-3 *Guest check returned with amounts face down.*

Figure 13-4 *Guest check—back side used to add check amount to room.*

In many hotel or motel dining rooms, the guest can sign the check and have the amount added to the total bill. (See Figure 13-4.) Payment is then made when the guest checks out. In such cases, be sure the room number is on the check.

Guest Check

In the food service industry, the bill or bill of sale is called a **guest check.** It is a list of items ordered and the cost of those items tallied when dining in a food service establishment. (See Figure 13-5.) In addition, a guest check will have other information listed on it. This information will be pointed out when explaining the types of checks usually used in the industry. The appearance of a guest check will vary from simple to elaborate depending on the type and kind of operation. From the roadside truck stop to the gourmet restaurant, guest checks are in use and presented at the conclusion of the meal. The one exception is the fast-food establishment, where the check is presented before or when the food is received.

Guest Check Responsibility

Guest checks are the responsibility of the waitperson. Although other employees are guided by the information listed on the check during and after the dining period, the waitperson is held responsible for its safekeeping. If a guest walks out without paying or if a check is misplaced or lost, the waitperson may be required to pay the amount due.

At the beginning of the dining period, the waitperson is issued a book or stack of blank checks with serial numbers on them. (See Figure 13-6.) Each individual check is numbered consecutively. The waitperson usually signs for each book or stack of checks received. In this way, management can account for each check issued. If a check is missing, it will indicate which person is responsible. At the end of the day or at the end of a service period, the checks are reviewed to determine whether any are missing or contain any errors. Numbering checks and being able to identify the person responsible for each check are also important in checking the daily receipts and assisting the accounting department or accountant in finding and correcting any errors. Never destroy or discard a check without receiving permission from your supervisor. Remember that controls are necessary in any business operation. Guest checks are just one device used.

TYPES OF GUEST CHECKS

There are basically three types of guest checks used in the food service industry. The information requested on them may vary from one operation to another. Basically they will all fit into the framework of one of three types: the blank check, the partly printed check, and the printed check.

Blank Checks

The blank check is used most often on the luncheon and dinner menu in quality restaurants that use computerized registers. Most of the information requested on the check is printed on it when the waitperson presses certain keys assigned to print out specific information.

Riverview Revolving Restaurant | Quality Hotel | Dock Side VI | Prime 'n Wine

065040 6

FRISCH'S RESTAURANTS, INC.
Motels & Specialty Restaurants
2800 Gilbert Avenue
Cincinnati, Ohio 45206

94-014583 NCR PATS. 4.259.569. D-261.007 R

ITEMS	SERV	PERS	LOC.	TABLE	TIME	DATE	CHECK NO.
65040	45	1	1	1	03:10	03/18/	650406

```
            ‡44 K BUR FF                1.50
            ‡44 K BUR FF                1.50
0398 TAX SUM .17
     CHECK SUM                          3.17

                 CHECK 650406 SETTLED
                          DIN PAID      3.17
     TAX                                 .00
             CHK TOTL                   3.17
     CSH TEND 3.17                BALNCE .00
   L1 45   T1 03:13PM 08/18/93 M1 0399
```

Riverview | Quality Hotel | Dock Side VI | Prime 'n Wine — DATE | AMOUNT

Figure 13-5 *Itemized guest check.*

LaRosa's

Date	Server	Table No.	No. Persons	No. 487176
1				
2				
3				
4				
5				
6				
7				
8				
9				
10				
11				
12				
13				
14				
15				
16				
17				
18				
19				
20				
21				
22			SUBTOTAL	
23			TAX	
24			TOTAL	
—				No. 487176
Date	Guest Receipt	Persons	Amount of Check	

LaRosa's

Figure 13-6 *Blank check.*

The blank check is inserted into a slot in the printer and the waitperson will press assigned keys that print vital information on the blank check such as: the date, server's number, table number or location, time, number of people served, check number, all food and drink items ordered, cost of each item ordered, state tax and the guest check total. It may also include any other information the owner or manager feels is necessary to keep track of cash or credit sales and assist the accounting department.

Before our modern computerized registers, the information requested on the blank guest check was handwritten. This procedure is still followed in some of the smaller operations that cannot afford computerized registers. Handwritten blank checks often cause a problem for the people that depend on the information listed. Consequently, it is important for the waitperson to have legible handwriting. The cook must be able to read it to fill the food order, the cashier must be able to understand the figures, the manager may wish to examine it for various reasons, and certainly the customer or guest will want to read the check.

Partly Printed Checks

Partly printed checks are used in food service operations that have a limited menu because most of the items listed are best sellers and appear daily. (See Figure 13-7.) This type of check speeds service and reduces errors. The standard menu items and the popular beverages that appear each day are listed, but their prices are not. If a computerized register is used, most of the information requested on the check is printed on the back when the waitperson presses specific keys. When this type of register is not available, the waitperson must record all or part of the information requested at the top of the check, list quantities and prices, find the subtotal, add the tax, and calculate the total.

Printed Checks

Printed checks have names or abbreviations of all food and beverage items printed on them. (See Figures 13-8 and 13-9.) This type of guest check is popular in fast-food operations, specialty houses, and ethnic operations. Printed checks are designed to speed service and reduce errors. Not too long ago, prices were also listed on this type of check, but that practice was eliminated when the cost of food started to fluctuate rapidly. The restaurants using printed checks feature a specialty menu with the same food and beverage selection each day. If the guest check shown in Figure 13-8 is used, the waitperson records any information requested at the top of the check, circles or underscores the selected items, writes in prices, finds the subtotal, adds tax, and calculates the total. At the bottom of that check is listed total 1st - 2nd - 3rd. This is for the convenience of the waitperson if totals must be changed. For example, if the waitperson has totaled the check, but the guest decides to purchase a dessert, the total would have to be changed.

The printed check shown in Figure 13-9 is one used for breakfast in an establishment that has a computerized register. When this type of register is used, as pointed out previously, the items purchased, prices, and tax are listed on the back of the check. Note that each item listed on this guest check has been numbered. These numbers are the ones that are pressed into the computer register when that item has been purchased by the guest. The computerized register is quite efficient, accurate, and fast, but all food service establishments cannot afford them. For this reason, it becomes necessary for the waitperson to be able to fill these checks out by hand.

ZINO'S 7833

Server	Table No.	No. Guests	No. Checks

PIZZA Large	Medium	Small	

D. D.	CLUB	STEAK	
SOLE	SUB.		
MTBL.	S.SUB		
TUNA	ZNVR.	F. F.	

G.P.	DU JOUR	ONION	
M. COAST	W. COAST		
TOSSED			

SP. SCE.	SP. MTBL.	
SP. MUSH.	LASAGNE	
V. PARM.		
	BROWN	
SEAFOOD	BEEF	
CHP. BF.	SPECIAL	

SOFT DRINK	LG	SM	
BEER	LG	SM	

SUBTOTAL
TAX
TOTAL

Figure 13-7 *Partly printed check.*

Frisch's® BIG BOY®

SERVER NO.	LOCATION	NO. PERSONS	CONTROL
			B 03655-12

SC. UP. O.L. O.M. O.W. H
USE THESE ABBREVIATIONS BELOW

1	TST. EGGS-2	H	B	S	HBR GT
2	TST. EGGS-2	H	B	S	JUICE
3	TST. EGG-1	H	B	S	HBR GT
4	TST. EGGS-2		10 TST. EGG-1		
5	CAKES-2 EGG-1	H	B	S	
6	CAKES-3	H	B	S	
7	CAKES-2		11 CAKE-1		
8	FR. TST.-3	H	B	S	
9	FR. TST.-1 EGGS-2				HBR GT
16	EGGS-2 TST.	17 EGG-1 TST.	H	B	S
18	EGGS-2 HBR-TST.	19 EGG-1 HBR-TST.			

BRK BAR CHILD FREE
SR #1 42 B S #2 43 B S #3 44 JUICE #4 45 B S
MINI 20 #1B 21 #1S 22 #2B 23 #2S
OMELETTE
13 PANCAKES 14 CAKES-2 15 CAKE-1
24 FR TOAST 25 2-SLICES 26 1-SLICE
SIDES 27 HAM 28 BAC 29 SAUS
30 HBR 31 BISC-GRAVY 32 GRITS
33 TOAST 34 BISC 35 ENG MUF
48 STK & EGG 428 FRT CUP
PASTRY 36 NUT 37 FRUIT CEREAL 38 DRY 39 OM
COF DECAF TEA HOT CHOC
MILK LG CHOC LG
40 SMALL JUICE 41 LARGE JUICE G LG T LG O LG
NCR Business Forms Division GRATUITY NOT INCLUDED #247 9/90

Figure 13-8 *Printed check (Courtesy of Frisch's Restaurant Inc.).*

TRELLIS RESTAURANT
MERCHANT'S SQUARE

0383 Table 42 #Party 8
BRYAN S SvrCk: 19 18:58 12/30/99

3 CLOS DU BOIS MERLOT	103.50
3 LENTIL APPETIZER	23.85
1 CHOWDER	4.95
2 SAUSAGE APPETIZER	17.50
1 SHRIMP APPETIZER	9.50
1 TROUT APPETIZER	8.95
6 PORK ENTREE	112.50
1 DUCK ENTREE, med well	24.50
1 WINTER SUPPER	20.00
2 ICE CREAM	7.90
1 BALLOON	4.95
1 PASTRY 5.95	5.95
4 DEATH BY CHOCOLATE	22.00
5 COFFEE	9.75
1 hot tea	1.95
1 GL/SUDUIRAUT	11.50
1 GALLIANO, rocks	5.00
Sub Total:	394.25
TX1:	37.45
12/30 20:29 TOTAL:	431.70

DESSERTS TO GO
DAZZLING CAKES BY THE SLICE
COLOSSAL COOKIES, ONE OR A DOZEN
ICE CREAM AND SORBETS BY THE CUP OR PINT

CHECK NUMBER: 383

Figure 13-9 *Printed check used for computerized cash register.*

6% SALES TAX COLLECTION BRACKET

Amt. of Sale	Tax	Amt. of Sale	Tax	Amt. of Sale	Tax	Amt. of Sale	Tax	Amt. of Sale	Tax
.09 to .24	.01	10.09 to 10.24	.61	20.09 to 20.24	1.21	30.09 to 30.24	1.81	40.09 to 40.24	2.41
.25 " .41	.02	10.25 " 10.41	.62	20.25 " 20.41	1.22	30.25 " 30.41	1.82	40.25 " 40.41	2.42
.42 " .58	.03	10.42 " 10.58	.63	20.42 " 20.58	1.23	30.42 " 30.58	1.83	40.42 " 40.58	2.43
.59 " .74	.04	10.59 " 10.74	.64	20.59 " 20.74	1.24	30.59 " 30.74	1.84	40.59 " 40.74	2.44
.75 " .91	.05	10.75 " 10.91	.65	20.75 " 20.91	1.25	30.75 " 30.91	1.85	40.75 " 40.91	2.45
.92 " 1.08	.06	10.92 " 11.08	.66	20.92 " 21.08	1.26	30.92 " 31.08	1.86	40.92 " 41.08	2.46
1.09 " 1.24	.07	11.09 " 11.24	.67	21.09 " 21.24	1.27	31.09 " 31.24	1.87	41.09 " 41.24	2.47
1.25 " 1.41	.08	11.25 " 11.41	.68	21.25 " 21.41	1.28	31.25 " 31.41	1.88	41.25 " 41.41	2.48
1.42 " 1.58	.09	11.42 " 11.58	.69	21.42 " 21.58	1.29	31.42 " 31.58	1.89	41.42 " 41.58	2.49
1.59 " 1.74	.10	11.59 " 11.74	.70	21.59 " 21.74	1.30	31.59 " 31.74	1.90	41.59 " 41.74	2.50
1.75 " 1.91	.11	11.75 " 11.91	.71	21.75 " 21.91	1.31	31.75 " 31.91	1.91	41.75 " 41.91	2.51
1.92 " 2.08	.12	11.92 " 12.08	.72	21.92 " 22.08	1.32	31.92 " 32.08	1.92	41.92 " 42.08	2.52
2.09 " 2.24	.13	12.09 " 12.24	.73	22.09 " 22.24	1.33	32.09 " 32.24	1.93	42.09 " 42.24	2.53
2.25 " 2.41	.14	12.25 " 12.41	.74	22.25 " 22.41	1.34	32.25 " 32.41	1.94	42.25 " 42.41	2.54
2.42 " 2.58	.15	12.42 " 12.58	.75	22.42 " 22.58	1.35	32.42 " 32.58	1.95	42.42 " 42.58	2.55
2.59 " 2.74	.16	12.59 " 12.74	.76	22.59 " 22.74	1.36	32.59 " 32.74	1.96	42.59 " 42.74	2.56
2.75 " 2.91	.17	12.75 " 12.91	.77	22.75 " 22.91	1.37	32.75 " 32.91	1.97	42.75 " 42.91	2.57
2.92 " 3.08	.18	12.92 " 13.08	.78	22.92 " 23.08	1.38	32.92 " 33.08	1.98	42.92 " 43.08	2.58
3.09 " 3.24	.19	13.09 " 13.24	.79	23.09 " 23.24	1.39	33.09 " 33.24	1.99	43.09 " 43.24	2.59
3.25 " 3.41	.20	13.25 " 13.41	.80	23.25 " 23.41	1.40	33.25 " 33.41	2.00	43.25 " 43.41	2.60
3.42 " 3.58	.21	13.42 " 13.58	.81	23.42 " 23.58	1.41	33.42 " 33.58	2.01	43.42 " 43.58	2.61
3.59 " 3.74	.22	13.59 " 13.74	.82	23.59 " 23.74	1.42	33.59 " 33.74	2.02	43.59 " 43.74	2.62
3.75 " 3.91	.23	13.75 " 13.91	.83	23.75 " 23.91	1.43	33.75 " 33.91	2.03	43.75 " 43.91	2.63
3.92 " 4.08	.24	13.92 " 14.08	.84	23.92 " 24.08	1.44	33.92 " 34.08	2.04	43.92 " 44.08	2.64
4.09 " 4.24	.25	14.09 " 14.24	.85	24.09 " 24.24	1.45	34.09 " 34.24	2.05	44.09 " 44.24	2.65
4.25 " 4.41	.26	14.25 " 14.41	.86	24.25 " 24.41	1.46	34.25 " 34.41	2.06	44.25 " 44.41	2.66
4.42 " 4.58	.27	14.42 " 14.58	.87	24.42 " 24.58	1.47	34.42 " 34.58	2.07	44.42 " 44.58	2.67
4.59 " 4.74	.28	14.59 " 14.74	.88	24.59 " 24.74	1.48	34.59 " 34.74	2.08	44.59 " 44.74	2.68
4.75 " 4.91	.29	14.75 " 14.91	.89	24.75 " 24.91	1.49	34.75 " 34.91	2.09	44.75 " 44.91	2.69
4.92 " 5.08	.30	14.92 " 15.08	.90	24.92 " 25.08	1.50	34.92 " 35.08	2.10	44.92 " 45.08	2.70
5.09 " 5.24	.31	15.09 " 15.24	.91	25.09 " 25.24	1.51	35.09 " 35.24	2.11	45.09 " 45.24	2.71
5.25 " 5.41	.32	15.25 " 15.41	.92	25.25 " 25.41	1.52	35.25 " 35.41	2.12	45.25 " 45.41	2.72
5.42 " 5.58	.33	15.42 " 15.58	.93	25.42 " 25.58	1.53	35.42 " 35.58	2.13	45.42 " 45.58	2.73
5.59 " 5.74	.34	15.59 " 15.74	.94	25.59 " 25.74	1.54	35.59 " 35.74	2.14	45.59 " 45.74	2.74
5.75 " 5.91	.35	15.75 " 15.91	.95	25.75 " 25.91	1.55	35.75 " 35.91	2.15	45.75 " 45.91	2.75
5.92 " 6.08	.36	15.92 " 16.08	.96	25.92 " 26.08	1.56	35.92 " 36.08	2.16	45.92 " 46.08	2.76
6.09 " 6.24	.37	16.09 " 16.24	.97	26.09 " 26.24	1.57	36.09 " 36.24	2.17	46.09 " 46.24	2.77
6.25 " 6.41	.38	16.25 " 16.41	.98	26.25 " 26.41	1.58	36.25 " 36.41	2.18	46.25 " 46.41	2.78
6.42 " 6.58	.39	16.42 " 16.58	.99	26.42 " 26.58	1.59	36.42 " 36.58	2.19	46.42 " 46.58	2.79
6.59 " 6.74	.40	16.59 " 16.74	1.00	26.59 " 26.74	1.60	36.59 " 36.74	2.20	46.59 " 46.74	2.80
6.75 " 6.91	.41	16.75 " 16.91	1.01	26.75 " 26.91	1.61	36.75 " 36.91	2.21	46.75 " 46.91	2.81
6.92 " 7.08	.42	16.92 " 17.08	1.02	26.92 " 27.08	1.62	36.92 " 37.08	2.22	46.92 " 47.08	2.82
7.09 " 7.24	.43	17.09 " 17.24	1.03	27.09 " 27.24	1.63	37.09 " 37.24	2.23	47.09 " 47.24	2.83
7.25 " 7.41	.44	17.25 " 17.41	1.04	27.25 " 27.41	1.64	37.25 " 37.41	2.24	47.25 " 47.41	2.84
7.42 " 7.58	.45	17.42 " 17.58	1.05	27.42 " 27.58	1.65	37.42 " 37.58	2.25	47.42 " 47.58	2.85
7.59 " 7.74	.46	17.59 " 17.74	1.06	27.59 " 27.74	1.66	37.59 " 37.74	2.26	47.59 " 47.74	2.86
7.75 " 7.91	.47	17.75 " 17.91	1.07	27.75 " 27.91	1.67	37.75 " 37.91	2.27	47.75 " 47.91	2.87
7.92 " 8.08	.48	17.92 " 18.08	1.08	27.92 " 28.08	1.68	37.92 " 38.08	2.28	47.92 " 48.08	2.88
8.09 " 8.24	.49	18.09 " 18.24	1.09	28.09 " 28.24	1.69	38.09 " 38.24	2.29	48.09 " 48.24	2.89
8.25 " 8.41	.50	18.25 " 18.41	1.10	28.25 " 28.41	1.70	38.25 " 38.41	2.30	48.25 " 48.41	2.90
8.42 " 8.58	.51	18.42 " 18.58	1.11	28.42 " 28.58	1.71	38.42 " 38.58	2.31	48.42 " 48.58	2.91
8.59 " 8.74	.52	18.59 " 18.74	1.12	28.59 " 28.74	1.72	38.59 " 38.74	2.32	48.59 " 48.74	2.92
8.75 " 8.91	.53	18.75 " 18.91	1.13	28.75 " 28.91	1.73	38.75 " 38.91	2.33	48.75 " 48.91	2.93
8.92 " 9.08	.54	18.92 " 19.08	1.14	28.92 " 29.08	1.74	38.92 " 39.08	2.34	48.92 " 49.08	2.94
9.09 " 9.24	.55	19.09 " 19.24	1.15	29.09 " 29.24	1.75	39.09 " 39.24	2.35	49.09 " 49.24	2.95
9.25 " 9.41	.56	19.25 " 19.41	1.16	29.25 " 29.41	1.76	39.25 " 39.41	2.36	49.25 " 49.41	2.96
9.42 " 9.58	.57	19.42 " 19.58	1.17	29.42 " 29.58	1.77	39.42 " 39.58	2.37	49.42 " 49.58	2.97
9.59 " 9.74	.58	19.59 " 19.74	1.18	29.59 " 29.74	1.78	39.59 " 39.74	2.38	49.59 " 49.74	2.98
9.75 " 9.91	.59	19.75 " 19.91	1.19	29.75 " 29.91	1.79	39.75 " 39.91	2.39	49.75 " 49.91	2.99
9.92 " 10.08	.60	19.92 " 20.08	1.20	29.92 " 30.08	1.80	39.92 " 40.08	2.40	49.92 " 50.08	3.00

Figure 13-10 *Sales tax collection table.*

Minimum Charge

Establishments featuring live music, a floor show, or some special type of entertainment usually add a **cover charge** to the check. The cover charge is a form of admission fee charged to each person to help pay for the cost of the entertainment. Another method of collecting for entertainment or service is by having a **minimum charge.** This means that a guest is required to spend a certain amount of money, once seated, even if the total check amounts to less. For example, if the minimum charge is $5.00, but the check amounts to only $4.25, the guest is still required to pay the $5.00 minimum charge.

Sales Tax

Sales tax, which is discussed in Chapter 19, is important in making out the sales check correctly. Most states have a sales tax; the rate varies depending on the state. Tax tables are made available to ensure that the amount of tax can be calculated quickly and correctly. An example of a sales tax collection table is shown in Figure 13-10.

TIPPING

Tipping, also referred to as a **gratuity,** is the giving of a fee for a service rendered. It is a voluntary act by the customer to express appreciation for a task well done. Tipping is used in the food service industry as a reward for courteous, prompt, and pleasant service. (see Figure 13-11)

Some people disagree with the practice of tipping and regardless of the quality of the service, refuse to leave a gratuity. They assume that the waitperson is paid an adequate salary by the employer to take the order and serve the food. However, this is not always the case. The salary is usually minimum wage. Other people do not feel obligated to tip but will leave a tip if courteous, prompt service is received. Therefore, the amount of tip received by a waitperson usually depends on the attitude of the guest towards tipping, as well as whether the meal was satisfactory and the quality of the service he/she received.

Figure 13-11 *Guest tipping a waitperson.*

Another factor that may have a bearing on tipping and the amount of the tip is the quality of the establishment. Tips seem to come more freely, and in larger amounts, in gourmet restaurants or night clubs. In the average family restaurant, or one with counter and booth service, the tips tend to be smaller.

Most people tip at a percentage of the total check. The accepted practice used to be 15 percent, but in recent years inflation has even found its way into this old custom. Now the accepted practice is 15 to 20 percent. Some establishments automatically add 15 to 20 percent of the check amount to the bill. If this is done, the guest should be made aware of this policy before they are served. Often, when the tip is added to the check, the guest is unaware of this policy, and still leaves a tip at the table.

For the guest who wishes to tip 15 or 20 percent of the amount of the check, or for the waitperson who is asked to figure the amount, there is an easy way to do this mentally. First, find 10 percent of the bill by moving the decimal point in the total bill one place to the left. Next, take half of the figure just found and add the two figures together if the tip is to be 15 percent. If the tip is to be 20 percent just double the 10 percent amount.

For example: The total bill is $18.00. To find 10 percent move the decimal one place to the left yielding $1.80. Half of $1.80 is $0.90. Add the two together, $1.80 + 0.90 = $2.70, the amount of the tip at 15 percent. If tipping 20 percent, take the amount found for 10 percent, $1.80, and double it. $1.80 + $1.80 = $3.60, the amount of the tip at 20 percent.

To simplify the matter of tipping the proper amount, one can purchase tip tables. These tables are of two types: a 15 percent table and a 15 to 20 percent tip table. They both list the total cost of meals from $1.00 to $100.00 and the amount of gratuity for each amount. (See Figure 13-12.)

Computerized registers may be programmed to print out suggested amounts of tips at the bottom of the receipt. (See Figure 13-13.)

15% & 20% TIP TABLE®

Check	15%	20%	Check	15%	20%
$1.00	$.15	$.20	$26.00	$3.90	$5.20
2.00	.30	.40	27.00	4.05	5.40
3.00	.45	.60	28.00	4.20	5.60
4.00	.60	.80	29.00	4.35	5.80
5.00	.75	1.00	30.00	4.50	6.00
6.00	.90	1.20	31.00	4.65	6.20
7.00	1.05	1.40	32.00	4.80	6.40
8.00	1.20	1.60	33.00	4.95	6.60
9.00	1.35	1.80	34.00	5.10	6.80
10.00	1.50	2.00	35.00	5.25	7.00
11.00	1.65	2.20	36.00	5.40	7.20
12.00	1.80	2.40	37.00	5.55	7.40
13.00	1.95	2.60	38.00	5.70	7.60
14.00	2.10	2.80	39.00	5.85	7.80
15.00	2.25	3.00	40.00	6.00	8.00
16.00	2.40	3.20	41.00	6.15	8.20
17.00	2.55	3.40	42.00	6.30	8.40
18.00	2.70	3.60	43.00	6.45	8.60
19.00	2.85	3.80	44.00	6.60	8.80
20.00	3.00	4.00	45.00	6.75	9.00
21.00	3.15	4.20	46.00	6.90	9.20
22.00	3.30	4.40	47.00	7.05	9.40
23.00	3.45	4.60	48.00	7.20	9.60
24.00	3.60	4.80	49.00	7.35	9.80
25.00	3.75	5.00	50.00	7.50	10.00

Check	15%	20%	Check	15%	20%
$51.00	$7.65	$10.20	$76.00	$11.40	$15.20
52.00	7.80	10.40	77.00	11.55	15.40
53.00	7.95	10.60	78.00	11.70	15.60
54.00	8.10	10.80	79.00	11.85	15.80
55.00	8.25	11.00	80.00	12.00	16.00
56.00	8.40	11.20	81.00	12.15	16.20
57.00	8.55	11.40	82.00	12.30	16.40
58.00	8.70	11.60	83.00	12.45	16.60
59.00	8.85	11.80	84.00	12.60	16.80
60.00	9.00	12.00	85.00	12.75	17.00
61.00	9.15	12.20	86.00	12.90	17.20
62.00	9.30	12.40	87.00	13.05	17.40
63.00	9.45	12.60	88.00	13.20	17.60
64.00	9.60	12.80	89.00	13.35	17.80
65.00	9.75	13.00	90.00	13.50	18.00
66.00	9.90	13.20	91.00	13.65	18.20
67.00	10.05	13.40	92.00	13.80	18.40
68.00	10.20	13.60	93.00	13.95	18.60
69.00	10.35	13.80	94.00	14.10	18.80
70.00	10.50	14.00	95.00	14.25	19.00
71.00	10.65	14.20	96.00	14.40	19.20
72.00	10.80	14.40	97.00	14.55	19.40
73.00	10.95	14.60	98.00	14.70	19.60
74.00	11.10	14.80	99.00	14.85	19.80
75.00	11.25	15.00	100.00	15.00	20.00

Target Promotions, Inc.
P.O. Box 1693
Santa Monica, CA 90406-1693
(213) 458-2152

Figure 13-12 *Tip table (Courtesy of Target Promotions, Inc.).*

T I P S . . . ***To Insure Perfect Solutions***

To quickly figure out a 15 percent tip:

1. Use the cost of the food and beverage on the guest check (example $240.00).
2. Take a look at the first two numbers, which equal 24.
3. Divide by 2, which equals 12.
4. Add the 12 to the 24; the 15 percent tip is $36.00.
5. If you get great service and want to leave a 20 percent tip, just take the first two numbers and multiply them by 2.

SERVICE AMERICA CORP

BEL AQU SAR RACTRACK 34

300 UNION AVE

SARATOGA SPRINGS, NY 12866

AMOUNT: $47.88

TIP TABLE PROVIDED FOR YOUR

CONVENIENCE

15%=$7.18 20%=$9.58 25%=$11.97

Figure 13-13 *Computerized register receipt with suggested tips.*

Summary Review

Find the amount of tip for each of the following bills if the tip equals 15 percent of the bill.

1. $12.00 ________	6. $52.85 ________
2. $20.00 ________	7. $70.65 ________
3. $24.25 ________	8. $82.60 ________
4. $30.25 ________	9. $105.40 ________
5. $32.50 ________	10. $125.50 ________

Using a percent to find the total amount of a check, when only the amount of the tip is known is a way for the waitperson to check if the customary tip was given. This is of little significance since tipping is a voluntary gesture on the part of a guest. This exercise, however, does provide an opportunity for the student to work with percents, and, as stated many times in this text, working with percents is an important function in a food service operation.

Using percentages to find the total amount of the check, divide the percent into the amount of the tip:

Amount of tip ÷ percent = amount of check

For example:

Mrs. O'Toole tipped her waitperson 15 percent. The amount of the tip was $2.00. How much was the check?

Solution:

Change 15 percent to 0.15. Divide 0.15 into the amount of the tip which was $2.00.

```
        $13.333
  0.15) 2.000
        1 5
        ----
          50
          45
          ----
           50
           45
          ----
```

This procedure will be the quotient, which is the total amount of Mrs. O'Toole's check: $13.33.

SUMMARY REVIEW

Find the total amount of each check.

1. For outstanding service, Ms. Hamlish left a 20 percent tip, which came to $8.00.

   Total check ____________________

2. Mrs. Abdul left a $4.50 tip, which was 15 percent of the total check.

   Total check ____________________

3. The service was poor, so Mr. Green left a 10 percent tip, which came to $2.25.

   Total check ____________________

4. Mr. Abrunzio left a $6.75 tip, which was 20 percent of the total check.

   Total check ____________________

5. The service was just fair; Mr. Vaughn left $3.50 or 15 percent of the total check.

   Total check ____________________

PART

V

ESSENTIALS OF MANAGERIAL MATH

People are attracted to a food service establishment because they have heard it has excellent food, competent, friendly service and positive price value relationship, and, perhaps, an attractive decor and atmosphere. The customers may keep coming, but this does not necessarily ensure a successful operation. Behind these necessary elements must be skilled management—an individual or team that can direct people, provide efficient service, and control both money and material so a profit can be made. In this section of the text, the emphasis is on the math functions that help management control money and material and at the same time provide the records necessary for a good accounting system. In addition, information will be presented concerning personal taxes and simple and compound interest—subjects that you should be familiar with to function in daily life.

Not all food service students have the desire or ability to manage a food service establishment. However, it is helpful to learn management procedures to better understand the functions of management and to know what makes a successful operation. With this knowledge you can become a better food service employee, which may lead to a more responsible position.

Daily Cash Reports and Bank Deposits

OBJECTIVES

At the completion of this chapter, the student should be able to:

1. Identify items on the daily cash report.
2. Identify and fill out a deposit slip.
3. Identify and balance a check register.
4. Write a check.
5. Identify the items on a bank statement.

At the end of each day or each service period, the cashier is required to fill out a **cashier's daily report.** The report is a tool used by management to keep track of cash and charge sales. Its purpose is to determine whether the actual amount of cash in the register drawer equals the total amount of cash sales made during a specific time period, as well as whether all sales (cash and charges) show the same total that the register prints out. In the past the largest percentage of sales used to be cash. Today, charge sales continue to increase.

The cashier's daily report may show a very small amount of cash over or under what should be in the cash register. With the constant exchange of cash between the guests and the cashier, small mistakes may occur. Usually, management only becomes concerned when amounts exceed a couple of dollars. The report is designed not only to protect the business operator from theft, but also the cashier. If the cashier makes a costly mistake, the error can usually be found by checking the daily report. The cashier's daily report shows information that will assist the accountant or accounting department when filling out financial statements at the end of a financial period.

Bank deposits are a system used to entrust accumulated money for safekeeping in a bank. It is a system used by both individuals and businesses. It is unwise to store money at home or on the premise of a business. This can be an invitation to theft, or loss by a disaster. After opening an account, a deposit can be transacted in person—by taking a completed deposit slip and money to the bank—or the deposit can be made automatically. These two methods will be discussed further in this chapter. Depositing money in an account is a way of holding money in reserve for future **expenditures.**

Chef Sez . . .

"Math is at the core of all successful businesses. We make decisions based on financial performance which is predicated ultimately on daily cash sales reports. We add, subtract, multiply, and divide to obtain food, labor, and controllable percentages. These percentages are the basis of decisions that will effect the bottom line of your operation. It makes sense—we must do the math and do it correctly.

All the hard work in both the front and back of the house would be for naught, without current, accurate, and verified bank deposits from the daily cash register tapes. If you are the owner, manager, or the chef manager, insist on accurate daily cash reports. Anything less and the integrity of your operation will be compromised. As managers, we are paid to make decisions. Without accurate, daily verified bank deposits, these decisions are jeopardized."

James V. Bigley
President
Quality Food Management, Inc.
Latham, NY

Quality Food Management, Inc. is a contract food management company servicing colleges, schools (private and public), health care facilities, and business settings with their food service needs. The company was started in 1982 by James Bigley with one account. It has grown to 50 accounts with more than 650 employees. Total yearly sales volume is 13 million dollars, with the purchase of food, paper, and beverages amounting to 4.5 million dollars.

The Daily Cash Report

There are many different types of cashier's daily reports in use since most establishments create their own form that is best suited for their particular operation. For example, some operations may keep charge sales separate from the cash sales so that the actual cash in the register drawer can be determined more easily. In general, however, all forms will contain the same general information. An example of a typical report is given in Figure 14-1. In this example, and also in the summary review, charge sales have been omitted to make it easier for you to follow the context of the form. Our interest is in determining the correct amount of cash in the register. However, students should be knowledgeable about accounting for credit card sales. Credit card receipts represent money taken in by the establishment in place of cash. On the daily cash report there should be a place to enter all credit card receipts. They should be broken down by companies, for example, American Express, Mastercard, etc. The total of each company's receipts should be listed on a separate line on the daily cash receipt form after Add—Bank. When the food service establishment pays out tips in cash to the waitstaff, the cash amount should be recorded as cash paid outs.

Items on the Daily Cash Report

The items listed on the daily cash report example are those most important to the food service operator. (See Figure 14-1.) These items will appear on most reports. An explanation of each is given.

Date ____________________	
Receipts (Register Readings)	
Food $450.00	
Liquor $290.00	
Misc. Items $120.00	
Sales Tax $38.70	
Gross Receipts	$898.70
Add—Start of Shift Money (Bank)	$ 25.00
Total Cash	$923.70
Less—Cash Paid Outs	$ 11.65
Total Cash in Drawer	$912.05
Cash—Actual	$911.65
Over—Short	$ .40
Record of Cash Paid Outs	
To *Whom* Paid	Amount
City Ice Co.	$ 2.90
Smith Candy Co.	$ 3.50
Watson Florist	$ 5.25
Total Cash Paid Out	$ 11.65
Weather *Cloudy and Cool*	
Customer Count *210*	
	Signed Jane Carson

Figure 14-1 *Cashier's daily report.*

Explanation of Items on Report **Receipts** (register readings). Receipts are taken from the register. With the versatile and sometimes computerized registers in use today, items can be categorized, rung up, and totaled separately or together. (See Figure 14-2.) The computerized registers available on the market are truly amazing considering all the tasks they can perform, but every food service operation cannot afford their high price tag. In just about any function of a food service operation, convenience can be acquired but carries a high price.

Gross Receipts. Gross receipts are a total of all separate register readings. The gross is the total before any deductions are made. In our example, gross receipts are a total of the amounts collected for food, liquor, miscellaneous items, and sales taxes. (See Figure 14-1.)

Add—Start of Shift Money (Bank). Starting change is added to the gross receipts. This money is placed in the register before any sales are made. It consists of both paper currency and coins. Its purpose is to assist the cashier in making change at the start of, and during, the dining period.

Total Cash. Total cash represents the amount of cash that should be in the cash register drawer before any paid outs are made. It is a total of gross receipts and change.

Less—Cash Paid Outs. This figure is acquired by totaling the amounts of money paid out of the register during the day. When a paid out occurs, a record must be made of the transaction by recording it on a report in the section headed "Record of Cash Paid Outs." For each cash paid out, the cashier should have a receipted bill, invoice, or cash

Figure 14-2 *Cashier ringing up a sale.*

payment voucher. Most registers have a key for recording paid outs. The total amount of paid outs on the report should equal the total amount of paid outs recorded by the register. Paid outs are subtracted from the total cash because this money was taken out of the register drawer.

Total Cash in Drawer. Total cash, less paid outs, gives the amount of cash that should be in the register at the end of the day or whenever the totals are taken.

Cash—Actual. The amount of cash that is actually in the cash drawer after all coins and paper currency, and checks are totalled.

Over—Short. If the amounts shown in Total Cash in Drawer and Cash—Actual are not equal, the difference is recorded as cash over or short. If amount shown in Total Cash in Drawer is more than Cash—Actual, there is a cash shortage. If the Cash—Actual is more than the Total Cash in Drawer, there is a cash surplus and the word (over or short) that correctly applies should be circled on the report.

Record of Cash Paid Outs. All money paid out of the register drawer is recorded here with the name of the person or company to whom it was paid. Items paid out of the cash register are usually small items that are needed in a hurry and picked up, such as flowers, ice, candy, candles, tips paid to the waitperson, etc.

Weather. A record is kept of the weather for each day because weather may influence the amount of business done. For example, suppose your food service operation is located in an office building and the weather is very poor, rainy or snowy. When the lunch hour arrives, most people will stay and eat in the building. On a clear, beautiful day, they will probably drive or walk to another location for a change of pace.

Customer Count. This figure is produced by the cash register. The cash register records the number of customers served as each sale is rung up on the register.

Signed. The cashier checks all the figures and is then required to sign the report.

SUMMARY REVIEW

Complete the following cashier's daily reports, using Figure 14-1 as an example.

1.

Date ________________		
Receipts (Register Readings)		
Food	$ 856.63	
Liquor	$ 474.68	
Misc. Items	$ 91.21	
Sales Tax	$ 64.01	
Gross Recipts		________
Add—Start of Shift Money (Bank)		$ 25.00
Total Cash		________
Less—Cash Paid Outs		________
Total Cash in Drawer		________
Cash—Actual		$ 1454.43
Over—Short		________
	Record of Cash Paid Outs	
To *Whom* Paid		Amount
City Ice Co.		$ 21.50
Smith Candy Co.		$ 16.85
Watson Florist		$ 18.75
		________
	Total Cash Paid Out	________
Weather *Rain*		
Customer Count *275*		
	Signed________________	

2.

Date ________		
Receipts (Register Readings)		
Food	$ 1275.65	
Liquor	$ 824.30	
Misc. Items	$ 116.45	
Sales Tax	$ 99.74	
Gross Recipts		________
Add—Start of Shift Money (Bank)		$ 75.00
Total Cash		________
Less—Cash Paid Outs		________
Total Cash in Drawer		________
Cash—Actual		$ 2351.54
Over—Short		________

Record of Cash Paid Outs

To *Whom* Paid	Amount
Jones Candle Co.	$ 13.92
City Ice Co.	$ 15.73
Watson Florist	$ 8.76
	________
Total Cash Paid Out	________

Weather *Clear and Cool*

Customer Count *420*

Signed________

3.

Date ________		
Receipts (Register Readings)		
Food	$ 3675.00	
Liquor	$ 785.90	
Misc. Items	$ 96.48	
Sales Tax	$ 177.87	
Gross Recipts		________
Add—Start of Shift Money (Bank)		$ 55.00
Total Cash		________
Less—Cash Paid Outs		________
Total Cash in Drawer		________
Cash—Actual		$ 3732.25
Over—Short		________

Record of Cash Paid Outs

To *Whom* Paid	Amount
Smith Candy Co.	$ 20.50
Watson Florist	$ 25.80
City Ice Co.	$ 10.40
	________
Total Cash Paid Out	________

Weather *Cloudy and Warm*

Customer Count *312*

Signed________

4.

Date ____________		
Receipts (Register Readings)		
Food	$ 6296.50	
Liquor	$ 1457.95	
Misc. Items	$ 117.86	
Sales Tax	$ 472.34	
Gross Recipts		________
Add—Start of Shift Money (Bank)		$ 65.00
Total Cash		________
Less—Cash Paid Outs		________
Total Cash in Drawer		________
Cash—Actual		$ 8361.42
Over—Short		________
Record of Cash Paid Outs		
To *Whom* Paid		Amount
Smith Candy Co.		$ 20.65
Watson Florist		$ 15.75
City Ice Co.		$ 11.75
		________
	Total Cash Paid Out	________
Weather *Cloudy and Warm*		
Customer Count *312*		
	Signed____________	

5.

Date ____________		
Receipts (Register Readings)		
Food	$10,650.00	
Liquor	$ 2,460.55	
Misc. Items	$ 127.25	
Sales Tax	$ 794.27	
Gross Recipts		________
Add—Start of Shift Money (Bank)		$ 75.00
Total Cash		________
Less—Cash Paid Outs		________
Total Cash in Drawer		________
Cash—Actual		$ 14,062.65
Over—Short		________
Record of Cash Paid Outs		
To *Whom* Paid		Amount
Smith Candy Co.		$ 15.40
Watson Florist		$ 20.35
City Ice Co.		$ 9.70
		________
	Total Cash Paid Out	________
Weather *Cloudy and Warm*		
Customer Count *312*		
	Signed____________	

BANK DEPOSITS

When a bank deposit is made, the money deposited is placed in a **savings** or **checking account.** If the deposit is made in person at a bank, the money being deposited is accompanied by a **deposit slip,** that provides the depositor and the bank with a record of the transaction. (See Figure 14-3.) If the deposit is made automatically, the transfer of funds is made through special communication lines set up between the depositor and the banking institution.

If the money deposited is placed in a savings account, it is held by the banking institution until the depositor wishes to withdraw some or all of the funds. While the money is in the savings account, the bank uses the money to make loans to customers for home or business improvements, the purchasing of new or existing homes, etc. At the same time, they pay you **interest** (the sum paid for the use of money) at a certain percent annually. This means that while your money is in the banking institution it is earning money. This money can be withdrawn at any time without a penalty.

If the money is deposited in a checking account, it is held in reserve to cover any check amount written by the depositor. A **check** is a written order directing the bank to make a payment for the depositor. The bank honors the check and makes the payment, providing the depositor has enough money on deposit in the checking account. A checking account is more active than a savings account because the money is usually on the move. That is, deposits are made, checks are written, and money is withdrawn.

Bills are usually paid by check whether they are for business, or personal and household expenses. Therefore, you should have some knowledge of how a checking account works. There are four important steps involved in using a checking account.

1. Filling out the deposit slip
2. Balancing the check register
3. Writing a check
4. Checking the bank statement

CHECKING ACCOUNT DEPOSIT TICKET

185206488 63631
ACCOUNT NUMBER

Robert Smith
NAME

DATE November 8 2001

CHECKS AND OTHER ITEMS ARE RECEIVED FOR DEPOSIT SUBJECT TO THE TERMS AND CONDITIONS OF THIS BANK'S COLLECTION AGREEMENT.

DEPOSITED IN

CASH →		201	50
CHECKS		20	40
		8	10
TOTAL FROM OTHER SIDE			
TOTAL ITEMS	TOTAL	230	00

29-8
213

USE OTHER SIDE FOR ADDITIONAL LISTING
ENTER TOTAL HERE

BE SURE EACH ITEM IS PROPERLY ENDORSED

⑆0213⑈0008⑆

DELUXE HD-14

Figure 14-3 *Deposit slip.*

If these steps are not completed properly, problems result for both the depositor and the banking institution. These problems can sometimes result in a fine for the depositor, especially if the account is **overdrawn** (to write checks upon an account for a greater amount than the money in the account).

The Deposit Slip

The **deposit slip** provides the depositor and the banking institution with a record of the transaction when money is deposited in the checking account. (See Figure 14-3.) When filling out the deposit slip, cash and checks are listed separately. After this is done, they are added to find a *subtotal.* ("Sub" means under, therefore this is a part of the total.) If cash is received when the deposit is made, the amount is subtracted from the subtotal, giving the net deposit or the amount you wish to place in the checking account. When receiving cash, some institutions require your signature on the deposit slips. In the upper left hand corner of the slip your name and address usually appear, and in the bottom left hand corner two groups of numbers appear. The first group is a routing number for the purpose of routing automatic deposits and checks to the correct institution. The second group is the customer's checking account number. (These numbers are not shown on Figure 14-3.) When deposits are made automatically, a deposit slip is not required, but the depositor would be required to know the proper route number. All deposit slips are not the same. Each institution has its own idea of arrangement and information desired. However, you will find that most are very similar. The banking institution supplies the deposit slips to the customer.

The Check Register

The **check register** is given to the depositor by the banking institution, so the depositor can record deposits and checks, knowing the balance of money on hand. (See Figure 14-4.) In this way, the depositor always knows the largest amount for which a check can be written and is less likely to overdraw the account.

The balance brought forward (shown at the top in Figure 14-4), is the balance from the previous page in the register. It shows a total of $283.00. On August 10, a check was drawn for $18.00, leaving a balance of $265.00. On August 13, another check was drawn for $175.00, leaving a balance of $90.00. On August 16, a deposit of $250.00 was made. This amount was added to the previous balance, creating a new balance of $340.00. On August 18, a check of $75.00 was drawn, leaving a balance of $265.00, and on August 20, another check of $135.00 was drawn. The remaining balance, $130.00, is the net amount against which future checks may be drawn.

Writing a Check

The check, as pointed out previously, is a written order directing the bank to make a payment for the depositor out of the money the depositor has in his or her checking account. The banking institution issues checks to the depositor. The depositor may be required to pay for the checks, or the bank may deduct the cost from the balance in the checking account. Sometimes the checks are free, if the depositor has a savings account or C.D. (Certificate of Deposit) at the same banking institution.

CHECK NO.	CHECKS DRAWN IN FAVOR OF	DATE	BAL. BRT. FRD.	✓	$ 283	00
111	TO Cinti Bell	8/10	AMOUNT OF CHECK OR DEPOSIT		18	00
	FOR Telephone Service		BALANCE		265	00
112	TO Allstate Insurance	8/13	AMOUNT OF CHECK OR DEPOSIT		175	00
	FOR Car Insurance		BALANCE		90	00
	TO Deposit	8/16	AMOUNT OF CHECK OR DEPOSIT		250	00
	FOR		BALANCE		340	00
113	TO Shillito Dept. Store	8/18	AMOUNT OF CHECK OR DEPOSIT		75	00
	FOR Charge Account		BALANCE		265	00
114	TO Norwood Building & Loan	8/20	AMOUNT OF CHECK OR DEPOSIT		135	00
	FOR House Payment		BALANCE		130	00
	TO		AMOUNT OF CHECK OR DEPOSIT			
	FOR		BALANCE			
	TO		AMOUNT OF CHECK OR DEPOSIT			
	FOR		BALANCE			
	TO		AMOUNT OF CHECK OR DEPOSIT			
	FOR		BALANCE			
	TO		AMOUNT OF CHECK OR DEPOSIT			
	FOR		BALANCE			
	TO		AMOUNT OF CHECK OR DEPOSIT			
	FOR		BALANCE			
	TO		AMOUNT OF CHECK OR DEPOSIT			
	FOR		BALANCE			

Figure 14-4 *Check register.*

When writing a check, always write neatly and clearly, using ink. (See Figure 14-5.) Be sure that all of the information listed on the check is complete and correct, such as amount, date, check number, account number, etc. Do not forget to sign the check. Without your signature, the payment will not be made.

TIPS . . . ***To Insure Perfect Solutions***

When writing a check, never use a pen with erasable ink. Anyone can change the information that you write on the check.

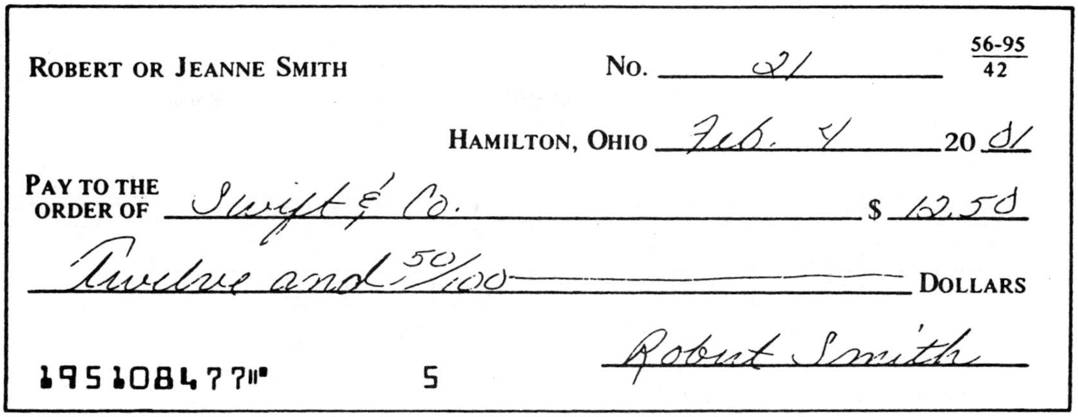

ROBERT OR JEANNE SMITH NO. 21 56-95/42

HAMILTON, OHIO Feb. 4 20 01

PAY TO THE ORDER OF Swift & Co. $ 12.50

Twelve and 50/100 DOLLARS

195108477" 5 Robert Smith

Figure 14-5 *Writing a check.*

The Bank Statement

At the end of a certain period of time (for example, one month, three months; each banking institution has its own regulations) the bank provides the depositor with a statement showing the activity of the account during that time period. In Figure 14-6 (time period of three months) the statement shows the checks drawn and deposits made during that period of time. The bank also returns all checks (canceled checks), or a copy of the checks issued during that period. The canceled checks are the depositor's receipts if proof is needed that payment was made. The bank statement is used to check the bank's figures against those recorded in the depositor's check register. In this way, mistakes can be detected before a problem arises or a fine is imposed.

The top left corner of Figure 14-6 shows the depositor's account number. In the center, the depositor's name and address are given. The balance brought forward shows that, as of May 20, there was no money in this account. This was probably when the account was opened at the bank. Deposits and credits show that during this period (May 20 to July 15) eight deposits were made totalling $1,710.32. This figure can be checked by finding the sum of all the amounts listed with a DP (deposit) before them. Checks and debits (a charge against the account) show that 25 checks were drawn on the account and the amount of those checks totaled $1,435.25. There is no service charge indicated by the bank during this period, which shows that the depositor received this service free of charge or paid for the checks when they were received. The current balance shows that as of July 15, $275.07 remained in the account. Other figures shown on this statement include the complete checking activity during this period of time, and the dates and amounts of all checks written. The bank statement shown in Figure 14-6 is a simplified one so that you could follow it without becoming confused. Most statements issued by banking institutions today are computer printouts and can be a little more confusing because they combine statements for both the checking and savings account and show a service charge for regular account maintenance.

486-174-8
Account Number

John or Jane Doe
9464 Stone Hill Dr.
Westchester, Ohio 45070

BALANCE FORWARD	DEPOSITS & CREDITS		CHECKS & DEBITS			CURRENT BALANCE
AS OF 05/20	NO.	AMOUNT	NO.	AMOUNT	SER. CHG.	AS OF 07/15
$0.00	8	$1,710.32	25	$1,435.25		$275.07

DATE	CHECK NO. OR CODE	AMOUNT	DATE	CHECK NO. OR CODE	AMOUNT	DATE	CHECK NO. OR CODE	AMOUNT
05 20	DP	200 00	07 05		50 00			
06 03	DP	200 00	07 05		139 88			
06 05		100 00	07 08		14 47			
06 07		132 00	07 09		10 50			
06 10	DP	500 00	07 10		14 44			
06 13		105 00	07 10		16 56			
06 13		110 35	07 10		18 40			
06 17	DP	200 00	07 11		50 00			
06 18		20 00	07 11		50 00			
06 19		255 92	07 15	DP	200 00			
06 24		10 00						
06 24		30 00						
06 24		50 00						
06 24		97 00						
06 27	DP	200 00						
06 28		25 16						
07 01	DP	200 00						
07 01		4 13						
07 01		7 00						
07 01		13 25						
07 01		100 00						
07 03	DP	10 32						
07 05		11 19						

Figure 14-6 *Bank statement.*

SUMMARY REVIEW

1. Prepare deposit slips for problems a through c. Follow the example given in Figure 14-3. If deposit slips are not available, make some by listing the necessary information on blank paper.

   a. On August 18, Duane Johnstone deposited the following in his checking account.

      2 twenty dollar bills
      4 ten dollar bills
      6 five dollar bills
      5 one dollar bills
      2 checks: $12.75 and $22.25
      2 half dollars
      8 quarters
      6 dimes
      7 nickels

   b. On October 6, Carmen Santi-Roberts deposited the following in her checking account.

      4 twenty dollar bills
      8 ten dollar bills
      7 five dollar bills
      4 two dollar bills
      9 one dollar bills
      1 check for $53.40
      6 half dollars
      3 quarters
      7 dimes
      9 nickels

   c. On November 10, Sonna Kozlowski, treasurer of the Cuisine Club, deposited in their checking account the following checks and money collected for dues.

      2 twenty dollar bills
      2 ten dollar bills
      8 five dollar bills
      6 one dollar bills
      3 checks: $10.40, $8.50, and $6.75
      5 half dollars
      5 quarters
      4 dimes

2. Prepare check registers for problems a through c. Follow the example given in Figure 14-4. If a check register is not available, make one by listing the necessary information on a sheet of paper.

a. Balance brought forward $520.65

October 2	Check No. 6 $43.50 Gas and Electric Co.
October 5	Check No. 7 $25.80 Best State Insurance Co.
October 10	Deposit $165.50
October 15	Check No. 8 $35.80 Albers Meat Market
October 20	Check No. 9 $265.00 Bill's Service Station

b. Balance brought forward $680.48

December 3	Check No. 15 $63.45 Swallen's Dept. Store
December 5	Deposit $183.20
December 8	Check No. 16 $158.00 Evanston Building and Loan Co.
December 9	Check No. 17 $178.25 Bay State Insurance Co.
December 12	Deposit $98.75
December 15	Check No. 18 $62.78 G.M.A.C.

c. Balance brought forward $728.60

January 4	Check No. 19 $15.34 Webster Insurance Co.
January 6	Check No. 20 $187.00 Home Savings and Loan Co.
January 9	Deposit $223.50
January 12	Check No. 21 $208.60 Joe's Service Station
January 14	Deposit $197.60
January 17	Check No. 22 $179.79 McMillians Dept. Store
January 20	Deposit $368.75
January 25	Check No. 23 $76.45 Metropolitan Hospital

Recipe and Food Costing

OBJECTIVES

At the completion of this chapter, the student should be able to:

1. Complete cost charts to determine the extension cost.
2. Find the total sales.
3. Find the amount of average sales.
4. Find the food cost percent.

In recent years the price of food has fluctuated rapidly, making it difficult for the food service operator to maintain a selling price for his or her food that will continue to show a profit. If a profit is not maintained, it means the owner is working for nothing and has no reason to stay in business. Ways must be found to keep up with changing prices. The answer to this problem could be to standardize and cost all recipes used in food service operations. This means staying current with the changing market prices so management will continually know the cost of the items to be sold. It is important in any business venture to *know your cost* before establishing a selling price. It also means a few extra hours of work each week. However, it is well worth the time if profits increase.

THE STANDARD RECIPE

A **standard recipe** is one that will produce the same amount, quality, and taste each time it is prepared. If consistency is a factor in the recipe, that too will be the same. The standard recipe provides assurance that the preparation will not fluctuate from one day to the next regardless of who is preparing the food. If the recipe is followed correctly, quality is maintained. This type of recipe is ideal for food preparation in schools, hospitals, nursing homes, retirement villages, in-plant food service, and other similar institutions.

Figuring the Standard Recipe

When figuring the cost of a standard recipe, the cost of each ingredient that goes into the preparation is totaled and a per-unit cost is calculated. (See Figure 15-1.) For example, when preparing a recipe that yields 50 servings, the cost of all the ingredients used in making these 50 servings are added together to obtain the complete cost of the preparation. The total cost of the preparation is then divided by 50 (the yield) to find

Hungarian Beef Goulash			**Approximate Yield: 50—6-ounce servings**
Ingredients	Amount	Market Price	Extension Cost
Beef Chuck	18 lb.	$2.25 per lb.	$40.50
Garlic, Minced	1 oz.	$2.52 per lb.	.158
Flour	8 oz.	.18 per lb.	.09
Chili Powder	$\frac{3}{4}$ oz.	3.65 per lb.	.171
Paprika	5 oz.	4.50 per lb.	1.406
Tomato Puree	1 qt.	1.88 per gal.	.47
Water	8 lb.	—	—
Bay Leaves	2	—	—
Caraway Seeds	$\frac{1}{2}$ oz.	5.72 per lb.	.179
Onions, Minced	2 lb.	.75 per lb.	1.50
Salt	1 oz.	.42 per lb.	.026
Pepper	$\frac{1}{4}$ oz.	5.18 per lb.	.081
		Total Cost	$44.581
		Cost Per Serving	.892

Figure 15-1 *Standardized recipe—costs included.*

the unit cost. The **unit cost** represents what one serving of this particular item costs to prepare. With this knowledge, the manager or food and beverage controller can establish a menu price. The formula for finding the unit cost is:

Total Cost ÷ Yield = Unit Cost

The form used to record the cost of a certain recipe may differ depending on the food service establishment. However, they all usually supply the same information: the exact cost to produce one serving. Of course, in order to obtain the proper yield and determine the correct unit cost, all servings must be uniform. (See Figure 15-2.)

A typical standardized recipe showing the market price of each ingredient, the extension cost, total cost, and unit cost per serving is provided in Figure 15-1. An explanation of the standardized recipe shown in this figure follows.

The first column in Figure 15-1 lists all the ingredients used in the preparation of this dish—in this case, Hungarian Beef Goulash.

The second column lists the amount of each ingredient needed to prepare 50 6-ounce servings.

The third column lists the current market price of each ingredient. These prices must be watched carefully because they fluctuate (go up and down) from time to time. The price is listed in quantities that are usually quoted by the vendor. For example, meat is always purchased by the pound, eggs by the dozen, milk by the gallon, and so forth.

The fourth column in Figure 15-1 is the extension cost of the quantity listed. This figure is found by multiplying the amount of the ingredient

Figure 15-2 *Uniform size allows the food service employee to determine the proper yield and unit cost.*

by the market price. Remember that when multiplying, both figures should represent the same quantity. That is, pounds multiplied by price per pound, ounces multiplied by price per ounce, and so on.

The following information explains how the cost was determined for one serving of Hungarian Beef Goulash.

The market price of beef chuck is $2.25 per lb. (pound). The amount is also in pounds (18). Since both the amount and market price are represented by the same quantity (in this case, pounds), the extension cost of $40.50 was determined by multiplying the amount (18) by the market price ($2.25).

The next ingredient, minced garlic, shows the amount and market price represented by different quantities—the amount in ounces and the market price in pounds. To determine the extension cost, a series of small steps must be performed. First, convert the market price to a cost per ounce. The garlic costs $2.52 per pound. Divide $2.52 by 16 (the number of ounces in a pound), which equals $0.1575. This is the cost of 1 ounce of garlic. (Note: the answer has *not been* rounded off.) Since both the amount and market price are in like quantities (ounces), the extension cost can be figured out. The next step is to multiply the $0.1575 (cost of 1 ounce) by 1 (amount of ounces that the recipe requires), which equals

$0.1575. Because we round off to the mill the extension cost of 1 ounce of garlic is $0.158.

Flour, chili powder, paprika, tomato puree, caraway seeds, onions, salt, and pepper also have the amount and market price represented by different quantities. Before extension costs can be calculated for these ingredients, the amount and market price have to be converted to the same quantities (ounces). All of the extension costs for these ingredients, except for the tomato puree, can be calculated by following the steps in the previous paragraph.

Tomato puree is slightly different. The amount is represented in quarts and the market price is represented in gallons, therefore both must be converted into like amounts. There are three quantities that gallons and quarts can be converted into: quarts, gallons, or ounces.

For example, the market price can be converted into a price per quart. There are 4 quarts in a gallon. Therefore, the market price of $1.88 per gallon is divided by the amount of quarts in a gallon (4). This equals $.47 per quart.

Or, the amount can be converted into gallons. One quart is equal to a $\frac{1}{4}$ (.25) of a gallon. To determine the cost of the tomato puree, .25 is multiplied by $1.88, which equals $0.47.

Finally, both the market price and the amount can be converted to ounces. There are 128 ounces in a gallon. The cost of a gallon, $1.88, is divided by 128 (amount of ounces in a gallon), which equals $0.0146875. This is the cost of 1 ounce of tomato puree. That cost of $0.0146875 is multiplied by the ounces in a quart (32). This results in a cost of $.47.

In calculating costs the authors have demonstrated that the three methods used above all result in the same answer. We used different methods to determine the correct answer. The one constant was that the amount and market price were represented in like quantities.

Once all of the extension costs have been calculated, the column is added to determine the total cost of the recipe.

To find the cost per serving, divide the total cost by the number of servings the recipe will yield. In this case, the yield is 50, so 50 is divided into $44.581 to get $0.892, which is the cost of each serving. (Note: prices have been carried to the tenth of a cent (mill), three places to the right of the decimal.)

In this type of standard recipe, where market price and extension cost are stated, the procedure or method of preparation is listed on the back of the card. This is done so that the card can be kept to a size that is easy to file. Other standard recipes that do not list market price and extension cost (the total cost of each ingredient used in the preparation) have the procedure or method of preparation listed on the face of the recipe. (See Figure 15-3.)

YIELD	**Fruit Sauce (Hot)**						
	Port	Oz.	Port	Oz.	Port	Oz.	
Ingredients	**25**	**2**	**100**	**2**			**Method**
Orange Juice	2 cups		2 qts.				1. Combine first 8 in-gregients. Bring to a boil.
Pineapple Juice	2 cups		2 qts.				2. Dissolve Cornstarch in cold water.
Water	$\frac{3}{4}$ cup		3 cups				3. Add to hot mix-ture, cook over low heat until thick and clear. Hold hot in bain marie. Taste.
Cloves, whole	2 ea.		4 ea.				*Note: Serve with Baked Ham, Canadian Bacon, Chicken*
Lemon Juice	1 Tbsp.		$\frac{1}{4}$ cup				
Salt	$\frac{1}{2}$ tsp.		2 tsp.				
Granulated Sugar	12 oz.		3 lbs.				
Fruit Cocktail (drained)	8 oz.		2 lbs.				
Cold Water	$\frac{3}{4}$ cup		3 cups				
Cornstarch	$2\frac{1}{2}$oz.		10 oz.				
Yield:	$1\frac{3}{4}$ qt.		$1\frac{3}{4}$ gal.				

Cooking Equipment: Sauce pan, Stock pot **Service Equipment:** 2 oz. ladle **Garnish:**
Temperature: 160°F **Color:** Multi-color **Date:**

Figure 15-3 *Standardized recipe — costs not included.*

SUMMARY REVIEW

Complete the following cost charts to determine the extension cost. When calculating the cost per ounce, per pound, etc.; do not round off at this point. Carry the price three places to the right of the decimal when calculating the extension cost, the total cost, and the cost per serving.

1. **Braised Swiss Steak** Approximate Yield 50 servings

Ingredients	Amount	Market Price	Extension Cost
6 oz. Round Steak	50 ea.	2.25 per lb.	________
Onions	12 oz.	0.75 per lb.	________
Garlic	1 oz.	2.52 per lb.	________
Tomato Puree	1 pt.	1.88 per gal.	________
Brown Stock	6 qt.	1.25 per gal.	________
Salad Oil	3 cups	6.57 per gal.	________
Bread Flour	12 oz.	0.18 per lb.	________
Salt	$\frac{3}{4}$ oz.	0.42 per lb.	________
		Total Cost	________
		Cost per Serving	________

2. **Salisbury Steak** Approximate Yield 50 servings

Ingredients	Amount	Market Price	Extension Cost
Beef Chuck	14 lb.	$2.25 per lb.	____________
Onions	3 lb.	0.75 per lb.	____________
Garlic	$\frac{1}{2}$ oz.	2.52 per lb.	____________
Salad Oil	$\frac{1}{2}$ cup	6.57 per gal.	____________
Bread Cubes	2 lb.	0.65 per lb.	____________
Milk	$1\frac{1}{2}$ pt.	2.18 per gal.	____________
Whole Eggs	8	0.89 per doz.	____________
Pepper	$\frac{1}{4}$ oz.	5.18 per lb.	____________
Salt	1 oz.	0.42 per lb.	____________
		Total Cost	____________
		Cost per Serving	____________

3. **Buttermilk Biscuits** Approximate Yield 6 dozen = 72 biscuits

Ingredients	Amount	Market Price	Extension Cost
Cake Flour	1 lb. 8 oz.	0.25 per lb.	____________
Bread Flour	1 lb. 8 oz.	0.18 per lb.	____________
Baking Powder	$3\frac{1}{2}$ oz.	1.68 per lb.	____________
Salt	$\frac{1}{2}$ oz.	0.42 per lb.	____________
Sugar	4 oz.	0.36 per lb.	____________
Butter	12 oz.	1.26 per lb.	____________
Buttermilk	2 lb. 4 oz.	1.23 per qt.	____________
		Total Cost	____________
		Cost per Dozen	____________
		Cost per Biscuit	____________

4. **Brown Sugar Cookie** Approximate Yield 14 dozen = 168 cookies

Ingredients	Amount	Market Price	Extension Cost
Brown Sugar	3 lb. 2 oz.	0.38 per lb.	____________
Shortening	2 lb. 4 oz.	0.48 per lb.	____________
Salt	1 oz.	0.42 per lb.	____________
Baking Soda	$\frac{1}{2}$ oz.	0.44 per lb.	____________
Pastry Flour	4 lb. 8 oz.	0.20 per lb.	____________
Whole eggs	9	0.89 per doz.	____________
Vanilla	$\frac{1}{4}$ oz.	1.77 per qt.	____________
		Total Cost	____________
		Cost per Dozen	____________
		Cost per Cookie	____________

5. **Soft Dinner Rolls** — Approximate Yield 16 dozen = 192 rolls

Ingredients	Amount	Market Price	Extension Cost
Sugar	1 lb.	$0.36 per lb.	________
Shortening	1 lb. 4 oz.	0.48 per lb.	________
Dry Milk	8 oz.	1.93 per lb.	________
Salt	2 oz.	0.42 per lb.	________
Whole Eggs	3	0.89 per doz.	________
Yeast	6 oz.	3.27 per lb.	________
Water	4 lb.	—	________
Bread Flour	7 lb.	0.18 per lb.	________
		Total Cost	________
		Cost per Dozen	________
		Cost per Roll	________

Chef Sez . . .

"Precost every penny before it goes on the menu."

Fritz Sonnenschmidt
Certified Master Chef, Chairman of the American Academy of Chefs
Culinary Dean, Culinary Institute of America
Hyde Park, NY

Fritz Sonnenschmidt is one of less than 60 Certified Master Chefs in the United States. In order to become certified, an individual must pass a complicated test of both practical and written work. Also, Chef Sonnenschmidt was the American Culinary Federation 1994 Chef of the Year. This award was created in 1963 to pay tribute to that active member whose culinary expertise and exemplary dedication have enhanced the image of the chef and his or her professional association; who commands the respect of his or her own peers because of character and performance; and whose accomplishments have been of benefit to the American Culinary Federation.

FOOD COSTING

In any food service operation, the two biggest expenditures are the cost of food and labor. If the operation is to have any chance for success, these two items must be controlled. It is not an easy task because it seems that both are constantly rising. One of the tools that is used to control the cost and use of food is the **daily food cost report,** the purpose of which is to show management the exact cost and amount of food used on any given day. This report is a guide that keeps the manager aware of cost, thus helping to control the cost of food being used in the establishment. The high cost of food coupled with waste on the part of employees makes it essential that tight controls be maintained on the items that can lead a food service operation to bankruptcy. There is more bankruptcy in the food service business than in any other business.

Customer Count	300		Date	January 15, 20
Average Sale	$1.20		Day	Thursday

Issues	Today	To Date	Last Month To Date
Storeroom			
Canned Goods	$ 25.50	$ 100.50	$ 95.25
Other Groceries	15.60	46.25	43.50
Meat	35.25	225.50	222.30
Frozen Foods	10.60	30.40	25.50
Direct Purchases			
Poultry, fresh	20.15	75.30	74.35
Seafood, fresh	21.30	58.60	57.60
Produce	8.00	39.25	35.20
Dairy Products	6.00	25.00	20.70
Bread and Rolls	5.00	20.35	18.40
Miscellaneous	4.00	10.50	10.45
Total Cost	$151.40	$ 631.65	$ 603.25
Total Sales	$360.00	$1,500.00	$1,400.00
Food Cost Percent	42.1%	42.1%	43.1%

Figure 15-4 *Daily food cost report.*

The daily food cost report also helps to provide a more accurate picture of the food service operation's monthly food cost pattern. That is, if the planned monthly food cost percent is set at a certain rate to ensure a profitable operation and each day this rate is exceeded, something is not right. It would therefore be apparent to management that all factors such as portion size, waste, theft, and food production must be investigated to find the cause.

There are several kinds of food cost reports in use. The simplified type is made up from the totals of storeroom requisitions and direct purchases for the day. (See Figure 15-4.)

A **storeroom requisition,** as explained in Chapter 11, is a list of food items issued from the storeroom upon the request of the production crew. These may be requests for certain meats, other groceries, canned foods, or frozen foods. The requisitions are priced and extended at the end of each day. The unit prices are usually marked on all storeroom items as they are received, or they may be stored on a disk if a computer is available. This way, the requisitioned foods can be priced immediately. **Direct purchases** are those foods that are usually purchased each day or every other day. They include produce, dairy products, fresh seafood, bread, rolls, and any other items that are considered perishable. The total for direct purchases can be obtained from the **invoice** (a list of goods sent to the purchaser with their prices and quantity listed) which is sent with each order.

Finding the Total Sales

In Figure 15-4, the total sales for the day is $360.00. This figure is found by totaling the register sales for the day. The figure can be checked by multiplying the average sales by the customer count.

Average Sales × Customer Count = Total Sales

$1.20	Average Sales
× 300	Customer Count
$360.00	Total Sales

Finding the Amount of Average Sale

The customer count is obtained by checking the register which records the total number of customers as sales are rung up. The amount of average sales for the day is found by dividing the customer count into the total sales.

Total Sales ÷ Customer Count = Amount of Average Sales

```
                      $1.20     Average Sales
Customer Count   300)$360.00    Total Sales
                      300
                       600
                       600
```

Purpose of Food Cost Percentages

Every food service operation should set a goal to determine how much money should be spent on buying food. Because of the great fluctuation in the volume of food sales it is impractical to state this goal in a dollar amount, such as $6,000 each month. One month the sales could be $40,000, while another month they may be only $3,000. Therefore, it is impractical to use a dollar figure because food service professionals would have a hard time understanding whether $10,800, $9,000, or $910.00 is a reasonable amount to spend on buying food. Instead, food service professionals use percentages to help them control and understand food costs. For example, a pizza operation sets a monthly food cost percentage goal of 27 percent. Regardless of how many pizzas are sold in that month, the raw cost of the food to prepare all the pizzas sold should be 27 percent of the amount of money received in sales dollars. If the number is lower than 27 percent, it could be that the cost of cheese has gone down. If the number is higher than the goal, it could be that an employee is giving away free pizzas to friends. There can be many reasons for the fluctuation in the food cost percentage. A manager knows that if the cost does not equal the goal, then an investigation must take place to determine why the cost is different from the goal.

To explain this further, at the end of a $40,000 sales month the cost of raw food should be 27 percent or $10,800, while in a $3,000 sales month the cost of food should be 27 percent or $810.00. As the student can observe, when the executive gets the report on his or her desk and the cost of food is reported as a percentage, it becomes easy to understand if the business is meeting the goal set by management.

Meaning of Food Cost Percentages

Food cost percentage is the cost of the food as it relates to the amount of dollars received in sales. In the previous section, we stated that our food cost percentage in the pizza shop was 27 percent. This means that for every $1.00 charged for a cheese pizza, it costs $.27 for the food to make that cheese pizza. So if our pizza shop sells the pizza to the customer for $5.00, we should pay 27 percent of $5.00 or $1.35 for the cost of food.

If the price of cheese and sauce goes up and causes the raw food of the pizza to be $.33, then the price of pizza must be increased or the food cost will rise.

Finding the Food Cost Percent

To find the individual menu food cost percent divide the menu price of the pizza into the cost of the food to prepare the pizza. The cost of the food to prepare the pizza is $.27. The menu price of the pizza is $1.00.

Menu Price $1.00) $.27 Cost of Food to Prepare Pizza = 27 Food Cost Percent

To find the food cost for a restaurant. The manager must add together the cost of all items issued for the day's food production (see Figure 15-4). If the total cost of food for the day is $151.40 and the sales for the day is $360.00, the food cost percentage is 42.1 percent.

Cost of Food ÷ Total Sales = Food Cost Percent

```
                    .4205 equals 42.1%    Food Cost Percent
Total Sales $360)151.4000                 Cost of Food
                 144 0
                   7 40
                   7 20
                     2000
                     1800
                      200
```

In addition to the daily food cost percent, some daily food cost reports also show the increasing totals for the month and the totals of the previous month to date. By including this information, the owner or manager has a clearer picture of the food cost pattern.

SUMMARY REVIEW

For the following daily food cost reports, find:

- Total cost of food for today, to date, and last month to date.
- Total sales for today.
- Food cost percent today, to date, and last month to date.

1.

Customer Count	390		Date	July 15, 20
Average Sale	$1.45		Day	Monday

Issues	Today	To Date	Last Month To Date
Storeroom			
Canned Goods	$24.30	$ 106.55	$ 98.40
Other Groceries	17.80	40.50	42.20
Meat	47.25	325.50	312.30
Frozen Foods	9.50	25.22	23.60
Direct Purchases			
Poultry, fresh	18.15	75.45	72.53
Seafood, fresh	20.35	52.60	48.22
Produce	10.56	37.65	34.25
Dairy Products	6.90	23.75	19.85
Bread and Rolls	5.85	24.43	23.46
Miscellaneous	6.20	12.24	11.47
Total Cost	—	—	—
Total Sales	—	$1,650.00	$1,560.00
Food Cost Percent	—	—	—

2.

Customer Count	290		Date	August 3, 20
Average Sale	$1.50		Day	Tuesday

Issues	Today	To Date	Last Month To Date
Storeroom			
Canned Goods	$30.24	$ 110.50	$ 112.25
Other Groceries	15.20	40.65	45.50
Meat	58.65	228.60	248.40
Frozen Foods	10.90	30.75	25.95
Direct Purchases			
Poultry, fresh	17.55	68.30	75.35
Seafood, fresh	25.40	59.42	65.75
Produce	15.50	49.25	52.20
Dairy Products	8.22	22.00	20.80
Bread and Rolls	8.45	18.80	21.50
Miscellaneous	6.30	12.43	13.65
Total Cost	—	—	—
Total Sales	—	$1,600.00	$1,700.00
Food Cost Percent	—	—	—

3.

Customer Count	380		Date September 8, 20
Average Sale	$1.35		Day Wednesday
Issues	**Today**	**To Date**	**Last Month To Date**
Storeroom			
Canned Goods	$36.75	$ 115.25	$ 116.35
Other Groceries	16.26	42.75	43.85
Meat	68.40	245.30	240.75
Frozen Foods	12.65	28.80	27.60
Direct Purchases			
Poultry, fresh	18.95	58.35	85.62
Seafood, fresh	24.15	46.12	58.14
Produce	18.85	39.25	48.20
Dairy Products	9.95	20.90	21.76
Bread and Rolls	10.22	18.80	22.87
Miscellaneous	7.50	9.20	13.70
Total Cost	—	—	—
Total Sales	—	$1,550.00	$1,590.00
Food Cost Percent	—	—	—

4. The menu price of a turkey sandwich is $5.95. The raw cost of food is $1.50. Find the food cost percentage.

____

5. A chicken marsella dinner has a menu price of $15.95. The raw cost of food is $3.89. Find the food cost percentage.

____

6. A lazy man's lobster dinner has a menu price of $19.95. The raw cost of food is $6.89. Find the food cost percentage.

____

7. A fajita platter has a menu price of $12.95. The raw cost of food is $2.22. Find the food cost percentage.

____

8. The total cost of all food purchased for the day is $1,020.00. Total sales for the day is $350.00. Find the daily food cost.

____

9. The total cost of all food purchased for the day is $367.00. Total sales for the day is $989.50. Find the daily food cost.

____

10. The total cost of all food purchased for the day is $20.00. Total sales for the day is $1,642.78. Find the daily food cost.

____

Pricing the Menu

OBJECTIVES

At the completion of this chapter, the student should be able to:

1. Identify the strategies to determine menu prices.
2. Find the menu price using the markup strategy.
3. Find the menu price using the food cost percent method.
4. Find the menu price using the multiplier strategy.
5. Find the food cost, food cost percent, or sales price using the Chef's Magic Circle.
6. Find the break-even point.

The **menu** is a detailed list of food served in a food service establishment. It should be organized in such a way that selections can be made in a short period of time. For example, the Desmond Hotel in Albany, New York, offers their guests two restaurants for dining. (See Figures 16-1 and 16-2.) Each item listed on a menu is priced for sale to customers, and in this chapter we will show how that price is determined.

PRICING THE MENU

In the past, pricing the menu was often done in a random fashion. Arriving at a selling price per item was based on your competition rather than your cost. If your competition charged $22.95 for prime rib of beef au jus, you would charge the same. Although there is still no one standard method of pricing items on a menu, food service operators must now determine their cost before deciding how much should be charged to make a profit. Many elements must be considered before a menu price is determined. The cost of all items purchased, rent, labor costs, equipment, taxes and so forth must be considered before establishing a price.

Large food service operations and chain operations doing a significant volume of business usually have accountants and computers to supply an accurate picture of the overall cost of maintaining a food service business. This makes pricing decisions easier for those involved. In smaller operations, however, the overall cost is more difficult to compute because controls are not always as tight as they should be and records are not always as accurate because of the time and cost involved.

.APPETIZERS

Iced Gazpacho Soup	$3.95	Stuffed Mushroom Caps	$5.95
New England Clam Chowder	$4.00	Crispy Potato Skins	$6.95
French Onion Soup	$4.25	Fresh Mozzarella Salad	$7.95
Soup of the Day	$2.75	Shrimp Cocktail	$7.95

Clams or Oysters on the Half Shell $6.95

SALADS

Caesar Salad $2.95
Chilled Romaine Lettuce tossed with a Classical Dressing
Topped with Grated Cheese and Seasoned Croutons

Spinach Salad $2.95
Fresh Spinach accompanied by Seasoned Croutons, Bacon and
Chopped Egg Served with Warm Bacon Vinaigrette.

VEGETARIAN ENTREES
All served with Simpson's salad with choice of dressing and vegetables of the day

Mediterranean Pizza $8.95
A Thick Pizza Crust Spread with a Sun-Dried Tomato Pesto and Topped with
Greek Olives, Grilled Fennel, Fresh Tomatoes, Smoked Mozzarella and Feta Cheese

Vegetable Stir-Fry $11.95
Fresh Vegetables Sauteed with an Oriental Flair
Served With Lo Mein Noodles

Bow-Tie Primavera $10.50
An Array of Fresh Vegetables Tossed with Bow-Tie Pasta and Light Cream Gratin

ENTREES
Each Entrée Includes Simpson's Salad with Choice of Dressing,
(Choice of Potato, Au Gratin, Baked Potato, French Fries or Rice Pilaf)
And fresh Vegetables of the day.

Seafood Pasta Alfredo $16.95
A Combination of Crabmeat, Baby Shrimp and Sea Scallops, Served in a Garlic Cream
Over Linguini Topped with Grated Parmesan Cheese

Grilled Swordfish $19.95
Fresh Swordfish Char-Grilled and Topped with Maitre D' Butter

Citrus Grilled Shrimp $18.95
Marinated Jumbo Gulf Shrimp Brushed with Citrus Butter and Chargrilled,
Accompanied by a Tropical Fruit Salsa

Figure 16-1 *Luncheon menu with weekly specials* *(continued)*

Fillet of Sole $15.95
Fresh Atlantic Sole, Broiled with Crushed Herbs and Topped with a
Sun Dried Tomato Butter

Herb Crusted Scallops $17.95
Large Sea Scallops Encrusted with Fresh Herbs and Broiled,
Served with Tomato-Caper Vinaigrette.

Grilled Salmon $17.95
Fresh Atlantic Salmon Fillet Basted with Dill Butter,
Char-Grilled and Served With Dill Hollandaise on the Side.

Prime Rib
Simpson's Specialty-Available while it Lasts
Choose the Portion of This succulent Aged Prime Rib, Cooked as you Like it,
Served With a Tangy Horseradish Sauce on the Side
12 ounce $17.95 16 ounce $19.95 Larger Cuts Available on Request

New York Sirloin Steak $17.95
A Thick 14-ounce Tender Aged New York Sirloin
Charbroiled to Your Liking, Served with Crispy Fried Onions
Piled High Served with Sauce Bernaise.

Filet Mignon $24.95
10 ounce Char-Grilled Center-Cut Filet Mignon, Served with Crispy
Fried Onions, Piled High and Served With Sauce Bernaise.

New York Sirloin Steak and Breast of Chicken Teriyaki $17.95
8-ounce New York Strip Steak Char-grilled to your liking
Served With Crispy Fried Onions Piled High and Sauce Bernaise ,
Combined with an 8-ounce Breast of Chicken Marinated in Teriyaki and Char-Grilled.

Cajun Style Steak $17.95
Center Cut New York Sirloin Rubbed with Cajun Spices and Char-Grilled.

Turkey Chop $16.95
Marinated and Char-Grilled, Served with Roasted Peach Chutney.

Barbecued Spareribs $16.95
Tender Rack of Ribs, Accompanied by Grilled Corn Bread.

Peppered Ribeye Steak $17.95
14 oz. Sauteed Ribeye Steak Served With Red Wine Au Jus.

Chicken Teriyaki $15.95
Boneless Breasts of Chicken Marinated in Teriyaki Sauce and Char-Grilled
Available Skinless Upon Request.

Creole Grilled Chicken Breast $16.95
Marinated with Fresh Herbs, Grilled and Topped with Tomato Creole.

Coffee, Tea, Soda, Milk Etc.

Figure 16-1 *Luncheon menu with weekly specials (Courtesy of the Desmond Hotel).*

Appetizers

Oysters Rockefeller	*$7.95*
Jumbo Shrimp Cocktail	*$8.50*
Clams Casino	*$8.50*
Escargot	*$7.50*
Smoked Norwegian Salmon	*$7.95*
Clams on the Half Shell	*$6.95*
Oysters on the Half Shell	*$6.95*
Wild Mushroom Ravioli	*$4.50*
Soup du Jour	*$2.95*
New England Clam Chowder	*$4.00*

Salads

Scrimshaw Salad
Radicchio Romaine, Boston Bibb, and Red Leaf Lettuce Topped with Sliced Mushrooms, Mandarin Oranges, Sliced Almonds, Cheddar Cheese and Our Own Creamy Garlic Dressing

Caesar Salad
Chilled Romaine Served with the Traditional Accompaniments and a Zesty Caesar Dressing

Traditional Entrees

Herb Roasted Rack of Lamb
Accompanied by wild rice and served with demi glaze *$27.95*

Veal Marsala *$19.95*
Prepared with a delicate marsala wine sauce and wild mushrooms

Veal Oscar *$21.95*
Topped with king crab, asparagus and a hollandaise sauce over a rich brown demi glace

Filet Mignon *$28.95*
A 12 ounce center cut served with sauteed mushrooms

New York Sirloin *$21.95*
A 16 ounce dry-aged center cut sirloin with maitre d' butter

Steak Au Poivre *$23.95*
A center cut sirloin served with a cognac cream and peppercorn sauce

Prime Rib
Petite 12 ounce cut *$19.95*
Gentlemen's 16 ounce cut *$23.95*

Chicken Francaise *$18.95*
Chicken Breast served with a lemon caper sauce

Figure 16-2 *The dinner menu from the Scrimshaw Restaurant* *(continued)*

Desmond Specialties

Broiled Seafood Platter Lobster Tail, Lemon Sole, Shrimp, Scallops and Clams		$32.50
Cedar Plank Salmon Fresh Atlantic Salmon broiled on a red cedar plank and served with a lingonberry port sauce		$20.95
Jumbo Shrimp Scampi Delicious Jumbo Shrimp sauteed over a flavorful rice pilaf		$21.95
Sea Scallops Broiled with Chardonnay		$18.95
Live Maine Lobster		
Grilled, steamed or baked & stuffed with	1 1/2lb	$24.50
crabmeat dressing	2 lb	$32.00
	Stuffed Add	$2.00

Surf and Turf Combinations

6 oz. Filet Mignon with a choice of	Shrimp Scampi	$25.50
	Lobster Tail	$32.50
	Broiled Scallops	$24.50
12 oz. Sirloin of Beef with a choice of	Shrimp Scampi	$23.50
	Lobster Tail	$32.50
	Grilled Chicken Breast	$20.50

All Entrees Served with Salad, Vegetable & Potato

SCRIMSHAW POTATO
A Flaky Puff Pastry Shell Filled with Caramelized Onions, Topped with Duchess Whipped Potatoes and Baked to a Golden Brown
or
Baked Potato, French Fries, Au Gratin or Rice.
All Entrees Served with Salad & Potato.

Figure 16-2 *The dinner menu from the Scrimshaw Restaurant (Courtesy of the Desmond Hotel).*

Determining the menu price per item is one of the most challenging and difficult tasks a food service professional will have to accomplish. As the previous paragraph states, large food service operations and chain operations have an easier time setting menu prices than smaller operations. One of the first questions asked by small operators, caterers, and students is, "How do I price my menu?"

Ideally, the food service professional should *figure out and know all the costs before* setting the menu price. Then the menu price can be determined based on costs, type of service, location, and other factors. The final question that has to be answered concerns the amount of profit that is desired. Small operators do not have this information available before the restaurant is opened.

However, there is one item a restaurant owner *can and must* do before setting the menu price of an individual entree or sandwich. Taking Chef Sonnenschmidt's advice from Chapter 15 (Chef Sez), the price of the raw food cost for each menu item *must* be determined. In other words, each food service business should know *exactly* how much it costs to place one meal in front of one guest. Once that is determined, the menu price can be calculated. This food cost must include the entree, starch, vegetable, and whatever else is included in the menu price. For example, if a restaurant is serving a lobster roll, the cost of the lobster meat, roll, and butter has to be included. A 3-ounce portion of lobster meat costs $2.50, the roll costs $0.10, and the butter costs $0.10. Therefore, it costs the restaurant $2.70 to serve one lobster roll to a guest.

The restaurant owner must also include all of the costs involved in serving one lobster roll to one guest. The cost of people to prepare the food (labor cost), paper plates, garbage removal, snow plowing, and so on must be figured into the equation before establishing a price for the lobster roll. Then an amount of money (the profit) must be added to the costs, and a final menu determination can be made.

When pricing the menu, food service professionals use three methods that take into account all of the factors listed above. They are *amount of markup using a percent, food cost percent, and multiplier effect.*

MARKUP

In menu pricing, the only standard is that cost must be established before a markup can be added to determine an item's selling price. **Markup** is the money added to raw food cost to obtain a menu price. The amount of markup usually varies depending on the type of establishment. A cafeteria might mark up all its items by one-half the cost to obtain a menu price; a gourmet restaurant might mark up all its items by two or three times the cost to obtain a menu price. The markup is not always figured using fractions. In many cases, percents are used because they are easier to work with and less mistakes are made.

Amount of Markup Using a Fraction

If the price of a raw food is $1.95 and the markup rate is $\frac{2}{3}$, markup is obtained by multiplying the cost by the markup rate. The formula for this is:

Step 1: Raw food cost × markup rate = markup amount
Step 2: Raw food cost + markup amount = menu or selling price

For example:

$$\frac{\$1.95}{1} \times \frac{2}{3} = \frac{\$3.90}{3} = \$1.30 \text{ markup amount}$$

$1.95 raw food cost + $1.30 markup amount
= $3.25 menu or selling price

Amount of Markup Using a Percent

If the markup is figured by using percent, the menu or selling price of an item is determined by multiplying the raw food cost by the percent and adding the markup to the raw food cost. The formula for this is:

Step 1: Raw food cost × percent = markup amount
Step 2: Raw food cost + markup amount = menu or selling price

When multiplying or dividing with percents, it is best to convert the percent to its decimal equivalent. This is done by removing the percent sign (%) and moving the decimal point two places to the left. For instance:

60% = 0.60

75% = 0.75

25.5% = 0.255

50.5% = 0.505

For example: If the raw food cost is $1.95 and the markup rate is 45 percent, convert 45 percent to 0.45 and multiply.

$1.95	Raw food cost
× 0.45	Markup percent
975	
780	
$0.8775	= $0.88 markup amount

Then add the markup ($0.88) to the raw food cost to determine the selling cost or menu price.

$1.95	Raw food cost
× 0.88	Markup Amount
$2.83	Menu or selling price

Food Cost Percent

Another method of menu pricing is to determine the monthly food cost percent and divide the food cost percent into the raw food cost. The formula for this is:

Raw food cost ÷ food cost percent = menu or selling price

For example: If the raw food cost is $2.90 and the monthly food cost percent is 35%, the menu price is determined by dividing 35 percent (or 0.35) into $2.90.

```
                             8.285   = $8.29 menu or selling price
Food cost percent 0.35)2.90000         Raw food cost
                       2 80
                        100
                         70
                        300
                        280
                         200
                         175
                          25
```

Many operators rely on the food cost percentage method of pricing the menu. In the example, our restaurant has set a goal of 25 percent for food cost for the lobster roll. That will leave 75 percent of the menu price to pay for all the expenses (plates, snow plowing, etc.) as well as make a profit.

$2.70 raw food cost ÷ .25 food cost percent
= $10.80 menu price

Our menu price of one lobster roll will be $10.80.

Multiplier Effect

In the past, many restaurant owners did not take the time or effort to figure out their exact costs before they priced the menu. An easier and quicker system was developed to price the menu called the **multiplier effect.** It works on the principle of food cost percentage, but instead of dividing, the restaurant owner multiplies the cost of the raw food by a number that corresponds to the food cost percentage goal. Therefore, to obtain a food cost percentage the restaurant owner takes the cost of the raw food and multiplies that number by the multiplier. In our example with the lobster roll, if we desire a food cost percentage of 25 percent, we take the cost of the raw food ($2.70) and multiply by 4 (see Figure 16-3).

$2.70	Cost of the lobster roll
× 4	Multiplier
$10.80	Menu price

This is the same menu price that was obtained by dividing the raw cost of food by the food cost percentage.

$2.70 raw food cost ÷ .25 food cost percent = $10.80 menu price

Raw food cost	Percent using a markup	Food cost percent	Multiplier effect	Menu price
$3.00	100%	50%	2	$ 6.00
$3.00	150%	40%	2.5	$ 7.50
$3.00	200%	33.3%	3	$ 9.00
$3.00	300%	25%	4	$12.00
$3.00	400%	20%	5	$15.00

Figure 16-3 *Pricing the menu.*

This method of pricing is sometimes used in a simpler manner by determining that to maintain a 33 percent food cost, the selling or menu price of a meal or item should be three times the raw food cost. If the food cost is 40 percent, the menu price should be $2\frac{1}{2}$ times the raw food cost, and for 50 percent food cost, the menu price should be two times the raw food cost. Using this method is quick, with less figuring involved.

For example: If the raw food cost is $2.90 and the monthly food cost is 40 percent ($2\frac{1}{2}$ times the raw food cost), the price is determined by multiplying $2\frac{1}{2} \times \$2.90$.

$$2\tfrac{1}{2} \times \$2.90 = \tfrac{5}{2} \times \tfrac{2.90}{1} = \$7.25 \text{ menu or selling price}$$

This problem can also be done by first converting $2\frac{1}{2}$ to the decimal 2.5 before multiplying.

$$\begin{array}{r} \$2.90 \\ \times\ 2.5 \\ \hline 1450 \\ 580 \\ \hline \$7.250 \end{array} = \$7.25 \text{ menu or selling price}$$

It has become a custom in the food service industry to price menu items so that they end in amounts of $0.25, $0.50, $0.75, or $1.00 to speed the totaling of checks. The customer can relate to the price faster, and in most cases less change is handled. This helps the establishment provide good service and maintain a more efficient operation. Thus, when a menu or selling price is determined to be $10.18, the price listed on the menu is usually $10.25. The exception to this custom has been fast food operations, which seem to like unusual prices such as $0.99 for their attention-getting quality. Examples of this custom are listed below.

Determined Price	Menu Price
$1.15	$1.25
$3.35	$3.50
$5.60	$5.75
$8.90	$9.00

Note that the price never reduces. It always moves upward.

Remember that prices are important in a customer's appraisal of a food service operation. It is essential that a price level be established that appeals to all types of potential customers. It must not only be a price customers can afford, but one that they feel is closely related to the quality of food and service they receive.

Remember, too, that the food service operator is in business to make a profit and that profits will usually result if an establishment is built on a solid foundation of quality food, attractive decor, fair prices, and good service.

Pricing the Menu

The three methods that can be used to price the menu: amount of markup using a percent, food cost percent, and multiplier effect will all yield the same final menu price. Figure 16-3 illustrates how each method is to be used.

For example: The cost of the raw food is $3.00. To find the menu price of the item with a markup of 100 percent, the $3.00 is multiplied by 100 percent which equals $3.00. This product of $3.00 is added to the original raw food cost to arrive at a menu cost of $6.00.

To find the menu price of the item using a 50 percent food cost, the 50 percent or .50 is divided into the raw cost of food ($3.00). The menu price with a 50 percent food cost is $6.00.

The easiest way to obtain the answer to the above questions is to use the multiplier. From the chart, the student can see that a markup of 100 percent or a food cost of 50 percent is arrived at by multiplying the raw food cost by 2. The menu price using 2 as a multiplier is $6.00.

T I P S . . . ***(To Insure Perfect Solutions)***

The Chef's Magic Circle

The Chef's Magic Circle (see Figure 16-4) was developed at the Community College of Southern Nevada by Certified Executive Chef Thomas Rosenberger. Chef Rosenberger is the Director of Food and Beverage Management Programs. He developed this technique to help students learn a method that is *easy to use* and *easy to remember.* This method was presented at a seminar at The American Culinary Federation's national convention in July 1999. The following material is reproduced from the handout given to participants at the convention.

The Method—Food Cost The Chef's Magic Circle is a paper calculator that allows for the easy calculation of Food Cost, Food Cost Percentage, and Sales Price. The method involves covering up what it is you want to find. Place your thumb over what you want to calculate on the circle, for instance Food Cost, and see what is left. Notice that Food Cost Percentage and Sales Price remain, separated by a vertical line. When calculating Food Cost, multiply Food Cost Percentage by Sales Price, with Food Cost Percentage expressed as a decimal. The vertical line indicates multiplication. In algebraic terminology this calculation would be expressed as FC = SP*FC%, but who wants, or needs, to remember formulae when you have the Chef's Magic Circle! Just plug in the numbers and perform the calculation indicated.

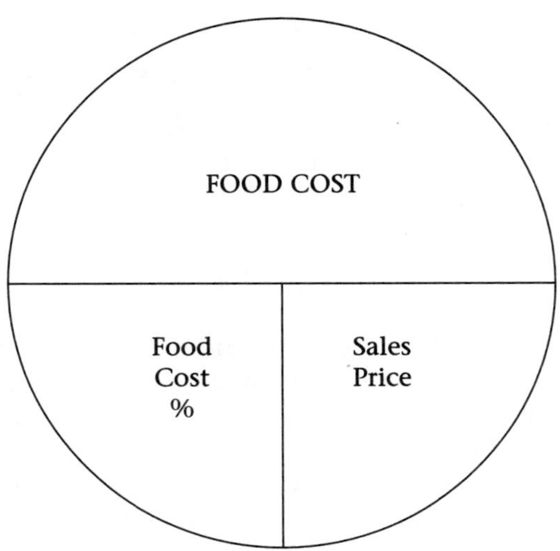

Figure 16-4 *The Chef's Magic Circle.*

The Method—Sales Price (or Menu Price) To calculate Sales Price, cover Sales Price on the circle and notice that Food Cost and Food Cost Percentage are divided by the horizontal line. When calculating Sales Price, divide Food Cost by Food Cost Percentage, which is expressed as a decimal. The horizontal line indicates division. In algebraic terminology this calculation would be expressed as SP = FC / FC%, but who wants, or needs, to remember formulae when you have the Chef's Magic Circle! Just plug in the numbers and perform the calculation indicated.

The Method—Food Cost Percentage To calculate Food Cost Percentage, cover Food Cost Percentage on the circle and notice that Food Cost and Sales Price are divided by the horizontal line. Again, the horizontal line indicates division. In algebraic terminology this calculation would be expressed as FC% = FC / SP, but who wants, or needs, to remember formulae when you have the Chef's Magic Circle! Just plug in the numbers and perform the calculation indicated.

Summary Review

Determine the menu price if:

1. The raw food cost is $4.20 and the markup rate is $\frac{2}{3}$.

____

2. The raw food cost is $6.60 and the markup rate is $\frac{5}{8}$.

____

3. The raw food cost is $3.25 and the markup rate is 43%.

____

4. The raw food cost is $5.55 and the markup rate is 60.5%.

____

5. The raw food cost is $4.96 and the markup rate is 38%.

____

6. The raw food cost is $3.72 and a 25% food cost is desired.

____

7. The raw food cost is $4.29 and a 59% food cost is desired.

____

8. The raw food cost is $12.72 and a 100% food cost is desired.

____

9. The raw food cost is $1.57 and a 43% food cost is desired.

____

10. The raw food cost is $5.63 and a 17% food cost is desired.

____

11. The raw food cost is $4.25 and a 25% food cost is desired.

____

12. The raw food cost is $4.25 and a 20% food cost is desired.

____

13. The raw food cost is $4.25 and a 40% food cost is desired.

____

14. The raw food cost is $4.25 and a 50% food cost is desired.

____

15. The raw food cost is $4.25 and a 33.3% food cost is desired.

____

16. The raw food cost is $4.25 and a 200% markup is desired.

____

17. What is the menu price using the multiplier of 3 if the raw food cost is $4.25?

____

18. What is the menu price using the multiplier of 2.5 if the raw food cost is $4.25?

____

19. What is the menu price using the multiplier of 2 if the raw food cost is $4.25?

____

20. What is the menu price using the multiplier of 5 if the raw food cost is $4.25?

____

Using the Chef's Magic Circle complete the following questions:

Question	Food Cost	Food Cost Percentage	Sales Price
21	$ 2.79	31.4%	$
22	$ 3.97	39.8%	$
23	$	24.9%	$ 7.35
24	$	19.4%	$24.95
25	$ 2.48	%	$11.95
26	$ 6.93	%	$19.95
27	$11.99	%	$49.95

28. In our restaurant we used a total of $43,189.00 in food last month. We earned revenue of $99,687.00. What was our food cost percentage for the month?

____

29. In May we spent $51,292.00 for food. Revenue for May was $109,213.00 and we have projected a 32.8% food cost percentage for the month. What was our food cost percentage for the month?

____

30. Next month we have forecasted a revenue of $61,484.00 and want a food cost percentage of 33.3%. What should our total expenditure of food dollars be for the month to achieve the desired food cost percentage?

____

BREAK-EVEN ANALYSIS

Break-even analysis is a mathematical method for finding the dollar amount needed for a food service operation to break even.

Break-even analysis calculates the level of economic activity where the operation neither makes a profit nor incurs a loss. It is based on a certain amount that must be achieved through total sales before a profit can be realized and below which a loss is incurred. This method is beneficial to the food service operator for planning profits. Planning profits is extremely important to any business operation when financial planning decisions must be made. In the food service industry, where bankruptcy is commonplace, the break-even figure could be a key to survival.

The concept of determining the break-even point of a food service operation can be expressed in this formula:

Step 1: Sales Revenue − Variable Costs = Gross Profit
Step 2: Gross Profit − Fixed Costs = 0 Break-Even Point

For example, using figures easy to follow:

Sales Revenue		Variable Cost		Gross Profit
$10,000	−	$5,000	=	$5,000
Gross Profit		Fixed Cost		
$5,000	−	$5,000	=	$0 Break-Even Point

Mathematical problems are expressed by formulas. If the formula is followed, a solution can be found. It is important to be able to identify, understand, and be familiar with each part of the break-even formula.

Sales revenue is the money received from the sale of all products, food, beverage, etc. It represents all of the money received over a certain period of time through cash sales.

Variable cost is the changeable cost or expenses that will increase or decrease with the level of sales volume. The greater the number of people served and meals produced, the greater the variable cost. Variable cost may be divided into two categories: cost of goods sold and serving expenses.

Cost of goods sold is the amount it costs the operator to provide food, beverages, etc., to serve customers. It is the operator's cost of goods to be sold.

Serving expenses are additional expenses incurred as a result of serving customers. These include:

- Laundry—tablecloths, napkins, kitchen towels, uniforms.
- Paper supplies—guest checks, report forms, register tapes.
- Payroll—labor cost.
- Tableware replacement—glassware, china, silverware.

Gross profit is the sales revenue minus variable costs. This is the total value before deducting fixed cost.

Fixed cost is the expenses that remain constant regardless of the level of sales volume. They may be divided into two categories: occupational expenses and primary expenses.

Occupational expenses, also called the cost of ownership, are those that continue whether or not the restaurant is operating. They include such expenses as property tax, insurance, interest on the mortgage, and depreciation of equipment, furniture, and building. There may be others depending on the local situation.

Primary expenses are those that result from being open for business. These expenses are constant whether serving a few customers or many. They include such expenses as utilities, basic staff (preparation, service, etc.), telephone service, repairs and maintenance, licenses, and exterminating costs.

As an example, if there is a $10,000 sales revenue and $5,000 variable expenses, the operation would have a $5,000 gross profit. If the fixed cost is $5,000, this restaurant would have zero profit and zero loss and thus break even. The $10,000 sales level is the break-even point for this business. Anything over this figure is profit; anything below is a loss.

The relationship between sales revenue, variable cost, and fixed costs must be known for profit planning purposes. It is necessary to find the percents that can be applied to these different dollar amounts.

Taking the figures given in our example and putting them into the form of an operating statement, the percents are as follows:

Sales Revenue	$10,000	100%
Less Variable Cost	$5,000	50%
= Gross Profit	$5,000	50%
Less Fixed Cost	$5,000	50%
= Net Income (loss)	-0-	(Breakeven)

Remember that percents are used by the restaurant operator because they give a clearer picture of the overall relationship between sales revenue and cost. The percents shown in the example were found in the following way:

Sales revenue always equals 100 percent. It represents all that is received. It was shown earlier in this text that to find a percent, the whole is divided into the part, so in this case $10,000 is divided into the variable cost $5,000.

$$\$5{,}000/\$10{,}000 = 50\%\ \text{Variable Cost}$$

Variable costs + gross profit = 100 percent. Next, $10,000 is divided into the fixed cost, $5,000.

$$\frac{\$5{,}000}{\$10{,}000} = 50\ \text{percent fixed cost}$$

Then the fixed cost of 50 percent is subtracted from the gross profit, to get 0 percent (breakeven).

In calculating the break-even point, two key facts should be remembered:

- Sales revenue always equals 100 percent.
- Once the gross profit percent is determined, it is easy to calculate the break-even point.

In this example, sales equal $10,000, which represents 100 percent. The gross profit is 50 percent which is determined by dividing the dollar amount of gross profit by sales.

$$\frac{\$5{,}000}{\$10{,}000} = 0.50 \text{ gross profit percent}$$

Having found the gross profit percent, it is then divided into the fixed cost to determine the break-even point.

$5,000	Fixed cost
0.50	Gross profit percent

	$10,000.00	Break-even point
Gross Profit Percent 0.50)	5,000.00	Fixed cost
	5 0	
	0	

Problem: The variable cost of the Blue Jay Restaurant is 40 percent of the total sales. The fixed cost is $18,000. What is the break-even point?

Sales − Variable Cost = Gross Profit Percent

Solution:	Sales	100%
	Variable cost	40% Given
	Gross Profit Percent	60% Found

Divide 60 percent (gross profit percent) into $18,000 (fixed cost) to find the break-even point.

	$30,000.00	Break-even point
Gross Profit Percent 0.60)	18,000.00	Fixed cost
	18 0	
	0	

Proof:

Sales	$20,000	100% Always
Variable Cost	$12,000	40% Known
Gross Profit	$18,000	60% Found
Fixed Cost (Known)	$18,000	
Net Income (Loss)	-0-	Breakeven

Of course, breaking even is not the reason a person is in business. One is usually in business to make a profit. Assume that the Blue Jay Restaurant did $50,000 in sales and determine the profit through break-even analysis. It is known that 40 percent of every dollar taken in is used to pay the cost of food and beverage. It is also known that the fixed cost is

$18,000. So knowing these figures it is simple to determine what the profit will be by following the formula given previously.

Sales Revenue	$50,000	100% Always
Less Variable Cost	$20,000	40% Known
Gross Profit	$30,000	60% Found
Less Fixed Cost (Known)	$18,000	
Net Income (Before Taxes)	$12,000	Profit

In this calculation, it is noted that in dollar amounts, variable cost is $20,000. The variable cost rate of 40 percent remains the same. Remember that the percent remains constant but the dollar amounts fluctuate with an increase or decrease in sales volume. This is because it costs more money (in food, beverage, laundry, tableware—all variable costs) to serve more people, and less money to serve less people.

The break-even point indicates that at a given sales volume the fixed cost has been met. Fixed means that a certain portion of cost does not change regardless of the volume of business.

Looking at the problem again, the following rule can be proven: All sales above the break-even point result in a profit (before taxes) of an amount equal to the gross profit percent.

Proof:

$50,000	Sales revenue
− $30,000	Break-even point
$20,000	Above break-even point (profit)

Gross profit rate (60%) times $20,000

$20,000	Above break-even point (profit)
× 0.60	Gross profit rate
$12,000	Net income (before taxes)

Yes, this is equal to the profit (net income) before taxes. The rule holds true. It always will.

There are times in the restaurant business when a loss occurs.

For example: Assume that the Blue Jay Restaurant did only $28,000 in sales.

Sales revenue	$28,000	100% Always
Variable cost	$11,200	40% Known
Gross Profit	$16,800	60% Found
Fixed cost (known)	$18,000	
Net Loss	($1,200)	

TIPS . . . ***To Insure Perfect Solutions***

When a loss occurs, the dollar amount is written inside parentheses on financial statements.

Note that although the variable cost percentage rate remained constant (40 percent) the dollar amount changed.

$28,000	Sales
× 0.40	Variable cost
$11,200	Dollar amount of variable cost

The change occurred because of a decrease in sales volume from $50,000 (when a profit was made) to $28,000 (when a loss occurred).

Chef Sez . . .

"Cost controls, math and numbers, are at the very heart of successful restaurants, regardless of their niche. The information and consequent knowledge gleaned from the numbers and their correct interpretation truly drives the restaurant's success."

Harold Qualters
General Manager
Troy Pub & Brewery
Troy, New York

The Troy Pub & Brewery (est. 1993) is a 300-plus-seat pub restaurant housed in a renovated 19th-century warehouse having a massive deck and overlooking the Hudson River. It is located in historic Troy, New York, the home of Uncle Sam. Harold Qualters is a past chairman of the New York State Restaurant Association and has served as chairperson for their annual food show held yearly in New York City.

SUMMARY REVIEW

For each problem given below, determine the break-even point, show proof, and find the amount of profit or loss. If a profit exists, see if the rule about gross profit percent holds true.

Before the student begins the break-even summary review, the following illustration will provide step-by-step directions for solving the problems.

Step-by-step directions for solving problem 1.

Step 1—Determine the percent of gross profit.

Sales are $80,000 which equals	100%	
Subtract variable cost which equals	− 40%	
The gross profit equals	60%	

Step 2—Determine the amount of the gross profit.

Sales are $80,000 which equals	100%	$80,000
Subtract variable cost which equals	40%	−$32,000
The gross profit equals	60%	$48,000

Step 3—Find the net profit.

Gross profit	$48,000
Subtract fixed costs which were given	−$24,000
Net profit	$24,000

Step 4—Determine the Break-even point

Fixed Costs	$24,000
Divided by the gross profit percent	÷ 60%
Break-even point	$40,000

Show the proof of the rule:

Sales	\$80,000
Minus break-even point	−\$40,000
	\$40,000
Multiplied by the gross profit percent	×.60
Equals the net profit	\$24,000

1. The Blue Bird Cafeteria did \$80,000 in sales. Their variable cost was 40 percent of the total sales and the fixed costs were \$24,000.

2. The Castle Restaurant did \$120,000 in sales. Their variable cost was 36 percent of the total sales and the fixed costs were \$32,000.

3. The Blue Angel Restaurant did \$32,000 in sales. Their variable cost was 40 percent of the total sales and the fixed costs were \$24,000.

4. The Red Gate Cafeteria did \$96,000 in sales. Their variable cost was 43 percent of the total sales and the fixed costs were \$63,600.

5. The Old Mill Restaurant did \$72,500 in sales. Their variable cost was 44 percent of the total sales and the fixed costs were \$28,112.

Inventory Procedures

OBJECTIVES

At the completion of this chapter, the student should be able to:

1. Identify perpetual inventory.
2. Identify physical inventory.
3. Find the cost of food sold.
4. Find the monthly food cost percent.
5. Identify computer applications for inventory procedures.

Inventory is a well-known business term because it is an activity that takes place in many business operations at least once a year. In a food service operation, it can be a continuous activity. An **inventory** is a catalog or itemized list of stock and its estimated value. An inventory of food service equipment may be taken from time to time, but the most important inventory concerns food. There are two kinds of inventories pertaining to food that are of major importance: the perpetual inventory and the physical inventory.

Chef Sez . . .

"When I enter mystery basket hot and cold food competitions, I may be given 70 or more food products and ingredients to prepare a meal. I never know how much or what type of ingredients will be available. In thirty minutes, I have to create a menu using all of the 70 ingredients and determine how much of each ingredient is needed to prepare the amount of food for the competition. A chef in these competitions must think quickly, respond appropriately, and choose the right ingredients and the correct amounts based upon the physical inventory he or she receives. The knowledge and use of math is used in every one of these competitions."

Jill K. Bosich
American Culinary Federation
Culinary Team 2000
Chef-Instructor, Orange Coast College
Costa Mesa, California

Chef Bosich is a member of the United States Olympic Culinary Team that competed in the 2000 Olympics in Berlin. She has her own culinary consulting, catering, and design company, "Currants." Chef Bosich has been awarded the prestigious DiRoNa standing while she was executive chef at Summer House Inn and Elario's Restaurant. The American Academy of Hospitality Sciences named her as "One of America's Best Chefs." She was captain of the 1996 Western Regional Culinary Team, USA.

Perpetual Inventory

A **perpetual inventory** is a continuous or endless inventory. It is a record that is taken in the storeroom to show the balance on hand for each storeroom item. (See Figure 17-1.) As a requisition from the production crew is received and the items are issued, the amounts are subtracted from the inventory balance. When new shipments of each item arrive and are placed on the shelves, they are added to the inventory balance.

If the food service operation does a large volume of business, a computer would probably be placed in the storeroom to handle these functions. If a computer is not available, the functions are done manually. At the end of each month, when the physical inventory of each item is taken, the physical inventory should match the perpetual inventory. If the two do not match, a problem exists. The problem may be poor bookkeeping, negligence in checking incoming orders, theft, or a similar situation. Keep in mind that in a business operation, control is a key word. The more departments, functions, or activities that can be controlled by management, the more profits will show up on the P&L sheet (Profit and Loss sheet).

Figure 17-1 *Storeroom inventory.*

Physical Inventory

The **physical inventory** is taken at the end of each month in order to determine the accurate cost of food consumed during that period. When doing a physical inventory, an actual count is taken of all stock on hand. The physical inventory figures are most important when making out the profit and loss sheet.

The inventory sheet should be prepared in advance using a standard form. This form should contain the name of each item, the quantity, size or bulk, unit price, and total price of items on hand. Two people usually take the inventory, one calling out the items on hand and the other recording the items and quantities. (See Figure 17-2.) While this task can be done by one person, it would be time consuming. The unit price for

Figure 17-2 *Two employees conducting an inventory of the storeroom.*

each item listed can be obtained from invoices and purchase records. When setting up an inventory sheet, most establishments classify the food and supply items into common groups such as:

- canned foods,
- other groceries,
- butter, eggs, and cheese,
- coffee and tea,
- fruits and vegetables,
- meat, poultry, and fish, and
- supplies.

When the total inventory value is found, this figure represents the cost of food still on hand or in storage. It is food that has not been sold during this inventory period. The inventory value is then used to find the monthly food cost percent. When computing the monthly food cost percent, this figure is referred to as the **final inventory.**

To find the monthly food cost percent, the purchases for the month are added to the inventory at the beginning of the month and the final inventory is subtracted to give the cost of food sold for the month. The food cost percent is then found by dividing the total sales for the month into the cost of food sold. The division should be carried four places to the right of the decimal to give the percent. (See Figure 17-3.)

Purchases + beginning inventory − final inventory = Cost of food sold

Cost of food sold ÷ total sales = Food cost percent

The amount of sales is found by totaling the register tapes for that particular month. It is the total of all sales made during that period. The purchases for the month represent the total of all the food purchased during that month. This is found by adding the totals of all invoices sent with each food purchase. The inventory at the beginning of the month is the final inventory from the previous month. (For an example of a physical inventory recapitulation see Figure 17-4.)

Sales	$2,550.00
Inventory at Beginning of Month	300.00
Purchases for the Month	895.00
Final Inventory	250.00

Step 1

To find the **Cost of Food Sold,** first add:

Inventory at Beginning of Month	$ 300.00
to Purchases for the Month	+ 895.00
	$1,195.00

Step 2

Then, from this sum	$1,195.00
Subtract the Final Inventory	− 250.00
Cost of Food Sold	$ 945.00

Step 3

To find the **Monthly Food Cost Percent**

Divide the Sales into the Cost of Food Sold

```
                .3705   = 37.1% Monthly Food Cost Percent
Sales  2,550)945.0000     Cost of Food Sold
             765 0
             180 00
             178 50
               1 5000
               1 2750
                 2250
```

Figure 17-3 How to find cost of food sold and monthly food cost percent.

Example of a Physical Inventory
(Prices are not current)
Weekly or Period Inventory Recapitulation

Week Ending August 9, 20___ — Period Ending August 31, 20___

Item No.	Item	Amount
1.	Canned Goods	$ 628.59
2.	Other Groceries	779.48
3.	Butter, Eggs, Cheese	42.44
4.	Coffee and Tea	45.69
5.	Fruits and Vegetables	294.12
6.	Meat, Poultry, and Fish	1140.14
	TOTAL FOOD	$2930.46
7.	Supplies	$ 590.77
	Total Inventory Value	$3,521.23

Called By___________ Extended by ___________
Manager ___________

Figure 17-4 Example of a physical inventory.

The following charts illustrate how the physical inventory for each item in Figure 17-4 (numbers 1 through 7) was calculated.

Canned Goods			
Quantity/Size	**Item**	**Unit Price**	**Extension**
8-#10	Apples	$ 3.52	$ 28.16
6-#10	Apricots	5.29	31.74
9-#10	Beans, Green	2.61	23.49
10-#10	Beans, Kidney	1.84	18.40
12-#10	Beans, Wax	2.07	24.84
14-#10	Bean Sprouts	2.79	39.06
4-#10	Beets, Whole	3.03	12.12
3-#10	Carrots, Whole	3.44	10.32
8-#10	Cherries	7.31	58.48
2-#10	Fruit Cocktail	4.10	8.20
3-#10	Noodles (Chow Mein)	2.74	8.22
6-#10	Peach Halves	3.71	22.26
5-#10	Peaches, Pie	3.60	18.00
5-#10	Pears	3.51	17.55
4-#10	Pineapple Tidbits	3.79	15.16
10-#10	Pineapple Slices	3.84	38.40
4-#10	Plums	3.24	12.96
6-#10	Pumpkin	3.85	23.10
7-#10	Sweet Potatoes	3.26	22.82
9-#10	Tomato Catsup	2.12	19.08
8-#10	Tomato Puree	3.67	29.36
3-#10	Tomatoes	3.41	10.23
6-#10	Asparagus Spears	6.50	39.00
8-#10	Cream Style Corn	2.08	16.64
12-#10	Whole Kernel Corn	2.15	25.80
24-#2	Salmon	2.30	55.20
		Canned Goods Total	$628.59

Item No. 1 *Canned goods.*

Groceries — Dry Bulk Goods			
Quantity/Size	**Item**	**Unit Price**	**Extension**
8 lb.	Baking Soda	$0.22	$ 1.76
9 lb.	Baking Powder	8.40	75.60
8 lb.	Cocoa	5.90	47.20
6 lb.	Coconut Shred	1.12	6.72
10 lb.	Cracker Meal	0.18	1.80
4 lb.	Chicken Base	1.12	4.48
7 lb.	Beef Base	1.15	8.05
6 lb.	Raisins	1.19	7.14
9 lb.	Cornmeal	0.15	1.35
12 lb.	Cornstarch	0.46	5.52
20 lb.	Tapioca Flour	0.22	4.40
63 lb.	Bread Flour	0.20	12.60
53 lb.	Cake Flour	0.25	13.25
74 lb.	Pastry Flour	0.22	16.28
15 lb.	Elbow Macaroni	0.49	7.35
18 lb.	Spaghetti	0.52	9.36
6 lb.	Rice	0.45	2.70
12 lb.	Noodles	1.13	13.56
		Subtotal	$239.12

Item No. 2 *Other groceries.*

Groceries — Oils and Fats			
Quantity/Size	**Item**	**Unit Price**	**Extension**
12 lb.	Margarine, 1 lb.	$50.52	$ 6.24
$1\frac{1}{2}$ tin	Shortening, 50 lb. tin	26.00	39.00
2 cans	Salad Oil, 5 gal. can	22.10	44.20
		Subtotal	$89.44

Item No. 2 *Other groceries.*

Groceries — Spices			
Quantity/Size	**Item**	**Unit Price**	**Extension**
$1\frac{1}{2}$ lb.	Allspice, Ground	$ 7.02	$ 10.53
$1\frac{3}{4}$ lb.	Bay Leaves	4.20	7.35
2 lb.	Chili Powder	4.35	8.70
3 lb.	Cinnamon	6.20	18.60
4 lb.	Cloves, Ground	6.95	27.80
$1\frac{1}{4}$ lb.	Ginger, Ground	4.50	5.63
$1\frac{1}{2}$ lb.	Cumin Seed	3.82	5.73
$2\frac{1}{2}$ lb.	Celery Seed	5.10	12.75
$2\frac{1}{4}$ lb.	Caraway Seed	2.90	6.53
$1\frac{3}{4}$ lb.	Mace	12.50	21.88
$2\frac{3}{4}$ lb.	Mustard, Dry	2.80	7.70
$1\frac{1}{2}$lb.	Marjoram, Dry	3.50	5.25
3 lb.	Nutmeg	8.50	25.50
4 lb.	Oregano	4.25	17.00
5 lb.	Pepper, White	6.00	30.00
3 lb.	Pepper, Black	5.00	15.00
2 lb.	Pickling Spice	4.18	8.36
$1\frac{1}{2}$ lb.	Rosemary Leaves	8.12	12.18
$1\frac{1}{4}$ lb.	Sage	10.82	13.53
$1\frac{3}{4}$ lb.	Thyme	5.89	10.31
		Subtotal	$270.33

Item No. 2 *Other groceries.*

Groceries — Dressing and Condiments			
Quantity/Size	**Item**	**Unit Price**	**Extension**
3 gal.	Mayonnaise	$ 8.44	$ 25.32
2 gal.	Dill Pickles	3.22	6.44
$1\frac{1}{2}$ gal.	Sweet Relish	4.60	6.90
4 gal.	Salad Dressing	3.88	15.52
$6\frac{1}{2}$ gal.	Vinegar	1.20	7.80
$1\frac{1}{4}$ gal.	Soy Sauce	6.48	8.10
4 gal.	Worcestershire Sauce	3.73	14.92
5 gal.	French Dressing	4.54	22.70
		Subtotal	$107.70

Item No. 2 *Other groceries.*

Groceries — Coloring and Extracts			
Quantity/Size	**Item**	**Unit Price**	**Extension**
$1\frac{1}{2}$ qt.	Caramel Color	$ 5.95	$ 8.93
$1\frac{1}{4}$ pt.	Yellow	3.12	3.90
$1\frac{3}{4}$ pt.	Red	2.82	4.94
2 pt.	Green	3.16	6.32
1 pt.	Lemon Extract	6.99	6.99
3 pt.	Vanilla Extract	11.89	35.67
$1\frac{1}{2}$ pt.	Maple Extract	4.09	6.14
		Subtotal	$ 72.89
		Other Groceries Total	$779.48

Item No. 2 *Other groceries.*

Butter, Eggs, and Cheese			
Quantity/Size	**Item**	**Unit Price**	**Extension**
8 lb.	American Cheese	$ 1.70	$ 13.60
15 lb.	Chip Butter	1.12	16.80
14 doz.	Eggs	0.86	12.04
		Butter, Eggs, and Cheese Total	$42.44

Item No. 3 *Butter, eggs, and cheese.*

Coffee and Tea			
Quantity/Size	**Item**	**Unit Price**	**Extension**
16 lb.	Coffee	$ 2.68	$42.88
$\frac{1}{2}$ pkg.	Tea — indiv. (100)	2.50	1.25
$\frac{1}{4}$ pkg.	Tea — iced (48)	6.24	1.56
		Coffee and Tea Total	$45.69

Item No. 4 *Coffee and tea.*

Fruits and Vegetables — Fresh			
Quantity/Size	**Item**	**Unit Price**	**Extension**
4 bu.	Carrots	$ 0.89	$ 3.56
3 lb.	Endive	1.45	4.35
7 head	Head Lettuce	0.89	6.23
8 lb.	Leaf Lettuce	1.25	10.00
20 lb.	Dry Onions	0.46	9.20
54 lb.	Red Potatoes	0.53	28.62
44 lb.	Idaho Potatoes	0.51	22.44
6 lb.	Tomatoes	0.88	5.28
3 bu.	Parsley	0.45	1.35
5 lb.	Green Peppers	0.48	2.40
8 lb.	Apples	0.83	6.64
7 lb.	Bananas	0.35	2.45
4 doz.	Lemons	2.25	9.00
5 doz.	Oranges	2.25	11.25
5 bu.	Radishes	0.35	1.75
3 bu.	Celery	0.89	2.67
		Subtotal	$127.19

Item No. 5 *Fruits and vegetables—fresh.*

Fruits and Vegetables — Frozen			
Quantity/Size	**Item**	**Unit Price**	**Extension**
9 lb.	Strawberries	$ 1.06	$ 9.54
12 lb.	Peaches	1.17	14.04
16 lb.	Blueberries	1.52	24.32
34 lb.	Lima Beans	1.23	41.82
25 lb.	Corn	0.63	15.75
18 lb.	Broccoli	0.78	14.04
12 lb.	Brussels Sprouts	0.87	10.44
18 lb.	Mixed Vegetables	0.57	10.26
22 lb.	Peas	0.56	12.32
16 lb.	Cauliflower	0.90	14.40
		Subtotal	$166.93
		Fruits and Vegetables Total	$294.12

Item No. 5 *Fruits and vegetables—frozen.*

Meat, Poultry, and Fish			
Quantity/Size	**Item**	**Unit Price**	**Extension**
15 lb.	Beef Ground	$ 1.72	$ 25.80
21 lb.	Beef Round	2.25	47.25
30 lb.	Beef Ribs	2.95	88.50
22 lb.	Beef Rib Eyes	3.20	70.40
19 lb.	Beef Chuck	1.95	37.05
15 lb.	Club Steak	3.58	53.70
14 lb.	Beef Tenderloin	6.20	86.80
28 lb.	Pork Loin	5.40	151.20
22 lb.	Boston Butt	2.20	48.40
36 lb.	Veal Leg	7.40	266.40
12 lb.	Veal Shoulder	6.22	74.64
14 lb.	Veal Loin	8.20	114.80
32 lb.	Ham	2.35	75.20
		Subtotal	$1,140.14
		Meat, Poultry, and Fish Total	

Item No. 6 *Meat, poultry, and fish.*

Supplies			
Quantity/Size	**Item**	**Unit Price**	**Extension**
4	Napkins	$ 41.00	$164.00
8	Butter Chips	5.48	43.84
22	Souffle Cups	7.80	171.60
15	Paper Bags	7.95	119.25
12 gal.	Bleach	1.24	14.88
13 gal.	Dish	3.89	50.57
21 lb.	Salute	0.58	12.18
5 ea.	Pot Brushes	2.89	14.45
		Supplies Total	$590.77

Item No. 7 *Supplies.*

Sales	$54,000.00
Inventory at Beginning of Month	6,780.50
Purchases for the Month	15,890.00
Final Inventory	3,521.23

Step 1

To find the **Cost of Food Sold,** first add:

Inventory at Beginning of Month	$ 6,780.50
to Purchases for the Month	+ 15,890.00
	$22,670.50

Step 2

Then, from this sum	$22,670.50
Subtract the Final Inventory	− 3,521.23
Cost of Food Sold	$19,149.27

Step 3

To find the **Monthly Food Cost Percent**

Divide the Sales into the Cost of Food Sold

```
                   .3546    = 35.5% Monthly Food Cost Percent
Sales  54,000)19149.2700    Cost of Food Sold
              162000
               294927
               270000
                249270
                216000
                 332700
                 324000
```

Figure 17-5 *How to find cost of food sold and monthly food cost percent.*

Now that the physical inventory has been taken and calculated, the monthly food cost can be determined. (See Figure 17-5.)

To explain the beginning inventory further and to clarify a point that can be confusing, let us use the months of October and November as examples. The final inventory for the month of October becomes the beginning inventory for the month of November. The final inventory, as stated before, is found from the physical inventory taken at the end of each month. To carry this point further, the final inventory for the month of November becomes the beginning inventory for the month of December.

The monthly food cost percent tells the food service operator what percentage of the total sales for that period was used to purchase food for the operation. This is a very important figure and one that must be controlled because the cost of food and labor are the highest costs in any food service operation.

SUMMARY REVIEW

In problems 1 through 5, find the cost of food sold and the monthly food cost percent. Carry percents three places to the right of the decimal.

1. | | |
   |---|---|
   | Sales | $48,500.00 |
   | Inventory at Beginning of Month | 4,890.00 |
   | Purchases for the Month | 41,465.00 |
   | Final Inventory | 3,682.00 |
   | Cost of Food Sold | ________ |
   | Monthly Food Cost Percent | ________ |

2. | | |
   |---|---|
   | Sales | $76,585.54 |
   | Inventory at Beginning of Month | 8,296.25 |
   | Purchases for the Month | 18,440.25 |
   | Final Inventory | 4,635.65 |
   | Cost of Food Sold | ________ |
   | Monthly Food Cost Percent | ________ |

3. | | |
   |---|---|
   | Sales | $9,760.00 |
   | Inventory at Beginning of Month | 1,495.00 |
   | Purchases for the Month | 2,025.00 |
   | Final Inventory | 675.00 |
   | Cost of Food Sold | ________ |
   | Monthly Food Cost Percent | ________ |

4. | | |
   |---|---|
   | Sales | $125,545.00 |
   | Inventory at Beginning of Month | 6,264.36 |
   | Purchases for the Month | 28,418.00 |
   | Final Inventory | 3,268.45 |
   | Cost of Food Sold | ________ |
   | Monthly Food Cost Percent | ________ |

5. | | |
   |---|---|
   | Sales | $66,342.50 |
   | Inventory at Beginning of Month | 4,615.15 |
   | Purchases for the Month | 22,728.00 |
   | Final Inventory | 3,785.00 |
   | Cost of Food Sold | ________ |
   | Monthly Food Cost Percent | ________ |

In this exercise, your instructor calls out the quantity and unit price of each item listed. Quantity and unit price may be true and current value or hypothetical. The instructor should also give the figures of sales, inventory at the beginning of month, and purchases for the month.

The student is asked to find the extension price, subtotals, totals, total food (on front of inventory), total inventory value (on front of inventory), and the monthly food cost percent.

Form to Use for Part B.
Weekly or Period
Inventory Recapitulation

Week Ending ____________ Period Ending ____________

Item No.	Item	Amount
1.	Canned Goods	
2.	Other Groceries	
3.	Butter, Eggs, Cheese	
4.	Coffee and Tea	
5.	Fruits and Vegetables	
6.	Meat, Poultry, and Fish	
		TOTAL FOOD
7.	Supplies	
	Total Inventory Value	

Called By____________ Extended by ____________
Manager ____________

Groceries — Dry Bulk Goods			
Quantity/Size	**Item**	**Unit Price**	**Extension**
lb.	Baking Soda		
lb.	Baking Powder		
lb.	Cocoa		
lb.	Coconut Shred		
lb.	Cracker Meal		
lb.	Chicken Base		
lb.	Beef Base		
lb.	Raisins		
lb.	Cornmeal		
lb.	Cornstarch		
lb.	Tapioca Flour		
lb.	Bread Flour		
lb.	Cake Flour		
lb.	Pastry Flour		
lb.	Elbow Macaroni		
lb.	Spaghetti		
lb.	Rice		
lb.	Noodles		
		Subtotal	

Groceries — Oils and Fats			
Quantity/Size	**Item**	**Unit Price**	**Extension**
lb.	Margarine		
lb.	Shortening		
lb.	Salad Oil		
		Subtotal	

Groceries — Dressing and Condiments			
Quantity/Size	**Item**	**Unit Price**	**Extension**
gal.	Mayonnaise		
gal.	Dill Pickles		
gal.	Sweet Relish		
gal.	Salad Dressing		
gal.	Vinegar		
gal.	Soy Sauce		
gal.	Worcestershire Sauce		
gal.	French Dressing		
		Subtotal	

Groceries — Coloring and Extracts			
Quantity/Size	**Item**	**Unit Price**	**Extension**
qt.	Caramel Color		
pt.	Yellow		
pt.	Red		
pt.	Green		
pt.	Lemon Extract		
pt.	Vanilla Extract		
pt.	Maple Extract		
		Subtotal	
		Other Groceries Total	

Butter, Eggs, and Cheese			
Quantity/Size	**Item**	**Unit Price**	**Extension**
lb.	American Cheese		
lb.	Chip Butter		
doz.	Eggs		
		Butter, Eggs, and Cheese Total	

Fruits and Vegetables — Frozen			
Quantity/Size	**Item**	**Unit Price**	**Extension**
lb.	Strawberries		
lb.	Peaches		
lb.	Blueberries		
lb.	Lima Beans		
lb.	Corn		
lb.	Broccoli		
lb.	Brussels Sprouts		
lb.	Mixed Vegetables		
lb.	Peas		
lb.	Cauliflower		
		Subtotal	
		Fruits and Vegetables Total	

Meat, Poultry, and Fish			
Quantity/Size	**Item**	**Unit Price**	**Extension**
lb.	Beef Ground		
lb.	Beef Round		
lb.	Beef Ribs		
lb.	Beef Rib Eyes		
lb.	Beef Chuck		
lb.	Club Steak		
lb.	Beef Tenderloin		
lb.	Pork Loin		
lb.	Boston Butt		
lb.	Veal Leg		
lb.	Veal Shoulder		
lb.	Veal Loin		
lb.	Ham		
		Subtotal	
	Meat, Poultry and Fish Total		

Supplies			
Quantity/Size	**Item**	**Unit Price**	**Extension**
	Napkins		
	Butter Chips		
	Souffle Cups		
	Paper Bags		
gal.	Bleach		
gal.	Dish		
lb.	Salute		
ea.	Pot Brushes		
		Supplies Total	

Sales . . . . ____________
Inventory at Beginning of Month . . . . ____________
Purchases for the Month . . . . ____________
Final Inventory . . . . ____________
Cost of Food Sold . . . . ____________
Food Cost Percent . . . . ____________

COMPUTER APPLICATIONS

As mentioned in Chapter 12, an important application of the computer involves the recording of the food service establishment's inventory. The calculations involved in completing an inventory sheet are very time consuming. The computer inventory sheet will eliminate most of the mathematical calculations, saving the establishment both time and money.

The format of the computer inventory sheet varies from the form used when taking inventory by hand. (See Figure 17-6.)

Groceries — Oils and Fats				
Quantity	**Item**	**Size**	**Unit Price**	**Extension**
	Margarine	32-lb. case	$ 16.64	
	Shortening	50-lb. tin	26.00	
	Salad Oil	5-gal. can	22.00	
			Subtotal	

Figure 17-6 *Computer inventory sheet.*

You will be responsible for entering the quantity. What is entered into the quantity column is determined by how much you have in stock, and by how the product is packaged. It is important that the quantity entered is in terms of the unit. For example, suppose you have 16 pounds of margarine in inventory, and the cost of the margarine is $16.64 for a 32-pound case. The amount you enter into the quantity column is 0.5, since the 16 pounds you have in inventory is one-half of the 32 pounds that is in one case.

Example: The following has been found in inventory:

- 8 lb. of margarine at $16.63 for a 32-lb. case
- 20 lb. of shortening at $26.00 for a 50-lb. tin
- 3 lb. of salad oil at $22.00 for a 5-gal. can

Figure 17-7 shows how the computer inventory sheet would look.

Groceries — Oils and Fats				
Quantity	**Item**	**Size**	**Unit Price**	**Extension**
0.25	Margarine	32-lb. case	$ 16.64	$ 4.16
0.4	Shortening	50-lb. tin	26.00	10.40
0.075	Salad Oil	5-gal. can	22.20	1.67
			Subtotal	$16.23

Figure 17-7 *Computer inventory sheet, completed.*

The computer spreadsheet will also calculate the Weekly or Period Inventory recapitulation. The following pages provide examples.

Weekly or Period
Inventory Recapitulation

Week Ending September 12, 20___		Period Ending September 30, 20___
Item No.	**Item**	**Amount**
1.	Canned Goods	$ 574.00
2.	Other Groceries	636.30
3.	Butter, Eggs, Cheese	39.12
4.	Coffee and Tea	52.01
5.	Fruits and Vegetables	290.30
6.	Meat, Poultry, and Fish	1080.25
	TOTAL FOOD	$2,671.98
7.	Supplies	$ 657.86
	Total Inventory Value	$3,329.84
Called By__________		Extended by __________ Manager __________

Canned Goods				
Quantity	**Item**	**Size**	**Unit Price**	**Extension**
6	Apples	#10	$ 3.52	$ 21.12
7	Apricots	#10	5.29	37.03
10	Beans, Green	#10	2.61	26.10
7	Beans, Kidney	#10	1.84	12.88
12	Beans, Wax	#10	2.07	24.84
13	Bean Sprouts	#10	2.79	36.27
5	Beets, Whole	#10	3.03	15.15
6	Carrots, Whole	#10	3.44	20.64
7	Cherries	#10	7.31	51.17
2	Fruit Cocktail	#10	4.10	8.10
1	Noodles (Chow Mein)	#10	2.74	2.74
4	Peach Halves	#10	3.71	14.84
6	Peaches, Pie	#10	3.60	21.60
5	Pears	#10	3.51	17.55
3	Pineapple Tidbits	#10	3.79	11.37
8	Pineapple Slices	#10	3.84	30.72
3	Plums	#10	3.24	9.72
5	Pumpkin	#10	3.85	19.25
7	Sweet Potatoes	#10	3.26	22.82
8	Tomato Catsup	#10	2.12	16.96
7	Tomato Puree	#10	3.67	25.69
4	Tomatoes	#10	3.41	13.64
6	Asparagus Spears	#2	6.50	39.00
10	Cream Style Corn	#22	2.08	20.80
8	Whole Kernel Corn	#2	2.15	17.20
16	Salmon	#2	2.30	36.80
			Canned Goods Total	$574.00

Item No. 1 *Canned goods.*

Groceries — Spices				
Quantity	**Item**	**Size**	**Unit Price**	**Extension**
1.25	Allspice, Ground	lb.	$ 7.02	$ 8.78
2.5	Bay Leaves	lb.	7.20	18.00
1	Chili Powder	lb.	4.35	4.35
3	Cinnamon	lb.	6.20	18.60
2.5	Cloves, Ground	lb.	6.95	17.38
1.75	Ginger, Ground	lb.	4.50	7.88
2.25	Cumin Seed	lb.	3.82	8.60
1.5	Celery Seed	lb.	5.10	7.65
3.25	Caraway Seed	lb.	2.90	9.43
0.25	Mace	lb.	12.50	3.13
1.25	Mustard, Dry	lb.	2.80	3.50
2.75	Marjoram, Dry	lb.	3.50	9.63
2	Nutmeg	lb.	8.50	17.00
3.5	Oregano	lb.	4.25	14.88
2	Pepper, White	lb.	6.00	12.00
4	Pepper, Black	lb.	5.00	20.00
3	Pickling Spice	lb.	4.18	12.54
2	Rosemary Leaves	lb.	8.12	16.24
1.74	Sage	lb.	10.82	18.83
2.25	Thyme	lb.	5.89	13.26
			Subtotal	$241.68

Item No. 2 *Other groceries.*

Groceries — Dressing and Condiments				
Quantity	**Item**	**Size**	**Unit Price**	**Extension**
4	Mayonnaise	gal.	$ 8.44	$ 33.76
2	Dill Pickles	gal.	3.22	6.44
3	Sweet Relish	gal.	4.60	13.80
3.5	Salad Dressing	gal.	3.88	13.58
7	Vinegar	gal.	1.20	8.40
2.75	Soy Sauce	gal.	6.48	17.82
5	Worcestershire Sauce	gal.	3.73	18.65
6.25	French Dressing	gal.	4.54	28.38
			Subtotal	$140.83

Item No. 2 *Other groceries.*

Groceries — Oils and Fats				
Quantity	**Item**	**Size**	**Unit Price**	**Extension**
0.43	Margarine	3-lb. case	$ 7.28	$ 3.13
1.5	Shortening	50-lb. tin	20.80	31.20
0.8	Salad Oil	5-gal. can	6.60	5.28
			Subtotal	$39.61

Item No. 2 *Other groceries.*

Groceries — Dry Bulk Goods				
Quantity	**Item**	**Size**	**Unit Price**	**Extension**
7	Baking Soda	lb.	$ 0.22	$ 1.54
1.6	Baking Powder	5-lb. box	8.40	13.44
1.6	Cocoa	5-lb. box	5.90	9.44
5	Coconut Shred	lb.	1.12	5.60
9	Cracker Meal	lb.	0.18	1.62
3	Chicken Base	lb.	1.12	3.36
8	Beef Base	lb.	1.15	9.20
5	Raisins	lb.	1.19	5.95
8	Cornmeal	lb.	0.15	1.20
13	Cornstarch	lb.	0.46	5.98
18	Tapioca Flour	lb.	0.22	3.96
0.58	Bread Flour	100-lb. bag	20.00	11.60
0.61	Cake Flour	100-lb. bag	25.00	15.25
0.75	Pastry Flour	100-lb. bag	22.00	16.50
13	Elbow Macaroni	lb.	0.49	6.37
16	Spaghetti	lb.	0.52	8.32
7	Rice	lb.	0.45	3.15
10	Noodles	lb.	1.13	11.30
			Subtotal	$133.78

Item No. 2 *Other groceries.*

Groceries — Coloring and Extracts				
Quantity	**Item**	**Size**	**Unit Price**	**Extension**
2	Caramel Color	qt.	$ 5.95	$ 11.90
1.5	Yellow	pt.	3.12	4.68
2.25	Red	pt.	2.82	6.35
3	Green	pt.	3.16	9.48
2	Lemon Extract	pt.	6.99	13.98
2	Vanilla Extract	pt.	11.89	23.78
2.5	Maple Extract	pt.	4.09	10.23
			Subtotal	$ 80.40
			Other Groceries Total	$636.30

Item No. 2 *Other groceries.*

Butter, Eggs, and Cheese				
Quantity	**Item**	**Size**	**Unit Price**	**Extension**
6	American Cheese	lb.	$ 1.70	$ 10.20
12	Chip Butter	lb.	1.12	13.44
18	Eggs	doz.	0.86	15.48
			Butter, Eggs, and Cheese Total	$39.12

Item No. 3 *Butter, eggs, and cheese.*

Coffee and Tea				
Quantity	**Item**	**Size**	**Unit Price**	**Extension**
18	Coffee	lb.	$ 2.68	$48.24
$\frac{1}{4}$	Tea — indiv. (100)	pkg.	2.50	.63
$\frac{1}{2}$	Tea — iced (48)	pkg.	6.24	3.14
			Coffee and Tea Total	$52.01

Item No. 4 *Coffee and tea.*

Fruits and Vegetables — Fresh				
Quantity	**Item**	**Size**	**Unit Price**	**Extension**
3	Carrots	bu.	$ 0.89	$ 2.67
2	Endive	lb.	1.45	2.90
8	Head Lettuce	head	0.89	7.12
9	Leaf Lettuce	lb.	1.25	11.25
18	Dry Onions	lb.	0.46	8.28
50	Red Potatoes	lb.	0.53	26.50
46	Idaho Potatoes	lb.	0.51	23.46
4	Tomatoes	lb.	0.88	3.52
2	Parsley	bu.	0.45	0.90
6	Green Peppers	lb.	0.48	2.88
9	Apples	lb.	0.83	7.47
8	Bananas	lb.	0.35	2.80
6	Lemons	doz.	2.25	13.50
4	Oranges	doz.	2.25	9.00
6	Radishes	bu.	0.35	2.10
4	Celery	bu.	0.89	3.56
			Subtotal	

Item No. 5 *Fruits and vegetables—fresh.*

Fruits and Vegetables — Frozen				
Quantity	**Item**	**Size**	**Unit Price**	**Extension**
8	Strawberries	lb.	$ 1.06	$ 8.48
10	Peaches	lb.	1.17	11.70
18	Blueberries	lb.	1.52	27.36
27	Lima Beans	lb.	1.23	33.21
30	Corn	lb.	0.63	18.90
17	Broccoli	lb.	0.78	13.26
11	Brussels Sprouts	lb.	0.87	9.57
19	Mixed Vegetables	lb.	0.57	10.83
23	Peas	lb.	0.56	12.88
18	Cauliflower	lb.	0.90	16.20
			Subtotal	$162.39
			Fruits and Vegetables Total	$290.30

Item No. 5 *Fruits and vegetables.*

Meat, Poultry, and Fish				
Quantity	**Item**	**Size**	**Unit Price**	**Extension**
16	Beef Ground	lb.	$ 1.72	$ 27.52
20	Beef Round	lb.	2.25	45.00
25	Beef Ribs	lb.	2.95	73.75
23	Beef Rib Eyes	lb.	3.20	73.60
20	Beef Chuck	lb.	1.95	39.00
16	Club Steak	lb.	3.58	57.28
15	Beef Tenderloin	lb.	6.20	93.00
27	Pork Loin	lb.	5.40	145.80
19	Boston Butt	lb.	2.20	41.80
33	Veal Leg	lb.	7.40	244.20
10	Veal Shoulder	lb.	6.22	62.20
13	Veal Loin	lb.	8.20	106.60
30	Ham	lb.	2.35	70.50
			Meat, Poultry and Fish Total	$1,080.25

Item No. 6 *Meat, poultry, and fish.*

Supplies				
Quantity	**Item**	**Size**	**Unit Price**	**Extension**
6	Napkins		$ 41.00	$246.00
9	Butter Chips		5.48	49.32
20	Souffle Cups		7.80	156.00
17	Paper Bags		7.95	135.15
6	Bleach	gal.	1.24	7.44
9	Dish	gal.	3.89	35.01
20	Salute	lb.	0.58	11.60
6	Pot Brushes	ea.	2.89	17.34
			Supplies Total	$657.86

Item No. 7 *Supplies.*

Finally, the computer spreadsheet will also be able to calculate the Monthly Food Cost Percent. (See Figure 17-8.)

Total Sales	$53,265.00
Inventory at the Beginning of the Month	6,525.35
Purchases for the Month	16,001.19
Final Inventory	3,329.84
Cost of Food Sold	19,196.70
Food Cost Percent	36.0%

Figure 17-8 *Monthly food cost percent.*

Financial Statements

OBJECTIVES

At the completion of this chapter, the student should be able to:

1. Identify listings on the profit and loss statement.
2. Find the cost of food sold, gross margin, total operating expenses, net profit, and the percent of sales.
3. Identify listings on the balance sheet.
4. Find total assets, total liabilities, net worth and total liabilities, and net worth-proprietorship.
5. Identify items that are budgeted.
6. Find the amount or percent of items budgeted.

Financial statements are the instrument used in a business operation to let management know its exact financial position. The figures tell a story of success or failure. There are two major financial statements that must be prepared and are essential to the operation of a business: the profit and loss (income) statement, sometimes referred to as the P&L sheet, and the balance sheet. These financial statements are especially important to the food service operation because of high labor cost and food prices that fluctuate quite rapidly.

THE PROFIT AND LOSS STATEMENT

The **profit and loss statement** is a summary or report of the business operation for a given period of time. The purpose of the statement is to determine how much money the business is making or losing. In the profit and loss statement, all income from sales is set off against expenses to determine the profit or loss. The following formula summarizes the profit and loss statement of a food service operation:

Sales − cost of food sold = Gross Margin
Gross Margin − total operating expenses = Net profit or loss

The net profit or loss is the figure that is of greater concern to the food service operator because it determines the success or failure of the business.

Most of the figures used to compile a profit and loss statement are taken from the daily records that are recorded and made available by

Figure 18-1 *Bookkeeper preparing financial records.*

the bookkeeper. (See Figure 18-1.) The daily records of the food service operation are kept in a book called the **cashbook.** The cashbook contains a record of all income and expenses. It is a means of keeping track of every sales dollar. The cashbook is also important for securing the figures needed for tax purposes and other financial obligations. Many food service operations have a computer available, and these cashbook records can be kept on a disk. The availability of a computer simplifies the task of record keeping. It can produce the most complicated figures immediately.

A profit and loss statement can be made up whenever the food service operator wants to know the business' financial situation or feels it necessary to review the financial situation. It can be done every month, every three months, every six months, or even once a year. However for control purposes, it is recommended that the profit and loss statement be completed each month. When the statement is completed, the food service operator analyzes all the figures and compares the dollar amounts in each category with those of previous months or years, looking for ways to cut costs for a more efficient operation. The operator may also wish to make a percent comparison of all figures with total sales, which represents 100 percent. The example of a profit and loss statement shows dollar amounts and percentages of the total sales. (See Figure 18-2.) As explained in a previous chapter, percents are usually the language spoken by the food service operator. Percents, rather than dollar amounts, give a clearer picture of the overall operation. It is suggested within the food service industry that a successful operation must hold its food and labor cost below 70 percent.

Profit and Loss Statement For the Month of September, 20__			
Total Sales		$96,000	100.0%
Food Cost:			
Inventory at Beginning of Month	$ 9,680		
Purchases for the Month	37,600		
Total	47,280		
Less: Final Inventory	6,000		
Cost of Food Sold		$41,280	43.0%
Gross Margin		$54,720	57.0%
Expenses			
Salaries	30,720		32.0%
Social Security Taxes	1,920		2.0%
Rent	4,800		5.0%
Laundry and Linens	672		.7%
Repairs and Maintenance	2,688		2.8%
Advertising	480		.5%
Taxes and Insurance	1,440		1.5%
Supplies	672		.7%
Depreciation	1,920		2.0%
Utilities	2,880		3.0%
Miscellaneous Expenses	1,440		1.5%
Total Operating Expenses		$49,632	51.7%
Net Profit		$ 5,088	5.3%

Figure 18-2 *Profit and loss statement.*

Chef Sez . . .

"Remember, we are banking dollars, not percentages."

Robert S. Faller
Director of Sales and Marketing
The Otesaga Resort Hotel
Cooperstown, New York

The Otesaga Resort Hotel of Cooperstown is one of New York State's most distinctive resorts. Since 1909, The Otesaga has offered distinguished service, dining, and memorable experiences to guests from around the world. With only a short walk or trolley ride from The Otesaga one can relive the memories of America's national pastime at the National Baseball Hall of Fame and Museum. The word *Otesaga* is derived from the Iroquois phrase for "the meeting place," which is consistent with the Otesaga Resort experience. The resort has 136 rooms, a golf course, a bar and grill, a lounge, a lakeside patio, and a dining room, as well as space for meetings and conferences.

Listings on the Profit and Loss Statement

Each item listed and explained below is an indispensable part of most food service profit and loss statements. Each item must be thoroughly understood whether it represents income or expense. Knowledge of these items will give you a better understanding of the importance of a profit and loss statement.

Total sales. Total sales are found by totaling the register tapes for that particular month. After business is completed each day, a total is taken of all sales. These totals are kept on file in the computer, on a disk, or in the cashbook.

Inventory at the beginning of the month. Inventory at the beginning of the month is acquired from the final inventory from the previous month. For example, the final inventory for the month of August is the beginning inventory for the month of September.

Purchases for the month. The total of all food purchased during the month are the purchases for the month. Total all invoices sent with each order. These figures may be kept in the computer on a disk or in the cashbook.

Total. The sum of the inventory at the beginning of the month and the purchases of the month is the total. It is a total of all food that was available during that month.

Final inventory. Final inventory is acquired from the physical inventory taken at the end of each month's operation. It represents the cost of food that is still in stock and was not sold. Since it represents food that was not sold, it is subtracted from the total cost of food available during the month.

Cost of food sold. When the final inventory is subtracted from the cost of food on hand, the result is the cost of food sold that month.

Gross margin. The gross margin or gross profit is found by subtracting the cost of food sold from the total sales. Gross means the total value before deductions are made. Margin is the difference between the cost and the selling price, so sales minus cost of food gives gross margin.

Salaries. Salaries or labor cost consists of all wages paid to all employees, including the owner's salary. You will notice it is the largest figure listed under expenses. Except for the cost of food, this is the most important item to control.

Social security taxes. Social security taxes are paid to the federal government for the purpose of retirement benefits. The employer must deduct a certain percent of the employee's salary for social security taxes and, at the same time, must match the amount the employee pays. The amount shown on the profit and loss statement represents only the amount the employer must pay.

Rent. Rent is a fixed amount paid at a certain time of each month to the owner of a property for the use of that property. If a food service operator owns the building in which the operation is located, this particular expense is not incurred. However, there may be a similar expense if the building is not paid for (for example, paying off the mortgage to a building and loan company or a bank). A food service operator who rents usually has a long term lease with the owner of the property. The operator can then be assured of continued occupancy for a specific period of time.

Laundry and linens. These items include the cost of cleaning or renting all uniforms, napkins, tablecloths, towels and so forth.

Repairs and maintenance. These are expenses that result from equipment failure or building repairs if the property is owned. If the property is rented, the owner may assume the responsibility for all repairs. This item is an essential part of any food service operation because equipment must be kept in good working condition at all times for an efficient operation.

Advertising. Advertising is an expense that is incurred when notifying the public about a place of business. The advertising may be done through the newspaper, television, radio, entertainment book, billboards, periodicals, Internet, or other media.

Taxes and insurance. These may be paid on an annual basis. If these are listed on the monthly statement, as shown in Figure 18-2, the monthly cost is found by taking one-twelfth of the yearly payment.

Supplies. Supplies are the cost of those items used other than food. These include janitorial supplies, paper products, and similar expenses.

Depreciation. Depreciation is the act of lessening the value of an item as it wears out. For example, if a new slicing machine is bought for $2,700.00, and is used constantly for one year, at the end of that year it is worth less than $2,700.00. It has been worn out slightly through use, and therefore has less value. There are several methods used for figuring depreciation, but the simplest and most practical is the straight line method.

In the **straight line method,** estimate the length of time a piece of equipment is expected to last, and the trade-in value it should possess at the end of its estimated life. The difference between the original cost of the equipment and its estimated trade-in value gives the total amount of allowable depreciation. For example: the slicing machine that was purchased for $2,700.00 is expected to last 15 years, at which time it will probably have a trade-in value of $600.00.

Original cost	$2,700.00
Estimate trade-in	− 600.00
Allowable depreciation	$2,100.00

The allowable depreciation $2,100.00 is divided by the number of years the item is expected to last (15).

```
    140.00   Amount that can be deducted each of 15 years
15)2100.00
   15
    60
    60
     0
```

Some food service operators estimate that all of their major pieces of equipment must be replaced every 10 or 12 years; instead of figuring depreciation on individual pieces of equipment, they figure it on the group. Thus, each year they charge off one-tenth or one-twelfth of the allowable depreciation. If a depreciation figure for a month is needed, find the depreciation figure for one year and take one-twelfth of that amount.

Utilities. Utilities include the cost incurred through the supply of gas, electricity, and water. These bills are usually based on monthly use and are presented to the customer on a monthly basis.

Miscellaneous expenses. These are usually smaller amounts than the others listed. They include licenses, organization dues, charitable contributions, and so forth. These amounts vary with the size and policy of the operation.

Total operating expenses. Total operating expenses are the sum of all the expenses incurred during the period or month that the P&L statement covered.

Net profit. The most important figure on the profit and loss statement, and probably the one first observed by the owner or manager is the net profit. This figure is found by subtracting total operating expenses from gross margin. In Figure 18-2, the profit is not a large one, but at least it shows that the business is heading in the right direction. Concern occurs when that figure shows a net loss, which may happen in the food service industry.

TIPS . . . *To Insure Perfect Solutions*

Percentage of Cost of Food Sold plus percentage of Gross Margin will equal 100 percent.

SUMMARY REVIEW

Prepare profit and loss statements using the amounts given in problems 1–3. Use the same form as shown in the example in Figure 18-2. Find the cost of food sold, gross margin, total operating expenses, net profit, and the percent of sales for each problem listed. Round percentages to the tenth.

1. The Manor Restaurant had total sales for the month of November of $15,500. Their inventory at the beginning of the month was $5,280. During the month they made purchases that totalled $8,200. The final inventory at the end of the month was $4,690.

   The Manor Restaurant had the following expenses during the month: salaries $3,220, social security taxes $115, rent $460, laundry $95, repairs and maintenance $421, advertising $75, taxes and insurance $195, supplies $120, depreciation $540, utilities $380, and miscellaneous expenses $210.

2. Connie's Cafeteria had total sales for the month of March of $25,830. Their inventory at the beginning of the month was $7,275. During the month they made purchases that totaled $10,900. The final inventory at the end of the month was $6,870.

   Connie's Cafeteria had the following expenses during the month: salaries $5,225, social security taxes $313.50, rent $540, laundry and linens $98, repairs and maintenance $268, advertising $78, taxes and insurance $218, supplies $120, depreciation $395, utilities $270, and miscellaneous expenses $168.

3. The Golden Goose Restaurant had total sales for the month of April of $75,300. Their inventory at the beginning of the month was $8,880. During the month they made purchases that totalled $25,500. The final inventory at the end of the month was $8,440.

   The Golden Goose Restaurant had the following expenses during the month: salaries $14,350, social security taxes $875, rent $650, laundry $225, repairs and maintenance $563, advertising $156, taxes and insurance $419, supplies $280, depreciation $690, utilities $345, and miscellaneous expenses $242.

The Balance Sheet

The **balance sheet** is a necessary part of any business operation, almost as important as the profit and loss statement. It is a statement listing all the company's **assets** (what they own) and **liabilities** (what they owe) to determine **net worth, proprietorship** (ownership), or **capital** (money). It is a dollar and cents picture of a company's financial status at a given time. The given time is usually December 31 if based on the calendar year, or June 30 if based on the fiscal year. A **fiscal year** is defined as the time between one yearly settlement of financial accounts and another.

A balance sheet can be prepared by a company at any time they wish to know their net worth. However, in most cases, this occurs only once a year. The balance sheet is not restricted for use in the business community. But it can also be used by individuals. It serves many purposes: to provide necessary information in reporting financial matters to the state and federal governments for income taxes, to secure loans from banks or building and loan companies, and in the case of many business operations, to provide the information stockholders and partners want to see or hear in the annual report.

The balance sheet is another financial report that can be simplified by using a computer and storing the information on a disk. Since every food service operation does not have a computer, it is to your advantage to learn how to perform the functions manually.

The formula for preparing a balance sheet can be expressed by the following equation:

Assets − Liabilities = Net Worth or Proprietorship

As the equation points out, a company totals all the money it owes and subtracts that amount from the total value of all it owns to find out its total worth.

To prove that the balance sheet has been prepared correctly, the liabilities are added to the net worth. The sum should equal the total assets. The relationship may be expressed by this equation:

Assets = Liabilities + Proprietorship

Two examples of balance sheets are shown in Figure 18-3. Example A is for an individual, and Example B is for a food service operation.

Listings on the Balance Sheet

The amounts shown on example A, the William Jones balance sheet of Figure 18-3, come from various sources, as indicated in the following sections. (See Figure 18-3, example A.)

Home. What a home is worth on the current market can be determined by a real estate adjuster or in some cases, a salesperson.

Home furnishings. This amount is more difficult to figure. The best method may be to list the original cost and deduct a certain percentage for age and wear.

Example A

William Jones
Balance Sheet, December 31, 20___

Assets		**Liabilities**	
Home	$165,000	Home Mortgage	$ 66,000
Home furnishings	19,470	Houseboat Loan	13,500
Certificates of Deposit	30,000	Auto Loan	4,500
Cash in savings account	13,500	Charge accounts (retail)	2,070
Cash in checking account	885		
Automobile	13,950	Total Liabilities	$ 86,070
Houseboat	26,325	Net Worth-Proprietorship	183,060
Total Assets	$269,130		
		Total Liabilities and Net Worth-Proprietorship	$269,130

Example B

Charcoal King Restaurant
Balance Sheet, June 30, 20___

Assets (Current)		**Liabilities (Current)**	
Cash in bank and on hand	$ 21,800	Accounts payable	$ 14,716
Accounts Receivable	6,700	Installment accounts or bank notes payable	48,624
Food and beverage inventory	10,340	Payroll and taxes payable	3,956
Supplies	1,680		
Total Current Assets	$ 40,520	Total Current Liabilities	67,296
Assets (Fixed)		Net Worth-Proprietorship	49,024
Stationary kitchen equipment	$ 41,288	Total Liabilities and Net Worth-Proprietorship	$116,320
Hand Kitchen equipment	9,824		
Dining room furniture and fixtures	13,548		
China glassware, silver and linen	11,140		
Total Fixed Assets	$ 75,800		
Total Assets (Current and Fixed)	$116,320		

Figure 18-3 *(A) Balance sheet for an individual*
(B) Balance sheet for a company

Certificates of Deposit. Certificates of Deposit are easy to total since the amounts are stated on each certificate. If the amount is difficult to find, just call your bank.

Cash in savings account. This figure is listed in the passbook or on your monthly statement received from the bank each month.

Automobile, houseboat. The current worth of an automobile or houseboat may be found by checking with the company from which they were purchased. There is a book available that will list the value of an automobile. It is called the blue book.

Liabilities. Liabilities are available by checking with the institution that made the loan.

Charge accounts. Statements of amounts owed are sent each month. If still in doubt, check with the company who issued the card.

The figures shown on the balance sheet for the Charcoal King Restaurant come from many sources, but can be obtained from records kept on file by the food service establishment in the computer, on a disk or in the cashbook. (See Figure 18-3, example B.) The bookkeeper will keep these figures, discussed in the following sections, current.

Cash. The cash amount is found in the cashbook, in the computer, or on a disk. This figure is kept up to date by the bookkeeper.

Accounts receivable. Accounts receivable refers to money that is owed to the company by various people or companies for various reasons.

Food and beverage inventory. This figure is taken from the profit and loss statement.

Assets (fixed). The value of the fixed assets listed (which in this case are for various kinds of equipment) can be acquired by referring to purchase contracts or equipment records.

Accounts payable. Accounts payable refers to money the food service operation owes for purchases made. (In other words, bills that have not been paid.) The amounts may be found by referring to the unpaid bill or invoice file.

Installment accounts or bank notes payable. These figures are found by referring to sales contracts or equipment records. Another possible source is the bank or company to whom the money is owed.

Payroll and taxes payable. These figures are found by checking with the bookkeeper or accountant who keeps these figures up to date.

Summary Review

Prepare balance sheets for problems 1–5, using the figures listed. Find total assets, total liabilities, net worth, and total liabilities and net worth-proprietorship.

1. Tim Wu had the following assets as of May 15 this year: home $138,000, home furnishings $26,085, automobile $12,750, speed boat $6,450, cash in savings accounts $38,670, cash in checking account $5,034 and stocks $4,825. His liabilities were as follows: home mortgage $85,500, auto loan $7,200, boat loan $3,900, note payable to loan company $4,500, and charge accounts $2,682.

2. Joe and Mary Hernandez had the following assets as of July 15 this year: home $157,500, house trailer $11,100, home furnishings $23,325, automobile $11,580, cash in savings account $18,795, cash in checking account $759, U.S. Savings Bonds $2,500, and certificates of deposit $15,000. Their liabilities were as follows: home mortgage $85,500, loan on house trailer $6,600, automobile loan $6,900, and charge accounts $2,691.
3. Robert and Dolores O'Shaunessey had the following assets as of December 31 this year: local home $116,250, vacation home $45,840, motor boat $8,400, automobile $19,650, home furnishings $17,970, certificates of deposit $20,000, cash in savings account $3,500, cash in checking account $1,695, and U.S. Savings Bonds $1,275. Their liabilities were as follows: local home mortgage $66,700, vacation home mortgage $31,650, motor boat loan $3,900, automobile loan $10,350, loan on home furnishings $5,400, and charge accounts $2,700.
4. Jim's Hamburger Palace had the following assets as of December 31 this year: cash $5,956, food and beverage inventory $4,800, supplies $392, equipment (stationary, hand, and serving equipment) $14,140, furniture and fixtures $5,000. The restaurant's liabilities were as follows: accounts payable $344.80, notes payable to First National Bank $3,900, note payable to Mike Bryce $1,120, sales tax payable $278, and taxes payable $1,040.
5. Bill's Oyster House had the following assets as of December 31 this year: cash $18,770, accounts receivable $2,186.32, food and beverage inventory $5,982, supplies $1,559.60, stationary kitchen equipment $21,797.40, hand equipment $1,714.20, dining room furniture and fixtures $14,453, and serving equipment and dishes $11,507. The liabilities were as follows: accounts payable $25,191.20, installment accounts payable $10,682, bank notes payable to First National Bank $30,100, sales tax payable $1,061.60, payroll tax payable $1,112, and taxes payable $243.80.

BUDGETING

Budgeting is a plan for adjusting expenditures to probable income for a calendar or fiscal year. It is a plan that works equally well for individuals, small businesses, and large corporations, for maintaining a fairly equal balance between income and expenses. Businesses use the budget not only to gauge expenses and income for the year, but also to keep all departments within the company on the proper financial track. Some companies even require department heads to submit a written report showing why they have exceeded their budget. The budget is just a plan, and like most plans, if followed, good results often happen. If one goes astray, problems will probably develop.

Not all food service operations find it necessary or advantageous to budget. Those that do are usually large corporations that operate their own food service for the benefit of their employees. Their goal for the operation is usually to break even or to hold their losses to a minimum.

In a budget, the areas listed under the two major components, **income** and **expenditures,** will vary, depending on the size of the overall operation. Generally included under income are the total of register receipts and income from sales that would not pass through the register, such as payment for a catered affair. These sales might be labeled supplemental income. These figures can be obtained from income records of the previous year.

Expenditures might include:

- total payoff or labor cost,
- total supplies (food, paper goods, cleaning supplies, etc.),
- telephone service,
- new equipment,
- service calls on equipment,
- workmen's compensation,
- utilities (gas and electric),
- printing service for menus, and
- fringe benefits (dental plan, hospitalization, etc.).

Many of the estimated figures required for these items can again be obtained from the records of the previous year. If, after checking the figures from the previous year, you are aware of or believe that an increase or decrease of funds will be required for the coming year, then adjustments are in order. Remember, the purpose of a budget is to give a general idea of what will happen. The budget is very seldom exact.

Using hypothetical figures, let us set up a budget as if it were a pie. The whole pie would be the food service operation's total income for a year. Two examples will be given. Example 1 will show a budget in percentages with the found dollar amounts. Example 2 will show dollar amounts with the found percent.

Example 1: A food service budget (break-even budget) is shown in Figure 18-4. The yearly income from register and supplemental sales is $300,000. The total dollar amounts budgeted for each item are listed.

Food and Supplies (30%)	= $90,000
Labor (25%)	= $75,000
Workmen's Compensation (3%)	= $ 9,000
Fringe Benefits (8%)	= $24,000
Utilities (9%)	= $27,000
Printing Service (5%)	= $15,000
New Equipment (10%)	= $30,000
Equipment Service (6%)	= $18,000
Telephone (4%)	= $12,000

When taking a percent of a whole number, in this case $300,000, we must multiply. For example:

$ 300,000	Yearly income
× 0.30	Food & supplies
$90,000.00	Amount budgeted for food & supplies

$ 300,000	Yearly income
× .25	Labor
1500000	
600000	
$75,000.00	Amount budgeted for labor

The other amounts shown in the budget are found by the same procedure.

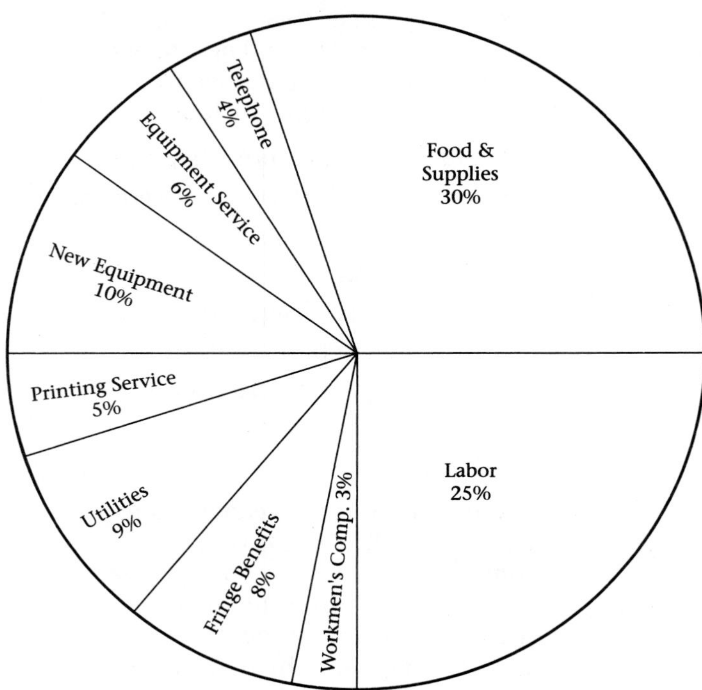

Figure 18-4 *Sample food service budget, example 1.*

Example 2: Another sample food service budget (break-even budget) is shown in Figure 18-5. The yearly income from register and supplemental sales is \$300,000. The percentage of the total income that was budgeted for each item is listed. The sum of the completed percentages should equal 100 percent.

Food and Supplies (\$75,000)	=	25%
Labor (\$69,000)	=	23%
Workmen's Compensation (\$24,000)	=	8%
Fringe Benefits (\$27,000)	=	9%
Utilities (\$33,000)	=	11%
Printing Service (\$9,000)	=	3%
New Equipment (\$45,000)	=	15%
Equipment Service (\$12,000)	=	4%
Telephone (\$6,000)	=	2%

To find what percent one number is of another number, divide the number that represents the part by the number that represents the whole. For example:

	0.25	= 25%
Represents the whole \$300,000	)\$75,000.00	Food & supplies
	60,000.00	represent the part
	15,000.00	
	15,000.00	

Thus, 25 percent is the percentage of the \$300,000 yearly income set aside for the cost of food and supplies. The other percentages shown in the budget are found by the same procedure.

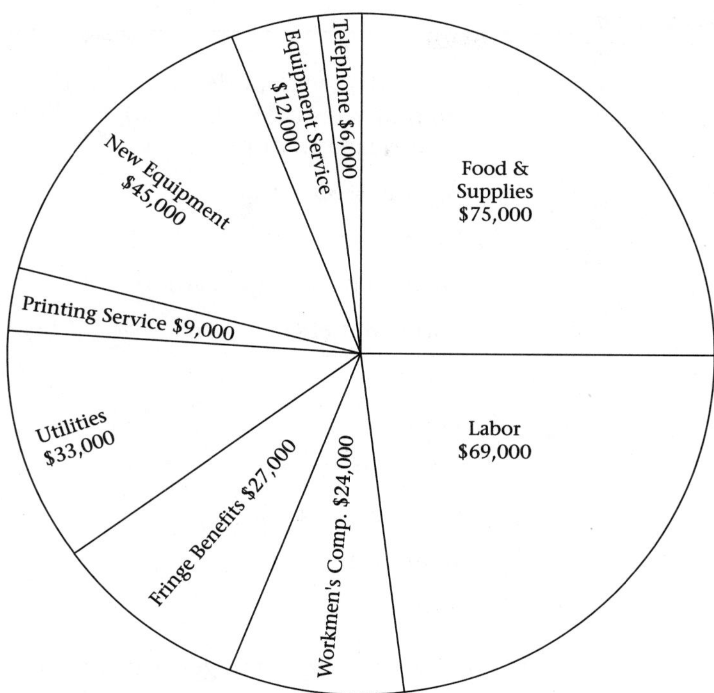

Figure 18-5 *Sample food service budget, example 2.*

Budgeting is also an important step in the proper management of personal affairs. The family income certainly should be budgeted so that money will be on hand when the bills are due. The family budget may be set up on a monthly or yearly basis, with a percentage of income or a dollar amount set aside for each important family expense.

Example: For a monthly income of $2,000.00, the budget might be as follows:

Item	**Percent**	**Dollar Amount**
Food	25%	$ 500.00
Clothing	15%	$ 300.00
Mortgage Payment	35%	$ 700.00
Recreation	9%	$ 180.00
Benevolences	5%	$ 100.00
Savings	11%	$ 220.00
	100%	$2,000.00

SUMMARY REVIEW

1. For a food service budget, the yearly income from register and supplemental sales is $550,000.00. Find the dollar amount that was budgeted for each item listed.

a. Food and Supplies	26%	$________
b. Labor	24%	$________
c. Workmen's Compensation	4%	$________
d. Fringe Benefits	8%	$________
e. Utilities	11%	$________
f. Printing Service	2%	$________
g. New Equipment	10%	$________
h. Equipment Service	5%	$________
i. Telephone	3%	$________
j. Profit	7%	$________

2. For a food service budget, the yearly income from register and supplemental sales is $725,000.00. Find the percentage of total income that was budgeted for each item listed.

a. Food and Supplies	$188,500	________%
b. Labor	$166,750	________%
c. Workmen's Compensation	$ 21,750	________%
d. Fringe Benefits	$ 65,250	________%
e. Utilities	$ 72,500	________%
f. Printing Service	$ 29,000	________%
g. New Equipment	$ 79,750	________%
h. Equipment Service	$ 43,500	________%
i. Telephone	$ 14,500	________%
j. Profit	$ 43,500	________%

3. The Piazza family has a monthly income of $2,400.00. What percentage of the monthly income was budgeted for each item? Prove that your percentages are correct by adding the results. The sum should be one hundred percent. Their monthly budget is as follows:

a. Food	$ 600.00	________%
b. Clothing	$ 432.00	________%
c. Charities	$ 144.00	________%
d. Savings	$ 192.00	________%
e. Mortgage Payment	$ 648.00	________%
f. Recreation	$ 216.00	________%
g. Utilities	$ 168.00	________%

4. The Fahy family has a yearly income of $28,975.00. Find the dollar amount that was budgeted for each item listed. The sum of the completed budget should equal the yearly income of $28,975.00. Their budget for the year is as follows:

a. Food	23%	$________
b. Mortgage Payment	27%	$________
c. Utilities	8%	$________
d. Clothing	13%	$________
e. Recreation	7%	$________
f. Family Welfare	6%	$________
g. Benevolences	3%	$________
h. Savings	9%	$________
i. Other Items	4%	$________

5. The Curran family has a monthly income of $2,260.00. What percentage of the monthly income was budgeted for each item? Prove that your percentages are correct by adding the results. The sum should be 100 percent. Their monthly budget is as follows:

a. Rent	$ 565.00	________%
b. Food	$ 519.80	________%
c. Clothing	$ 429.40	________%
d. Utilities	$ 180.80	________%
e. Entertainment	$ 248.60	________%
f. Insurance	$ 67.80	________%
g. Doctors' Fees	$ 90.40	________%
h. Savings	$ 158.20	________%

Personal Taxes and Payroll

OBJECTIVES

At the completion of this chapter, the student should be able to:

1. Identify and understand the concept of employees withholding tax (federal, state, local).
2. Identify and understand the concept of employees income tax (federal, state, local).
3. Identify and understand the concept of F.I.C.A. (Social Security) tax.
4. Identify and understand the concept of sales tax.
5. Identify and understand the concept of licenses (state, local).
6. Identify and understand the concept of personal property tax.
7. Identify and understand the concept of occupational tax.
8. Identify and understand the concept of real estate tax.
9. Calculate gross wages.
10. Calculate net pay.
11. Calculate salary plus commission.

There is a lot of truth to the old saying that "The only sure things in this life are death and taxes." Everyone pays, except perhaps a few people who can somehow find loopholes in the law. For those of us who do pay, these taxes are necessary to operate our federal, state, and local governments as well as our school districts and other services necessary to our daily lives.

In general, we are faced with the obligation of paying taxes to the three levels of government mentioned above: federal, state, and local (city and county). The following is a list of the taxes that food service operators and their employees are required to pay or the employer is required to collect by deductions from the employee's paycheck:

Federal Taxes

Employees Withholding Tax
Income Tax
Social Security

State Taxes

Employees Withholding Tax
Income Tax
Sales Tax
Various Licenses

Local Taxes

Employees Withholding Tax
Income Tax
Personal Property Tax
Occupational Tax
Various Licenses
Real Estate Tax

Since these taxes affect you, the employee, as they show up in the form of deductions on your paychecks, it is important to learn as much as possible about them. Many people do not understand why all this money is taken out of their paychecks. In this chapter, the goal is to acquaint you with these taxes and provide enough information to help you understand their importance.

Federal Taxes

These are taxes collected by the federal government. They are established and enforced by federal law so that each individual citizen pays what he or she properly owes to support the functions financed by the federal government.

Employees Withholding Tax

Employees Withholding Tax is money withheld from each employee's paycheck during the year to pay for the income tax that they owe the federal government at the end of the year. The money withheld is sent to the government by the employer and is credited to the employee's account. Paying the tax as the money is earned, called "pay as you go," is a system devised by the federal government to ensure that your tax money is available when your taxes are due. At the end of the calendar year (December 31) and before January 31 of the following year, the employer sends each employee a W-2 form (wage and tax statement) indicating the total amount of money earned during the year, as well as how much money was withheld for taxes, social security payments, and any other money withheld such as state and city income taxes. (See Figure 19-1.) If a person has worked steadily for just one employer the whole year, the amount of taxes withheld will probably equal the amount owed at the end of the year. In this case, when the employee files his or her income tax return on or before April 15th of the following year, what is owed the federal government has already been paid.

Sometimes the employer deducts too little or too much money from the employee's paychecks during the year. If too little money was deducted and money is owed the government, a check for the amount owed must be sent to the Internal Revenue Service (IRS) with the employee's federal tax return. If the amount owed is less than the amount deducted from the paychecks, the government sends the individual a check for the amount overpaid after the return is processed.

The W-2 form annually received from the employer usually comes in four parts. One copy is to be filed with the employee's federal return, one with the state return, one for local use and one for the individual's personal files.

a Control number	Void	OMB No. 1545-0008		
5621	☐			
b Employer's identification number			1 Wages, tips, other compensation	2 Federal income tax withheld
138-71-8521			72,665.88	16,828.15
c Employer's name, address, and ZIP code			3 Social security wages	4 Social security tax withheld
John Phillips Restaurant 3567 Meadowcreek Drive Albany, NY 12203			7,260.00	4,501.20
			5 Medicare wages and tips	6 Medicare tax withheld
			72,665.88	1,053.66
			7 Social security tips	8 Allocated tips
d Employee's social security number			9 Advance EIC payment	10 Dependent care benefits
022-35-6241				
e Employee's name, address, and ZIP code			11 Nonqualified plans	12 Benefits included in Box 1
Carlita Alverez 287 Third Avenue Albany, NY 12203			13 See Instrs. for Form W-2	14 Other
			15 Statutory employee / Deceased / Pension plan / Legal rep. / Deferred compensation	

16 State	Employer's state I.D. No.	17 State wages, tips, etc.	18 State income tax	19 Locality name	20 Local wages, tips, etc.	21 Local income tax
NY	138-71-8521	72,665.88	4,114.53			

Department of the Treasury—Internal Revenue Service

Form **W-2** Wage and Tax Statement 1998

Copy D For Employer

For Privacy Act and Paperwork Reduction Act Notice, see separate instructions.

Figure 19-1 *Form W-2 wage and tax statement.*

Income Tax

The main source of income for operating the federal government is obtained from taxes levied on the income of individuals and corporations. Income tax returns must be filed by all people who earn over a certain amount of money. These individuals are required by law to file a federal income tax return with the Internal Revenue Service on or before each April 15th. If an employee does not earn enough money to pay taxes, he or she must file an income tax return to get the money back that was withheld by their employer for taxes.

Since it is impossible to discuss all the problems that might arise when preparing a federal income tax return, we will discuss only the major points here. If more information is desired, it can either be obtained from your local Internal Revenue Service office or by calling the number for your area listed in the instruction booklet published by the Internal Revenue Service and usually sent to your home the last week of December. The office that you contact will provide assistance in making out tax returns as well as answering any questions you may have. Help can also be obtained from accountants who are licensed by the state to fill out returns for a fee. Remember that, although another person may make out your return and sign it, you are also required to sign and are held responsible for any mistakes, so it would be wise to read those parts of the instruction booklet that apply to your situation.

There are a variety of income tax forms that are used to report income. The form to be used depends on the amount and source of the income and whether deductions are itemized by the individual. Specific requirements should be obtained from the Internal Revenue Service. Each individual who earns an income has the responsibility of submitting a tax form. Failure to submit a form may result in a monetary fine or a prison sentence.

Depending upon the income earned, tax forms can be submitted electronically, by using the telephone, or by sending the forms through the mail. Many individuals with limited income file simple forms, which are fairly easy to prepare and submit. For individuals with a high amount of income and deductions, tax forms can be confusing and difficult to complete. For those individuals, the authors recommend that an accountant or qualified person be hired to prepare the taxes.

A major concern for food service employees is that income tax must be paid on all tips received. The employee must give to the employer a written statement declaring how much money was received in tips during the pay period. The employer deducts from the employee's paycheck the proper amount of withholding tax for these tips, or the employee pays the employer the amount of tax due out of the tips collected.

The cost of meals furnished to the employee by the employer is also considered part of the employee's income. It is, therefore, subject to income tax unless it can be shown that the employee was given the meals for the convenience of the employer.

The authors advise all employees to consult the current tax code concerning tips, as well as any other questions that employees may have, in order to be in compliance with the tax laws. This is because the law may (and usually does) change from year to year.

F.I.C.A. (Social Security) Tax

The letters F.I.C.A. stand for the Federal Insurance Contribution Acts, which became law in 1935. This act established the social security system and tax. The social security system provides for the payment of retirement, survivor, and disability insurance benefits. It also provides hospital insurance benefits for persons age 65 and over who meet its eligibility requirements. This insurance, commonly known as Medicare, provides coverage for both hospital and doctor visits. Funds for payment of these benefits are provided by taxes levied on employees and their employers as well as self-employed persons.

Under the terms of the Social Security Act, the employer is required by law to deduct a certain percentage of the employee's wages each payday and remit the amount deducted to the federal government. For a self-employed person, the percentage is doubled. Each self-employed person has to pay the F.I.C.A. rate as an employer and an equal amount as an employee.

The term *wages* means "that which is paid or received for services" and includes salaries, commissions, fees, bonuses, tips, etc. For example:

Bill Clark, manager of the Red Gate Restaurant, is paid a salary of $550.00 per week, plus a 2 percent commission on the private party business in excess of $6,000 per week. During the first week of June, the restaurant's private party business was $10,500. Assume that the social security tax rate is 7.65%. How much F.I.C.A. tax was deducted from Bill's earnings for that week?

Salary	$550.00	
Commission	90.00	(2% of 4,500)
Total Earnings	$640.00	
7.65% of $640.00 =	$ 48.96	F.I.C.A. tax

The amount of social security tax deducted from Bill's earnings that week was $48.96.

Besides the money deducted each payday from the employee's paycheck, a tax equal to that amount is levied on the employer. The tax is computed at the same rate as the employee's tax and is based on the total taxable wages paid by the employer. For example:

During the month of June, the Red Gate Restaurant paid out \$10,650.00 in taxable wages. If the social security rate is 7.65 percent, the owner must pay the federal government \$814.73.

$$\$10,650 \times 0.0765 = \$814.73$$

Self-employed persons must also pay social security taxes on income, but as pointed out previously, at double the rate.

In the food service industry, once a knowledge of food preparation and managing is acquired it is a fairly easy step to go from employee to employer. However, with tax obligations such as these, much thought must go into taking that big step.

SUMMARY REVIEW

Calculate the following problems concerning social security tax. Round answers to the nearest cent.

1. The cook at the Sea Shore Restaurant is paid a salary of \$395.00 per week, plus 2 percent commission on all food sales for the week in excess of \$20,000. During the second week of March, the food sales amounted to \$25,000. If the social security tax rate is 7.30 percent, how much social security tax was deducted from his earnings for that week?

____

2. Bill Walters, a waiter at the Red Gate Restaurant, is paid a salary of \$150.00 per week, plus tips. During the first week of July his tips amounted to \$220.00. Assuming that the social security tax rate is 7.30 percent, how much F.I.C.A. tax was deducted from Bill's earnings for that week?

____

3. Jean Curran, a hostess at the Red Gate Restaurant, is paid a salary of \$120.00 per week, plus tips. During the first week of May her tips amounted to \$155.00. Assuming that the social security tax rate is 7.30 percent, how much tax was deducted from Jean's earnings for that week?

____

4. Fred Hartzel, manager of the Kentucky Inn, is paid a salary of \$525.00 per week, plus $2\frac{1}{2}$ percent commission on the food and beverage business in excess of \$12,500 per week. During the second week of November, the business amounted to \$24,600. Assuming that the social security tax rate is 7.30 percent, how much tax was deducted from Fred's earnings for that week?

____

5. The catering manager of the Gourmet Catering Company works on a 3 percent commission of total sales for each week. During the first week in June total sales were $24,000. What were her total earnings?

   ____

   How much social security tax did she pay if the rate is 7.30 percent?

   ____

STATE TAXES

These are taxes collected by the state government. The taxes collected are for the purpose of operating all the state functions and agencies. Each agency submits a budget outlining how their money will be spent. Each state government operates independently from each other. The state governing body (generally the governor and state legislature) determines the amount of tax revenue required to operate and how those taxes will be imposed upon its citizens.

Employees Withholding Tax

Employees Withholding Tax is money withheld from each employee's paycheck by the employer during the year for the purpose of paying the employee's state income tax at the end of the calendar year. It is done for the same purpose as the employee's federal withholding tax. The amount of money withheld from each individual's paycheck is determined by the amount of income earned and the percentage set by the state. The tax is always lower than the amount withheld for federal tax.

Income Tax

Most states have an income tax. The income tax laws in most states are patterned after the federal income tax laws. The percentage of tax collected on each individual's adjusted gross income varies from state to state, but it is usually a percentage that graduates with the increase of income and it is always less than the amount paid to the federal government. Your state income tax is paid to the state in which you live even though the money may be earned in another state.

SUMMARY REVIEW

For the following problems, compute the state income tax due on net income. Use statements (a) through (e) as a guide in solving these problems.

(a) Net income is \$3,000 or less; your tax is 2 percent.

(b) Net income is over \$3,000, but not over \$4,000; your tax is \$60, plus 3 percent of excess over \$3,000.

(c) Net income is over \$4,000, but not over \$5,000; your tax is \$90, plus 4 percent of excess over \$4,000.

(d) Net income is over \$5,000, but not over \$8,000; your tax is \$130, plus 5 percent of excess over \$5,000.

(e) Net income is over \$8,000; your tax is \$280, plus 6 percent of the excess over \$8,000.

State Taxes Due

1. Net income \$12,990. ______________
2. Net income \$7,950. ______________
3. Net income \$19,589. ______________
4. Net income \$7,460. ______________
5. Net income \$45,980. ______________

Sales Tax

Most states have a **sales tax.** The tax is added to most items purchased. However, in some states, food, prescription drugs, and clothing are exceptions. The amount of the tax is added to the amount of purchase made within that state. For example:

Bob and Dolores received a dinner check at the Blue Star Restaurant for \$30.75. The sales tax for that particular state is 6 percent. How much tax did they pay? What was the total bill?

\$30.75	Cost of two dinners
× .06	6% sales tax
\$1.8450	= \$1.85 amount of tax

\$30.75	Cost of two dinners
+ 1.85	Amount of tax
\$32.60	Total bill

Amount purchased + amount of tax = Total bill

To help cashiers and salespeople find the total amount of tax due, each state publishes and distributes a tax chart showing the amount of purchase and the tax due on that purchase. An example of a sales tax chart is shown in Chapter 13.

The business owner is asked to collect this sales tax and give the receipts to the state government. In some states, a small percentage of the amount collected is given to the business owner as compensation for collecting the tax.

Backing Out Sales Tax

Some business owners include the price of the sales tax in the total menu price. The business owner will have to back out the tax from the menu price in order to know how much must be paid to the government. The following example will demonstrate how to do this:

The menu price for an entree is $15.00, which includes the sales tax of 7.5 percent. How much money is collected in sales tax? How much money is left for the price of food minus the sales tax?

Step 1: Convert 7.5% to a decimal

7.5% = .075

Step 2: Add 100% or 1 to the decimal of .075

1 + .075 = 1.075 (divisor) sales tax rate

Step 3: Divide the menu price by the (divisor) sales tax rate

$15.00 divided by 1.075 = $13.95 (which equals the price without the tax)

Step 4: Subtract the results from the original menu price, which equals the sales tax owed.

$15.00 − $13.95 = $1.05 (sales tax owed)

To prove the formula:

Step 1: Multiply the price obtained, $13.95, by the sales tax rate of 7.5%.

$ 13.95	Price
× .075	Sales tax rate
6975	
+ 9765	
104625 = 1.04625 = $1.05	

Step 2: Add the sales tax amount to the price of the food.

$ 1.05	Sales tax
+ $13.95	Price
$15.00	Original menu price

SUMMARY REVIEW

Solve each of the following problems by finding the amount of sales tax and the total cost of the item purchased.

1. Judy Brown purchased a new VCR at a price of $325. The sales tax was 6 percent. What was the amount of sales tax paid?

   ____

   What was the total cost of the VCR?

   ____

2. John Curry purchased a new slicing machine for $2,400. He paid cash and received a $2\frac{1}{2}$ percent discount. If the sales tax was $3\frac{1}{2}$ percent, what was the amount of tax paid?

   ____

   What was the total cost of the slicing machine?

   ____

3. Dale Warren, the chef at the Red Lion Inn, purchased a new steam table for $4,900. He was given a $1\frac{1}{2}$ percent discount. The sales tax was $4\frac{1}{2}$ percent. What was the amount of sales tax paid?

   ____

   What was the total cost of the steam table?

   ____

4. The Paridiso Restaurant charged $18.00 for its veal marsala, tax included. If the sales tax was 3.2 percent, what was the amount of sales tax paid?

   ____

   What was the price without the sales tax?

   ____

5. A banquet (tax was included) cost $10,100. If the sales tax was 8 percent, what was the amount of sales tax paid on the banquet?

   ____

Licenses

Although the term **licenses** is used here, in reality it is another form of taxation. These licenses will vary from state to state, but usually are required to practice a profession such as medicine, law, or dentistry, or to operate a business such as a convenience store, taxi service, or butcher shop. Since most states require some type of license to serve food and drink, the food services industry is affected by licensing requirements.

LOCAL TAXES

Local taxes are collected for the purpose of operating municipal governments (city, town, county). Like the state, city departments and agencies submit a budget each year detailing how much money is needed to operate and how that money will be spent. The governing body of the local government determines the amount of tax dollars required to operate and the method used to collect the taxes.

Employees Withholding Tax

Employees Withholding Tax is money withheld from an employee's paycheck by an employer during the year to pay for the income tax that is assessed by the locality where the employee works. Everyone who works within the city limit pays the tax whether they live within that area or not. This money is rarely refunded even if the employee lives in another state. The amount withheld is generally smaller than either the federal or state withholding taxes.

Income Tax

Local income tax is money paid to the local government to help pay for the cost of operating the municipality. The money is usually paid to the municipality in which the employee works and the tax rate is relatively small.

Personal Property Tax

Personal Property Tax may be assessed by the state or county in which the employee lives. It is a tax on certain pieces of personal property, such as an automobile, furniture, or out of state investments. The amount of tax is usually based on the present value of the property. For example, a new automobile is taxed more heavily than an older one.

Occupational Tax

Occupational tax is assessed by the city in which a business is established. It is a tax that must be paid in order to operate any business within that city.

Licenses

Licenses are an official document given to an individual or group, for a fee, for permission to engage in a specified activity, perform a specific act, etc. Those licenses required vary from city to city. They may be required for operating a car, putting on a certain type of show, or having a pet and, in most cases, operating a food and beverage establishment.

Real Estate Tax

If you own property, you will be paying a real estate tax. This tax impacts decisions regarding purchasing property. If you like the property and are to the point of making an offer, the next question is usually, what are the taxes? In some communities the tax rate is so high that it can discourage a purchase.

Real estate tax is usually assessed by the local government, but the money paid is distributed among the state, city, county, and township. This tax provides the money to operate schools, pay teachers, firefighters, police officers, and local officials. The money is also used for local projects such as improving streets and sewers, and building playgrounds. Real estate tax provides most of the revenue needed to operate local governments. It is a tax that affects the property owner most, because it is believed they are the ones who benefit most from local services and improvements.

Real estate or property taxes are collected once a year or every six months, depending on the area in which the property is located. The tax rate is based on the amount of money required to meet the operating budget of the city, county, school district, and so on, for the next year. Each unit of local government plans a budget for the following year and sets a tax rate that will meet these expenses. The total of these individual rates makes up a combined rate that is charged to the property owner.

Each piece of property in the area is assessed for its value by the county assessor. The property is usually assessed at 35 to 40 percent of the actual amount it would bring if sold. Some areas assess property at its market value, but this is not usually the case.

Property tax rates may be expressed either as a percent, or as a certain amount of money for every $100 or $1,000 of assessed valuation.

Example No. 1:

$85,000	Value of house if sold (market value)
$34,000	Assessed valuation (40% of market value)
$35	Tax rate (per **$1,000 of assessed value**)

$34,000 ÷ **$1000 = 34**

$35	**Tax rate per $1,000**
× 34	Times $1,000 goes into $34,000
$1,190	Cost of real estate taxes for one year

Example No. 2:

$85,000	Value of house if sold (market value)
$34,000	Assessed valuation (40% of market value)
$5.20	Tax rate (per $100 of assessed value)

$34,000 ÷ $100 = 34

$5.20	Tax rate (per $100 of assessed value)
× 340	Times ($100 goes into $34,000)
20,800	(Tax rate is based on each $100)
1560	
$1,768.00	Cost of real estate taxes for one year

Example No. 3:

$85,000	Value of house if sold (market value)
$34,000	Assessed valuation (40% of market value)
$5.5%	Tax rate of the assessed valuation

$34,000	Assessed valuation
× 0.055	Tax rate
170000	
170000	
$1,870.000	Cost of real estate taxes for one year

SUMMARY REVIEW

Find the amount of real estate tax due in problems 1 through 5 using the facts provided in each problem.

1. The value of the house if sold equals $95,000. Assessed valuation is 40 percent of the market value. The tax rate is $38.00 per $1,000 of assessed value. Find the annual taxes due.

   ____

2. The value of the house if sold equals $125,000. Assessed valuation is 36 percent of the market value. The tax rate is $36.00 per $1,000 of assessed value. Find the annual taxes due.

   ____

3. The value of the house if sold equals $136,000. Assessed valuation is 42 percent of the market value. The tax rate is $5.325 per $100 of assessed value. Find the annual taxes due.

   ____

4. The value of the house if sold equals $112,500. Assessed valuation is 38 percent of the market value. The tax rate is 4.65 percent of assessed value. Find the annual taxes due.

   ____

5. The value of the house if sold equals $79,500. Assessed valuation is 30 percent of the market value. The tax rate is $28.00 per $1,000 of assessed value. Find the annual taxes due.

   ____

Payroll

The purpose of explaining certain points concerning payroll is to help you understand how your money is earned and what happens to a portion of that earned income before it is placed in your hands in the form of a *paycheck*. When your earned income is calculated in the payroll department, certain *deductions* are taken from your *gross pay* (pay before any deductions) before arriving at your *net pay* (take-home pay after deductions) and before a paycheck is issued.

Many young people enter the world of work without understanding the payroll system. They become confused and sometimes angry when they receive their first paycheck and find that it does not meet their expectations. The points to be discussed in this section are those that may affect a food service employee.

A **payroll** is a record of earnings kept by the employer on all persons classified as employees. The employer is required by law to record and maintain complete, up-to-date, accurate records on all employees. How this information is recorded and maintained is up to the employer. In a small operation they may be kept up to date by an individual bookkeeper, controller, or accountant using customary office machines. Or the operation may hire a bank or company that offers a payroll service for a fee that is based on the number of employees on the payroll. In a large or chain operation, a computer would be used. Forms and methods used in compiling a payroll will vary from company to company and even from state to state. State laws and company policy differ in certain areas.

Wages refer to a payment made for a service rendered, usually referring to payment for total hours of work at a designated hourly rate. When a person accepts employment by a company, an agreement is made on wages. The wages will be based on a specific amount for each hour worked and usually an 8-hour day and 40-hour week.

When the term **salary** is used, it usually refers to payment set for a week, month, or year. When payment is based on salary the work may exceed 8 hours a day or 40 hours a week. When beginning a new salaried job, you will probably be given a job description outlining your duties and responsibilities. If it takes more than the customary hours in a day or week to satisfy these responsibilities, it is of little concern to the employer because the employee does not receive overtime pay. In a food service operation, employees involved in supervision and management usually work for a straight salary.

When an employee is paid on an hourly basis, a definite amount of money is paid for each hour worked. As pointed out previously, the total number of hours scheduled to work each day is usually eight or forty for a week. These are called regular hours or *straight time*. Hours worked over these regular hours are called **overtime** hours. In accordance with federal wage and hour laws, companies that engage in interstate commerce or companies that have union contracts with an overtime clause must pay overtime at a rate of time and a half for work over eight hours a day or forty hours a week. Some union contracts specify that when an employee works on certain days such as Sunday and holidays they receive *double time*. That is, the employee is paid two times his or her regular rate of pay for each hour worked.

```
 5 MALTSEV, SERGEY
TIMECARD # 2              PAGE  1
- - - - - - - - - - - - - - - - - - -
 IN/OUT    TIME    #HRS DAY/PERIOD

 1 IN   MON FEB21 10:26AM
        5/1 SERVER
 1 OUT  MON FEB21 02:32PM
        5              4.10/4.10
```

Figure 19-2 *Time card.*

The hours that an employee works are usually recorded on a *time card,* that is punched on a *time clock* when the employee reports to work, and again when he or she leaves for the day. (See Figure 19-2.) When a time clock is used, the company will have a set policy on time limits for punching in and out before a penalty is imposed. Another method of recording employees' hours worked is by computer. The employee punches a certain number assigned to them when arriving and leaving work and the computer records the time.

Calculating Gross Wages

To compute an employee's wage, the hourly rate of pay is multiplied by the number of hours worked.

Hourly rate × hours worked = Gross pay

For example:

Thomas Payne is paid $9.75 per hour. He works a regular 40-hour week. To calculate his gross pay for one week:

$40 \times \$9.75 = \$390.00$

$9.75	per hour worked
× 40	hours worked
$390.00	Gross pay

When overtime is involved, gross pay can be calculated in two ways but with the same results:

1. Multiply the number of hours over the regular work time of 40 hours by $1\frac{1}{2}$ (for time and a half) or by 2 (for double time). Multiply this result by the hourly rate. Add the overtime pay to regular pay.

   Overtime hours × $1\frac{1}{2}$ = Total regular hours
   Total regular hours × hourly rate = Overtime pay
   Overtime pay + regular 40 hours pay = Gross wages

For example:

Tim Macke earns \$9.00 per hour for a regular work week of 40 hours with overtime pay at time and a half. To calculate his gross wages for a week in which he worked 48 hours:

Overtime hours $8 \times 1\frac{1}{2}$ = 12 regular hours
12 × \$9.00 hourly rate = \$108 overtime pay

Overtime pay	\$108.00
Regular pay (40 × \$9.00)	+ 360.00
Gross wages	\$468.00

or

2. Multiply the hourly rate by $1\frac{1}{2}$ or 2 = overtime rate.
   Then multiply the number of hours over 40 (regular time) by the overtime rate = overtime pay. Add overtime pay to regular pay = gross pay.

   Hourly rate × 1.5 = Overtime rate
   Overtime rate × overtime hours = Overtime pay
   Overtime pay + regular pay = Gross pay

For example (using the same problem as example number 1):

\$9.00 hours rate × 1.5 = \$13.50 overtime rate
\$13.50 × 8 overtime hours = \$108.00 overtime pay

Overtime wages	\$108.00
Regular wages (40 × \$9)	+ 360.00
Gross wages	\$468.00

In comparing the two methods of calculating overtime pay, you will notice that the results are the same and that only the method used differs.

SUMMARY REVIEW

1. Bill Miller, a cook at the Blue Boar Restaurant, earns \$9.50 per hour for a 40-hour week, with time and a half for all hours worked over 40 hours per week. This past week he worked a total of 46 hours. What was his gross wage for the week?

   ____

2. Faiza Khan, a fry cook at the Conservatory Restaurant, works on a 40-hour a week basis with time and a half for all overtime. Her regular hourly rate of pay is \$8.75 per hour. Last week she worked a total of 49 hours. What was her gross wage for the week?

   ____

3. Gloria Luran, a salad person at Lang's Cafeteria, works on an 8-hour per day basis, plus time and a half for time worked over 8 hours in any one day. Her regular hourly rate of pay is $6.50 per hour. This past week her time card recorded the following hours:

S	**M**	**T**	**W**	**TH**	**F**	**S**
	12	9	8.5	8	10	

What was her gross wage for the week?

____

4. Mario Astor, the sauce cook at the Metropole Hotel, worked a total of $49\frac{1}{2}$ hours during a recent week. He is paid $12.25 per hour plus time and a half for all hours over 40 hours per week. What was his gross wage for the week?

____

5. Jacob Rowe, a salad person at the Gibson Hotel, worked 7 consecutive days, 8 hours a day, from Monday through Sunday. His regular pay rate is $5.75 per hour. The hotel pays time and a half for all hours worked on Saturday and double time for all hours worked on Sunday. What was his gross wage for this period of work?

____

◆ *Chef Sez . . .*

"Math is very important to the chef or the cook. All ordering and purchasing are based upon math. Supplies from dry goods may have to be converted from pounds to the metric system. It is a must to know math! Even what you get paid is based upon numbers. Math is important when you get your paycheck."

Kevin Gee, Certified Executive Chef
Corporate Executive Chef
Organic Foods, Inc.
Little Rock, Arkansas

Chef Gee in his vast career has had the privilege of cooking meals for four presidents of the United States. During his career in Arkansas, he cooked for Ronald Reagan, Jimmy Carter, George Bush, and Bill Clinton. In addition, he has cooked for the press corps, Secret Service, and many other presidential candidates.

Calculating Net Pay

Gross wages are the amount of money you earn before any deductions (the amount taken away) are made. After deductions are made, the result is called **net pay** (net meaning free of all deductions). An employer is required by law, or in some cases by clauses in a union contract, to make certain required deductions. Any deductions beyond those required must be authorized by the employee. Some of the required deductions are F.I.C.A. (Social Security) taxes, federal withholding taxes (income tax), state income tax, city income tax, health insurance and retirement fund. Some of the deductions that you may authorize include union dues, contributions to charitable organizations, credit unions, and company stock purchases.

To calculate net pay, all deductions are subtracted from gross wages. Net pay is the figure that will appear on your weekly, semi-monthly, or monthly paycheck. The formula for calculating net pay is as follows:

Gross wages − deductions = Net pay

For example:

Jerry Roth, an employee of the Terrace Plaza Hotel, receives $7.45 an hour for a regular 40-hour work week with time and a half for overtime. Last week Jerry worked 52 hours. Deducted from his gross wages were: $31.54 F.I.C.A. (Social Security) taxes, $64.81 federal withholding taxes, $21.65 health insurance, and $25.93 state income tax.

To determine Jerry's gross wage and net pay follow Step 1 and Step 2.

Step 1:

52	Total hours worked
− 40	Regular hours
12	Overtime hours
12	Overtime hours
× 1.5	Time and a half
60	
12	
18.0	Overtime hours converted to regular hours
+40	Regular hours
58	Total regular hours worked
$7.45	Per hour
× 58	Total regular hours
5960	
3725	
$432.10	Gross wages

Step 2:

$ 31.54	F.I.C.A. tax
$ 64.81	Federal withholding tax
$ 21.65	Health insurance
+ $ 25.93	State income tax
$143.93	Total deductions
$432.10	Gross wages
− 143.93	Total deductions
$288.17	Net pay (take-home pay)

As you can see by comparing the two steps to solving this problem, there is a great deal of difference between gross wages and net or take-home pay.

Sometimes the payroll department may not have all the proper schedules, tax guides, and tables put out by the various tax agencies of the federal and state governments. In such cases, they may be required to calculate deductible dollar amounts using percentages.

For example:

Jerry Roth, an employee of the Terrace Plaza Hotel, receives $7.45 an hour for a regular 40-hour work week with time and a half for overtime. Last week Jerry worked 52 hours. Deducted from his gross wages were: 7.30 percent for F.I.C.A. (Social Security) taxes, 15 percent for federal withholding taxes, 5 percent for state income tax, and $1\frac{1}{2}$ percent for city income tax.

To determine Jerry's gross wage and net pay follow Step 1 and Step 2.

Step 1:

52	Total hours worked
− 40	Regular hours
12	Overtime hours
12	Overtime hours
× 1.5	Time and a half
60	
12	
18.0	Overtime hours converted to regular hours
+40	Regular hours
58	Total regular hours worked
$7.45	Per hour
× 58	Total regular hours
5960	
3725	
$432.10	Gross wages

Up to this point, the calculations are the same as in the previous example. The difference lies in calculating the deductions because dollar amounts must be found when deductions are given in percents.

Step 2:

F.I.C.A. 7.30% × 432.10 gross wages	=	$ 31.54
Federal withholding tax 15% × 432.10	=	$ 64.82
State income tax 5% × 432.10	=	$ 21.61
City income tax 1.5% × 432.10	=	$ 6.48
Sum of deductions	=	$124.45

$432.10	Gross wages
− 124.45	Sum of deductions
$307.65	Net pay or take-home pay

SUMMARY REVIEW

1. The chef at the Metropole Hotel is paid a salary of $3,500 per month and receives a paycheck twice a month. On a recent paycheck, the deductions from his total earnings were as follows: $127.75 F.I.C.A. tax, $350.00 federal withholding tax, $87.50 state income tax, and $26.25 city income tax.

   What was his gross wage for this pay period? ____________

   What was his net pay? ____________

2. For each of the following, find gross wages and amount of net pay based on a 40-hour work week with time and a half for all hours worked over 40.

Name	Total Hours Worked	Hourly Rate	Gross Wages	Total Deductions	Net Pay
Tisha Adams	46	$ 5.95	$	$ 79.95	$
Rafael Romero	56	$ 7.50	$	$120.10	$
Rose Fahery	45.5	$ 9.25	$	$126.90	$
Paul Brown	49.5	$10.75	$	$137.50	$
Kim Lee	57	$12.25	$	$142.60	$

3. The head salad person at the Kemper Lane Hotel is employed on the basis of 8 hours per day, with time and a half for all overtime hours. Her regular hourly pay rate is $6.50. In a recent week she worked the following hours:

S	M	T	W	TH	F	S
—	9.5	9	10.5	8	12	—

   Deducted from her gross wages were F.I.C.A. tax $21.00, federal withholding tax $76.70, state income tax $10.95, and health insurance $16.90.

   What was her gross wage?____________

   What was her net pay?____________

4. John Linsdale, a waiter at the Sands Hotel, receives a base salary of $125.00 per week plus tips. Last week his tips amounted to $260.00. From his gross wages the following deductions were made: F.I.C.A. tax 7.30 percent, federal withholding tax 15 percent, state income tax 4 percent, and $20.45 for health insurance.

   What was his gross wage?____________

   What was his net pay?____________

5. Elsa Suarez, a baker at the Chesapeake Hotel, works on a 40 hour per week basis, with time and a half for all overtime. During this past week she worked 49 hours. Her regular pay rate is $6.95 per hour. The following deductions were taken from her gross pay: federal withholding tax $65.60, F.I.C.A. $27.14, health insurance $12.95, and union dues $7.00.

   What was her gross wage?____________

   What was her net pay?____________

Figure 19-3 *Controller compiling salary with commission information for a food service employee.*

Calculating Salary Plus Commission

There are situations in the food service industry where an employee is paid a salary plus a commission (generally a percentage of sales for a given period). These situations usually occur to motivate supervisors and managers to increase production and sales. Commissions are calculated by the financial officers usually referred to as controllers in the Hospitality Industry (see Figure 19-3).

To calculate a gross wage when a commission is involved, the amount of the commission is added to the basic salary. To find the amount of the commission, sales are multiplied by the percent of commission. The formula for calculating gross wages involving commission is as follows:

Amount of sales × percent of commission = Amount of commission

Amount of commission + salary = Gross wages

For example:

The banquet manager at the Alms Hotel is paid a salary of \$590.00 per week plus a $1\frac{1}{2}$ percent commission on the private party business in excess of \$5,000.00 per week. In a recent week the party business amounted to \$12,000. To determine the gross pay refer to the following example.

\$12,000	Total sales
− 5,000	Amount deducted
\$7,000	Amount on which commission is paid
× .015	Percent of commission
35000	
7000	
\$105.00	Amount of commission
\$590.00	Weekly salary
+ 105.00	Amount of commission
\$695.00	Gross pay

SUMMARY REVIEW

1. The catering manager at Elegant Fare Catering Company receives a basic salary of $950.00 per month plus a 2 percent commission on all the catered business. Last month the catered business amounted to $35,000.00. What was her gross wage?

____

2. The manager of a local fast-food restaurant receives a monthly salary of $1,600 plus a commission of $0.12 for every sandwich sold during the month. Last month, 1,200 sandwiches were sold. What was his gross wage for the month?

____

3. The manager of the food concession at the local swimming club receives a small weekly salary of $125.00 plus a commission of 6 percent on all food sales for the week. Last week the food sales amounted to $7,550. What was her gross wage for the week?

____

4. The preparation cook at Bob's Catering Company receives a salary of $350.00 per week plus a commission of $1\frac{1}{2}$ percent on all the catered party business. In a recent week the catered party business amounted to $15,000. Deducted from her gross wages were the following: F.I.C.A. tax $41.98, federal withholding tax $126.50, and city income tax $8.63.

   What was her gross wage?

   ____

   What was her net pay?_______________

   ____

5. The food and beverage manager at the Fountain Square Hotel receives a salary of $2,800.00 per month plus a commission of $\frac{1}{2}$ percent on all food and beverage business for the month. Last month the food business amounted to $24,500. The beverage business was $8,600. What was her gross wage for the month?

____

Simple and Compound Interest

OBJECTIVES

At the completion of this chapter, the student should be able to:

1. Identify and understand types of interest.
2. Calculate simple interest.
3. Calculate compound interest.

Interest is defined in banking circles as the price of money, a rental payment, or a charge placed on borrowed money, by the lender, for the use of money. It could also mean something extra given or money paid for the use of someone else's money for a certain period of time. Regardless of how it is defined, it is an important factor in the economy. Without interest, money could not be loaned to individuals to start a business, buy a house, or get a college degree. Moreover, savings accounts would not earn interest.

Earning interest or paying interest on borrowed money has become a way of life in the United States. Interest can be an asset or a problem depending on the individual or company doing the borrowing. When done moderately, borrowing can be an advantage. Excessive borrowing, however, can cause financial ruin because interest, being a fixed charge, if not paid, entitles the creditors to legal recourse in case of **default** (failure to pay a debt). To many, interest is a reward for thrift, that is, a payment made to lenders to encourage them to save their money so that money can be made available to others.

Interest rates that banks charge for borrowing money can fluctuate almost as rapidly as food prices, but by smaller amounts. Banking institutions usually have an interest rate change once a week. There is a lot of uncertainty in interest rates, and without expertise it is difficult to predict whether the rates are going up or coming down. The secret for acquiring a good interest rate on a home or business loan is to watch how rates fluctuate each week, and when they reach a point that you feel you can afford, make your move.

TYPES OF INTEREST

There are two types of interest: simple and compound. **Simple interest** is money paid only on the **principal** (the amount of money loaned or borrowed). **Compound interest** usually associated with savings accounts and Certificates of Deposit (CDs) is interest that is added to the principal (with interest then paid on a new principal). In other words, each time the interest is paid, it is added to the previous principal to obtain a new and higher principal. Compound interest has no association with borrowing or taking out a loan.

The rate of interest paid on a loan is usually expressed in terms of an annual rate of percentage on the principal. Thus, if $8.00 is paid for the annual use of $100, the rate is 8 percent. The $8.00 is the difference between what was loaned and what was repaid. This percentage interest rate is determined and kept current by various factors. The most important being the relationship between the supply of money available to lend and the demand for borrowing. The same factor controls most pricing—the law of supply and demand.

Calculating Simple Interest

To calculate the amount of interest charged or paid, use the following formula:

Principal × rate × time = Amount of interest

The principal is the amount borrowed, rate is the percentage of the principal charged, and the time is usually one year, unless otherwise stated.

The interest year may be expressed as an ordinary year (360 days) or as an exact year (365 days). The type of interest year becomes important when the time of the loan is expressed in days. When days are mentioned you must first find the amount of interest for one year and divide this amount by either 360 (ordinary) or 365 (exact) days to find the amount of interest per day. The amount of interest charged per day is then multiplied by the number of days mentioned in the loan.

Expressing these calculations as a formula:

Amount of interest for one year ÷ ordinary or exact days per year = Interest per day

Interest per day × number of days of loan = Amount of interest paid

For Example:

James Baker borrowed $8,650.00 at 8 percent interest for a period of 60 days. What amount of interest would he pay if he borrowed the money at (a) ordinary interest? (b) at exact interest?

For part (a) we have:

$8,650.00	×	.08	=	$692.00 ÷ 360 =
principal	×	rate	=	interest ÷ days per year =
$1.9222222	×	60	=	$115.333332 or $115.33
interest per day		days		total interest for 60 days when rounded to the nearest cent

For part (b) we have:

$8650.00	×	0.08	=	$692.00 ÷ 365
principal		rate		interest per year days exact year
$1.8958904	×	60	=	$113.753424 or $113.75
interest per day		days		total interest for 60 days when rounded to the nearest cent

Note: Do not round off the amount of interest per day until it is multiplied by the number of days stated in the loan. In this way, an exact total can be obtained.

The yearly interest for both ordinary and exact interest is the same, but a difference occurs in the amount of interest per day because of the difference in the divisor.

The difference in interest per day will, of course, show a difference in the amount of interest charged for a 60-day period, as shown below. In some cases this difference can be substantial, so be aware of the method used to determine days in a year when borrowing money. Remember that interest calculated on ordinary interest will always be slightly more than calculated on exact interest. For our example the difference is:

$115.33	ordinary interest
− 113.75	exact interest
$1.58	difference

If the time of a loan period is stated in months, then the amount of interest for one year is divided by 12 to obtain the amount of interest charged per month. The result is then multiplied by the number of months stated in the loan period.

For example:

Mr. Pete Jackson borrowed $5,680.00 at 9.5 percent interest for a period of six months. What was the total amount of interest paid?

$5,680.00 principal	×	.095 rate	= $539.60 interest per year	÷ 12 = months in year
$44.966666 interest per month	×	6 months loan time	= $269.7999996 or $269.80 total interest for 6 months when rounded to the nearest cent	

Note: Do not round off the amount of interest per month until it is multiplied by the number of months stated in the loan. In this way, an exact total can be obtained.

As stated previously, time is a very important factor in determining the amount of interest paid. It is therefore essential that the time factor be calculated accurately. To calculate the exact number of days between dates stated in a loan period, subtract the starting date from the number of days in that particular month and continue to count the days until you have arrived at the ending date. For example:

How many days are there in a loan period that starts on May 5th and ends of August 15th?

31	days in month of May
− 5	starting date of loan
26	days left in May
30	days in month of June
31	days in month of July
+ 15	August ending date of loan
102	number of days between starting date and ending date of loan period

TIPS . . . ***To Insure Perfect Solutions***

Months with 31 days:

January, March, May, July, August, October, and December.

Months with 30 days:

April, June, September, and November.

February is a month with 28 days, except for Leap Year when it has 29 days.

What is the amount of interest charged on a loan of $760.00 at 12.5 percent ordinary interest if the money is borrowed on April 15th and is to be repaid on September 15th?

Calculate the time:

31	days in April
− 15	April starting date
15	days left in April
31	days in May
30	days in June
31	days in July
31	days in August
+ 15	September ending date of loan
153	number of days between starting date and ending date of loan period

Calculate the interest after finding the time:

$760.00	×	0.125	=	$95.00	÷	360
principal		rate		interest per year		days ordinary year

$.2638888 = interest per day

$.263888	×	153	=	$40.37
interest per day		number of days		interest for 153 days when rounded to the nearest cent

What is the amount of interest charged on a loan of $2,500.00 at 10.5 percent exact interest if the money is borrowed on August 12th and is to be repaid on October 26th?

Calculate the time:

31	days in August
− 12	August starting date
19	days left in August
30	days in September
+ 26	October ending date
75	number of days between starting date and ending date of loan period

Calculate the interest after finding the time:

$2,500.00	×	0.105	=	$262.50	÷	365
principal		rate		interest per year		days in exact year

$0.719178 = interest per day

$0.719178	×	75	=	$53.43835 or $53.94
per day		number of days		interest for 75 days when rounded to the nearest cent

Summary Review

Answer each of the following:

1. Peter Chan borrowed $7,540.00 at 8.5 percent ordinary interest for a period of 60 days. What amount of interest was paid?

 ____

2. Meryl Macke borrowed $5,455.00 at 7.5 percent exact interest for a period of 80 days. What amount of interest was paid?

 ____

3. Carlos Kistler borrowed $10,550 at 6.5 percent interest for a period of six months. What was the total amount of interest paid?

 ____

4. How many days are there in a loan period that starts on March 21 and ends on October 20th?

 ____

5. What is the amount of interest charged on a loan of $880.00 at 12.5 percent ordinary interest if the money is borrowed on April 20th and is to be repaid on September 20th?

 ____

Find the answer to each of the following problems by finding the amount of interest paid using ordinary (360 days) interest.

	Principal	Interest Rate	Time	Interest Paid
6.	$ 960.00	7%	75 days	________
7.	$1,290.00	9%	110 days	________
8.	$2,470.00	10.5%	150 days	________
9.	$3,650.00	12.5%	April 15th to July 10th	________
10.	$4,255.00	14%	July 5th to November 12th	________

Find the answer to each of the following problems by finding the amount of interest paid using exact (365 days) interest.

	Principal	Interest Rate	Time	Interest Paid
11.	$ 985.00	6%	60 days	________
12.	$1,370.00	7.5%	90 days	________
13.	$2,225.00	11.5%	130 days	________
14.	$3,845.00	12.5%	April 2nd to July 20th	________
15.	$4,735.00	13%	August 7th to Dec 5th	________

Calculating Compound Interest

Compound interest, as stated previously, is interest payments added to the principal, with interest then paid on the new principal. The new principal is used each interest period to calculate the amount of interest paid for that period. With interest payments being added onto the principal, the principal will constantly increase. Consequently, the amount of interest for each interest period will also increase. This method can be used to let money earn more money. Keep in mind, what has been mentioned before, compound interest is usually associated with savings accounts and Certificates of Deposit (CDs). It is not associated with borrowing or taking out a loan.

Interest may be compounded as follows:

- Annually—once a year
- Semiannually—twice a year
- Quarterly—four times a year
- Monthly—twelve times a year
- Daily—every day

When computers became popular, banks and other lending institutions started offering daily compounding on savings accounts. The daily interest earned is usually entered into the account at the end of each quarter as a single amount.

When interest is compounded annually, ordinary simple interest is computed for the first year and then added to the original principal to become the new principal for computing interest for the second year. This procedure is repeated for as many years as stated in the contract.

For example:

Find the amount of compound interest at the end of three years on a principal of $2,000.00 compounded annually at 8 percent interest.

$2000.00	×	0.08	=	$160.00	+	$2000.00
original principal		interest rate		interest 1st year		original principal

= $2160.00 amount on deposit at end of 1st year new principal

$2160.00	×	0.08	=	$172.80	+	$2160.00
new principal		interest rate		interest 2nd year		new principal

= $2332.80 amount on deposit end of 2nd year new principal

$2332.80	×	0.08	=	$186.62	+	$2332.80
new principal		interest rate		interest 3rd year		new principal

= $2519.42 amount on deposit end of 3rd year

$2519.42	amount on deposit at the end of 3 years
$2000.00	original principal
$ 519.42	amount of interest earned over the 3-year period

Note: Each time the interest is paid, round off to the nearest cent.

When interest is compounded semiannually, the same general procedure explained for compounding annual interest is followed. However, the interest is figured twice a year with the time being six months or half a year. The total number of periods is twice the number of years stated in the contract period. The interest rate per period would then be half the stated annual rate.

For example:

Find the amount of compound interest at the end of two years on a principal of $2,000.00 compounded semiannually at 8 percent interest.

$2000.00	×	0.04	=	$80.00	+	$2000.00
original principal		interest rate half year		interest 6-month period		original principal

= $2080.00 amount on deposit at end of 6 months ($\frac{1}{2}$ year) new principal

$2080.00	×	0.04	=	$83.20	+	$2080.00	=	$2163.20
new principal		interest rate 6-month period		interest 2nd 6-month period		new principal		amount on deposit end of 2nd 6-month period of 1 year new principal

$2163.20	×	0.04	=	$86.53	+	$2163.20	=	$2249.73
new principal		interest rate 6-month period		interest 3rd 6-month period		new principal		amount on deposit end of 3rd 6-month period new principal

$2249.73	×	0.04	=	$89.99	+	$2249.73	=	$2339.72
new principal		interest rate 6-month period		interest 4th 6-month period		new principal		amount on deposit end of 4th 6-month period or 2-year new principal

$2339.72	amount on deposit at the end of 2 years with interest compounded semiannually
− 2000.00	original principal
$ 339.72	amount of interest earned over a 2-year period when compounded semiannually

When interest is compounded quarterly, the interest is figured four times a year or every three months. The total number of interest periods is four times the number of years stated in the contract period. The interest rate per period would then be $\frac{1}{4}$ the stated annual rate.

For example:
Find the amount of compound interest at the end of one year on a principal of $2,000.00 compounded quarterly at 8 percent interest.

$2000.00 ×	0.02	=	$40.00	+	$2000.00	=	$2040.00
original principal	interest rate per quarter		interest 1st quarter		original principal		amount on deposit end of 1st quarter new principal

$2040.00 ×	0.02	=	$40.80	+	$2040.00	=	$2080.80
new principal	interest rate per quarter		interest 2nd quarter		new principal		amount on deposit end of 2nd quarter new principal

$2080.80 ×	0.02	=	$41.62	+	$2080.80	=	$2122.42
new principal	interest rate per quarter		interest 3rd quarter		new principal		amount on deposit end of 3rd quarter new principal

$2122.42 ×	0.02	=	$42.45	+	$2122.42	=	$2164.87
new principal	interest rate per quarter		interest 4th quarter		new principal		amount on deposit end of 4th quarter

$2164.87	amount on deposit at the end of one year with interest compounded quarterly
– 2000.00	original principal
$ 164.87	amount of interest earned over a 1-year period when compounded quarterly

When interest is compounded monthly, it is figured 12 times a year at $\frac{1}{12}$ of the yearly rate. When interest is compounded daily, it is figured every day at $\frac{1}{365}$ of the yearly rate. In daily compounding, exact simple interest is used rather than ordinary simple interest, which is used when compounding for the other time periods. For other time periods, such as quarterly or semiannually, ordinary simple interest is used.

Compound interest can be calculated by using the interest formula as shown in the previous examples or by using a compound interest chart. (See Figure 20-1.) The chart is used in many cases to cut down the lengthy process of computing compound interest. It saves time and eliminates confusion. The chart, when used correctly, gives amounts of interest based on one dollar. Figure 20-1 shows a total of 25 periods and a percentage rate from 1 percent to 7 percent. The number of periods and the compound interest rates listed in these charts will vary.

Number of Periods	1%	1.5%	2%	2.5%	3%	3.5%	4%	5%	6%	7%
1	1.010000	1.015000	1.020000	1.025000	1.030000	1.035000	1.040000	1.050000	1.060000	1.070000
2	1.020100	1.030225	1.040400	1.050625	1.060900	1.071225	1.081600	1.102500	1.123600	1.144900
3	1.030301	1.045678	1.061208	1.076891	1.092727	1.108718	1.124864	1.157625	1.191016	1.225043
4	1.040604	1.061364	1.082432	1.103813	1.125509	1.147523	1.169859	1.215506	1.262477	1.310796
5	1.051010	1.077284	1.104081	1.131408	1.159274	1.187686	1.216653	1.276282	1.338226	1.402552
6	1.061520	1.093443	1.126162	1.159693	1.194052	1.292255	1.265319	1.340096	1.418519	1.500730
7	1.072135	1.109845	1.148686	1.189686	1.229874	1.272279	1.315932	1.407100	1.503630	1.605781
8	1.082857	1.126493	1.171659	1.218403	1.266770	1.316809	1.368569	1,477455	1.593848	1.718186
9	1.093685	1.143390	1.195093	1.248863	1.304773	1.362897	1.423312	1.551328	1,678479	1.838459
10	1.104622	1.160541	1.218994	1.280085	1.343916	1.410599	1.480244	1.628895	1.790848	1.967151
11	1.115668	1.177949	1.243374	1.312087	1.384234	1.459970	1.539454	1.710339	1.898299	2.104852
12	1.126825	1.195618	1.268242	1.344889	1.425761	1.511069	1.601032	1.795856	2.012196	2.252192
13	1.138093	1.213552	1.293607	1.378511	1.468534	1.563956	1.665074	1.885649	2.132928	2.409845
14	1.149474	1.231758	1.319479	1.412974	1.512590	1.618695	1.731676	1.979932	2.260904	2.578534
15	1.160969	1.250232	1.345868	1.448298	1.557967	1.675349	1.800944	2.078928	2.396558	2.759032
16	1.172579	1.268986	1.372786	1.484506	1.604706	1.733986	1.872981	2.182875	2.540352	2.952164
17	1.184304	1.288020	1.400241	1.521618	1.652848	1.794676	1.947900	2.292018	2.692773	3.158815
18	1.196147	1.307341	1.428246	1.559659	1.702433	1.857489	2.025817	2.406619	2.854339	3.379932
19	1.208109	1.326951	1.456811	1.598650	1.753506	1.922501	2.106849	2.526950	3.025600	3.616528
20	1.220190	1.346855	1.485947	1.638616	1.806111	1.989789	2.191123	2.653298	3.207135	3.869684
21	1.232392	1.367058	1.515566	1.679582	1.860295	2.059432	2.278768	2.785963	3.399564	4.140562
22	1.244716	1.387564	1.545980	1.721571	1.916103	2.131512	2.369919	2925261	3.603537	4.430402
23	1.257163	1.408377	1.576899	1.764611	1.973586	2.206115	2.464716	3.071524	3.819750	4.740530
24	1.269735	1.429503	1.608437	1.808726	2.032794	2.283329	2.563304	3.225100	4,048935	5.072367
25	1.282432	1.450945	1.640606	1.853944	2.093778	2.363245	2.665836	3.386355	4.291871	5.427433

Figure 20-1 *Compound interest chart.*

Using the compound interest chart is a fairly simple procedure. The steps to take are as follows:

1. Divide the annual interest rate by the number of times the interest will be paid per year. This will give you the percent column to use on the table.
2. Find the total number of interest periods to determine the line to use in the number of periods column.
3. When both columns are determined, place your finger on the number line and move your finger to the right until it comes to the correct rate column. The figure shown where the two columns meet is the compounded interest for $1.00.
4. Multiply this figure or factor by the amount of the original principal to determine the total amount on deposit.

Jim Kottman deposited $2,000.00 in a savings account paying 8 percent interest compounded quarterly. What will be (a) the total amount on deposit, and (b) the amount of interest earned at the end of two years?

Step 1:
Find the percent column to use. Divide the annual interest rate by the number of times the interest will be paid in one year.

8 percent annual interest rate ÷ 4 payments per year
= 2 percent column to use.

Step 2:
Find the total number of interest periods.
2 years × 4 quarters per year = 8 interest periods.

8 is the number to use in the number of periods column.

Step 3:
Locate the number 8 in the number of periods column and follow that line to the right to the interest rate column for 2 percent to find the factor \$1.171659.

Step 4:
Multiply the factor by the amount of the original principal to determine the amount on deposit at the end of the 2-year period.

\$1.171659 × \$2,000.00 = \$2343.318 amount on deposit at the end of two years.

Thus, the answer to part (a) is \$2,343.32. For part (b) we write:

\$2343.32	total amount on deposit at the end of the 2-year period
\$2000.00	original principal
\$ 343.32	amount of interest earned over a 2-year period at 8 percent interest per year

SUMMARY REVIEW

1. Find the amount of compound interest at the end of 2 years on a principal of \$3,550.00 compounded annually at 7.5 percent interest.

   ____

2. Find the amount of compound interest at the end of $1\frac{1}{2}$ years on a principal of \$4,500.00 compounded semiannually at 10.5 percent interest.

   ____

3. Find the amount of compound interest at the end of 2 years on a principal of \$9,550.00 compounded quarterly at 5.5 percent interest.

   ____

4. Bob Smart purchased a \$10,500.00 certificate of deposit paying 10.5 percent interest compounded monthly for two years.

   What is its total value at maturity?

   ____

   What was the total amount of interest earned?

   ____

5. Yuna Yi opened a savings account with a deposit of $6,450.00. The bank paid interest at 7 percent compounded quarterly. The money was left on deposit for 15 months. What was the amount on deposit at the end of 15 months?

____

What was the total amount of interest earned?

____

For each of the following problems, find the amount on deposit at the end of the time period and the amount of interest earned. Use the compound interest table.

	Principal	Interest Rate	Interest Paid	Time in Years	Amount on Deposit	Interest Earned
6.	$ 960.00	6%	Quarterly	1	______	______
7.	$ 5,175.00	12%	Monthly	$1\frac{1}{2}$	______	______
8.	$ 795.00	10%	Quarterly	6	______	______
9.	$16,230.00	5%	Annually	4	______	______
10.	$ 6,335.00	14%	Semiannually	3	______	______

◆ *Chef Sez . . .*

"The key to sustainability in food service is profit. Profit is the cost of doing business. With out profit you die . . . disappear. There is a cycle in this business. To have great quality you have to pay for it. If you pay peanuts you get monkeys. This business is very detailed and focused. We need to know every day what each item on the menu will return in dollars. A space on the menu is equivalent to a seat on an airplane. For example if roast chicken is sold for $16.50, it must return us $8.25. The contribution margin of every dish is the key ingredient. We have to focus on the cost at the micro level. The culinary professional needs to understand the cost of goods and cost of labor. The restaurant that doesn't make money disappears."

Charles E. Henning
Managing Director
SONOMA MISSION INN & SPA
Sonoma, California

Mr. Henning is the Managing Director of Sonoma's only full-service Resort, Spa, and County Club. Built in the 1920s on the wooded site of a natural hot spring, Sonoma Mission Inn & Spa is an intimate, luxurious, and romantic oasis nestled in the heart of the wine country. It offers luxury accommodations, European-style spa, 18-hole golf course, two award-winning restaurants, and outstanding meeting and wedding facilities, all located just one hour from San Francisco. In 1999, Mr. Henning was responsible for completing an expansion of the Inn that cost $20,000,000.

Posttest: Math Skills

The Posttest determines the extent of the student's improvement during the course. In most cases, improvement will be noted.

To earn a competency in each of the 40 math skills presented, a student must work three of the four problems presented correctly. If this is achieved, the student will earn a + (plus) for that particular math skill. If this goal is not achieved, a − (minus) will be recorded. A profile sheet on both the pre- and posttests are kept on file by the teacher for reference by both the student and the teacher. The pluses earned are recorded in either blue or black ink on the profile sheet under the proper math skill. The minuses are recorded in red ink.

1. Add the following numbers.

29	18	8,426
+ 58	48	3,268
	+ 15	+ 6,349

49 + 138 + 5,579 + 43,684 = ______________

2. Subtract the following numbers.

69	529	73,840
− 37	− 263	− 12,425

42,229 − 17,483 = ______________

3. Change the mill to the nearest cent.

$.049 ______________ $6.834 ______________

$.137 ______________ $726.533 ______________

4. Multiply the following numbers.

43	79	883
× 8	× 36	× 132

3,450 × 46 = ______________

5. Divide the following numbers.

$14\overline{)168}$ $\qquad$ $26\overline{)6{,}864}$

$125\overline{)81{,}250}$ $\qquad$ $2{,}232\overline{)618{,}264}$

6. Reduce the fractions to the lowest terms.

$\frac{3}{12}$ = ______________ $\qquad$ $\frac{18}{96}$ = ______________

$\frac{54}{108}$ = ______________ $\qquad$ $\frac{80}{128}$ = ______________

7. Convert each mixed number to an improper fraction.

$7\frac{1}{8}$ = ______________ $\qquad$ $18\frac{4}{7}$ = ______________

$5\frac{3}{8}$ = ______________ $\qquad$ $45\frac{7}{8}$ = ______________

8. Convert each improper fraction to a whole number or to a mixed number.

$\frac{45}{9}$ = ______________ $\qquad$ $\frac{176}{110}$ = ______________

$\frac{32}{6}$ = ______________ $\qquad$ $\frac{280}{22}$ = ______________

9. Find the equivalent fractions.

$\frac{5}{9} = \frac{?}{54}$ = ______________ $\qquad$ $\frac{5}{8} = \frac{?}{40}$ = ______________

$\frac{2}{3} = \frac{?}{18}$ = ______________ $\qquad$ $\frac{3}{16} = \frac{?}{32}$ = ______________

10. Add the following fractions and reduce the answer to the lowest terms.

$$\begin{array}{r} \frac{7}{8} \\ +\ \frac{5}{8} \\ \hline \end{array} \qquad \begin{array}{r} 3\frac{3}{8} \\ +\ 4\frac{3}{4} \\ \hline \end{array} \qquad \begin{array}{r} 1\frac{15}{16} \\ +\ 6\frac{1}{4} \\ \hline \end{array} \qquad \begin{array}{r} 3\frac{1}{2} \\ 5\frac{5}{16} \\ +\ 6\frac{5}{8} \\ \hline \end{array}$$

11. Subtract the following fractions and reduce the answer to the lowest terms.

$\frac{11}{12}$	7	$14\frac{1}{4}$	$36\frac{21}{32}$
$-\frac{5}{12}$	$-2\frac{3}{8}$	$-6\frac{3}{16}$	$-24\frac{3}{16}$

12. Multiply the following fractions and reduce the answer to the lowest terms.

$\frac{2}{5} \times \frac{5}{6} =$ ______________ $6\frac{3}{4} \times 2\frac{7}{8} =$ ______________

$7 \times \frac{5}{9} =$ ______________ $9\frac{2}{3} \times 3\frac{1}{4} =$ ______________

13. Divide the following fractions and reduce the answer to the lowest terms.

$\frac{5}{9} \div \frac{1}{4} =$ ______________ $4\frac{3}{4} \div \frac{4}{5} =$ ______________

$3\frac{1}{4} \div \frac{1}{8} =$ ______________ $15\frac{3}{4} \div 1\frac{5}{8} =$ ______________

14. Convert each decimal to a fraction.

0.8 = ______________ 0.008 = ______________

4.25 = ______________ 0.86 = ______________

15. Convert each fraction to a decimal.

$\frac{3}{16} =$ ______________ $6\frac{1}{6} =$ ______________

$\frac{5}{8} =$ ______________ $2\frac{3}{8} =$ ______________

16. Convert each fraction to a percent.

$\frac{4}{5} =$ ______________ $\frac{7}{9} =$ ______________

$2\frac{3}{5} =$ ______________ $\frac{7}{10} =$ ______________

17. Convert each decimal to a percent.

0.0076 = ______________ 5.3 = ______________

0.63 = ______________ 0.074 = ______________

18. Convert each percent to a decimal.

9.6% = ______________ 14.8% = ______________

22.3% = ______________ 24% = ______________

19. Add the decimals.

$$\begin{array}{r} 8.5 \\ 3.7 \\ +\ .9 \\ \hline \end{array} \qquad \begin{array}{r} 7.096 \\ +\ 15 \\ \hline \end{array}$$

$0.5 + 7.4 + 14 =$ ____________

$0.0036 + 0.035 + 4.26 =$ ____________

20. Subtract the decimals.

$$\begin{array}{r} 8.09 \\ -\ 2.68 \\ \hline \end{array} \qquad \begin{array}{r} 245.08 \\ -\ 7.4 \\ \hline \end{array}$$

$44.6 - 10.53 =$ ____________

$6 - 0.07 =$ ____________

21. Multiply the decimals.

$$\begin{array}{r} .295 \\ \times\ 18 \\ \hline \end{array} \qquad \begin{array}{r} 8.35 \\ \times\ 2.5 \\ \hline \end{array}$$

$7.5 \times 0.35 =$ ____________

$12.75 \times 0.65 =$ ____________

22. Divide the decimals.

$.08\overline{).956}$ $\qquad$ $7.5\overline{).5842}$

$.43\overline{).5453}$ $\qquad$ $18\overline{)9.762}$

23. Use percents to find the total number.

25% of what number is 9? ____________

15% of what number is 36? ____________

70% of what number is 56? ____________

35% of what number is 105? ____________

24. Find the percent of a number.

    38% of 20 = ______________

    7.5% of 48 = ______________

    $15\frac{1}{2}$% of 95 = ______________

    85% of 220 = ______________

25. Find the percent of two given numbers.

    What percent of 60 is 36? ______________

    What percent of 90 is 54? ______________

    What percent of 120 is 36? ______________

    What percent of 260 is 91? ______________

26. Measurement equivalents—ounces

    8 Ounces = ______________ Quart or Quarts

    128 Ounces = ______________ Gallon or Gallons

    16 Ounces = ______________ Pint or Pints

    32 Ounces = ______________ Quart or Quarts

27. Measurement equivalents—cups

    16 Cups = ______________ Gallon or Gallons

    2 Cups = ______________ Pint or Pints

    4 Cups = ______________ Quart or Quarts

    6 Cups = ______________ Quart or Quarts

28. Measurement equivalents—spoons

    48 Teaspoons = ______________ Cup or Cups

    16 Tablespoons = ______________ Cup or Cups

    8 Tablespoons = ______________ Cup or Cups

    3 Teaspoons = ______________ Tablespoon or Tablespoons

29. Find cost per serving.

    A $2\frac{1}{2}$-pound box of frozen corn costs $4.20. How much does a $3\frac{1}{2}$-ounce serving cost?

    ____

    A $2\frac{1}{2}$-pound box of frozen peas and carrots costs $.68 per pound. How much does a 3-ounce serving cost?

    ____

A 5-pound box of frozen peas costs \$3.95. How much does a $3\frac{1}{2}$-ounce serving cost?

____

If frozen asparagus spears cost \$12.90 for a 5-pound box, how much does a 3-ounce serving cost?

____

30. F.I.C.A. (Social Security Tax)

If the Social Security Tax rate is 7.30%, how much tax is paid on the following weekly salaries?

\$668.00 ____________

\$720.00 ____________

\$585.00 ____________

\$428.00 ____________

31. Sales tax

Find the amount of sales tax paid on the following purchases if the sales tax rate is $5\frac{1}{2}$ percent.

\$2,587.50 ____________

\$3,229.60 ____________

\$1,650.00 ____________

\$ 935.80 ____________

32. Chain calculations—using calculator

$82 + 320 - 78 \times 2 \div 2$ = ____________

$1{,}360 - 482 + 125 \div 2 \times 5$ = ____________

$245 \times 22 - 165 + 341$ = ____________

$\$3{,}524.50 - 1{,}415.25 \times 0.04$ = ____________

33. Metric conversion

1 gram = ____________ ounces

1 kilogram = ____________ pounds

28 grams = ____________ ounce or ounces

1 liter = ____________ quart or quarts

34. Determine the total cost of each meal.

A tip of $3.00 was 15% of the cost of the meal. ____________

A tip of $6.00 was 20% of the cost of the meal. ____________

A tip of $5.00 was 20% of the cost of the meal. ____________

A tip of $9.00 was 15% of the cost of the meal. ____________

35. Interest

Find the simple interest on $585.00 at 5% interest for 1 year.

____

Find the simple interest on $945.00 at $4\frac{1}{2}$% interest for 1 year.

____

Find the amount of compound interest at the end of 2 years on a principal of $4,000.00 compounded annually at 3% interest.

____

Find the amount of compound interest at the end of 3 years on a principal of $3,500.00 compounded annually at 3.5% interest.

____

36. Find the Cost of Food Sold and Monthly Food Cost.

Sales . . . . $ 2,000.00
Inventory at Beginning of Month 150.00
Purchases for Month 650.00
Final Inventory 200.00
Cost of Food Sold . . . . ________
Monthly Food Cost Percent . . . . ________

Sales . . . . $ 5,000.00
Inventory at Beginning of Month 250.00
Purchases for Month 3,000.00
Final Inventory 450.00
Cost of Food Sold . . . . ________
Monthly Food Cost Percent . . . . ________

Sales . . . . $ 2,550.00
Inventory at Beginning of Month 300.00
Purchases for Month 895.00
Final Inventory 250.00
Cost of Food Sold . . . . ________
Monthly Food Cost Percent . . . . ________

Sales . . . . $ 6,725.00
Inventory at Beginning of Month 700.00
Purchases for Month 3,785.00
Final Inventory 550.00
Cost of Food Sold . . . . ________
Monthly Food Cost Percent . . . . ________

37. Determine Menu Price

Raw Food Cost is $2.98 and markup rate is $\frac{3}{4}$. ____________

Raw Food Cost is $4.20 and markup rate is 35%. ____________

Raw Food Cost is $3.35 and markup rate is $\frac{2}{3}$. ____________

Raw Food Cost is $5.65 and markup rate is 40%. ____________

38. Serving portions

How many 6-ounce Swiss Steaks can be cut from a beef round weighing 42 pounds (A.P.) if 5 pounds 4 ounces are lost in boning and trimming?

____

A 12-pound (E.P.) pork loin is roasted, 2 pounds 7 ounces are lost through shrinkage. How many 2-$\frac{1}{2}$-ounce servings can be obtained from the cooked pork loin?

____

An 8-pound (A.P.) beef tenderloin is trimmed, 8 ounces are lost. How many 8-ounce filet mignons can be cut from the loin?

____

A 6-pound (E.P.) beef tenderloin is roasted, 12 ounces are lost through shrinkage. How many 3-ounce servings can be obtained from the roasted loin?

____

39. Calculating Gross Wages

Mario Astor, the sauce cook at the Metropole Hotel, worked a total of 52$\frac{1}{2}$ hours during a recent week. He is paid $10.75 per hour, plus time and a half for all hours over 40 per week. What are his gross wages for that week?

____

Jerome Miller, a cook at a local restaurant, earns $8.50 per hour, with time and a half for all hours worked over 40 per week. The past week he worked a total of $48\frac{1}{2}$ hours. What are his gross wages for the week?

____

John Wall, a cook at a local restaurant, earns $9.75 per hour, with time and a half for all hours worked over 40 per week. Last week, he worked 47 hours. What were his gross wages for that week?

____

Anna Li, a salad person at the Gibson Hotel, worked 7 consecutive days, 8 hours a day, from Monday through Sunday. Her regular pay rate is $6.50 per hour. The hotel pays time and a half for all hours worked on Saturday and double time for all hours worked on Sunday. What was her gross pay for that week?

____

40. The Constant function—using calculator

What is the amount of sales tax on the following amounts, if the 5.5 percent sales tax rate is used as the constant?

$ 296.00 ______________

$ 89.50 ______________

$2,218.95 ______________

$5,350.00 ______________

Math Skills—Profile Sheet

The following should be listed on the Profile Sheet for the Posttest.

1. Addition
2. Subtraction
3. Changing the mill
4. Multiplication
5. Division
6. Reducing fractions
7. Converting to improper fractions
8. Improper fractions to mixed numbers
9. Finding equivalent fractions
10. Addition of fractions
11. Subtraction of fractions
12. Multiplication of fractions
13. Division of fractions
14. Converting decimals to fractions
15. Converting fractions to decimals
16. Converting fractions to percent
17. Converting decimals to percent
18. Converting percent to decimals
19. Addition of decimals
20. Subtraction of decimals
21. Multiplication of decimals
22. Division of decimals
23. Percents to find number
24. Finding percent of a number
25. Finding percent of two given numbers
26. Measurement equivalents—ounces
27. Measurement equivalents—cups
28. Measurement equivalents—spoons
29. Cost per serving
30. F.I.C.A. (Social Security Tax)
31. Finding sales tax
32. Chain calculations—using calculator
33. Metric conversion
34. Cost of meal
35. Interest

36. Inventory procedure
37. Menu price
38. Serving portions
39. Calculating gross wages
40. The Constant function—using calculator

Appendix A

Formulas

Addition—Addend plus addend = Sum

Assets—Liabilities plus proprietorship

Break-Even Analysis—Sales revenue minus variable costs = Gross profit. Gross profit minus fixed costs = Break-even point

Check amount based on tip—Money amount of tip divided by percent of tip

Containers needed—Ounces needed divided by ounces in one container

Converting Celsius temperature to degrees Fahrenheit—Multiply the Celsius temperature by $\frac{9}{5}$ and add 32 to the result

Converting Fahrenheit temperature to degrees Celsius—Subtract 32 from the given Fahrenheit temperature and multiply the result by $\frac{5}{9}$

Converting standard recipes—Multiply each ingredient in the original recipe by the working factor to find the new desired quantity

Cost of food sold—Beginning inventory plus purchases minus final inventory

Cost, ounce—Total cost divided by total ounces

Cost per serving—Cost of 1 ounce times number of ounces served

Cost, total (per pound)—Number of pounds times cost per pound

Division—Dividend divided by divisor = Quotient

Edible portion (E.P.)—Weight of product after trimming or processing.

Food cost—Sales (or menu) price times food cost percentage

Food cost percentage—Food cost divided by sales or menu price

Gross pay—Hourly rate times hours worked

Gross profit percent—Sales minus variable cost

Interest—Principal times rate times time

Interest paid—Interest per day times number of days of loan

Interest per day—Amount of interest for 1 year divided by ordinary or exact days per year

Menu pricing using the food cost percent method—Raw food cost divided by food cost percent

Menu pricing using the markup amount method—Raw food cost times markup rate. To obtain menu price: add the markup amount to the raw food cost

Multiplication—Multiplier times multiplicand = Product

Net pay—Gross pay or wages minus deductions

Net worth or proprietorship—Assets minus liabilities

Number of ounces required—Amount of portion times number of people served

Number of servings—Total weight of all ingredients used divided by serving portion size.

Number to order—Number of ounces required divided by ounces in container

Ounces needed—Number of people to be served times portion size

Ounces in one container—Pounds in container times 16

Ounces, total—Total weight times 16

Percent of ingredient—Weight of ingredient divided by weight of flour

Pounds needed—Number of ounces needed divided by 16

Price, extension—Quantity of items multiplied by the unit price

Recipe yield—Total weight of preparation divided by weight of portion

Salary plus commission—Amount of sales times percent of commission equals amount of commission. Salary plus amount of commission equals gross wages

Sales, average—Total sales divided by customer count

Sales price or menu price—Food cost divided by food cost percentage

Sales, total—Average sales multiplied by customer count

Subtraction—Minuend minus subtrahend = Difference

Unit Cost—Total cost divided by yield

Working factor—New yield divided by old yield

Glossary

A

abbreviation—The shortened form of a word or phrase.

account, checking or savings—A record in which an individual's or a business' money is deposited or withdrawn usually in a financial institution.

accountant—A person skilled in keeping, examination of, and adjustment of financial records.

accounts payable—Money owed by the business operator for purchases made.

accounts receivable—Money owed to the business operator by customers.

addressing (in data communication)—A computer term by which you are selecting another computer to send data via modem.

adhere—To stick fast; to become attached or cling to.

a la carte—Foods ordered and paid for separately; usually prepared to order.

analysis—The division or separation of a thing into the parts that compose it.

annual—Pertaining to a year; happening once in 12 months.

A.P. weight—As purchased weight. The weight of an item before processing.

approximate—To come near to, nearly correct.

aspic—A clear meat, fish, or poultry jelly.

assess—To fix or determine the amount of a tax, fine, or damage; to rate or set a certain charge upon, as for taxation.

assessor—A person appointed to estimate the value of property for the purpose of taxation.

assets—Things of value; all the property of a person, company, or estate that may be used to pay debts.

automation—The automatic control of production processes by electronic apparatus.

B

backup—A spare copy of data or a program.

baker's balance scale—An instrument to weigh ingredients used in baking.

balance—Difference between the debit and credit sides of an account; an amount left over.

balance sheet—A written statement made to show the true financial condition for a person or business by exhibiting assets, liabilities or debts, profit and loss, and net worth.

bank note—A note issued by a bank that must be paid to the bearer upon demand. Bank notes are used as money.

breading—A process of passing an item through flour, egg wash (egg and milk), and bread crumbs, before it is fried.

break-even analysis—A mathematical method used to find the dollar amount needed for a food service operation to break even.

budget—A plan of systematic spending; to plan one's expenditures of money, time, etc.

C

calculate—To reach a conclusion or answer by a reasoning process.

calculator—One who computes; a machine that does automatic computations.

calendar year—A period that begins on January 1 and ends on December 31; consisting of 365 days, in a leap year, 366 days.

capacity—Power of holding or grasping; room; volume; power of mind; character; ability to hold cubic content.

capital—Amount of money or property that a person or company uses in carrying on a business.

captain—A service individual in charge of a station or stations.

carryover—Have left over; keep until late.

cashbook—A book containing records of all income and expenses of a business operation.

cashier's daily report—A tool used by management to keep track of cash and charge sales.

Celsius—A term used to measure temperature in the metric system of measuring; graduated or divided into 100 equal parts called degrees; previously called centigrade.

cent—A term used to represent the value of one hundredth part of a dollar.

centigrade—A term used to measure temperature in the metric system of measuring; graduated or divided into 100 equal parts called degrees. The term now used is celsius.

centimeter—The one hundredth part of a meter.

certificate—Issued by a bank to a depositor indicating that a specific amount of money is set aside and not subject to withdrawal except on surrender of the certificate, usually with an interest penalty.

chaud-froid—Jellied white sauce, used for decorating certain foods that are to be displayed.

check—A written order directing a financial institution to make a payment for the depositor.

check register—A form given to the depositor by the financial institution so the depositor can record deposits and checks, knowing the balance of money on hand.

cipher—Zero.

commission—Pay based on the amount of business done.

compensation—Something given in return for a service or a value.

competency—The state of being fit or capable.

complex—Not simple, involved, intricate.

compound interest—Money that is added to the principal (with interest then paid on a new principal).

compressed—Made smaller by applying pressure.

computer—Any of various mechanical, electrical, or electronic devices for computing; specifically one for solving complex, mathematical problems in a very short time.

computerized—To use, perform, operate, etc., by means of a computer or computers.

configuration—A group or series of machines and programs that make up a complete data processing system.

concept—A mental idea of a class of objects.

Constant Function—A calculator key used to multiply or divide repeatedly by the same number.

convert—Change; to turn the other way around.

corporation—A group of persons who obtain a charter giving them (as a group) certain legal rights and privileges distinct from those of the individual members of the group.

cost of food sold—monetary value of food on hand at beginning of the month, plus the purchases for the month, minus the monetary value of food in the final inventory.

cover charge—An admission fee charged for entertainment.

cubic centimeter—A measure of volume in the metric system with sides 1 centimeter long.

cubic meter—A measure of volume in the metric system with sides 1 meter long.

currency—Money in actual use in a country. In the United States, the term usually applies to paper money, although technically, it is both coins and paper money.

cursor—A short, blinking line that appears underneath the space where the next character is to be typed or deleted. The cursor indicates that the computer is ready for the input of the command.

D

daily food cost report—A tool to show management the exact cost and amount of food used on any given day.

data—A collection of information, facts, statistics, or instructions arranged in definite terms suitable for processing by manual or automatic means.

data base management—The sorting and categorizing of information or data.

debit—The entry of an item in a business account showing something owed or due.

decimal—A system of counting by tens and powers of ten. Each digit has a place value ten times that of the next digit to the right.

decimal fractions—Fractions that are expressed with denominators of 10 or powers of 10.

decimal point—A point (.) used to indicate a decimal fraction.

decimeter—A metric measure of length equal to one tenth of a meter.

deduction—The process of taking away.

default—Failure to pay when due.

dekameter—A metric measure of length equal to 10 meters.

denominator—The bottom number of a fraction.

deposit—Put in a place for safekeeping. Money put in a bank is a deposit.

deposit slip—A form that provides the depositor and the financial institution with a record of the transaction when money is deposited in the checking account.

depreciation—Lessening or lowering in value.

designate—Point out; indicate definitely.

diameter—The length of a straight line through the center of a circle.

difference—the answer in a subtraction problem.

digit—Any one of the figures 0-1-2-3-4-5-6-7-8-9.

direct purchases—Those foods that are usually purchased each day or every other day.

disc—A flat, circular plate used in computers for the purpose of magnetically recording information on one or both sides.

diskette—A thin, flexible magnetic disk, sometimes called a floppy disk. Information can be recorded onto and played back from a diskette.

dividend—(1) Money to be shared by those to whom it belongs. If a company shows a profit at the end of a certain period, it declares a dividend to the owners of the company. (2) Also the number to be divided by the divisor.

division—Act of giving some to each. Process of dividing one number by another.

divisor—A number by which another (the dividend) is divided.

E

economic—Pertaining to the earning, distributing, and using of wealth and income, public or private.

entree—The main dish of a meal.

E.P. weight—Edible portion weight. The usable portion after processing.

equation—To make equal.

equivalent—Equal in value or power.

estimate—A judgment or opinion in determining the size, value, etc., of an item.

evaluate—Find the value or amount of; fix the value.

expenditure—That which is spent.

extension—To stretch out, lengthen, or widen.

F

fabricated—Made up; in food service, standardized portion.

facsimile—To make an exact copy of. A rapid way of communicating, allowing one to send and receive any type of text or graphic information over telephone lines.

factor—One of the two or more quantities, which when multiplied together, yield a given product. Example: 2 and 4 are factors of 8.

Fahrenheit—A term used to measure temperature in the standard system of measuring; graduated or divided into 212 equal parts called degrees.

file—Put away and kept in any easy-to-find order.

final inventory—The total value of all goods on hand (e.g. in the storeroom). It is the food that has not been sold during the inventory period.

finances—Money; funds; revenues; financial condition.

financial—Having to do with money matters.

financial statements—Instruments used in a business operation to let management know its exact financial position.

fiscal year—The time between one yearly settlement of financial accounts and another. In the United States, a fiscal year usually starts July 1 and ends June 30 of the following calendar year.

fixed assets—Those assets (things of value) that stay firm and do not change.

fixed costs—Those costs (price paid) that stay firm and will not change.

fluctuate—Change continually.

food cost percentage—The cost of food as it relates to the amount of dollars received in sales.

food production report—a form used to find how much product is produced and sold.

forecast—A prophecy or prediction.

format—Size, shape, and general arrangement of a book, magazine, etc.

formula—A rule for doing something; a recipe or prescription.

fraction—One or more of the equal parts of a whole; a small part or amount.

function—A quantity, the value of which varies with that of another quantity.

G

garnish—To decorate, such as food.

gelatin—An odorless, tasteless substance obtained by boiling animal tissues. It dissolves easily in hot water and is used in making jellied desserts and salads.

gourmet—A lover of fine foods.

graduated—Arranged in regular steps, stages, or degrees.

gram—Metric system unit of weight (mass). Twenty-eight grams equal one ounce.

gratuity—A present or money given in return for a service; also called a tip.

gross—With nothing removed or taken out. Gross receipts are all the money taken in before costs are deducted.

gross margin—Sales less the cost of food gives the gross margin. It is the margin before other deductions are taken.

gross pay—Money earned before any deductions are removed or subtracted.

gross wages—Money paid to an employee for services before deductions.

guest check—The bill or bill of sale used in a restaurant.

H

hectometer—Measure of length in the metric system equal to 100 meters.

horizontally—Parallel to the horizon; at right angles to a vertical line.

host/hostess—An individual who receives guests at a private or public function.

hypothetical—Something assumed or supposed.

I

improper fraction—A fraction whose numerator is larger than its denominator and whose value is greater than a whole unit.

income—All payments received for services provided.

indicator—One who or that which points out.

ingredient—One part of a mixture.

installment—Part of a sum of money or debt to be paid at certain regular times.

interest—Money that is paid for the use of borrowed money.

inventory—A detailed list of items with their estimated value.

invert—To turn upside down.

invoice—A list of goods sent to a purchaser showing prices and amounts.

itemize—To state by items, as to itemize a bill.

K

keyboard—A bank of number, alphabetic, or function keys of a typewriter or computer. On the computer, they are used to enter information into the computer terminal.

kilogram—A metric measure of weight equal to 1,000 grams.

kilometer—A measure of length in the metric system equal to 1,000 meters.

L

ladles—Tools used to serve foods or to control portion size.

lease—A written contract whereby one party grants to another party the use of land, buildings, or personal property, for a definite consideration known as rent, for a specified term.

least common denominator—The smallest number that is a multiple of both denominators.

legumes—Vegetables; also refers to dried vegetables such as beans, lentils, and split peas.

liability—A state of being under obligation; responsible for a loss, debt, penalty, or the like.

licenses—A form of taxation that individuals or businesses are required to obtain in order to conduct business.

like fractions—Fractions that have the same denominator.

liter—A measure of volume in the metric system. One liter equals 1.0567 quarts in customary liquid measure or 0.908 quarts in dry measure.

M

maitre d'—Person in charge of dining room service.

manual—Pertaining to, or done by hand.

margin—The difference between the cost and the selling price of an article.

markup—Marked for sale at a higher price.

medicare—A federal health insurance program for people 65 or older and certain disabled people.

Memory Function—A calculator key used to retain figures.

menu—A list of the various dishes served at a meal.

meringue—Egg whites and sugar beaten together to form a white, frothy mass; used to top pies and cakes.

meter—Unit of length in the metric system equal to 39.37 inches.

metric system—The system of measurements based on the meter.

mill—The third place to the right of the decimal when dealing with monetary numbers. It represents the thousandth part of a dollar, or one tenth of one cent.

milligram—Pertaining to the metric system of measure. It is the thousandth part of a gram.

milliliter—Pertaining to the metric system of measure. It is the thousandth part of a liter.

millimeter—Pertaining to the metric system of measure. It is a lineal measure equal to the thousandth part of a meter.

minimum charge—A fee charged to the guest who is required to spend a certain amount of money even if the total check amounts to less.

minuend—The original number in a subtraction problem.

mixed decimal fraction—A number that is made up of a whole number and a decimal fraction.

mixed number—A whole number mixed with a fractional part.

modem—An electronic device that makes possible the transmission of digitized data from one location to another over telephone lines.

monetary—Pertaining to money or coinage.

monitor—A computer output device. Various information is shown on the monitor.

mortgage—Claim on property given to a person who has lent money in case the money is not repaid when due.

mouse—A computer device that will fit in the palm of your hand. When rolled on a flat surface, it will move the computer cursor. It relays signals that move the cursor on the computer screen.

multiple—A number that contains another number a certain amount of times, without a remainder; example: 16 is a multiple of 4.

multiplicand—In multiplication, the number or quantity to be multiplied by another number called the multiplier.

multiplier—Number by which another number is to be multiplied.

multiplier effect—A method used to obtain a menu price.

N

net—Amount remaining after deducting all necessary expenses.

net pay—Money paid to an employee for services after deductions.

net worth—Excess value of resources over liabilities; also called net assets.

numeral—Symbol for a number.

numerator—The top number of a fraction.

O

occupational tax—A fee that must be paid in order to operate any business within a certain city.

operating system—Directs the flow of information to and from various parts of the computer and is needed by the computer to run programs.

overdrawn—To draw from an account (bank) more than one has a right.

overtime—Time beyond the regular hours.

P

pasta—A dried flour paste product. Example: spaghetti, vermicelli, and lasagna.

payroll—List of persons to be paid and the amounts that each one is to receive. Total amounts to be paid to them.

percent—Rate or proportion of each hundred; part of each hundred.

period—A group of three digits set off by commas in a large number.

periodical—Magazine that is published regularly.

perpetual inventory—A continuous or endless record to show the balance on hand for each storeroom item.

physical inventory—A count taken of all stock on hand.

P and L sheet—Another name for a profit and loss statement.

portion—A part or share.

portion control—A term used to ensure that a specific or designated amount of an item is served to a guest.

portion scale—A tool used for measuring food servings.

portion size—The amount or quantity of prepared food.

prefix—A letter, syllable, or group of syllables placed at the beginning of a word to modify or qualify its meaning; example: deci in front of meter indicates 1/10 of a meter.

primal cut—One of the primary divisions for cutting meat carcasses into smaller cuts.

primary—First in time; first in order; first in importance.

principal—Sum of money on which interest is paid.

printer—An output device for the computer. Prints out required information.

procedure—A way of proceeding; method of doing a task.

product—The result obtained by multiplying two or more numbers together.

production formula—A standardized formula used to prepare foods in quantity.

profile—An outline or contour.

profit—Gain from a business venture. What is left when the cost of goods and carrying on the business is subtracted from the amount of money taken in.

program—Pertaining to the computer, a plan of related instructions or statements that is brought together as a task.

proper fraction—A fraction whose numerator is smaller than its denominator.

property tax—An amount of money collected from individuals or businesses based on the present value of the property.

proportion—Relation in size, number, amount, or degree of one thing compared to another.

proprietorship—Ownership.

purchase order—A written form that indicates to the vendor how many items are to be delivered to an establishment, and lists the prices for each item.

purchase specifications—A detailed description of requirements for items being purchased.

purveyor—One who supplies provisions or food.

Q

quantity—Amount; how much.

quotient—Number obtained by dividing one number by another; the final answer of a division problem.

R

ratio—Relative magnitude. The ratio between two quantities is the number of times one contains the other.

real estate tax—See *Property tax.*

receipt—A written statement that money, a package, a letter, etc., has been received.

recipe—A set of directions for preparing something to eat.

recipe file number—The number placed on the recipe for easy access when it is filed.

reconstitute—To rebuild the way it was originally, to put back into original form; example: to reconstitute dried milk, the water is put back.

recourse—Person or thing appealed to or turned to for help or protection.

reduce—To make less in value, quantity, size, or the like.

remainder—The number less than the divisor that remains after the division process is completed.

report—An account officially expressed, generally in writing.

requisition—A demand made, usually in written form, for something that is required.

revenue—Money coming in; income.

rotating menu—Menu that alternates by turn in a series. The series is usually set up on a yearly basis.

roux—A thickening agent consisting of equal parts of flour and shortening.

royalty—Share of the receipts or profits paid to an owner of a patent or copyright; payment for use of any of various rights.

S

salary—A regular, periodical payment for official or professional services rendered.

sales revenue—Money coming in from the sale of certain items.

sales tax—Money collected on purchases of goods from consumers or businesses by governments.

saute—To cook in shallow grease.

scoops or dippers—Tools used to serve foods or to control portion size.

simple interest—Money paid only on the principal.

simplification—A method used to express a fraction in lower terms without changing the value of the fraction.

simplify—To reduce from the complex to the simple; to make plainer to understand.

software—A general term for programs that direct a computer operation. A set of instructions given the computer to perform a given task.

solar—Working by means of the sun's light or heat.

specification—A detailed statement of particulars.

spreadsheet—A printout similar to an accountant's ledger containing rows and columns of important calculations and financial information.

standard recipe—A recipe that will produce the same quality and quantity each and every time.

standardize—To make standard in size, shape, weight, quality, quantity, etc.

stations—Serving sections in a restaurant.

status—Condition, state, or position.

stockholder—Owner of stocks or shares in a company.

storeroom requisition—A list of food items issued from the storeroom upon the request of the production crew.

straight-line method—The simplest method to use when figuring depreciation on an item such as a piece of equipment.

subproduct—Sub means under, below, or before. Product is the result of multiplying.

subtraction—An operation that tells the difference between two numbers.

subtrahend—The number removed from the minuend.

sum—Total of two or more numbers or things taken together; the whole amount.

summarize—Express briefly; give only the main points.

symbol—Something that stands for or represents something else.

T

table d'hote—A meal of several courses at a set price. The dinner menu in most restaurants is served table d'hote.

taxes—Money collected from individuals or businesses by governments to pay for public services.

technology—The application of science and technical advances in industry, the arts, etc.

terminology—The special words or terms used in a science, art, business, etc.

trading (borrowing)—To make a group of ten from one of the next highest place value, or one from ten of the lowest place value.

triplicate—To make threefold; three identical copies.

U

unit—A standard quantity or amount.

unit cost—The amount that one serving of a particular food costs to prepare.

unlike fractions—Fractions that have different denominators.

utilities—Companies that perform a public service. Railroads, gas and electric, and telephone companies are utilities.

V

variable cost—Costs that are changeable.

variation—The extent to which a thing changes.

vendor—One who sells a product.

verbally—Stated or expressed in words.

versatile—Turning easily from one action, style, or subject, etc., to another; able to do many tasks well.

vertical—Straight up and down.

volume—Space occupied.

voucher—A written evidence of payment; receipt.

W

wages—That which is paid or received for services.

whole numbers—Numbers such as 0, 1, 2, etc., that are used to represent whole units rather than fractional units.

withholding tax—A deduction from a person's paycheck for the purpose of paying yearly income taxes.

word processing—The system of recording, storing, and retrieving typewritten information.

Y

yield—Amount produced.

Index

Q

R

W

Y